Collective
Search
for Identity

Collective
Search
for Identity

ORRIN E. KLAPP
San Diego State College

Holt, Rinehart and Winston, Inc.
New York   Chicago   San Francisco   Atlanta
Dallas   Montreal   Toronto   London   Sydney

COPYRIGHT ACKNOWLEDGMENTS

The author wishes to thank the following copyright holders for permission to reprint extracts from the listed works:

The American Sociological Association and the authors for James S. Bossard and Eleanor S. Boll, "Ritual in Family Living" in *American Sociological Review*, Vol. 14 (1949).

The Bodley Head Limited for Charles Chaplin, *My Autobiography*.

Life for Winthrop Sargeant, "Holy Man" in *Life* (May 30, 1949).

Harold Ober Associates for a statement by Malcolm Muggeridge in the *Observer* (June 26, 1966). Reprinted by permission of Harold Ober Associates Incorporated. Copyright © 1966 by Malcolm Muggeridge.

Simon & Schuster, Inc., and Laurence Pollinger Limited for Alexander King, *Mine Enemy Grows Older*. Copyright © 1958 by Alexander King.

A. Watkins, Inc., for Roger Eddy, "On Staying Put" in *Mademoiselle* (May 1966). Copyright © 1966 Roger Eddy.

To Evelyn, Merrie, and Curtis

PREFACE

This book is about identity-seeking movements of modern society. It deals with such things as fashions, fads, poses, ritual, cultic movements, recreation, heroes and celebrities, and crusades, from the point of view of what they tell about the identity search of a mass society. My view, briefly, is that a collective identity search is symptomatic of the fact that some modern social systems deprive people of psychological "payoffs," the lack of which, expressed by terms such as alienation, meaninglessness, identity problem, motivates a mass groping for activities and symbols with which to restore or find new identity. People grope because they do not really know what is wrong, especially when there is physical prosperity *yet* a sense of being cheated. When mass movements become concerned with identity, they develop certain characteristics, such as "ego-screaming," concern with costume and self-ornamentation, style rebellion, concern with emotional gestures rather than practical effects, adulation of heroes, cultism, and the like, with which I shall deal. Such signs show that ordinary economic and political solutions are not what is wanted. People feel the futility and irrelevance of such measures, yet do not know quite what else to do.

The sense of being cheated is not explainable in economic terms because it is a *shortcoming in meaning.* When there is a shortcoming in meaning in a social system, it is not easily remedied just by changing the distribution of goods or by changing one's social position—even from very poor to very rich. A shortcoming in meaning can be experienced by people in almost any position: business executives, youths with all the "advantages," ghetto dwellers, suburban dwellers, successful movie actresses; it can be experienced when goods and luxuries pile up—the question remaining, What is the meaning of these goods and luxuries for *me*? So there comes a sense of futility about "success." Young people may view the opportunities and careers laid out for them by parents and say, "Not for me." I have chosen to examine in this book, then, certain activities which plainly show a turning away from "sensible" economic and political measures toward a search for meaning to oneself, for oneself, in oneself. Some of them, like cultic movements, are relatively successful; others, like ego-screaming and faddism, seem to fail. The basic viewpoint from which such things are judged is a theory of symbolism (conditions for symbols, what feedback is necessary for identity symbols, the balance of discursive and nondiscursive symbols). The idea is that collective behavior is not just expressive, nor is it merely practical; but it is an effort, more or less successful, to create symbols which give meaning to oneself, hence, on the larger scale, to restore symbolic balance to the society.

So this book is written with the idea that there is a disturbance of symbolic balance—a loss of nondiscursive symbolism—behind the identity problem of modern times. This is an important reason why it may be said that society "cheats" in being unable to "pay off" emotionally. Few today pay attention to symbols, concerned as they are with economic, political, and similar practical matters. But if man is a symbolic animal, then when things go wrong with him, it is likely that his symbols will also go wrong—cause, effect, or both. Identity, as I see it, is a symbolic matter—a meaning attached to a person, or which he is able to attach to himself, with the help of the responses of others, as explained by the well-known theory of George H. Mead. Disturb these responses, disturb these meanings, and you disturb the man. A society fails to supply adequate identity when symbols are disturbed to the extent that they no longer give reliable reference points (in such things as status symbols, place symbols, style models, cultic values, mystiques) by which people can locate themselves socially, realize themselves sentimentally, and declare (to self and others) who they are. We now live in a world in which catastrophic changes are occurring in reference symbols, yet the notion persists that you can change a man's style, teach him new languages and a new religion, run tractors under his window wiping out a landscape, and he will still be the same man—with a little sophistication added perhaps. Symbolic catastrophes are happening not just in acculturating and war-torn countries; they are happening in the most prosperous lands, exploding like inaudible bombs in the quiet of suburbia. Among the casualties are those pervasive symbols—mystiques—that make the others, more tangible and verbal, significant. The unfortunate thing about symbols is that they are not replaced as easily as tires, rebuilt as easily as houses, or easily manufactured; often they are better when older. Although technology has a mystique of its own—of science, chrome, and efficiency—so far it has not supplied man with identity and a sense of belonging to the world. On the whole, technology has been much better at wiping away symbols than making them.

This book is not a critique of technology, however, but an effort to say what people in the mass do when identity symbols are disturbed. First, no doubt, they reassert them and cling to them; then, failing to find confirmation, they search for new ones. In describing this search, we shall begin with the paradox of unrest in *abundant* societies—"rebellion with no place to go"—then, after stating it as an identity problem due to symbolic disturbances rather than material shortcomings, we shall go on to describe mass responses to the disturbance of identity, concluding with a theory of symbolic balance and imbalance.

But what, in the name of symbols, are people searching for? In this book I make certain assumptions about what the need for identity consists of, namely, a need for a socially confirmed concept of self (adequate ego symbolism); fullness of sentiments, including mystiques; and centering or devotion, so that a person's life is focused on a point where he recognizes some highest value (*summum bonum,* perhaps a supreme "kick"). Then his life has "meaning"—and he has identity. To achieve such goals, a dissatisfied member of mass society enters various activities, seeking objectives which are largely nonrational, but nevertheless of great importance.

This book gives cultic movements, ritual, and mystiques more prominence than many writings do because I believe, as a sociologist, that they are important—far more so than one might judge if one took modern society on its own terms: bureaucracy, technology, and all that. To my view, modern society is so rationalistic and positivistic in its assumptions that (unlike Durkheim, a good positivist who emphasized the importance of cult) most writers are unwilling to put cultic activity on a par with practical activity. This is reflected in the literature of sociology, psychology, and semantics. But this, as I see it, does not dispose of cults and mystiques; it merely makes them thrive under other names, such as "fun," or "therapy," or possibly "science."

Identity-seeking behavior seems neurotic in such aspects as anxiety, pose (misplaced theatricalism), exhibitionism, identification with supermen—and so it is; but I do not thereby regard it as "abnormal"; at least it is very common among "normal" members of our society. Misplaced theatricalism is an effort to glamorize a life by using symbols in which there is not much confidence. But why is there not confidence? This, I would say, is a symbolic problem of society, not just a psychological illness of the individual. Rather than regarding identity search as psychologically abnormal, it is better to say that it is a collective search *outside the organizational and institutional channels* (regularized status passages) provided by work, school, church, organized recreation, therapy, penal institutions, and so on; and more in "leisure" very broadly conceived. This is collective behavior, technically defined by sociologists as outside organization. This area, of course, includes some deviance, much of the identity search consisting of peculiar and disreputable activity. But much of it is also just plain "fun."

Yet the peculiar directions taken by some people's identity search lead to a line of demarcation—a battle, if you like—between "square" and "nonsquare" in matters of style, which is now a fundamental feature of our society. From this point of view, this book is not about the "organization men" but the "outsiders," not about the "good scholars" but the "drop-outs"—though many are still hanging their coats reluctantly in the school cloakroom. Outsiders include a vast legion of restless, alienated, escapist, albeit conforming, people. Indeed, it might be that they make up a majority of the crowd which is masquerading, adventuring in play, or seeking some form of cult experience. They do this perhaps only as a vacation from their roles in square society. Leisure is a maze of identity-seeking activities under the aegis of "fun." Such paths taken by individuals are "streams," if we think of collective processes, by which people move in search of solutions, consciously or unconsciously. The general assumption is that this is what collective behavior is, an opportunity to free identity and find oneself anew. The assumption is that organizations fix identity, collectivities[1]* unfreeze it.

Though the thread of identity runs through all man's concerns and enterprises, leaving its signature on everthing he does, there is today a new preoccupation with identity; people are worrying about it. Identity is like wealth; when you have it you do not need it, but when it is gone, you know you do not have it. There has been a curious shift in concern in the last fifty years, from "making one's way" (in the Dick Whittington sense) to finding oneself. The urgent question of the twentieth century, in its looming age of leisure, is not What can I do? but Who can I be? "Who" questions are now becoming more important than "what" questions. And a new right has been defined (of which Jefferson never heard) to *be what one pleases*. But it is hard to realize this new right entirely within the conventional structure of success—for reasons such as the decline of employment, alienation from work, together with the competition of interesting, offbeat directions which conflict with work. So it seems likely that the new identities of the twentieth century will be sought more in leisure, possibly in religion, than in work. This throws all the more emphasis on collective behavior—people looking for things to do—the retired man getting out his golf bag or taking dancing lessons; the playboy buying fast cars and chasing thrills; the modernist trying new gadgets, hats, faces; the spiritually minded seeking second birth; the intellectual sifting ideas; the other-directed seeking crowds and social sets.

The rise of interest in identity problems has rather paralleled, but followed, interest in sexual neurosis; just as one did not know one had a neurosis until Freud and his followers began their work, so awareness of the identity problem had to wait for theories of the social self of James, Baldwin, Cooley, and G. H. Mead. The sequence came not just from the work of theorists, however. Exhaustion of reaction to sex helped create the identity problem. That is, as people lost taboos and became more familiar with sex, they lost their fascination with it—either its mystery or the sense of sin and rebellion against Puritanism. So one of the sources of personal meaning was taken away. Sex has been explored (therapeutically by some, hedonistically by others) and found to be neither a proof of manhood nor a sacrament nor a fertility cult nor diabolism, but a biological outlet, a mere convenience; or perhaps just an orgy of the League for Sexual Freedom. The loss of mystery in such things as sex has simply added to the need for mystiques with which to fill the void. For many, the old formulas for "saving" people will not do. A modernist cannot be satisfied by sin-and-salvation revivalism (what Marcus Bach calls the "conscience cults"), which require the mystique of sin. Freud helped the humanist movement to finish that. Nor will national identity serve true modernists. So the identity problem is taking shape as an ever larger task, of defining an identity for everyone in the world, hopefully without using obsolete goals like nationalism.

In this book we do not predict how identity will be achieved, but analyze what is going on now. To do so, we use certain concepts, sometimes special terminology, which may be useful to mention here. One concept is that of *groping*[2] as a form of social action. Groping rather nicely conveys the idea that a search is going on which is more or less in the dark, that what is being sought is not clear, that even having found it people are not quite sure what they have seized. The forms of collective behavior are the fingers of this exploration. The view of collective behavior as groping conflicts somewhat with its "outburst" character.[3] The groping view which stems from Robert E. Park, as developed by Herbert Blumer, is that collective behavior is basically concerned with building or rebuilding a social order, and emphasizes its symbolic or consensual goal, rational or nonrational. Le Bon implied as much when he said that the crowd creates gods. Such a view is also in accord with Sumner's treatment of the crescive growth of mores. Identity-seeking collective behavior belongs within this building. The groping idea of social action also comes in part from the pragmatism of John Dewey and George H. Mead, which asserts that truths and objects emerge from actions that do not know their goals in advance. No doubt the "outburst" theory fits some forms of collective behavior, such as panic. The purpose of this book was to select forms which identity seeking fits best.

A *seeker*, then, is taken as a person who is more or less actively, whether or not consciously, searching for a new self; his mobility and mass-mindedness reflect this preoccupation. *River* is a metaphor for the collective groping process, embodied in myriad seekers. *Social types* are considered as emergent or perfected styles which can serve as models for seekers. *Sym-*

bolic leaders are those whose public gestures and styles present an identity solution (not just a practical solution) to seekers; the leader having "found himself," perfected a style, offers it to the masses (or, rather, they use him) as a model. Such a leader might be a statesman, sports champion, playboy, hipster, beatnik, faddist, fashion plate, *guru,* devotee, crusader, rebel, crowd spellbinder, entertainer, or a therapist of some kind. *Group identity,* distinguished from individual identity, is an established conception which members may have of themselves as "we," which can serve as a superidentity or alter ego for them. *Poses* refer to identity experiments in which a person takes a role which is not his own, supported or unsupported by peers, group response, or models others supply. Every pose, however eccentric, is regarded as part of mass identity experimentation. A *grail symbol* is one which carries a mystique, offering an answer to life's meaning and redemption of identity, at the end of a quest. Seekers are unconsciously looking for a grail symbol, if only in wheat germ or Zen. *Mystique* refers here to that semantic "beyond" which ritual refers to and cultic movements aim at; which discursive symbols are unfitted for and rational techniques do not achieve. *Summum bonum* is used for any value high enough to be taken as the center and purpose of life ("it"), used to integrate the individual and as a basis of cult, secular or sacred. A *cult* refers to any group of devotees who use ritual to center on a highest value and realize and organize their lives by "it." Cult is used generically for a variety of activities beyond religion as ordinarily conceived, one of the prime goals of the collective groping process. Finally, *square* and *nonsquare* are used here in a technical sense to designate the position and direction of a seeker, whether within or outside the conventional social structure. I accept the viewpoint of the outsider as being a valid viewpoint, whether or not legitimate, as to what is going on in modern society; it may be that some of the most important identity solutions are antisquare.

Such definitions may be enough to give the reader a quick view of the ideas to be developed in this book and the way phenomena of collective behavior are to be treated as part of the search for identity.

In offering this book, with a scope indicated by the title, *Collective Search For Identity,* I must admit gaps in its coverage. One is that nationalistic movements, obviously an important part of the subject, are not treated as such, though many of the observations would apply to nationalistic movements. I am content with what, I hope, is a modest aim: I have tried mainly to develop an idea, following the thread of identity search in collective behavior, carrying on where I think writers such as Erik Erikson, Anselm Strauss, and Erving Goffman left off. The germs of the idea of the collective search for identity, of course, are found in many writings—by Charles H. Cooley, George H. Mead, Erich Fromm, Eric Hoffer, Herbert Blumer, Gustave Le Bon, William G. Sumner, Emile Durkheim, and Max Weber, to name only a few. Obviously I cannot claim to have empirically researched all areas treated in this book; it is better described as an arrangement of materials for a theoretical purpose, an effort to fit pieces together—exemplification, not proof. It has not been done before on this scale; it is important to those who see social behavior in symbolic terms—a society based on symbols and self as a symbol; and it should be interesting to the many readers who are today becoming conscious of the identity problem.

O. E. K.

Athens, Greece
December 1968

CONTENTS

PART I PROBLEM

1 Seekers

Know thyself.—Socrates

Be yourself.—Will Rogers

I yam what I yam, and that's all I yam.—Popeye

Which you am I talking to now?—James Thurber

He never knew who he was.—Arthur Miller

Take a look at yourself in the mirror and tell me what class you belong to—what your place is in society.—Jesùs Sanchez[1]

THE IDENTITY PROBLEM OF MODERN SOCIETY

My father lacked many things, but one thing he did not lack was a definite conception of himself. I am sure it never occurred to him (nor, perhaps, did it to your father, since we are dealing with a generational difference) to ask "who he was"; and he would have thought it odd, to say the least, that anyone should be concerned with such a problem. His problems—of which he had his share—were with external affairs; he had no time for introspection. Today attention is turning inward; more and more people are becoming aware that they have identity problems. Best-selling books with titles like *Modern Man in Search of a Soul, The Divided Self, The Supreme Identity,* and *The Magic Power of Self Image Psychology* show the concern of the public with finding itself. Identity is a fashionable topic for conversation in intellectual, artistic, and religious circles. We are more aware of a difference between our role and our true self—whatever that is. We present ourselves, put on faces, and play roles with great facility,[2] not regarding ourselves as hypocritical, as the older generation would. As a result, "Who are you?" is not just a televised game for celebrities—it is coming to be a fair question that might be asked of a housewife, an auto worker, a businessman. Indeed, in our modern society it is more fashionable to have an identity problem than a sexual neurosis.

It is paradoxical that our society, as it gains in abundance, should be losing knowledge of itself in the spiritual sense. Perhaps it is only as material problems are solved that we get time to sit around and ask questions about ourselves. Abundance also means freedom to pursue new interests, luxury, frivolity, mobility, emancipation from status obligations—unemployment for some—so there are many reasons why an abundant society should have identity problems. Whatever the causes, few can disagree that in America a vast uncertainty—about goals, the fitness of careers, the fitness of mates, the rightness of judgments, the right thing to tell children, what kind of person one is—has taken the place of that simple assurance which any tribal native or peasant feels. As a professor of philosophy once confessed to me, in talking about the meaning of life with a Minnesota farmer, "As I looked him in the eye I felt ashamed that he knew exactly where he stood but I didn't."[3]

In view of this uncertainty, it is ironical to see underdeveloped countries marching into the future as though they were going to receive the blessings of technology and abundance without the price of self-doubt that seems to go with them. Probably they would say, "Give us the tractors first and we'll be glad to take on the luxury of worrying about identity problems." No doubt, too, a Utopian dream of a good society—especially for Marxists—helps make this prospect palatable. But already, looking at Kenya Negroes, or Indonesians, or Latin Americans, it is hard to tell how much of their problem is hunger, and how much thwarted pride.

Many social scientists are intrigued with the idea of a *frustration ratio* as a measure of discontent and political instability—not of absolute deprivation, but the discrepancy between what one expects and what one is, has, or can do. In a frustration ratio, a purely intangible thing such as the idea "I am no longer the man I was" or "I am not the man I could be" can weigh more than a thousand dollars or a thousand bushels of wheat. Therefore, to frame the problem of frustration in terms of physical satisfactions without attention to the problem of identity seems meaningless. The fact that collective misery may have more to do with self images than politics or even economics[4] contradicts the whole outlook of economic determinism, which seems to be the implicit philosophy of those who put material problems first.

The American Negro is in a parallel predicament as he struggles toward equality though, in his case, the question is more pertinent because he is moving directly into the very situation where identity problems seem to thrive. No doubt his answer would be, "Give us the Thunderbirds and split-level homes, and we'll worry about the identity problem later." Moreover, it must be admitted that to trade a stigma on identity and status of menial for a mere confusion about identity may be a bargain.

At any rate, the stock answer of modernists—whether called progress lovers, culture exporters, imperialists, or missionaries—to any spiritual malaise arising from acculturation seems to be a naive one, namely, "Let people solve material problems and they will get around to the philosophical and psychological ones later." This is why the American case is so pertinent. For underdeveloped peoples it is a glimpse into the future: The world's most prosperous people seem not only to have not gotten around to solving their identity problem but do have a greater one than many of the unfortunate peoples to whom they are so generously extending help. That is why it is so important to see what Americans as leaders of modernization are doing about their own identity problems. A beacon light to the world? Or the blind leading the blind?

What, then, is an identity, and why should its problems not be solved by material progress? It seems plain that identity is not in any special way connected with possessions, but is any generally satisfactory answer to the question, Who am I? (Who are you?). While possessions may signify identity, lack of possessions may also do so, as in the case of a monk. Strictly it includes all things a person may legitimately and reliably say about himself—his status, his name, his personality, his past life. But if his social context is unreliable, it follows that he cannot say anything legitimately and reliably about himself. His statements of identity have no more reliability than a currency which depends upon the willingness of people to recognize and accept it. We feel that we can count on our identity not only because of habit but because we can count on people responding to it. As habit is a memory, in others it is an expectation, both of which are concepts. Since identity consists of concepts, rather than inherent qualities like eye color, it is always to some extent arbitrary, challengeable, and changeable—when people change their minds.[5] While identity does not require agreement, it does require a certain conjuncture or coincidence between what a person claims for himself and where others place him.[6] Fictions may give an illusion of constancy to identity[7] If indeed identity is a concept, it does not rest so much upon its accuracy as upon whether it is challenged: If I am in love with Jane and think she is beautiful, while she thinks I flatter her enormously, this does not constitute an identity problem for Jane; her identity as a beautiful woman rests upon the constancy of her admirers. Nor does it matter how much identity changes, provided that the feeling of continuity is preserved and all parties are reasonably satisfied by it. In short, identity rests far more upon satisfaction to self and others—a pragmatic relationship—than it does either upon actual qualities of a person or the physical circumstances in which one is placed. Indeed, far from being a God-given quality fixed in us by birth, as so many regard it, it is actually a fragile mechanism whose equilibrium needs constant maintenance and support from the proper environment, and it is quite easy for something to go wrong with it.

What, then, is an identity problem? At the simplest level, it is any serious dissatisfaction with the kind of person one is (rather than a mistake that can be rectified without changing one's self). And this is almost always associated with unsatisfactory "feedback" from others. Willie Loman's tragedy was not that he was a business failure but that he could not rectify the kind of person others saw him to be. On the other hand, a person can achieve a satisfactory identity through the physical destruction of himself, as in the case of a martyr who achieves a reputation highly satisfactory to himself and others although he is not around to enjoy it.[8] A person who has a serious identity problem needs, more than remedying a mistake, a kind of rebirth through an experience which washes away the blemished features of his self image which are a source of discontent to him as well as giving him a better reputation. But all achievements which produce better reputation do not produce rebirth.

Charles Chaplin's career might be regarded as a symbol of success to the common man, yet it shows poignantly the identity problems of a boy who makes good in Horatio Alger fashion—not only problems along the way but unresolved ones at the end. His life reveals at least three identity crises. First, there was the crisis of developing a stage personality—the Charlie Chaplin the public knows. Like many entertainers, he had not only to perfect skills but to throw away a style or two before he found the right one. Knowledge of who he was professionally was revealed in a horrifying crisis which he referred to as "the nightmare at the Forresters" Music Hall. It came during his overconfident debut as a Jewish-type comedian wearing false whiskers.

> After the first couple of jokes the audience started throwing coins and orange peel and stamping their feet and booing. At first I was not conscious of what was going on. Then the horror of it filtered into my mind. I began to hurry and talk faster as the jeers, the raspberries, and the throwing of coins and orange peel increased. When I came off the stage I did not wait to hear the verdict from the management; I went straight to the dressing room, took off my makeup, left the theatre and never returned, not even to collect my music books. . . . I did my best to erase that night's horror from my mind, but it left an indelible mark on my confidence. That ghastly experience taught me to see myself in a truer light; I realized I was not a vaudeville comedian, I had not that intimate, come-hither faculty with an audience; and I consoled myself with being a character comedian.[9]

Given another chance, at the London Coliseum, he discovered the right stage personality almost by accident:

> In an emotional chaos I went on. One either rises to an occasion or succumbs to it. The moment I walked onto the stage I was relieved, everything was clear. I entered with my back to the audience—an idea of my own. From the back I looked immaculate, dressed in a frock coat, top hat, cane and spats—a typical Edwardian villain. Then I turned, showing my red nose. There was a laugh. That ingratiated me with the audience. I shrugged melodramatically, then snapped my fingers and veered across the stage, tripping over a dumb-bell. Then my cane became entangled with an upright punching bag, which rebounded and slapped me in the face. I swaggered and swung, hitting my self with my cane on the side of the head. The audience roared.

Now I was relaxed and full of invention. I could have held the stage for five minutes and kept them laughing without uttering a word. In the midst of my villainous strutting my trousers began to fall down. I had lost a button. I began looking for it. I picked up an imaginary something, then indignantly threw it aside: "Those confounded rabbits!" Another laugh. . . . When the curtain came down, I knew I had made good.[10]

As we would say, he "found himself" as an actor. But is this really such a different kind of discovery from what any teenager makes who goes through an embarrassment and then succeeds? All roles and selves require testing before an audience, and it is sometimes hard to say whether failure on or off stage is the worst crisis.

The second crisis in Chaplin's autobiography came after his theatrical one, this time in real life, when he posed as a British aristocrat for a brief, glorious stay at the Astor Hotel in New York.

I took a room at the Hotel Astor which was quite grand in those days. I wore my smart cutaway coat and derby hat and cane, and of course carried my small suitcase. The splendor of the lobby and the confidence of the people strutting about it made me tremble slightly as I registered at the desk.

The room cost $4.50 a day. Timidly I asked if I should pay in advance. The clerk was most courteous and reassuring: "Oh no, sir, it isn't necessary."

Passing through the lobby with all its gilt and plush did something to me emotionally, so that when I reached my room I felt I wanted to weep. I stayed in it over an hour, inspecting the bathroom with its elaborate plumbing fixtures and testing its generous flush of hot and cold water. How bountiful and reassuring is luxury!

I took a bath and combed my hair and put on my new bathrobe, intending to get every ounce of luxury out of my $4.50 worth . . . if only I had something to read, a newspaper. But I had not the confidence to telephone for one. So I took a chair and sat in the middle of the room surveying everything with a feeling of luxuriant melancholy.

After a while I dressed and went downstairs. I asked for the main dining room. It was rather early for dinner; the place was almost empty but for one or two diners. The maitre d'hotel led me to a table by the window. "Would you like to sit here, sir?"

"Anywhere will do," I said in my best English voice.

Suddenly an industry of waiters whirled about me, delivering ice water, the menu, the butter and bread. I was too emotional to be hungry. However, I went through the gestures and ordered consomme, roast chicken, and vanilla ice cream for dessert. The waiter offered me a wine-list, and after careful scrutiny I ordered a half bottle of champagne. I was too preoccupied living the part to enjoy the wine or the meal. After I had finished, I tipped the waiter a dollar, which was an extraordinarily generous tip in those days. But it was worth it for the bowing and attention I received on my way out. For no apparent reason I returned to my room and sat in it for ten minutes, then washed my hands and went out.

It was a soft summer evening in keeping my mood. As I walked sedately in the direction of the Metropolitan Opera House. "Tannhauser" was playing there. I had never seen grand opera, only excerpts of it in vaudeville—and I loathed it. But now I was in the humor for it. I bought a ticket and sat in the second circle. The opera was in German and I did not understand a word of it, nor did I know the story. But when the dead Queen was carried on to the music of the Pilgrims' Chorus, I wept bitterly. It seemed to sum up all the travail of my life. I could hardly control myself; what people sitting next to me must have thought I don't know, but I came away limp and emotionally shattered.

I took a walk downtown, choosing the darkest streets, as I could not cope with the vulgar glare of Broadway, nor could I return to that silly room at the hotel until my mood had worn off. When I recovered I went straight to bed. I was emotionally and physically exhausted.[11]

Then Chaplin returned to the "old grind" after his day of "graceful living." This pose shows his desire for a different self, as well as the crisis in a fraudulent claim of identity with "neurotic" symptoms. It was not just the nervousness of a rookie trying a role for the first time but a trespass into an identity to which he had no right—at least at this point. However, it was not a serious fraud, like Fred Demara's, but an identity vacation.

After Chaplin's success—one might say transforming a Cockney boy into an English gentleman by successfully playing the role of an American tramp—he had a third major identity crisis, this one revealed by Francoise Gilot, Pablo Picasso's mistress. Growing old in body had made it impossible for Chaplin still to be the little clown. Picasso comments:

The real tragedy lies in the fact that Chaplin can no longer assume the physical appearance of the clown because he is no longer slender, no longer young, and no longer has the face and expression of his "little man," but that of a man who's grown old. His body isn't really him anymore. Time has conquered him and turned him into another person. And now he's a lost soul—just another actor in search of his individuality; and he won't be able to make anybody laugh.[12]

So Chaplin really did not achieve a permanently satisfactory identity by his image as "Charlie," but had to go through the crisis of a has-been who is no longer up to his role.

We draw on Chaplin's case not only because he is a symbol of every man searching for a self by trying on roles, but because it shows that success of a role, even as a celebrity, is not necessarily a solution to an identity problem. Judging from the number of famous people whose lives have become more tangled and miserable after success, there is little reason to believe their luck is better on the whole than that of those who seek themselves without the limelight. The public role may be a poor fit, or it may require a sacrifice of something else that the person wanted to do. Jack Benny, the American comedian, comments on his passion for violin playing:

I'm probably the greatest violinist who stopped studying at the age of twelve and didn't pick it up again until fifty years later . . . you have to understand something. The violin is my great love. I've often wondered—even brooded—what would have happened if I had made a career of it. You know what some critics now say? They say they can tell from the way I play certain passages that I would have been a great violinist.[13]

Picasso himself, for all his creative self-fulfillment, was apparently not as successful at coming to terms with himself as his friend Matisse. Francoise Gilot describes Matisse's inner peace and self-contentment—almost like that of an Oriental sage—in contrast with Picasso:

Pablo had almost a reverence for Matisse because Matisse's manner reflected an inner balance, a calm that brought peace even to a man such as Pablo. . . . I think that Matisse had eliminated from his thinking any sense of rivalry, and this made their friendship possible. His detachment from self was certainly the positive element in their relations.[14]

A bewildering succession of styles and "periods" may reveal that an artist has not found himself. Yet one does find celebrities—like the unforgettable Will Rogers or the jazz artists Erroll Garner and Louis Armstrong—who are so refreshingly themselves that it is a delight to see *them* as well as their performance. Armstrong says:

> When I pick up that horn the world's behind me. I don't concentrate on nothin' but that horn. I mean I don't feel no different about the horn than I did when I was playin' in New Orleans. No, that's my life and my livin'. I love them notes.[15]

Not shifting styles, nor a fixed style, nor even creativity, is a sign that an artist has found his identity; rather it is an immediate authenticity. Another jazz artist, Ahmed Jamal, says:

> People do seem to spot my sound right off. I think it's my approach. It's a certain touch, the same touch I've had since I started piano at age three. Whatever the touch is, I'm sure it has something to do with my extreme fondness for the piano. I always want to touch the keys with that fondness expressed in the sound. Even at my most percussive, the fondness will always be there.[16]

So people without identity problems, famous or not, have certain characteristics. They have a definite style with which they are satisfied. They don't doubt themselves or engage in soul searching of the kind which raises the question who am I or what should I be? They are not "shopping around," because their satisfaction comes from within themselves. They may, of course, have *been* through a period of searching and posing.[17] Still, a person who has really settled his identity problem may evince a spirit of dedication like that of Albert Schweitzer, Madame Curie, or Billy Graham. It may be that some cultures, eras, or classes supply their members with such satisfactory styles that relatively few have identity problems— for an example, think of the jokes about the extreme self-satisfaction of the Victorian Englishman, who took his toast, tea, and architecture with him wherever he went—even to Africa or the Himalayan highlands.

It may be useful to list the common symptoms of identity trouble.[18]

One is a feeling of being blemished, or that there is something wrong with one's self. For example, whether or not there is a physical basis,[19] a child might dislike his own name or face, or feel ugly because of moles or freckles. To the extent that a person carries feelings like this, his life becomes an effort to manage his tensions created by feelings of inacceptability in the eyes of others. A second unmistakable sign of an identity problem is self-hatred. A third is touchiness, oversensitivity, being easily wounded.[20] Such touchiness is because the ego is like an easily tipped canoe. The overcompensation Alfred Adler attributed to the inferiority complex is another aspect of this instability. A fourth sign of an identity problem is excessive self-concern, as when a person looks in the mirror too often, is self-conscious and easily embarrassed, is too fastidious about his appearance or style, or eats up flattery because he needs reassurance (sometimes called narcissism). Fifth is a feeling of alienation, a sense of being at war with the world or a stranger to one's own society, which implies that one has the wrong identity not only for the social structure but perhaps for all the roles offered in one's society. Sixth is the feeling of unrealized potentiality, that "nobody appreciates me," as illustrated by Ralph Ellison's *Invisible Man*. Seventh is a hankering to be somebody else, a high or remote aspiration that is actually a wish for another life rather than just success in a career. The wish might also be a yearning downward, or for another culture, era, or ethnic group.[21] Eighth is excessive consciousness of role-playing (awareness of self as an actor) in real life a feeling of fraudulence in roles voluntarily assumed, as illustrated by Chaplin's Hotel Astor pose. An interesting aspect of this, bearing on the celebrity's difficulty in finding himself, is the "hero's neurosis."[22] Ninth is excessive other-directedness, as described by David Riesman, or "role diffusion."[23]

A college sophomore says:

> I found early in life that a good way to be popular was to mirror the personalities around me, to assume their values, viewpoints and actions. With the pious I was pious, with the bawdy I was bawdy. As a person I was a hypocrite, getting along with almost everyone. I took on the role of student leader in high school. As president of the student body, one of my duties was chairman at the judicial committee, to prescribe punishment for those who violated the norms set by the student council and deans. The role of judge was extremely hard for me, having to impersonally pass sentence on a great many who were my friends.

By graduation one might say that I had reached my goal, being elected campus favorite by my classmates. But no, I was not at peace with myself. I could go on no longer as a bundle of contradictions. After a riotous first year of college, much drinking and contemplation, I have finally assumed the role of the semi-isolate, academic student, closer to self and reality, and closing in on happiness.

Such other-directedness may be expressed in a chameleon-like shifting of style, manners, and attitudes; or a tinkering with one's self as in faddism; or a "shopping around" for faiths and cults. Tenth is an identity crisis in which the grounds of one's self-assurance are shaken and the assumptions on which one has based one's life are felt to be untenable. This might result from a withdrawal of familiar social cues, or a rebuff by others on whom one has counted:

> Rosamond, while these poisoned weapons were being hurled at her, was almost losing the sense of her identity, and seemed to be waking into some new terrible existence. . . . All her sensibility was turned into a bewildering novelty of pain; she felt a new terrified recoil under a lash never experienced before. . . . When Will had ceased to speak she had become an image of sickened misery: her lips were pale, and her eyes had a tearless dismay in them. . . . The poor thing had no force to fling out any passion in return; the terrible collapse of the illusion towards which all her hope had been strained was a stroke which had too thoroughly shaken her: her little world was in ruins, and she felt herself tottering in the midst of a lonely bewildered consciousness.[24]

Eleventh is an unresolved ethical dilemma so severe that it is in fact an identity crisis, in which a person can't decide which self to be, epitomized by Sergeant York's paralysis until he chose between military and Christian. Twelfth, despair in the absence of a physical threat to existence or career is probably a sovereign symptom of an identity problem.[25]

Identity despair implies that "there is something about me I cannot do anything about." Such despair might come late in life to a man who has two cars, two homes, two television sets, and still is not what he wanted to be; it might come to an artist whose creativity is dead, who feels that he has nothing else to live for. While identity despair may lead to suicide, it is very likely that many more lead lives of what Thoreau called "quiet desperation." It is plain that feelings like these may strongly motivate one to leave one's old life, to seek experiences by which to change one's self, to engage in collective behavior or social movements which are not part of the old structure; in short, these symptoms in a mass society produce the behavior which is the focus of this book.

SOURCES OF IDENTITY PROBLEMS

Another thing (besides motivation to engage in new experience) which seems plain from such symptoms is that identity problems are not troubles an individual gets into by using or misusing his mind, but result from a social milieu—perhaps a lack of structure or feedback—which makes it harder for individuals to define themselves satisfactorily, even when they use their minds properly and even when they have plenty of time to sit around and wonder who they are. Why, indeed, should we have so many identity problems in modern life? It cannot be for lack of rationality for we have more rational information and techniques than ever: in terms of scientific inquiry, numbers of people with access to education and psychiatry, control of nature, and rationalization of institutions.[26] The problem has shifted from philosophy (Socrates' "Know thyself") into psychology, psychiatry, and sociology: defining the kinds of situations which make it harder for normal people to find themselves. If a situation is unfavorable enough, relatively few people, no matter how clever, can achieve satisfactory identity. If a social system is defective in role casting, it becomes like a play in which most of the actors are dissatisfied with their parts; or, worse, extras standing around with no parts at all. If a social system is inadequate in feedback and symbolization, it cannot give individuals an adequate sense of meaning—of others or of themselves. If it is defective in the support it gives to individuals, they have no solid basis for the feeling of belonging.

Therefore, people easily feel outside and have to search for roles and identities. In such a world, an Einstein has only a slightly better chance of finding who he is than a Willie Loman or a Jesùs Sanchez. All this has little to do with either rationality or abstract justice. We may find the paradox that a society which treats men unequally and rather unfairly may give them a stronger sense of identity than one which treats men equally but fails to define roles clearly. For example, the English, to an American, may seem to put people into their place, whatever it is. An English teacher will tell a child quite firmly, "You have no talent in mathematics," or "I wouldn't advise you to take the O-level examination." There is a sense of finality about such placements. (An American child in an English school responded almost with panic to this.) Englishmen act with reserve and concern themselves with correctness because they expect to be placed by their deportment and speech. By contrast, an American is freer to let himself go and is more blurred in his sense of social place. He is never quite sure where to put people (including himself) or whether they will stay. One advantage of this, of course, is openness of opportunities; but one might make the case that a sharp, clearly defined classification may settle more questions about who one is than a vague promise to develop abilities which may or may not be there and which, when developed, may not find a place waiting.

In this light, we recognize common kinds of situations which generate identity problems. One is the breaking up of old traditions in connection with modernization and acculturation.[27] This represents not merely a political and economic change but an explosion of identity needs, in which people may be seeking both an individual and a collective self image. Modernizing societies should be expected to generate identity problems in proportion to their rate of modernization. "Japanese women are confused," says a feminine graduate student at the University of Tokyo. "They are not Westerners. They are no longer Japanese. They are in the middle." But those over 45 keep to the old ways. In a similar predicament, Hindu women try to preserve their identities by insisting on the traditional costume as a symbol of femininity, even when it is inconvenient or uncomfortable. Asked why she persisted in wearing the sari for business, even riding a bicycle, an Indian woman admitted:

> It isn't for esthetic reasons, nor even for practical ones. We go on wearing the sari because we are not just women but Indian women. The sari is our flag. To give it up would be a betrayal—as if we were giving up our nationality.

Beatnik movements and troublemaking by university students in developing countries likewise need to be interpreted in the light of the effort to preserve or fabricate new identities—a need perhaps accentuated in females.

A second familiar situation generating identity problems is that of a minority group with an unsatisfactory identity imposed by prejudice and discrimination, in which members feel outside a society whose values they have none the less accepted. Few have been more outspoken than James Baldwin in expressing this kind of grievance among American Negroes:

> We are afraid to reveal ourselves because we trust ourselves so little. . . . The person is desperately trying *not* to find out what he *really* feels . . . the truth cannot be told . . . about one's attitudes: we live by lies. . . . Nothing more sinister can happen, in any society, to any people. And when it happens, it means that the people are caught in a kind of vacuum between their present and their past—the romanticized . . . past, and the denied and dishonored present. It is a crisis of identity. And in such a crisis . . . it becomes absolutely indispensable to discover, or invent . . . the stranger, the barbarian, who is responsible for our confusion and our pain. Once he is driven out—destroyed—then we can be at peace. . . .[28]

The American Negro, says Essien-Udom, has a sense of "two-ness." He "cannot choose both" white culture and Negro subculture;[29] so for him separation as a Black Muslim and hating whites is one move toward unity. Likewise, one may see the significance of jazz "soul" music as an expression of yearning for authentic identity. On the other hand, the Hopi Indians of Arizona chose to withdraw to isolation at Oraibai to preserve their image of themselves and avoid two-ness. For the ethnic minority which, instead of separating, tries to stay and compete, carrying the subtle burden of a prejudice which denies opportunities, the price is often group self-hatred, as pointed out by Kurt Lewin. The paradox, then, in an age of anxiety over identity, is that ethnic *solidarity* acquires new importance. People may grasp at it even when it carries the price of conflict or persecution.[30] The dilemma seems to be that a clear identity, even with discrimination, seems better than "nothing-ness." Yet "nothingness" could be like the ritual bath in which new identity is found—if only people will let go, immerse—though it by no means follows that every whirlpool is a baptism.

A third broad kind of situation generating identity problems may be called mobile pluralism: great movement of persons from one status, subculture, class, community, job, church, school, family, or association to another in a milieu with great variations. This means pressure to adjust one's identity with situations, rather than holding fast to one image. The experience of Japanese exchange students visiting America illustrates disturbance of identity as they are plunged into not discrimination, but acceptance. Some developed a "double identification," perceiving their own identity as a blend of American and Japanese traits; some developed a "double alienation" without clear identity, whether Japanese or American; some returned to Japan more strongly identified with American than with Japanese ways—the women's

> . . . whole approach to life had altered. Their attitudes toward the roles of the sexes had changed: they were no longer so timid, and sometimes in mixed company they preferred the companionship, the intellectual level, of men. They demanded equal treatment from men and were frequently considered too "forward." . . . They were often regarded as Americanized and defeminized.

And some returned to Japan disillusioned with America and more strongly Japanese. Those who suffered the greatest stress were the "idealists" who, critical of Japan and wishing to reform it, tried hard to find satisfying relations with Americans and to find themselves, saw themselves as avant-garde intellectuals or modernists, and often wound up alienated from both Japan and America. Less disturbed were "adjusters," who played American roles but kept their Japaneseness intact—meeting Americans with casual freedom, accepting egalitarian cues—and "constrictors," who remained conservatively Japanese, avoided intimate contact with Americans, and smiled politely at everything that was said.[31]

So there are strategies for preserving identity in a mobile pluralistic setting—such as withdrawal, or learning to play roles without involving oneself (which may become such a skill that a person takes pride in role-playing *per se* and it becomes for him a source of integrity). But the challenge and threat are always there, for the question is endlessly repeated: How much revision of identity and alienation from one's old self are necessary for adjustment to each new group? How much will each new association claim? And how much will it give—or fail to give—in return? Is the price of new memberships a weakening of all identities based upon membership and reference groups? Does mobility, then, mean a richer identity or merely a wallet full of membership cards that don't mean anything? A critical point seems to be reached when people enter statuses at a faster rate than they can grow the loyalties, self images, character, habits, and life styles that go with them.

A fourth common threat to identity, especially important to modern, as contrasted with modernizing, societies, is lack of employment and the opportunity to prove oneself by work—an especially serious crisis for people raised in the Protestant ethic. Automation, as we all know, is an unparalleled threat today, which leads us to expect that, in societies where it is a great force, there will be a surge of discontent and restless mass groping for new kinds of significance—in recreation, furious play, religion and cultic activity, associations, community activity, fad and fashion, misbehavior, sexual promiscuity, rebellion, and, more hopefully, education and the arts.

Then there are the identity problems that seem to center around the rational and formal nature of roles in a technological and bureaucratic order: a person may have a very well-defined goal—and in material terms a just one—without deriving satisfaction from it. Such dissatisfactions include the feeling that one is a "cog" in a machine; loss of femininity in business and mechanized work; loss of joy and pride in craftsmanship; and the mediocre, essentially unheroic, self image of "bureaucrat" and "white collarworker".[32]

These are five very common situations threatening identity that might be found in any modern or modernizing society. America herself has a grand combination of them—with some emphases of her own. We have a society in which people are badgered by advertisers into being as discontented with themselves as possible. There is also the stimulation from celebrities we experience through mass communication: we may imitate their styles, hanker to be entertainers and stars, and glamorize careers of fashion models, disc jockeys, and rock-and-roll musicians. These intensify the struggle for status symbols as almost everyone presumes above his station. But the furious pursuit of status symbols does not guarantee that people will find identity. Standards of style dissolve, even with the help of tastemakers[33] and social arbiters.[34] Not only that, but the reference groups and places and status symbols change continually. The tractors are always at work and whatever you have done may be wiped away tomorrow: your home, your name on the office door. So you get that status symbol; but no one notices your new hat in church, the neighbors don't know you got that promotion, the Lincoln Continental arouses respect but no one recognizes who is in it. In the midst of all this movement and insecurity, the illusion persists: "There is some status and identity which is right for me; I just haven't found it yet." So yearning for identity, and a certain amount of dissatisfaction with it, are permanent minor harmonies to the melody of pursuit of happiness.

This is the heady brew of freedom that intoxicates the immigrant to America dreaming of opportunities, then stuns him with its disregard of style and ambiguities (such as pervasive friendliness, imprecise English, changing fashions) which make it difficult for him to place people or to define himself. Once he has weathered Ellis Island, he is usually eager to trade his firm self conception (as a Greek, Syrian, Swede, Irishman, and so forth) for the blurred identity which will be offered to him, or at least to his children. For one cannot argue that abundance of goods guarantees integrity of style, any more than that rummaging through piles of clothing on a bargain counter make it likely that one will come out with a good fit. It is an abundance of "status symbols" which in fact give very little status. Guidelines, reference points, and feedback for identity are needed; and these may be just what the immigrant is giving up as he spends his first paycheck in the basement of a New York department store. Is there any reason to be sure that his grandson, with three times as much income and a college education, will find these guidelines?

To attempt to pinpoint all the sources of identity problems recognized by sociologists, psychologists, psychiatrists, philosophers, and theologians.[35] would take us too far afield. I merely wish to treat identity disturbance in general terms as part of a *meaning vacuum* which results from defective symbolic responses of one kind or another. We do not usually receive the kinds of responses from our fellows that will permit us to feel ourselves: deeply (in warm relationships or strenuous tests) as a unity or whole (continuously as the same kind of person), of inherent worth (creatively fulfilling inner potential), and living "for" something (a cause, value, or ideology in which one deeply believes). To the high school senior who says, "I have found it very hard to find my place in the world, a cause that would give me a reason for being here," the Christopher movement replies:

> Have a purpose in life, and, having it, throw such strength of mind and muscle into your work as God has given you. (Thomas Carlyle) Whether you are in the home, at work or in school, you owe it to yourself and others to give of your best. Don't let frustration, hardship or opposition deter you from living up to your responsibilities with the quiet enthusiasm that can transform the humdrum of everyday life into a meaningful challenge. There is no substitute for you! "Everyone has his own specific vocation or mission in life; everyone must carry out a concrete assignment that demands fulfillment. Therein he cannot be replaced, nor can his life be repeated. Thus, everyone's task is as unique as his specific opportunity to implement it" (Victor Frankl).

One must relate the loss of sense of purpose to symbolic conditions of modern life (applying just as much to the average person as to those who are poor or underprivileged) which often deprive one of the feedback one needs to define oneself satisfactorily as a person. There are lacks of symbolic self-reference to be found in: (1) information accumulation, (2) modernism, (3) mobility (transforming "place" into "space"), and (4) lack of ritual for emotional intensification and self-definition, which contribute to the sense of emptiness in modern life. These are all essentially symbolic failures, largely at the nondiscursive, or "silent,"[36] level, in providing status symbolism, interactive feedback, and ritual mystique, as we will explain later.

LACK OF IDENTITY IN ACCUMULATING INFORMATION

A leading "rock" group, "The Rolling Stones," complain in one of their best known songs about the deluge of irrelevant information— that a man comes on the radio telling one more and more which gives no satisfaction because it does not drive one's imagination. Thus they express, in terms eloquent for teenagers, what many of us feel about public communication, whether advertising, news or education. The paradox we have already noted is that with increasing knowledge modern societies have not gained in self-knowledge and assurance, that the knowledge explosion of modern times is associated with an increase in identity problems. By ordinary reasoning, as knowledge of the world and the past increases, man should know himself better, and feel more a part of the world he knows. But this does not seem to be the case. As the number of potential reference points has multiplied, the ability to refer oneself to these points has declined. The knowledge explosion of modern life has not been accompanied by a self-knowledge *im*plosion. On the contrary, as with Faust, when man knows the most he begins to suffer an identity problem.

History provides one example, offering the paradox that as historical knowledge accumulates, a sense of familiarity with the past lessens. When we feel the obvious pride the English take in battles like Waterloo or in the defeat of the Spanish Armada—or the Americans in the Boston Tea Party, or the Greeks in "Ochi Day"—we see that history is a series of events which can greatly intensify a people's sense of who they are. The formation of the state of Israel was a tremendous shot-in-the-arm to the Jewish identity. Yet, in spite of this obvious function that historical knowledge can have for identity, people today are getting out of touch with *their* past. Our society is becoming, in a real sense, traditionless and historyless; history and tradition are becoming less relevant to what we do as a people. There is a break with the past at precisely the time when books of history, as of other kinds of information, are being published by the hundreds. There seems to be less reference to the past of the kind that can identify one with the past.

The key is in the distinction between knowledge as information and knowledge which identifies. It seems at first glance nonsense to say that any people could be free from their own history, unless we bear in mind that a people's behavior is not just the effect of causes in the past but also the effect of continual reference to the past which makes them more or less traditional, more or less characteristic as a people, and more or less predictable. On the one hand, it would be absurd to deny that causation chains ever stopped, that there is any discontinuity in the causations of time. All the causes operating in any historical period are carried into the next, and in this sense, nothing ever escapes from the past. But, on the other hand, people can lose culture and knowledge of the past: for example, the Mayan Indians of Yucatan today, although they speak the Mayan language, are unable to recall anything of the grandeur of the culture they once had, and cannot even explain the architecture and artistic ruins found in the jungle. In this sense, it is a very real possibility to lose the past.

But this isn't the problem in a civilization with a vast amount of printed and broadcast information. It is, rather, that very little of this information can be claimed as "mine" or "ours." It lacks personal connection. One uses it to describe what happens to "some people", not to "my people." The knowledge of today is information *about*, not knowledge which *identifies*, which creates a sense of union. Objective knowledge is neutral, it excludes the subject and his feelings, it is factual rather than poetic. By contrast, knowledge which identifies creates a sense of union, takes a person into the subject; it may not be factual at all. For example, a movie we call a "tear jerker" takes a person into an experience. So does a letter from home, which is more than knowledge about certain people. Empathic knowledge involves you, heightens the sense of "I" and "we." But it seems plain that today most information is impersonal: even the history of one's country or region, even the description of the community in which one was born lacks that "hometown" feeling. Further, most empathic experiences are with strangers, with whom one can feel no personal bond.

This is the reason, it seems to me, that we can have today the paradox of accumulating history and decline of tradition. I define tradition as the sense of living continuity with the past, the feeling of ownership that goes along with ideas from the past, normally the record we call history is part of tradition; but it is possible to lose tradition and still gain history. History, when it is not tradition, becomes a dead record of the ages and generations which we do not feel as ours. It is remote, irrelevant; our ancestors might as well be some other people. Yet traditionless history is, I think, taught today both at the high school and the university level. Debunking great men and criticizing the legendary aspects of history merely add to the alienation. Did Betsy Ross make the first flag? Did Dame Frietchie do what Whittier said she did? Was Lincoln an idealist?

"No" to such questions means that another warm link with the past has been sundered. Traditionless history poses a problem of teaching history and making it come alive. But how can you make history come alive in a society that assumes the past is dead, antique, mythical, or irrelevant? If the past becomes dehumanized, impersonal, and irrelevant, even though we know about it, there is still a general loss of touch with the past as a source of we-feeling, ancestral pride, as roots of identity for the collectivity and the person.

What I am saying applies, of course, not only to history but to sociology, psychology, biology, and the other, less human, sciences. In short, the creators of objective knowledge (and to a great extent this is true also of art) are producing a body of information with which *no one can identify* in a personal way—not even (final irony!) the author himself. Such a mass of impersonal information is incapable of being forefather, father, mother, brother, comrade, friend—let alone God. So knowledge explodes beyond the mind, but not into the heart of man. Always we are outside, and even when we enter such knowledge we do so as strangers. Obviously the pursuit of mystiques—Yoga union, LSD "trips," group catharsis—counteracts such knowledge and represents an effort to get to the heart of things.

Traditionless history and inhuman knowledge illustrate the fact that it is possible for society to accumulate knowledge and things in such a way that they do not help people to establish identity—and may even stand in the way of it. The question is one of symbolic reference points; whether our society is supplying enough reference points for people to identify themselves, or whether it is erasing them too rapidly. Identity—the answer to the question, Who am I?—depends upon symbolic reference points which enable a person to remember who he is. For example, a diary—you go back to a diary to find out how you felt and how you thought in past days. It is a symbolic reference point for you. But what is happening to the symbolic reference points of modern life? Are we losing them in our knowledge of the past and our relations with people?

MODERNISM: PLACE INTO SPACE

Those who are optimistic about modernization, such as Daniel Lerner, think of it as bringing an increased freedom to imagine oneself as a kind of person (or in a situation) different from what is. But the other side of the question is whether, in gaining such freedom, people lose symbolic ties with the meaning of their lives. For example, anthropologists note that corn is not just a utilitarian economic good among American Indians but a means of worshipping the gods. When we teach them to shift to other kinds of cash crops, we may give them more income but deprive them of a meaningful area of their lives. Here is a similar example that applies to more Americans. It is a statement by a Connecticut dairy farmer about what happened to the meaning of his life. One might call it a sentimental essay in favor of rootedness. He speculates on why few people who live where they were born commit suicide:

> Too many of their ancestors are watching as they load the gun or mix the poison. Natives of a place feel themselves in the presence of a continuing life force larger than they are. Someone cares. Surrounded by sights, sounds, and people totally familiar to him, the man who lives where he was born is rarely alone. No matter what a failure he may be—and everyone broods on failure as he measures himself against what he once hoped to accomplish—no matter how wasted his life may have been, it is difficult for the man who lives where he was born, be it city, town, or tiny village, not to derive pleasure from something each day of his life. A tree he saw planted—now sixty feet tall—the first patch of grass that sets green early in the spring, a bunch of boys playing baseball in the same lot where he once played baseball.
>
> The town or village native knows many secrets. He knows, for instance, who lived in what is now a funeral parlor. He knows where the old road went before the new one was built. Let the air be filled with the smell of sewage, he will tell you whose septic tank is overflowing. He can also tell you when it's going to rain. Considered one by one, these secrets have little value. Taken as a whole, however, they can be as priceless as life itself. Furthermore, the man who lives where he was born, when he hears a train whistle or a church bell or the voices of children as they are let out of school, can in the merest of instants, relive his entire life. Sounds that are inaudible to most ears can make him young again. He possesses an indestructible immortal contentment.
>
> People need the familiar just as they need food. Most people would truly rather see the same places, the same things, the people every day of their lives than be exposed to the new and different.
>
> In my New England city, one of our more prominent citizens was persuaded by his family to take a round the world cruise. He saw

London, Paris, Rome, the Near East, the Far East, all the oceans, and most of the wonders produced by man. Home at last and having appeared at his club where for forty years he had sat at the same table and eaten the same lunch being served by the same waiter, he was asked how he had enjoyed his trip. "Oh," he said, with an obvious lack of enthusiasm, "it was okay, I guess, except all I could think about was all the fun I was missing at home."

What should we feel for this citizen? Contempt for his provincialism? Should we scorn him because he prefers his own house to the Taj Mahal? Or should we instead envy him his contentment? Hamlin Garland describes his emotions as he returned to the prairy home of his boyhood. He was depressed to find how much everything had changed at the hands of even so few enterprising settlers. The prairy, trackless and wild when he was a boy, had been tamed and plowed. Where there had been only crossroads, there were now towns, and towns had become cities. It took him a full day of searching to discover even a small patch of virgin prairy sod. But if progress was unsettling to an absentee Garland, one may well imagine how distressing these same changes are to the man who remains in his birthplace and who, therefore, sees them happen. This being the era of the bulldozer, if a patch of prairy sod or any sod at all is to be preserved, it must be declared a national monument.

However, just as it is impossible for almost any man to live where he was born and be totally miserable, so it is impossible for him to be totally happy. He lives in a state of constant outrage against those who are confining his childhood memories in concrete pipes all in the name of flood control. He resents the miles of plywood he sees snaking over the land. "Where are the trees on which I carved my initials?" he asks. As he looks about his birthplace, he feels the bulldozers crush him as well. He feels himself being engulfed by the inexorable tide of men and machinery. The man who lives where he was born prefers things that have not changed to those which have. It may now take him only eight minutes to reach the center of the city instead of thirty-five, but he prefers to remember what was under the new road. He sees growing numbers of people as a skin disease. Secretly, he longs for a plague to stop every bulldozer dead in its tracks. Only his ever dwindling supply of secrets sustains him. Perhaps it would have been better if he had moved. Every day on his way to work, the man who lives where he was born passes the grave of his ancestors and their aspirations, noble or ignoble, by some osmosis become part of his own. He is a sentimentalist and an increasingly frustrated one. Of course, all those who live where they were born are, like philosophers, without immediate honor in their own community. We still have in our city, for instance, a native son who may shortly become the president of one of the richer corporations in the world. Only 45, but already a director of a score of companies, the father of four children and the owner of a yacht, the recipient of a dozen national awards in his chosen profession, he has everything that it is possible for a generous providence to bestow—except the respect of those who went to school with him, because he cried, he *cried* on his graduation day when he failed to win the good posture prize. He should, of course, have moved away and triumphed elsewhere, because just as others who live where born know many secrets about you, you also know many secrets about them.[37]

This New Englander's complaint about the destruction of the scene of his boyhood illustrates what I mean about the loss of the symbolic reference points of identity. What is one to say about his complaint? Why doesn't he welcome the bulldozer? Is it mere sentimentality, a fear of the newfangled, a wish to hold up progress and turn the clock back? I think it is a mistake to put this issue in terms of progress versus antiprogress. If we do so, we shall miss the real issue. It seems to me he has a legitimate complaint. He is expressing an injury to his integrity which came from wiping away the symbols that made *his* environment meaningful and *his* kind of identity possible. He has, in a sense, been robbed of identity—a loss which to some extent applies to practically everyone in the United States. This injury to integrity comes not from progress, but from a too rapid and indiscriminate sweeping away of symbols. In the accumulation of new things, it is possible for society to pass the optimum point in the ratio between the new and the old: between piling up information and material wealth on the one hand and old things which have merely souvenir value; between innovation and acculturation on the one hand and tradition on the other. Beyond this optimum point, where a society is roused to creativity by introduction of new elements, is a danger point where consensus and integrity of the person break down. At such a point, too many symbols lose their meaning and there begin to be questions about whether life is meaningful, life styles become unstable and confused, there is excessive faddism and a general loss of touch with the past and the present as a source of we-feeling. Much of this comes not from progress *per se*, but from insufficient recognition of the symbolic problem: that symbols are important, and cannot be replaced by mere things. The only intelligent way to replace a symbol is to build another symbol. Who worries about this?

We suffer in America from rampant, dogmatic modernism; we look with complacency, if not pleasure, at the fact that we are a country of vanishing traditions—with perhaps the fewest traditions in the world. One aspect of this is faddism; the rate of change in American styles is too fast to be good even for a modernist. We find, for example, the curious phenomenon of the old learning from the young. Passing a dancing school in Santa Monica, California, I looked in to see a number of men and women of 40 to 60 dancing with young instructors and instructresses. A person not born in America could not help but think it strange that there is a reversal of the usual socialization pattern, in which we find the old turning to the young for knowhow, if not wisdom—with style change among the young so rapid that the old feel out of date and can get "with it" only by turning to the young for guidance. I thought no more about this until I went to a party and found the hostess, who was well over 50 years in age, announcing that they were going to do some of the new dances; and the lady had, in fact, brought in three teenagers to teach the new steps. This phenomenon of the old looking to youth for guidance raises questions about the dignity and integrity of identity in America, and whether the optimum ratio of change has not been passed. Not only is the rate of change too fast for persons over 40, but there is a melange of styles borrowed from almost everywhere—for example, in popular music—which makes it hard to identify a national style even of the moment. With such a style melange, the natural question for the person is, Which style identifies me? Which identifies my class? My people? In the light of such ambiguity, we see a nostalgia for tradition in the fad of folk singing, which has the ability to transport a person momentarily back to the frontiers, to the cotton fields, to a Mississippi River boat, to the feeling of a lonely cowboy or a Civil War campfire—to a sense of the living past to which one belongs. But pseudofolk singing is only a pseudosymbol and creates only a pseudopast.

Modernism acting upon the American scene is symbolized by the bulldozer and the ever-changing faces of billboards. The call to bring in the bulldozer is linked with slogans like "live modern, smoke a———." This modernism rides roughshod over every consideration that is not economically and politically organized. Aside from a few antiquarian and historical interests, there is no voice, no pressure group, for symbols as such. Bulldozers wipe away every scene and the reference points that make local identity possible. It is commonplace that the wide-open spaces are disappearing in the United States (that even camping is coming to have an uncomfortable resemblance to apartment-house dwelling). It is not yet so keenly realized, however, that *places* are disappearing even faster than space in the United States.

What is a place? A place is a space with a sense of locality and identity. It is a recognized territory of symbols: my old neighborhood, Plymouth Rock, Canterbury Cathedral where Becket was murdered. Stepping over the battefield at Vicksburg, one is aware one is in a place. Obviously, bulldozers, as they clear spaces for tract housing, high-rise apartments, and parking lots, for hordes of strangers moving in, destroy places because they destroy the symbols and sense of familiarity with the territory. As America becomes one vast suburbia, high-rise center, and parking lot, it will cease to be a place and become a modernized space. Even Hilton Hotels, grand as they are, seem more space than place. Space is *in* human geography (just as history can be traditionless). A geographer, Philip Wagner, remarked, "I wonder if geography is not working at cross purposes with history?" By this he meant that the tendency of geography to treat places in an indifferent way, like other places, deprives them of their identity.

In this sense much of Los Angeles is a space, not a place. Some slums are not much to look at, but they have the distinction, at least, of being places. Disneyland, though fun to go to, a children's mecca perhaps, might be called a pseudoplace, really more space than place—a lot of ingeniously arranged concrete that creates the illusion of somewhere one has been. My point is that space—perhaps even pseudoplace—robs identity. Place, on the other hand, nurtures it, tells you who you are—either "I belong" or "This is foreign to me, I am an outsider"—and one achieves identity by differentiation. Will the trend from place into space continue? Will the future world become a modernized space rather than a place? One sees already phenomena such as Aswan Dam drowning historic monuments in Egypt. A traveler may wake up some morning and not know where he is—Egypt, South Africa, Japan, or Los Angeles. In the light of these considerations, I cannot see a gain for identity in modernization as a destroyer of place. It still is an open question whether new human symbols can be devised which will replace local sense of place.

MOBILITY: PERSON INTO CATEGORY

The conversion of place into space is, of course, closely associated with the well-known mobility and "rootlessness" of Americans. And this mobility is associated with an ambiguity of the person, which may not be such a crisis to Americans as it is to foreigners in America because we natives are used to it. Daniel Boorstin calls it the "ideal of the undifferentiated man"; it is not a shock to find a judge shoeing a horse, the boss playing baseball with employees, the housewife who is also a business executive. We do not expect people to maintain differences, be status-conscious, hold themselves apart. (By contrast, Kurt Lewin noted that a German customs official in a bathing suit is still a customs official.) You cannot place a man by where he comes from, his antecedents, even the status symbols he displays. It is entirely up to him. "Prove yourself. Who are you?"

But ambiguity is perhaps a terrible burden for a social system to bear. I wish to analyze here how it is a problem for the reference points and feedback which identity needs. Mobility, of which American society provides such good examples, is one of the favorite concepts of the sociologist. He distinguishes physical mobility as movement in space from social mobility as contact with different groups, classes, and kinds of people (including what I would call places). To take a familiar example, a society doctor meeting charity cases at the county hospital is contacting classes of people different from himself and is highly mobile socially. The history of our country is a kind of story of physical and social mobility, of the immigration of pilgrims and other settlers, the movement westward, the escape into the frontier, the success story of Babbitt, the status revolutions of new classes rising into power—*nouveaux riches* overthrowing Tories, Whigs, and Mugwumps; the rise of bureaucrats, technicians, and manangers; the overthrow of society by "publiciety," as described by Cleveland Amory. There are also what might be called the convection currents of population—such as the drift from land to the towns, the flight from the central cities to the suburbs, the movement of migratory workers, the daily motions of commuters, even grandma and grandpa on wheels in their retirement. I have asked my sociology classes whether they intend to follow their parents' occupation. The answer, as you may expect, is almost unanimously No. Ask them how many changes of residence they have had since they were born, and the median is sometimes ten or eleven moves.

Now the centrally significant psychological fact about social mobility of any kind is that you can't move without leaving a place, therefore losing a place; and you can't make new contacts without in some way lessening or disrupting old relationships. Thus mobility pulls roots, and *makes particular persons less important* in their relationships with one another. In very mobile societies, there is a feeling of "Bye bye, I won't see you long." It can be illustrated by the experience of changing schools: the student makes friends all over again—are his new friends the same as the friends he left in his previous school? Or it is illustrated by a series of love affairs and marriages: Is the first the same as the fifth and the tenth?

We have the general affect of numbers in similar relationship, as pointed out by sociologists. As long as only one person is in a relationship, he is "somebody special"; if others can share it or replace him, it is a class of relationship. If you have a hundred or a thousand people in the same relationship, you begin to have a mass. As greater numbers are encountered in a category, there is a dilution of attention and concern which results in impersonality and mass-likeness of human relations. So the students become just one in a class of a hundred, and a patient becomes just case number fifteen in a ward. But this mass-likeness, as we well know, is not just found in large groups, but also in America has entered friendly and personal relationships. If you are lucky enough still to be living with the twenty or so people that you were raised with, you probably still feel you are "somebody special," but the majority of people are not living and working with lifelong friends, but merely with acquaintances.

Indeed, it is becoming characteristic of our society that nobody really knows anybody. The "friendship" is only a role, a categorical relationship. People with hundreds of "friends" suddenly discover that they didn't know one of their "friends" had been ill or separated, or alcoholic, or psychotic; or they find to their discomfort that after they had been away for months they had not been missed (unless their role had been called for). Worse, yet, is the discovery that one's category—to which he may have given his life—can be so easily filled by someone else. Now this awareness that "friendship" is only a role played on certain occasions and the feeling that "they can get along without me" lead to a sense of insignificance. A categorical, refillable status is incapable of giving a person the feeling of being "somebody special"—indeed, even really *there* as a person. And the more easily refillable the status, the more this is so. Americans live and try to maintain identities in such shallowness of relationship[38] in which even "intimates" are transitory—like telephone operators replaceable at either end of the line. Facile and enthusiastic playing of the role is the limit of commitment and "sincerity," which easily leads to the feeling that one cannot get through to people, can't reach the "real man"—only façades and masks are presented. The frustration of excessive mobility (in dating) is well expressed by this statement of a television actress:

> You can go out every night with a different guy, but after a while you're bound to get tired of it, because all the running around you're doing is in a circle. Really, you don't get anything. You don't get to learn anything about people. You'll find six months of it is a very long time. After that, you're asking yourself, "What's going on? What's it all about?"[39]

In such mobility, people cannot answer their emotional questions; they find their insight into others dulled rather than deepened. Finally, in frustration, people seek group therapy or to "tune in" with LSD. Such shallowness, based on skillful (and impenetrable) role-playing, combined with mobility converting a person into a category, is a milieu in which identity easily perishes from lack of the assurance of being somebody special that everyone needs.

Aggravating, rather than helping, this is the furious pursuit of status and ego symbols which, past a certain point, becomes a vicious circle. It is now true, in our land of ambiguous identity, that anyone may adopt almost any status symbol which he can afford. He may have his Cadillac, the new look of fashion, the fashionable address, the fancy letterhead. He announces and maintains any identity that he can get away with. But to consider the ultimate effect of free adoption of symbols on identity itself, we might imagine a play in which the actors were free to costume themselves as they pleased. Would it not soon become impossible to tell who was really who? Would not the action become, instead of a meaningful play, a confusing masquerade? The changeability of symbols makes life like a masquerade. That employee I intend to hire, that person I want to marry, that friend—who is he really? Life acquires a Fred Demara–like quality of pose. When everybody is adopting symbols, how does one tell who one really is? The paradox seems to be that when anybody can be anybody, nobody can be "somebody."

Another detrimental influence on identity from mobility in a pluralistic setting is inconsistency and unreliability of signals. From the conflict of subcultures, confusion of styles, rapidity of changes, diversity of viewpoints, shifting of positions, and difficulty of sorting out poses, a person has a hard time feeling he is right—whether he follows or rejects a certain position. He has trouble, first, in deciding which persons, styles, and authorities are right and true among the poses, pretexts, and rationalizations of those playing "games." Secondly, when he takes a position, he doesn't know whether the expressions of opinion and concern of others are sincere, so he doesn't know whether he will be really supported or whether he is "going out on a limb." An undetermined number of people with whom he deals in a mobile society are "phonies" (inauthentic role-players)[40]—he cannot be sure which—and their responses do not help him become authentic by sincere revelation or, ordinarily, by challenging encounter. Like the polite applause that does not tell an entertainer how good his act is, such signals do not tell a person what he needs to know. Seeking adequate signals from others, he becomes other-directed, anxious about what people think but not, even when conforming, having assurances he is really right; he is gullible to tastemakers and opinion pundits, but their advice does not help him build sound judgment or know his own position at all—or where his real comrades are among the poseurs.

This is like putting one's foot into the soft mud of a lake bottom seeking a firm place to stand—and not finding it. Since, in such a milieu, one doesn't really know where people stand, one cannot say what "people think"—cannot, in the terminology of George Herbert Mead, build a realistic generalized other. One builds instead a pragmatic concept of roles which get by; and a concept of oneself as a conforming performer (expert role-player) who is "making it" socially but has not had a chance to check his real feelings against what people really think, let alone infer from their deceptive responses what is right to think. The whole thing means weakness and fragmentation of the generalized other (which Mead said is the basis of some rather important qualities such as objectivity, truth, morality, and justice).

Excessive mobility also makes family relations fragile which, of course, strikes at the heart of identity. Divorce, serial marriage, desertion of children, alienation of youth from parents, dispersion of kin, insecurity of old people deprive a person of the ability to define himself by relations which should be most reliable, intimate, and meaningful. Even when kinship structure is not destroyed, mobility brings in the whole problem of "adjustment"—of mate to mate, parent to child, neighbor to neighbor, man to work (relationships which in stable societies are simply taken for granted; you don't adjust to Uncle Henry or the person you marry or the baby you have because it is simply in the order of things to get along with them—anyway, you have lived with that kind of person all your life). As mobility increases, it becomes a problem to make relationships work which a person ought to be able to count on and not worry about. He has a need for "contacts," role-playing—the Dale Carnegie problem. We do not dwell here on those disturbances of parent-child and sibling relationships which produce the severest identity problems—neuroses and psychoses—about which psychologists have written so much, because our focus is on those general societal conditions which affect "normal" people (sufficiently ordinary to be a mass), the meaning of life and happiness of almost anyone. Doubtless such conditions as loss of tradition, shallowness of relationships, inadequacy of feedback, which make normal people unhappy, are crises with which it may be impossible to cope for those who were cheated in their first relationship.

LACK OF IDENTIFYING RITUAL

Modern society also fails to give a person an adequate conception of himself through a lack of identifying ritual. The average person today is unlikely to experience many ceremonies which intensify his awareness of shared mystiques or his awareness of himself as a person. Most of our participations in art, drama, mass entertainment, and other "language of the emotions" are as strange and "outside" as impersonal information. Even when they are emotionally moving and involving, one gets little sense of belonging to something from them, and even less sense of being somebody. And many of the ceremonies which *are* supposed to increase our sense of identification with groups (for example, church and patriotic) are, for reasons I shall explore in Chapter 4, formalistic and boring, or otherwise lacking in significance. Though church attendance is high, there is a general decline of significant rites of passage; people are denied adequate "rebirth" rituals by a society that is largely secular-minded and anticeremonial. Mircea Eliade says:

> Modern man no longer has any initiation of the traditional type . . . a ritual death followed by resurrection or a new birth. . . . For archaic thought . . . man is *made*—he does not make himself all by himself. It is the old initiates, the spiritual masters, who make him. But these masters apply what was revealed to them at the beginning of time by the supernatural beings . . . this birth requires rites instituted by the supernatural beings; hence it is a divine work . . . the puberty initiation represents, above all, the revelation of the sacred . . . the new man is no longer a "natural man."[41]

Of course, modern man does not hanker for primitive initiation rites; but what many people seem to be striving for in strenuous and dangerous play—not to say sex and other things not usually thought of as sports—is some kind of ritual by which to prove themselves, some test which requires a person to extend his whole self, not merely play a role. This test element is the mystique of many sports, perhaps even of some crimes. But, on the whole, though modern American society offers many models by which a person can try to make himself as he pleases—with the help of such peer groups as will accept him—relatively few of these have initiatory or rebirth rites. The majority of roles a man takes are "grown into" or contracted for without his ever having a clear impression of himself as having "made it," or having been created, remade, reborn—without, in other words, a distinct experience: "I am a new man."

Such factors as I have mentioned—lack of identity in accumulating information, modernism changing place into space, mobility changing person into category and supplying unreliable signals, and lack of ritual—work toward a kind of emotional emptiness in America, a situation in which nobody "counts." I have tried to point to some of the most obvious things that defeat identity in America—deficiencies in interaction and symbols, which mean insufficient feedback for personal integrity and emotional well-being. As I said before, I am not concerned with deficiencies of interaction which would result in severe personal and mental disorder, but only with those which stand in the way of the ordinary man's having a satisfyingly meaningful life.

SOLUTIONS?

Once one recognizes it, what does one do about an identity problem?

Some people think of it primarily as a solo operation ("I must do it for myself. Who else can do it for me?"). They study philosophy, theology, or psychology; scrutinize themselves, meditate, introspect; and see a psychiatrist if it gets too much for them. Existentialists, especially, lean to the view that the individual can find himself only within and by himself. They reject formulas and the help of society. Everyone is on his own, with or without God. If freedom is all you have, advises Sartre, make the most of it: "human freedom is a curse, but that curse is the unique source of the nobility of man." Or take the "courage of despair," advises Tillich, to proceed on one's way. Yet it now appears that if the solution is to be an individual one, it is not a rational (Socratic) one. Since Freud we have known that no amount of piling up of facts or of careful reasoning about one's position is going to spare a J. S. Mill, a Kierkegaard, a Tolstoi, a suicidal crisis; indeed, by intellectualizing, a man might as easily lose as find his identity. Religious mystics (including Jung) also recommend a lonely route, but they stress something repugnant to many existentialists as well as rationalists: avoiding thought and willful choice, losing one's ego in order to find a higher identity that is not personal—a Buddha-nature, Divine Ground, Atman, Supreme Identity,[42] which is almost misnamed to be called self. Even Christian mystics deny that true identity is the self. Says Meister Eckhart, "One work remains to a man truly and properly, that is the annihilation of himself."

But once identity troubles are recognized as common to millions of people, they become a societal problem and a question of social policy. One can see that a lot of solos, even if successful, do not add up to an orchestration. Just as an individual must do something about himself, he must also do something about the groups he associates with. Here in the realm of interaction are two general directions. One is to restrict the groups with which one associates, some kind of closure—of which the outcome is controlled and organized—whether insularism (the Oraibai solution of the Hopi Indians), sectarianism, or on a larger scale the closed totalitarian system.[43] The other general direction is to plunge into encounters of one sort or another in an "open" manner—that is, not knowing precisely the outcome. This is the direction of group therapy; non-directive counseling (Carl Rogers), sensitivity training, "I-thou" relationships (Martin Buber), and the theories of C. H. Cooley and G. H. Mead about the self being an image which is developed and enlarged through social feedback. There may be a vague restlessness for involvements: to change careers, to join a cause, to stand up and be counted, to assert oneself, to reaffirm one's position in a church or seek another faith, to have an emotional experience, to play to an audience, to undergo some kind of test or ordeal. In any case, for those who seek the open route, it is felt that identity is like the pearl that will not form in the closed oyster.

To discover true identity, no doubt the dive of introspection and the plunge into encounters must both be taken, each to check and enrich the other. Yet, though they are all we have, neither route is entirely to be trusted. "Closer to others" leads to as many pitfalls as "deeper within." Society projects many false selves upon an individual; he may have to seek solitude, as did Thoreau:

> I went to the woods because I wished to live deliberately, to front only the essential facts of life, and see if I could not learn what it was to teach, and not, when I came to die, discover that I had not lived. I did not wish to live what was not life, living is so dear; nor did I wish to practice resignation, unless it was quite necessary. I wanted to live deep and suck out all the marrow of life, to live so sturdily and spartan-like as to put to rout all that was not dear, to cut a broad swath and shave close, to drive life into a corner, and reduce it to its lowest terms, and, if it proved mean, why then to get the whole and genuine meanness of it, and publish it, or if it were sublime, to know it by experience, and be able to give a true account of it . . . for most men, it appears to me, are

in a strange uncertainty about it, whether it is of the devil or of God, and have *somewhat hastily* concluded that it is the chief end of man here to "glorify God and enjoy him forever."[44]

But the individual who relies on intuition has no sure guide, neither his own perception nor a *guru*, to tell him which introspections and which interactions offer true identity. This, I think, was the burden of T. S. Eliot's *The Cocktail Party*: that we are neither the image created by ourselves nor that projected upon us by others—both are misses; but somehow, by encounters and introspections, we can get there (the psychiatrist in the piece, however, is an unrealistically omniscient *deus ex machina*). Discontent with introspections and social roles leads the individual to seek further encounters and introspections, without assurance that he will find what he is looking for. In an alienated society such as ours, it is quite possible to go through life feeling "lost," "dead," or "cheated."

Teenage identity problems show in exaggerated form the risks of too much trust in interactions. Rebelling against the definition of themselves parents offer, with a Holden Caulfield's eye for what is phony, they turn to peers for a truer image; they bleach, cut, or grow their hair savagely, drive freakish cars, switch from one fad to another, scream at heroes handling a ball or twirling a baton or twanging a guitar, or plunge into activities like surfing which may interrupt their careers. The wish for popularity, for finding identity in groups, may result in identity diffusion[45] from too many models, or identity dislocation by rebellion based on an inappropriate model. Does anyone seriously suppose that the social images adults offer to one another are more to be trusted? The master of ceremonies for a teenage television show remarked significantly, "I do not see any difference between these kids and the grownups." Paul Goodman, in *Growing Up Absurd*, indicts adult roles and takes the view that the identity adults offer youth is not good enough for them.

STREAMS OF THE SAME RIVER

Nevertheless, activity must go on. We assume that man is a meaning-seeking animal, not satisfied with material goods and facts unless they supply him with a sense of realness as a person.[46] Insistence on something "more" makes him not only philosophical but cult-prone, ritualistic, meditative, faddish, crusading in spirit, romantic—searching in various directions for the mystique that will add meaning to his life. It is neither necessary to deprecate this as illusion, as did Freud, nor to extoll it as pragmatic truth, as did William James, but merely to postulate it for the majority of humans—whether it shows them to be less hardy or more wise than the few who can do without meaning. Beyond meat-packing, let us say, as an economic process, there must be a cult of the sausage—a salami mystique, so to speak. The mystifying process is not, as Marxists hold, merely a result of the need to disguise naked economic interests; rather, it is the need for meaning, that humans seek something "higher" or beyond themselves which cannot easily be stated in matter-of-fact terms.

This need for meaning and mystique, as I conceive it, is only another name for the claim to identity with something beyond oneself as presently perceived. Conscious or unconscious, it is the thread of careers, perhaps the prime motive; when rationally recognized, it becomes the *summum bonum* of which Aristotle wrote, the self-realization that is either synonymous with, or the basis of, happiness. When frustrated, the need becomes compulsive, desperate, bizarre, slavish, the thing sought in therapy.[47]

The intertwining of such motives leads to the building of a new social order, with such features as cult, we-feeling, fashion, and various kinds of social movements.

Where does a man look for meaning? In nature and himself first, perhaps; but almost unavoidably he turns to collectivities where he can get reassurance and consensus, and have emotional experiences to become a new man or confirm the old one. He looks for soulmates, comrades, fellows, partners-in-crime. As Everett C. Hughes said, "We are in a time when part of the very struggle to be a man is the search for one's others."[48] But finding one's true others is not easy in a mass society, nor do the searchers all manifest themselves in the same way: some "play it cool," withholding themselves in alienation; some affirm themselves visibly and vocally in some action such as protest; some "shop around," consciously or unconsciously, for something better—a "kick," or an escape. We are concerned mostly with the shoppers who have made their pursuit of identity explicit in collectivities which they join or form.

Whatever he does, there seem to be three main tactics that a searcher for identity can use when he wishes to use the interaction path: (1) He can try to change himself, using others as models, perhaps by instruction, the fashions of a peer group, or hero worship without personal interaction. The use of models does not require direct interaction. (2) He can seek an interactive confrontation in which to project and validate or discover by feedback a new image, or remedy a discrepancy between his self image and what others think of him. He might do this in small groups (friendship, therapeutic, religious, and so forth.) or try to find himself as a performer before a large audience, even by projecting an image to the public which they accept.[49] This fed-back identity comes from how he perceives what others think.[50] (3) He can seek deep feelings, "kicks," emotions, ecstasies, by which to fill the emptiness, or phoniness, of his life. Let us call this personal intensification. Such intensification may come from interaction itself (a process value, as sociologists like to call it); but it might also come from some kind of thrill chasing, indulgence in stimulants, audience experience that is not primarily interactive; from deviation from what others do; or from art, meditation, creativity, achievement, adventure alone. That is, filling the emotional dimension overlaps but does not coincide with the interactive. These three goals can be achieved at the same time, but they are analytically separable. The first is copying from a model, with or without interaction; the second is essentially human or public relations with feedback; the third is emotional intensification by any means, individual or social.

These three possible tactics of identity search follow from our theory that identity is a functioning system of three basic variables: (1) what a person thinks about himself introspectively; (2) what he projects or sees imaged or accepted in the eyes of others (his social identity); and (3) his feelings, validated when "real to me" and when shared with others. A person is necessarily concerned with these things and looking for ways to improve them. If he has an identity problem, the remedy depends on which dimension is particularly lacking. If he does not see himself clearly, he might turn to interior exploration and soul searching, try artistic self-expression, dash off a letter to an editor, or try to pattern himself on a model. If he is not sure about the image he projects (his social identity), he will almost surely turn to some kind of interaction or encounter to find out. If he does not feel his own sentiments as valid, he must look for some experience to intensify them. A man might be stronger on two of these points and yet have an identity problem because he is weak on the third. For example, take a man who is a "pillar of the church." He has a clear image of himself as a confirmed church member; people agree on this so feedback supports his self image. Yet something is missing. It makes him a little uncomfortable to realize he does not feel the "brotherly love" and "presence of God" that others talk about. He, therefore, cannot feel altogether genuine in his role and may reproach himself for slackness, even for being a fake. "Something is wrong with me" seems the inevitable conclusion of anyone who fails to feel appropriately his accepted role—how much, indeed, does this apply to roles in business, industry, military service, school, and so on?

It may be that shallowness of emotion and lack of fellow feeling connected with shallowness of interaction are the most serious dimensions of the American identity problem. Many with clear self roles and validated social identities yet feel that something is missing from the meaningfulness of life on the score of valid sentiments. We live in a society where sentiments of all kinds are in doubt: romantic love, kin feeling, fellow feeling,[51] patriotism, morality, religious faith, school spirit, civic spirit, feelings for what is beautiful. There seems to be a conspiracy against the expression of emotion—even where it should be displayed, as in modern funerals. Some of this emotional impoverishment is doubtless due to the formalism of bureaucracy, and some to neurosis traceable to early family life.[52]

But, once interactional and symbolic deficiencies are recognized as a source of identity problems, it is natural to turn to relationships, trying to improve them technically (with the help of ministers and psychiatrists) or to find new forms of relationships that will be more meaningful. From this standpoint, individual pursuits such as philosophy and theology, and collective ones such as fashion, recreation, religion, and mass movements are *streams of the same river*. They are part of a search for identity going on all the time—not only among disappointed and alienated people, but among many squares who feel meaninglessness. From the standpoint of the Establishment, the main choice of direction in identity search is between ways in and ways out: on the one hand, institutionalized role models and status passages,[53] and, on the other hand, ways which are deviant, emergent, uninstitutionalized. Why should a person choose ways "out" rather than "in"? My basic theory is that the modern social system deprives many people of identity (cheats) in varying degrees, which have little relationship to economic rewards; that is, those who are well paid may feel emptiness. Such people are the first to become alienated, feel outside; the first to turn to rebellion, fads, poses, "fun," "kicks," or cults for meaning; and most likely to look outside to exotic, eccentric, nonsquare—it may be deviant—opportunities. Choosing such ways out, they may undergo identity dislocation—develop a character which does not fit them for their society or their careers. Such dislocations might come from a conversion experience, from "hero worship," from associating with people who introduce one to a new way of life, or from an exciting audience experience—either as performer or member. Most of the phenomena sociologists call "collective behavior" offer such opportunities—especially those into which one throws oneself emotionally because they give process values or "kicks."

Seekers, as considered in this book, are those for whom the identity search has become the melody line in the harmony or disharmony of their life activities. Consciously or unconsciously, they are groping, gravitating, shopping, drifting, browsing—they are on the lookout for change. At least, they are vulnerable to influence, available—amenable, in the sense of Mr. Weller of *Pickwick Papers*—as opposed to apathetic (apathy only describes their attitude toward the existing role structure). Job- and careerswitching may reflect identity search.[54] Likewise religious shopping, when it takes the form of trying out religions the way one might soap flakes. A woman convert to Jehovah's Witnesses says:

I have been looking for the right church. I went to almost every church I could find. They all talked and talked but something was always missing. I had just about given up hope when a woman came to my door with a *Watchtower* magazine.

Question: What was so special about the magazine, Mrs. K.?

Answer: Oh, it just had the truth. I can't really explain it but I felt it right away. All of a sudden it was there. I knew I had found what I was looking for.

A desire to change oneself might be seen in a person who goes from one therapist to another, who plunges deeply into expressive art, such as modern dance or amateur theater, or an artist who continually changes styles. A political shopper seeks more than just a party with which to align himself on issues; he has an almost religious need for a faith, fellowship, and higher reality with which to identify himself—as in Arthur Koestler's trials of communism and Yogism.[55] The beatnik goes "on the road," looking someplace else than churches or parties for his image of himself:

> He had packed a rucksack and gone off by himself into the desert . . . and given himself over to meditation for days at a time. He had listened for it in the music of Bach and the music of jazz, with equal attentiveness and absorption. He had sought for it in sex and pot. He was young, only in the beginnings of the quest, but he had a pretty good idea what he was looking for and it wasn't all gathered from books. There were birds in his experience, and deserts and mountains and danger and fatigue. He knew he had a long way to go. After all, he was only nineteen! But he was "on the road."[56]

A scientist might have a mystique about his work that reflects a quest for identity, as did Madame Curie:

> Life is not easy for any of us. But what of that? We must have perseverance and above all confidence in ourselves. We must believe that we are gifted for something, and that this thing, at whatever cost, must be attained.[57]

Such a mystique is not just a curiosity about what lies beyond but a sense of special identity, of being set apart for something better, achieved through the search. It is the theme of the Grail hunter—taking the Grail as a mystical symbol of self-fulfillment and redemption. A Grail, by definition, lies beyond existing social structure; its quest is always a transcendental adventure.[58] The feeling of the quest is well expressed in the statement of this woman who made her search by reading:

> As I grew older, it (my life) was filled with an indefinable wonder about the mystery at the heart of things . . . inseparable from a feeling of expectancy . . . that there was something far more real and permanent

than what appeared to be the trivial, unpredictable and shifting adult world, and which I might discover. This feeling of expectancy I have never quite lost . . . it was this sense that I was just on the point of discovering something of peculiar significance that gave me an incurable persistence when in my middle years I spent the leisure of twenty of them in reading some 250 works which promised to shed light on these tremendous questions. For I experienced as keen a desire for my quarry as the drunkard feels for the bottle and the lover for his mistress. This desire possessed my earliest waking moments and haunted my pillow before sleep came to interrupt the chase.[59]

Likewise, an English convert to Buddhism says:

. . . The longing for Enlightenment . . . might manifest itself as a vague sort of longing. Being essentially a feeling of the heart, the intellect does not know what to do with it. There arises mistrust and fear about this feeling, so it is suppressed as much as possible. But it will pop up again and again, preparing the way to doubt—the great doubt. What am I? What is life all about? What am I here for? . . . And the search begins. The search of the intellect—the search of the heart. Not that the heart really needs much searching—but in the early stages of this period of great doubt, which can be very black indeed, the heart has not much say. The *I* cherishes desires of a completely different nature from the heart— desires for the glorification and enrichment of the *I*—and thus the heart is silenced again and again. The feeble spark of longing for Enlightenment is suppressed by the all-powerful *I*. And the constant fight from within is on. It is exactly at this juncture that many of us came in contact with Buddhism.[60]

An identity quest is probably the secret of the crusader[61] as well as of the cultist. Yet, if you ask people, "Would you like to be converted?" very few would say yes, because conversion implies giving way to an influence, losing self-control. But a great many would like to be reborn or renewed, if the matter could be put in acceptable terms. Call it education, realization, self-improvement, a fad, a new hobby, and it is quite all right to try to remake oneself consciously. Yet the change sought in oneself may be more than one can accomplish rationally; it may require a profound, sweeping, emotional self-reevaluation. Such a rebirth needs a trigger, a midwife. A person with such a desire had better honestly face the fact that he is a seeker for some kind of conversion and be as rational about it as he can, considering that it cannot be brought about just by thinking.

From the standpoint of availability of people for mass movements, Figure 1 may express how I would classify the population of modern society. The seekers are those in categories III and IV; they are most likely to plunge into the river of identity search.

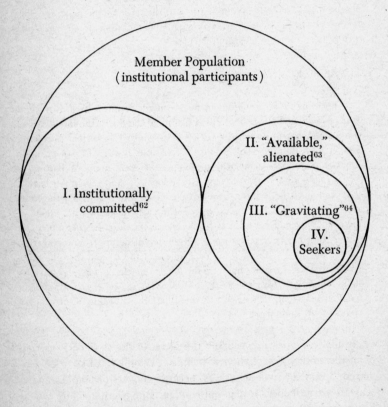

Member Population
(institutional participants)

I. Institutionally committed[62]

II. "Available," alienated[63]

III. "Gravitating"[64]

IV. Seekers

The more people there are in categories III and IV, the broader and deeper becomes the river of identity search—the greater the potentiality for radical change.

Streams of the river are phenomena of identity search viewed collectively as things which go on in society, perhaps without people realizing it; but, from the standpoint of the individual, there are certain tactical choices he can make as he shops around, depending on the aspect of identity in which he feels weak. If he doesn't like his own appearance, he may seek to revise himself in terms of external symbols and styles, a "look" offered by fad or fashion; style rebellion and eccentricity; a pose which fools others; improvisations of ego and status symbols, many of which one can achieve without support of a peer group—though a peer group may demand a certain fashion for acceptance (to keep "in"), and style rebellion may need the cohesiveness of comrade-in-arms to face a hostile world. Or, if a person is short on feeling himself as real, he may seek experiences which intensify and enrich emotional life: collective (sharing interaction or emotion in a primary group, crowd, or audience response, or ego-screaming in a mass, as I shall explain); vicarious (voyages of identity by means of heroes and dramas); or private (such as by artistic creativity or drugs). In such ways he can come to feel more alive. Another choice for emotional intensification is between action ("doing things") and symbolism which doesn't accomplish anything practically—such as ritual, cultism, and vicarious experience. And in the sector of action, we find a great range between bureaucracy, which is lacking in the ability to intensify feelings, and violent forms of "fun" or conflict or crusades which give a person a chance to prove himself by commitment, encounters, and ordeals. Yet another tactical choice is between square and offbeat groups. If a person feels weak in the sense of belonging, does not feel himself to be a "regular fellow," he has a choice between trying to win acceptance by "regular" people, according to conventional standards, or turning to seek acceptance by "characters": beatniks, hippies, style rebels, or other deviant or criminal groups. We suppose that the more alienated a person feels—the more hollow he feels are the games played for "success," the more he feels cheated—the more he leans to offbeat directions and to seeking his comrades among the dropouts and *declassé*. But whether he turns to squares or offbeat groups, if belongingness is what he needs, he should be expected to seek types of interaction which provide intense or candid feedback, as information about himself in the eyes of others, and indications of recognition and acceptance; they may confirm his identity through tests, ordeals, membership tokens, brotherhood ritual, badges, and insignia.

A person's identity search may be: (1) stylistic (modifying appearance, looks; pose, role to audience) versus inner self-exploration and realization; (2) square versus offbeat or radical directions requiring a break with old identity; (3) activities on one's own, or supported by a peer group; (4) real action versus vicariously living in the roles of dramas and heroes; and (5) practical achievement versus ritual or cultic symbolism aiming at emotional intensification and rebirth.

Such choices of course, are made, within a milieu of social pressures and opportunities. Clearly these will vary, depending on whether one is an urbanite or a rural villager; literate or illiterate; heavily or lightly exposed to news, fiction, and television; living in a traditional or a modernizing, pluralistic culture; slum dweller or jet-set member; mobile or static in occupation; and living in a police state or a democracy. The chapters of this book reflect identity search Americans and others in modern Western societies commonly take when there is considerable freedom to revise oneself plus wealth, mobility, and exposure to mass media. In the following chapter, "The American Revolutionary Potential," I shall try to explain why the tactical choices of so many Americans today lean in stylistic, offbeat, vicarious, and cultic directions—rather than toward practical political rebellion and economic reform. Chapter 3 deals with external stylistic revision in terms of fad, fashion, style rebellion, and pose. Chapters 4 and 5 deal with ritual and cultic movements aiming at emotional enrichment of the inner life and rebirth. Chapter 6, "Secular Cult," carries the cultic theme into identity-seeking activities in recreation, and health and knowledge seeking. Chapter 7 deals with vicarious voyages of identity through heroes and celebrities. Chapter 8 treats crusades as a type of collective practical action especially adapted to the pursuit of identity.

2   The American Revolutionary Potential: What Has Happened to the "Spirit of '76"?

THE INCREDIBLE REBELLION

If Thomas Jefferson could have returned to America in 1967, he would have been astounded to find a land echoing with gunfire, smoking from Molotov cocktails and "pot," and filled with 200 million people, most of them crowded in cities and not liking it much. Though Jefferson himself had said that "a little rebellion now and then is a good thing," he would have been puzzled by the absence of what he would have considered good and sufficient reasons for it—namely, tyranny. Some of the slogans he might have understood: "civil rights," "we shall overcome," "freedom now," "black power." Others would doubtless have baffled him: "make love, not war," "turn on, tune in, drop out," "do not fold or mutilate," "legalize pot." Even the faddism and music of youth had a rebellious quality. Folk singers seemed to have a chip of protest on their shoulders. Plainly a revolution of some kind was afoot and Jefferson would have been astounded that 200 years of progress and democracy had come to this.

He would have been astonished also to note that rebellion was not concentrated in the economic and political have-nots, but had spread widely in the middle classes—even upper status groups, especially the radical right. Indeed, it would have puzzled him that so many of the rebels had—in material terms—nothing to complain about. And, even if they had something to complain about, it was hard to explain the particular courses their complaint took.

The rebellion in Detroit, during the "violent summer" of 1967 (by August there had been riots in over 30 cities, climaxed by Detroit in which 1300 buildings were razed and 2700 businesses looted), showed how hard it was—by sensible economic and political reasoning—to explain entirely the reasons for revolt in terms of injustice, or to explain the course it took. Some of the curious features of the Detroit rebellion were that it was not a "race" riot but an aggressive outburst in which whites and Negroes joined in "integrated" looting, that it expressed the alienated spirit of a mass of have-nots sharing a subculture of poverty; that there was an emotional satisfaction in burning and destruction for its own sake (mood of nihilism, carnival spirit, "burn, baby, burn!") which made it clear that psychological rather than mere economic explanations were needed; and, finally, that this peak outburst had occurred in a city where progress in racial reconciliation had been perhaps greatest in the nation.

Equally puzzling was the "hippie" rebellion, disclaiming economic goals, defying the law to use psychedelic drugs, strewing flowers, and preaching, "Make love, not war."

The basic fact was that the new radicalism of the 1960s did not run along classic political, economic, class, or racial lines. It had a sociology, no doubt; but there was no generally understood ideology that could state its premises or stake out its objectives and program—legitimate or otherwise. It was, in fact, an incredible rebellion in the eyes of a Greek or Arab or Congolese, who might have said, "You have all that prosperity and yet you're rebelling!" or "You say we have had a revolution. What do you have?"

I propose to appraise the revolution of today along lines we laid out in the last chapter: considering that the rebels of today suffer more from identity problems than tangible economic or political injustice; that the appropriate responses are, therefore, not necessarily—only incidentally—political or economic; and that the forms of the new revolution are appropriately vague, inchoate, groping, symbolic in objective (occasionally using economic symbols), and focused on life-style change, moral and ethical questions, meaning, and cultic values—all matters of identity.

I also propose to consider the frustrations of today in the light of the facts that in modern society: (1) The hard-work ideology is breaking down (the idea you have to work hard for what you get, and have a right to what you work for); now the idea is looming that society owes a man a living, and the state hands out benefits, whether or not he works. (2) There has been an explosion of expectations at all levels of society. Everyone feels he is entitled to "happiness" and individual self-expression (what I shall later call the new romanticism), and feels an accentuated hankering for identity—even those with highest status (for example, debutantes and princesses). Everyone therefore feels entitled to adopt the symbols and style of any status group he pleases if he can afford them; there are no hard and fast lines separating classes, professions—even sexes—from one another. (3) Uncertainty about identity and loss of "togetherness" (nonrational consensus) seem greater than ever, as pointed out in the previous chapter. It is thus easy to see that the frustrations of practically anybody—old, young, rich, poor, male, female, white, black—might rise to intolerable levels. And it is quite possible that "civil rights" or economic equality is way down the list of what the shouting is all about.

MAIN FORMS OF THE REBELLION

What, then, are the nature and source of the revolutionary ferment with which America seems to be bubbling? It seems to me that we have not sufficiently distinguished the forms: we have, for example, tended to lump together socialists, "action" rebels, and style rebels; we have overstressed material problems at the expense of the psychospiritual. There were at least five widespread, socially significant forms of rebellion in the United States in the late 1960s, which had the character of mass movements: (1) contagious ghetto violence, (2) new left activism, (3) radical right extremism, (4) style rebellion, and (5) the dropout movement, most conspicuously the "hippies."

The first—which in 1967 came to be called the "mindless violence" of the urban ghettoes—comes closest to the stereotype of an impoverished proletariat "throwing off the chains" of economic and class injustice. It occurred among people who had been "left out" (to use Franklin Delano Roosevelt's phrase)[1], sharing an alienated subculture and expressing the irresponsibility and crime-proneness of the mass. A chief characteristic of this kind of rebellion was a "mob" type of leadership, a shifting leadership by "spokesmen" and hotheads who emerged at the moment, often to attack the established leaders (such as Martin Luther King, James Farmer, Roy Wilkins, even the leaders of SNCC) as "Uncle Toms" and confound their plans and commitments for responsible leadership. Black Nationalist extremists had their day, though they were usually rejected by the rank-and-file Negroes. The "mindless violence" was expressed in the pronouncement of one of the new leaders, H. "Rap" Brown, "We're going to burn it if we don't get our share of it."[2] It seemed clear that the trouble was not *just* racial and economic injustice, but an exaggeration of expectations plus the idea one does not have to work for things ("Society owes me. If I don't get it, I'll take it"). As one policeman said, Detroit's was not a race riot but a riot of thieves. The methods, which destroyed so much more property than was seized, seemed justifiable by no defensible economic ideology, constituting a kind of nihilism, injurious to the self, but in which a psychological gratification to the ego was evident—the prideful joy of "burn, baby, burn!"

The second major form of rebellion in the United States during the 1960s might be called new left activism, sometimes referred to as "The Movement."[3] Participating groups included Students for a Democratic Society (SDS), the Vietnam Anti-War Campaign, the Free Speech Movement, Americans for Democratic Action, the Student Nonviolent Coordinating Committee (SNCC), and other fighters for civil rights. The members were mostly of college age. Their thought was expressed in publications like *Ramparts* magazine, seeking to formulate an ideology for a "new politics." Yet this movement, so often called "new left," fell short of a classic radical left revolution on several counts—indeed, it was a most curious revolution because its members were, on the whole, highly educated, prosperous, middle class, with good career outlooks, all their rights, and full dinner pails.[4] Its chief characteristics were a commitment to action on the basis of moral concern and direct personal responsibility; mistrust of big organizations, bureaucracy, centralization, ideology, and planning; pragmatism, in the sense of lack of concern with ideology and sustained program; and the fact that much of its activity was confined to moral protest—by rallies, parades, sit-downs, sit-ins, blockades, draft-card burning, and other forms of civil disobedience. Unlike the ghetto have-nots, these rebels were not concerned with seizing wealth, but rejected the comforts they were used to. Jacobs and Landau say:

> That these young people reject the affluent society which produced them is one of The Movement's most startling characteristics. This generation has not grown up in a depression world, as did the youthful radicals of the '30's. Their drive is not to go from rags to riches; they know about poverty only because they adopt it as a way of life and not because they were born into it. And their repudiation of the American value system is so serious that they have forced thoughtful elements in society to re-examine their own acceptance of America, to discover what it is in American life that is so unattractive, so distasteful as to make these young people turn their backs on it and call for a revolution to replace it.[5]

This movement seemed unable to phrase its goals in terms of ideology; the old left seemed irrelevant, yet a new politics did not clearly emerge. As one spokesman of the new left explained:

> Most of us radicals of the 1960's would agree with Daniel Bell that the postwar years have witnessed the "end of ideology." . . . The old left is dead . . . contemporary "liberalism" is impotent . . . we are tired of the stereotyped responses of the Marxists. . . . In a sense we are lost, for we do drift about in rough and uncharted seas. We are fearful that if we do establish a steady course it may take us somewhere we do not want to go. . . . Conservative tradition and state authority may weaken, or even destroy us. Perhaps this is why we have only a dissenting ideology. We unhesitantly express what we are against, but are less sure of what we are for. Because of this, we are rather more reformists than revolutionaries. We tend to believe in nonviolence not only because it is effective, but also because it is inherently good. To be sure, most of us are uncommitted—except to humanism, rationality, and an action program.[6]

The lack of ideology and long-range program in the new left seemed to go with an existentialist concern with realizing oneself by action. For these reasons it was hard to see the new left as simply a radical economic or political movement.

The third major form of rebellion in the United States made even less sense as a revolution of have-nots, or of those who had suffered economic or political injustice. It consisted of those who had done rather well and/or were at least symbolically loyally attached to the status quo—the radical right.[7] This movement, as Lipset points out, included such people as capitalists with a nineteenth-century concept of laissez-faire, small businessmen losing the battle with taxes and big corporations, agrarians losing ground to urban interests, religious fundamentalists, Southern whites, especially poor whites—all having the common bond of getting the worst of it in the mainstream trend of the United States toward what is commonly called the welfare state or Great Society and therefore suffering a loss of status relative to the gains of the left. The left, for all their protests, peace marches, sit-ins, teach-ins, and "dirty word" demonstrations, were getting much of what they wanted; they were moving in the sense of welfare measures attained. Not so the right, looking back with increasing frustration on a disappearing golden age of laissez-faire and religious fundamentalism, in the midst of a trend of society that meant for them shrinking privileges, lost freedoms, and vanished glory. Though the economic position of many members of the radical right was quite good, they were suffering an identity loss and a status loss relative to the gains of the left.[8] Toward this vanishing image of themselves as independent entrepreneurs and self-made men in a golden age of laissez-faire, their attitude was intensely patriotic and moralistic. They saw contemporary society as morally sick and themselves as Paul Reveres saving it—at least spreading the alarm. They were "paranoid" about communism as a cause of all the trouble. On the far right, extremist groups formed, and their supplies of weapons and military uniforms and exercises spoke for their intentions.

The fourth major form of rebellion visible in the United States and many modern countries was style rebellion, which took various forms: such as flamboyant and garish (even deliberately offensive) costumes, manners, music, dances, art, and comedy, with which people announced their rejection of prevailing "good taste" and placed themselves symbolically (if not politically and economically) outside the Establishment. For example, beards (beatnik, Castro, Hell's Angel) became important among some men as an announcement of outsideness, perhaps symbolizing unrestrainable wildness and indifference to social forms. Male youths allowed their hair to grow to shocking lengths, dismaying teachers, barbers, even health authorities. Bare feet—symbolizing poverty or, more likely, negligence in clothing—became a part of styles such as those of the beatnik and the surfer. Barbarism (implied by symbols like death's heads and swastikas and names like The Animals and The Plague) was part of the style of many groups. Also prominent were "effeminacy" in boys' hairdos and boy-girl-look-alikes (to be dealt with in Chapter 3). Teenagers' music developed a caterwauling style, marked by the stridency of electric guitars, loudness of amplifiers, and a vulgar style of singing and dancing; it was not only an assault upon the senses but plainly announced, "We don't want *your* music, or your respectable culture either." Probably never before had a generation so repudiated the music of its elders. In its technique—or lack of technique—there was a deliberate primitivism, a turning of the back on school music and refined taste. Such rebel styles were all defiant toward established taste, with a thumb-to-nose symbolism; subversive in impact on conventional manners; and intensely self-concerned, with rebels defining themselves in ways different from those offered by the prevailing "success" models.

An important aspect of style rebellion is that it symbolizes a mystique of private experience which squares do not understand. So style rebellion has not the political significance of a gesture like Thoreau's tax refusal or the Boston Tea Party. It is not an abstract claim of a political right or a program for action. The spirit of Joan Baez is not the spirit of Eugene Debs. Style rebels are not so much seeking to overthrow the organization as to find their own meaning and assert their own integrity by expressing scorn for the conventional way of life. Don't be square means do not join it spiritually. The beatniks, the weirdos, as well as the dandyish "mods," were saying, "Let me live as I please; stay out of my hair, you squares; if I want to go in bare feet, let my hair grow long like a girl, smoke pot or take a trip with LSD, what's it to you?" But their claim to live as they please, even if we ignore the assault aspect, was spiritually, if not politically, anarchic.

The fifth form of rebellion made least sense of all in terms of economics and politics. It consisted of a substantial and growing dropout movement, with uncounted numbers of people—many from the middle classes—quietly dropping out of the system of "prosperity" and its rewards. It was the fashion to make fun of the Bohemians of the 1930s and the beatniks of the 1950s, but by the '60s there were rather too many dropouts to dismiss as arty eccentrics or oddballs. The "hippies" became publicly visible, on Haight Street, San Francisco, sometimes gathering by the thousands for "trip festivals," "happenings," marijuana "smoke-ins." But there were others—some among the antiwar protestors, some in Sexual Freedom Leagues, and large numbers of other young people of college and high school age,[9] some wearing Ivy League, some surfer, styles, as well as many in the middle and upper classes outside of school age—who showed their great interest in dropouts by adopting many of their styles and reading their literature. No small part of the dropout movement was to be found in churches, monasteries, sectarian groups, and new religious thought of one kind or another. Intellectuals, too, contributed a large membership, though their sanctuary was the ivory tower. Indeed, it was hard to tell how far the tidal pull of dropping out was felt within the Establishment, in the alienation of those who were working hard without quite knowing why. J. B. Priestley noted that the real

> lost souls don't wear their hair long and play guitars. They have crew cuts, trained minds, sign on for research in biological warfare, and don't give their parents a moment's worry.[10]

Indeed, the origin of the dropout movement could easily be dated from Henry David Thoreau, or even from the Shakers of New England; but it was psychedelic drugs that really precipitated the movement on the American scene in the 1960s, and gave it a religious and esthetic mystique, so well expressed in Timothy Leary's slogan, "Turn on, tune in, drop out." This brought the movement to a head, especially when it came in conflict with the law in civil disobedience—whether in flagrant use of LSD or in other forms such as antiwar protest and strewing flowers in the path of policemen and soldiers. The hippie made especially clear to the public the orientation of the dropout movement which, unlike the activists of the new left, was not to fight for causes but to "tune in," "be in," "swing," "make love, not war"; not to achieve anything practically but to advocate having one's own esthetic or mystical experience, to "dig," or "grok"—defined by Herbert Gold as to "enjoy, float and relish the scene for that's what's happening baby."[11] Unlike the forward looking of progressives, and the backward looking of the radical right, the dropout movement looked to the present—"the real is now." Far from developing polemics in its criticism of the system, it was antiword, with a preference for "cool" experience as defined by Marshall McLuhan, where "little is given and . . . much has to be filled in by the listener."[12] But the peak of it all, that made dropping out easier and more interesting than it had been when only the methods of monasticism were available, was the new adventure, the "private sea,"[13] offered by psychedelic drugs.

The spread of these new drugs and the conversions ("quick Nirvana," "instant mysticism") led to a great increase in psychedelic drug use, including a new popularity of marijuana with claims of its legitimacy and a movement to legalize "pot" by leaders such as Leslie Fiedler and Timothy Leary. Psychedelics also made a new contribution to style rebellion in art and clothing fashions. The movement reached such proportions that, by midsummer 1967, just as the riots were bursting forth in the urban ghettoes, national magazines like *Life* were offering feature articles with such titles as "Marijuana: Millions of Turned-On Users." Conservatives still viewed this as a badly aggravated "drug problem," a kind of crime wave. But note the difference between the older attitude toward drug addicts and the following account of police action against a "smoke-in" in Manhattan in August 1967:

POLICE WATCH A MARIJUANA "SMOKE-IN." The sweet, heavy smell that indicates burning marijuana drifted over Tompkins Square Park on the lower east side of Manhattan yesterday evening. The hippies were having a "smoke-in" and seven policemen were standing by doing nothing about it. About 200 young people gathered between two gnarled trees and smoked marijuana for over three hours. No arrests were made, though possession or smoking of marijuana is either a misdemeanor or a felony, depending upon the quantity involved. One officer said an arrest would "cause more trouble than it was worth." . . . The smoke-in began at about 7:15 p.m., when a band called the Pteradactyls began playing electric guitars. They called for the audience to come onstage and play the drums and five Puerto Ricans heeded the call. "That's the best part of this," one marijuana-smoking hippie said. "The hippies and the Puerto Ricans have one thing in common—grass." . . . (There was) a smoke-in last Sunday and the Sunday before. Each started with the smoking of banana peels (a relatively new hippie craze), but marijuana was smoked each time before the evening was out. This time, though, the grass was handed out at once. At one point, two boys walked into the crowd with two large brown paper bags full of cigarettes made of marijuana. They threw the marijuana up in the air and the crowd of 200 grabbed and scrambled for the falling cigarettes. A minute later, two policemen walked into the crowd to "see what those cigarettes were." Five people opened a circle in the crowd and offered five burning objects to the policemen. Two were filter cigarettes, but three looked very much like marijuana. One of the policemen waved his hand and both walked out of the group. They were given an ovation by the smokers.[14]

So, in 1967, America began to see mass participation in open drug use comparable to that of alcohol at a picnic.

The shock of conservatives deepened, however, when they began to realize that this was not just a drug problem but a challenge to the very foundations of the modern social order: values such as the desirability of maximum production, spending as much as you can afford, working for status symbols, modernization and progress, monogamy, conventional religion, and reason as a prime method of thought (versus intuition). The most alarming thing of all, perhaps, was that the dropout movement was seducing youth from "success" to voluntary poverty and mysticism. Hippies were only part of a larger, more pervasive (and older) movement, including beatniks, hipsters, surfers, some folk singers, dandies, poseurs, jacket boys, and other style rebels, going back to cynics, mystics, and monastics of older times. The chief characteristics of the dropout movement were a concern with inner values and experiences (kicks), disinterest in politics (in spite of the movement to legalize "pot"), personal freedom of expression and style, and a concern with finding oneself and living a better life privately (the new romanticism), with retreat from obligations and antagonism to the Establishment. Perhaps the most positive thing one could say about the dropout movement was that the use of psychedelics engendered missionary zeal to spread "love" and "illumination" to other people, and that its members cared enough about their mission to engage in illegal acts and risk arrest for it, with the apparent hope of ultimately creating a society of "turned-on" people.

These five forms of rebellious mass movement in America show many differences: in class and ethnic makeup, position of their members in the social structure, tactics, orientation, and conception of the world. But common features are also notable, among which are: protest or enmity against the existing order, whether called "the Establishment" (as the left defines its villain) or moral and ideological corruption and the welfare state (as the right defines its villains); rejection or suspicion of "progress" (whether seen as the danger of organization and bureaucracy to the individual, liberal hypocrisy, or the road to socialism, as seen by the right); and the rejection of affluence by all but the ghetto rebels (even the radical right stressing austerity, thrift, Puritanism, and the corruption of hedonism and luxury). But, more important, all seem to suffer from a deficiency of ideology, an intelligible public philosophy. All seem to have no place to go. This is seen in the "mindless violence" of the urban ghetto; the pragmatic humanism of the new left, without a program, searching for a "new politics"; the hankering of the radical right for a past which can never return; and style rebellion, which has gestures but no rationale at all; while the dropouts, especially the psychedelic ones, have quit working altogether and live like the "lilies of the field," without plans or social security. In this series of incredible rebellions, perhaps civil rights makes the most sense—but not quite enough sense to justify the actions. All these movements have shown, and perceived themselves, that they have no place to go within the sensible alternatives of radical or conservative political and economic action. They cannot get a real, slambang political revolution started. They lack a program of step-by-step (or even one shot) action that can bring reasonable promise of a new world. All, frustrated, seem to turn to irrational directions, and seem more concerned with style, slogans, and emotional outlet than with practical progress. A common denominator was a feeling, however vague, of being for something that could not be achieved through conventional politics—"new politics" maybe, but no one seems to know exactly what that could be.

REBELLION WITH NO PLACE TO GO

In this sense, then, our society is generating rebellion which has no place to go within the conventional alternatives of political and economic radicalism. Its expressions are peculiar and, in the eyes of some, morbid. Perhaps this is what Senator J. William Fulbright meant when he said, "The Great Society has become a sick society," trying to cope with the Vietnam war and internal rebellions at the same time. He commented on the confused and baffled state of mind of the younger generation, seeing so much wrong and not quite knowing what to do about it.

> Unlike so many of their elders, they have perceived the fraud and sham in American life and are unequivocally rejecting it. The hippies have simply withdrawn, others are sardonic and skeptical, but still others are striving to keep alive the traditional values of American democracy.[15]

I would like to explain here why a sincere radical of the 1960s had a hard time visualizing any kind of practical program to drastically reorient the society of which he disapproved. The truth was that the sources of radicalism—material and ideological, so lush in the nineteenth century—had about dried up.

For one thing, prosperity was being attained at a rapid rate through technology alone by nations which had reached the "take off" stage (to use Walter Rostow's phrase)—free enterprise or socialism, ideology or no ideology—as many economists have pointed out. The accumulation of capital, gross of corporate organization, development of skills, process of invention, and increased efficiency of technology went on almost regardless of (often in spite of) the political perspective and economic theories of those who headed the system. Such prosperity, attainable more by science and technology than politics, was like a cornucopia spilling its abundance and raising the floor of mass consumption without theories of whether the system was "fair" or not. It developed a mystique of faith in technology and at the same time deprived the mass of reasonable rebellion based on poverty. It became, rather, a matter of waiting for the standard of living to rise. Even for those who remained poor,[16] there was a compensatory kind of pseudoprosperity, created by such things as advertising, credit buying, and watching the life of the jet set and wealthy celebrities (comparable to vicarious participation in the life of royalty). So, to the rebel who had the temerity to protest the economic system, the answer became: "You've never had it so good, what are you complaining about?" or "Wait a little, you'll get yours yet." In short, the economic rebel was in the position of kicking the cornucopia—or, if I may change the metaphor, how can you kick a slot machine that is coughing nickels at you all the time? There seemed no sensible way to go for those who wanted to go better and faster than down the mainstream of welfare, bureaucracy, and technology, where everybody was hastening anyway.

Another reason that the sources of radicalism had about dried up—in the United States at least—was, as pointed out by Bell[17] and others, that the welfare state had pre-empted so many of the economic and social reforms demanded by socialism. The labor movement had given up its early radicalism for bread-and-butter gains. American pragmatism had helped devise ideological monstrosities like TVA, that put a lion's head on a sheep's body and made it viable. Books like John Kenneth Galbraith's *The New Industrial State* (1967) showed how far free enterprise had gone away from a market economy toward planning and government intervention that could as easily be labeled socialism as capitalism. So socialism was like a sled that had run out of snow. The vast majority of educated liberals (who might have been socialists in another era) could see no sense in a radicalism that was not much different from visibly approaching welfare state measures such as civil rights, antipoverty, and guaranteed annual income. The only sensible course seemed down the mainstream—more rapidly perhaps, but surely no need for drastic portages over rocky land to get to another stream.

On the other hand, for those radicals who wanted to draw their inspiration for rebellion from the doctrine of unalienable rights and the limited state—that civil disobedience and "treason" are legally justified when tyranny invades natural rights (so familiarly stated by Jefferson)[18]—there was another source of difficulty: the natural rights idea had in the twentieth century suffered a serious loss of confidence. The Declaration of Independence, for example, was regarded as "controversial" in America. Once it was removed from the wall of the lobby of a certain western State House for this reason, until protest had it put back, according to an anecdote by Justice William O. Douglas. I have asked college classes whether they would sign the Declaration of Independence or the United Nations Declaration of Rights; invariably the vast majority say No, regarding such statements as Utopian and unrealistic, if not, in some cases, subversive. The prevailing opinion seems to be that rights are relative to culture and socially bestowed (therefore can be taken away), not unalienably possessed. Nor did it help the status of Jeffersonian doctrine to see slogans of natural liberty used by such ultraconservative, dubious groups as the Liberty Leaguers and Minute Men—even the Ku Klux Klan. And the natural rights doctrine fared no better among scholars than with the man on the street.

At the intellectual level, I think it is safe to say that the majority of scholars no longer believed in the physical or metaphysical existence of natural rights, as distinguished from rights which are socially bestowed. The historian Merle Peterson said that Rufus Choate's phrase, "glittering generalities," "summed up a growing reaction against" the Declaration of Independence and the idea of natural rights; the Declaration was "the great creative myth of the American people." Carl Becker rejected the "self-evidence" of natural rights and regarded it as naive to ask whether they were true or false since their purpose was propagandistic—to justify American independence.[19] The impact of science, especially positivism, did much to weaken the idea of natural rights. C. E. M. Joad, the English philosopher, said:

> Our age does not believe in the dignity of man. It does not assign him a special place in a purposeful universe, but thinks of him after the mode that science has made fashionable, an accident of evolution, a complex of reflexes, a puppet twitched into love or war by the showman who pulls the strings, or, as the behaviorists would have us believe, a by-product of chemical and physiological processes pursuing his course across a fundamentally alien and brutal environment and doomed ultimately to finish his pointless journey with as little significance as in the person of the amoeba his ancestors once began it.[20]

In other words, although there was scientific basis for saying that man was the highest primate, there was none for placing him outside the animal kingdom in the matter of unique rights; he was only the star performer in the zoo. Suppose, then, someone put him in a cage or made a slave of him; was there any biological or sociological law which said this could not be done? To the extent that moderns came to doubt the absoluteness of rights, considering them merely social, the whole concept had become philosophically soft.

There was a lack of rock-like assurance, therefore no fulcrum for leverage against the state. "Rights" were only a desideratum, an idea of what you liked or what you thought you had coming to you—one among many values such as power and welfare, not a categorical imperative. To this extent, they were lame as a revolutionary principle and could not serve as a powerful lever of protest, rebellion, or reform in the world.

Nor was that all. Even more unfortunate for political and economic radicalism, sociologists noted that *all* ideology, not just natural rights doctrine, seemed to be drying up—at least in America.[21] The grand notions about history that so entranced the intellectuals of the nineteenth and early twentieth centuries were seen as "glittering generalities." College youths were being raised on the anti-ideological theories of Pareto, Freud, and, ironically, Marx, interpreted by the sociology of knowledge of Karl Mannheim. Pragmatism was in the air. Except for closed and sectarian societies, there was a general loss of belief in fine principles. Richard Hofstadter said that "No new conceptions of comparable strength have taken root" to replace the old "ideology of self-help, free enterprise, competition and beneficent cupidity upon which Americans have been nourished since the foundation of the Republic." He noted the rudderless and demoralized state of American liberalism.[22] Americans were not especially embarrassed by lack of ideology; they even took pride in it, regarding it as a blessing. Arthur Schlesinger, Jr., said:

> America has the good fortune not to be an ideological society. . . . Most of the time Americans have foxily mistrusted abstract rationalism and rigid *a priori* doctrine. Our national faith has not been in propositions but in processes. In its finest hours, the United States has, so to speak, risen above ideology. . . . This skepticism about ideology has been a primary source of the social inventiveness which has marked so much of our development. . . . American social thought has been empirical, practical, pragmatic.[23]

Foreigners noted the lack of ideology among Americans. The anthropologist Clyde Kluckhohn said:

> Japanese . . . complained to me that it was difficult to understand American democracy because Americans seemed to lack an explicit ideology that they could communicate. The Japanese contrasted the Russians who

could immediately give a clear account of their system of belief. Various Americans have remarked that what the United States needed more than a good five cent cigar was a good five cent ideology. Such political ideology as we have derived largely from the political radicalism of the late 18th century. We repeat the old words. . . .[24]

If this is the way things were, then it is no surprise to find ideas like Jeffersonianism or Marxism, however radical, a poor launching pad for revolution in America in the 1960s—and for much of the rest of the world. They suffered from a general malaise of ideology that made all programs for a Utopian future, or reaching a "natural and right" order of things, suspect. Even if one believed in the doctrine of natural rights, it was, at best, only a short-run basis for revolution—a matter of collecting the last delayed installment on the Emancipation Proclamation. Where then? (One may note that most of the rebellious spirit of the new left was for ideas no more novel and advanced than civil rights.)

The only kind of ideology that seemed to stir much enthusiasm among college students and intellectuals—in America at least—might be broadly characterized as a kind of humanism, or concern for man as such, for exploring his potentialities—without labels, without color or class, and without nation. I feel that existentialism, liberalism, scientific positivism, psychoanalysis, and religious mysticism, insofar as they appeal to the rebel spirit, are all imbued with a humanism that hopes for what man will become when he outsteps his present limitations—well expressed, for example, in Thomas Henry Huxley's *Trans-Humanism*. Such humanism, realizing man's true well-being, makes many kinds of short-run radical stands and idealistic proposals meaningful: protests of the Vietnam war, sit-ins in segregated restaurants, efforts to legalize abortion, ekistics,[24a] a call for more human cities. But what is mainly lacking in revolutionary humanism is a program of what to do when short-run goals and protests are achieved. Humanism lacks features which help action programs, such as patriotism or loyalty to organizations, so it cannot motivate programs for the benefit of one nation or party in disregard (or at the expense) of another; sacrifice of humans now for a revolutionary goal later; and lack of faith in politics. In this lack of willingness to use men for political purposes, humanism is weaker than Marxism. So, if humanism were to become as effective a basis of revolution as Marxism, it would not only have to develop a program but overcome its lack of faith in politics (using men as means).

Hence, in spite of all the smoke and fire of rebellion and unrest, the United States in the 1960s was not a very good place for a revolution based on classical ideas of political or economic injustice (such as encroachment of natural rights, or a proletariat ground into poverty by capitalism). A Lenin or a Tom Paine would have been in despair.

THE REAL PROBLEM AND APPROPRIATE RESPONSES

From examining the forms of the incredible rebellion, the conclusion seems inescapable that there is a source of frustration in America that is not remedied by material prosperity and progress, and that it may grow even worse. What is this frustration? In my opinion, it comes mainly from two psychological ingredients: (1) The explosion of expectations and capacity to dream (psychological mobility), made possible by physical welfare and stimulated by mobility and mass communication, *combined with* a lowered norm of effort in a technological society: the idea that one does not have to work for what one gets, that one has things coming to him (stimulated, no doubt, by advertising which says, "You've got it coming to you," "You deserve this," "Pamper yourself".[25] Thus many people stimulated to expect more are at the same time unfitted to put forth the effort that might have gotten it for their fathers, who believed in working hard for a living. (2) The identity problem, an inability to define oneself successfully in a milieu of inadequate symbolism—which means that even people in wealth and luxury (how much more likely in squalor and poverty!) come to feel that life is empty, boring, that somehow they have been cheated, yet they can't say why. This is because of the disintegration of interactions and symbols that make life and self meaningful at the nondiscursive level (sentiments, mystiques).

Were these two problems solved, Midas' misery might disappear and man could live in his world of golden gadgets grasping luxury with real felicity.

I think the rebels of our modern affluent society are reacting to a frustration compounded of a sense of relative deprivation, from comparing themselves with others and their own exploding expectations, and from symbolic disturbances to identity. Only a fraction of this frustration is attributable to sheer economic hardship or political injustice.

In the light of these considerations, there is a certain naïveté in the idea that equalizing things economically and politically for the "disadvantaged"—whether nations or individuals—is going to solve the problems of frustration and rebellion in the modern world. If there are causes of frustration that have little or nothing to do with economic or political equality or inequality, then rebellion will continue to flower and will seek new excuses when the old ones are gone. It is rather like buying toys for brothers who fight; after they have exactly the same toys and privileges, they will find something else to fight about. Indeed, from the standpoint of identity, it may be that differentiated, unequal relationships are just as satisfying as sameness. The sexes are a case in point. I do not wish to overdraw it, merely to say that equality *may* be irrelevant to the question of whether relationships are meaningful and satisfying.

Because of this, it is understandable that, especially with the drying up of faith in ideology, political scientists should be coming to attach more importance to frustration than to rationally perceived injustice as a source of political instability. They are turning to the idea of a *frustration ratio*, a purely psychological equation, making people dissatisfied with their lot and inclined to extremism, which is not sheer hardship or absolute lack of something, but a ratio between expectations and the available means of satisfying them.[26] The important point is that, since the frustration ratio is a psychological and not just a physical fact, abundance and middle-class comforts are no guarantees against a revolutionary potential. The princess sleeping on twelve mattresses can be just as unhappy as the peasant on straw. And, on the material score, even disregarding the identity problem, it is clear that, although we have an abundant society, we also have one geared to making people discontented. All the diabolical arts of Madison Avenue are devoted to raising the level of expectations. (Whereas, by contrast, Buddhism in the Orient is a restraining force, its lesson being, as we well know, "He who sleeps on the floor will never fall out of bed.")

Both the American pursuit of happiness and Marxism by its emphasis on material well-being are exacerbating to discontent. All the more so for those who have extra lead in the saddle in the race with galloping expectations. But, for all of this, as I have said, material deprivation theory alone does not very well fit the American picture.

To repeat, the real problem in an advanced country like America is *exaggerated expectations* compounded by *boredom*. These are two very real kinds of frustration, reinforcing each other ($F = E \times B$). Neither is reducible to "injustice" as usually conceived. It is for this reason that boredom has such a prominent place in the complaints of the new left beside the rational injustices of the social order. So Mario Savio, leader of the Berkeley student revolt, comments:

> It is a bleak scene . . . American society in the standard conception it has of itself is simply no longer exciting. The most exciting things going on in America today are movements to change America. America is becoming evermore the Utopia of sterilized, automated contentment. . . . "Futures" and "careers" . . . are for the most part intellectual and moral wasteland. This chrome-plated consumer's paradise would have us grow up to be well behaved children.[27]

A student newspaper at San Diego State College says:

> Many are indeed "dropping out" of the ordinary life styles of the sterile "middle class"; get up in the morning, go to work for eight hours, come home and watch TV until the week is over and the weekend of fun and games ends and the cycle starts over again. The denial of this sterile way of life and the search for a new "life style" is a threat to the existing society.

David A. Shannon, commenting on the decline of American communism, says, "The era of the picture window and the tail-finned automobile has produced its own dissatisfactions and frustrations but not the kind that leads one to seek salvation in Left Wing politics."[28]

And Viktor Frankl, it seems to me, puts his finger exactly on the problem when he says the "existential vacuum" of modern man "manifests itself mainly in a state of boredom. . . . Boredom is now . . . bringing to psychiatrists more problems to solve than is distrust."[29]

In spite of improving technological organization and growth of national product, what, indeed, is there to appeal to an idealistic university student who wants a vision of a better world, that is more than a vast, unending prospect of bureaucracy, however improved? It must be admitted that this is a boring prospect. Even science (which has exhausted its wonders since H-bombs and Mars-shots) is becoming boring. Except for the really underprivileged, welfare is boring. And, for the better off, "success," the American dream, has become boring: commuting in two hours of smog between bureaucracy and suburbia; the white-collar worker replacing the self-made man; the land pioneer on his fifty-foot lot; the great exciting unpredictability of how a horse opera will come out. I am not saying the American dream is a bad dream, mind you, just not a very exciting one. So many American college students seek "free universities" where they can get more excitement. The Free University of New York states in its catalog that "this school exists in response to the intellectual bankruptcy and spiritual emptiness of the American educational establishment."

And yet I would not imply by this that American college students are unusually revolutionary; most of them are the best mannered, nicest, blandest people one could expect to find in a university. Because their frustration ratio is relatively low and there is no believable programmatic radicalism to stir them up, they are on the whole better behaved, and less political, than students in countries where there is really something to complain about. For example, sociologist David Nasatir has compared student rebellions in Latin America and North America. In Latin America, student rebellions spread to the community-at-large whereas American student rebellions tend to be localized on campuses; Latin American student rebellions are intensely political whereas American student rebellions tend to be apolitical; Latin American student rebellions make use of small arms, knives, and Molotov cocktails as standard equipment whereas these are less usual in American student rebellions; in Latin American student rebellions siege situations are common, with the campus a sanctuary from the police, whereas American student rebellions are promptly controlled by police action; Latin American students have a large voice in academic affairs, can fire professors, feel their oats, whereas American students have a less active role (though the take-over of Columbia University in April 1968 may indicate a change toward the Latin American pattern).[30]

However, when $F = E \times B$ predominates over injustice as a social problem, there comes a time when politics and economics are seen failing as adequate responses. They fail because they themselves do not directly meet the problem and because they are seen to lack meaning, to be banal, are even felt as immoral; and because the social fabric (togetherness) has disintegrated (anomie) to a point where economic and political measures do not remedy it. But it was first necessary to exhaust material solutions before it became plain that they were not the answer, that even with prosperity, something was still missing. Exaggerated expectations and boredom create a new kind of problem, afflicting rich and poor alike. People do not know what to do about such a problem, whereas they could figure out what to do about injustice and poverty. So the motive of the incredible revolution is to find a different solution than remedying the inequity of the distribution of goods or power. So rebellion has no place to go; it may hide its boredom under protests about "injustice" and grope for more appropriate solutions—but what?

This is what I think was happening in America in the late 1960s: People were perceiving the inadequacy of political-economic responses and turning to others. It is a variant of the Toynbee thesis, if you please, a turning to spiritual and religious response in time of crisis. But not just religious in the narrow sense: The range of activities we review in this book shows the varieties of nonpolitical, noneconomic gropings—which might be likened to fingers of exploration, or arrows in the dark—by which the mass tries to solve its psychospiritual problems, many of which seem disloyal or heretical because they are a turning away from stock solutions.

Now we get back to LSD and things like that. What does a young person do when a situation is boring, lacking in challenge, when there is no place to go in terms of exciting ideology, the university seems a great machine with pipelines into the organization world, and suburbia is the prospect of the good life? When a person is bored with the kind of life he lives and the kind of person he is, he is likely to liven up his existence by style rebellion. A "trip" via LSD is another way out of a society where there is no exciting place to go. Cultic movements are not primarily concerned with rebelling but with adding meaning and mystique to a life which is boring. It is wrong, therefore, to associate either beatniks and other style rebels, or hippies, with communism; they couldn't care less. That is square, too, as is all politics. Cultists and style rebels are retreatists from the political and economic point of view: they are concerned with finding a private life of their own, or their own group; they express the fact that rebellion has switched to esthetics and religion for those who see no place to go economically and politically. In such movements, thousands of people try to throw off— not the chains of political or economic servitude but—the chains of banality, bureaucracy, and prosperity itself in a search for personal significance and identity, a claim for a right their fathers never heard of: the right not to be bored, to have an interesting life, to be personally fulfilled—each and every one.

But style rebellion and cultic movements are not the only appropriate responses in a society which suffers from boredom. Many interesting opportunities for radical experimentation are offered in fashion, faddism, posing, shocking art (pop, "junk" sculpture, "happening"), orgiastic fun, riot, crime, civil disobedience, crusading. Most of these mass responses, however, are efforts of people to find identity without working through politics or economics or commitment to ideologies. Vicarious participation in the lives of celebrities is an enormously important way in which people seek identity, largely irrelevant to politics or economics (though when a political movement uses the cult of personality it shoots with both barrels). The crusading type of movement, to which we devote a chapter, involves a commitment to action which redeems identity as well as achieving practical results; but the crusade is inherently a kind of movement which cannot be reckoned solely in practical terms, because a psychological payoff to identity may loom larger.

So, in conclusion, I would say that, though there is much unrest in our abundant society, it is not the kind which is likely to lead to programmatic political rebellion. The real goals of this revolution are nondiscursive (speechless). It is too early to say where it is going. Perhaps all one can say is that the responses of a society with identity problems do not fit very well within the practical programs of politics and economics, and may drain off energy from them. Which is not to say, of course, that a political movement such as fascism cannot use them.

But what is the real threat of the incredible revolution? It seems to me that it is by no means necessarily fascism or communism. The Constitution is relatively safe, I would say, from this kind of rebellion. Style rebels will not storm the barricades. But there is a treasonable challenge to the images of "progress" and "success." The incredible revolution is against the very image of "success": it rejects the expense-account luxury and satrapy of the business executive, the social life of the clubwoman, the safe job of the bureaucrat, and the happy family life of suburbia. "What, indeed, is the world coming to?" the hard-working, conscientious businessman has a right to ask. The world is being filled with "fun"-lovers, thrill-seekers, playboys, dandies, cultists, and others who live *primarily* for goals which the older system condemned ("living it up," "loafing," the life of the wastrel). The incredible revolution is also a challenge to rationalism (planning, technology, science, logic); it rejects the intellect as a sole valid method (the premise of Socrates, Descartes, J. S. Mill), indeed, blames it for some of the troubles of the life of "one-dimensional man" (Herbert Marcuse). In short, the incredible revolution is a rejection of "progress" as the eighteenth and nineteenth centuries conceived it. It is, therefore, "treasonable" at the deepest levels, with which the conventional logic of Americans cannot argue successfully. The real threat of the incredible revolution is working as hard as you can to get as much as you can—practical materialism. As far as it is concerned, capitalism can go hang (and so can socialism)—it may die of neglect, but not of expropriation.

It may be that the appropriate responses to the meaning problem, which are now mostly nonrational, will be developed into a rational program. However, we appear not to be in a position yet (in spite of the new romanticism) to recognize the identity problem on its own terms, as on a par with political and economic problems, and to see that restoring identity and the symbolism necessary for it could be made into a program of rational, radical reform—just as intelligible as reforming capitalism was to a socialist or restoring civil rights was to a liberal in the early twentieth century. In this book, however, we are concerned with movements now bursting forth, with the identity problem only dimly perceived, with trying to remedy boredom and meaninglessness, and the symbolic and interactional deficiencies which give rise to it, and with trying to get some glimpse of where modern man is going and what he is groping for, now that abundance has been achieved.

PART II RESPONSES

3   Fashions and Masquerades

Starch is the man.
Beau Brummell

This chapter is concerned with how fad and fashion symptomatize a restlessness about identity which is becoming characteristic of much of the modern world. Folk and rural traditions are disappearing, the focus of life is shifting to cities "where the action is." More and more people are being drawn into a whirl of style change, invited—even pressured—to revise themselves. Out of the urban milieu come new styles and types competing for attention— first noticed in visible "leaders"—some of which hit, like arrows a bull's-eye, what the mass is groping for. Some of the types are strange, offbeat, weird, irrational, shocking to what used to be called good taste. These extravagant styles reflect not only changing tastes but the fact that growing abundance in many countries makes it possible for more people to enter the fashion race and indulge their taste for novelties, including the vanity of wishing to be somebody else; psychological mobility (the ability and wish to imagine oneself in another's place)[1] is stimulated by radio, movies, television, advertising, education, and the example of celebrities (see Chapter 7); increasing leisure offers new opportunities for escapes and adventures of identity. So, whereas in the past only a small minority of aristocrats, dandies, artists, theatrical people, and bohemians concentrated their energies on the fashion race or went to extremes of style to dramatize themselves, now more and more people are becoming conscious stylists, studying fashion magazines, watching celebrities and dandies for guidance, patronizing exclusive shops and boutiques, and adopting status symbols or defying lines of status. The upshot is that status symbols are less often reminding people who they are and where they belong, and more often expressing a claim or wish to be somebody else. The range of material subject to fashion—that can be used as dramatic props, so to speak, for a new life—seems to be widening too: automobiles, gadgets, home furnishings, areas to live in, places to travel, sports gear, hobbies, foods, beverages, art, music, books, topics of conversation, slang, points of view, types of medical treatment—anything that can figure in one's life style as status symbol. Such things are more abundant, easier to manufacture and imitate, and offered and bought more consciously on the market as status symbols. So fad and fashion as means of revising identity seem to be on the rise. Style revision is ceasing to be a rich man's game; the common man is getting into the act. The race for new identity symbols is on for just about anybody who can get a credit card.

Which is not to say that the average man may not still feel outside of all this. He may not read fashion magazines or shop at boutiques. He may pride himself on buying economically, "being himself," resisting change. (Roughly 18 percent of university students, for example, classed themselves as highly fashion-conscious, 55 percent as moderately, and 26 percent as little or not at all so; women were more fashion-conscious than men. Three-quarters said they tried to stay in the middle in fashion, neither behind nor too far out in front; three-quarters also said they tried to achieve "looks" by fashion.)[2] However, even the resistant person feels some pressures of fashion upon his identity—perhaps to throw away a perfectly good suit, to trade in an automobile that only last year was his faithful friend, to stay "with it" in whatever may be the latest points of view and topics of conversation. He is usually aware, too, of "keeping up with the Joneses". So lack of fashion consciousness is not proof one is outside fashion. We are all to some extent afloat in a sea of fashion change, the currents of which are marked by leaders moving most rapidly, but the tide at last swaying all but a very few stubborn eccentrics.

It is among the extremists, however, that we find the most interesting movements in fashion. Here the experiments are most daring, gestures most flamboyant; the identity claims (to be noticed, to be somebody else) fairly scream. One sees such extremes not only among elites (jet set, international rich, *nouveaux riches*, café society, show people) but in the lower ranks—underprivileged classes, ethnic minorities, beatniks—drawing heavily from youth at all levels. The hypothesis seems valid that fashion is most important for those who have something to prove about themselves—especially when they cannot prove it by other means. But some distinctions are in order. When style is devoted to maintaining a social position to which one has a reasonably valid claim, it may be called *front.* The majority of fashion conformers try to stay in the vogue (maintain the front) of their social set, rather than go too far ahead or behind. *High fashion* goes to extremes that are sometimes grotesque, expressing the bravura of an actual or would-be fashion leader who feels sure enough of his position and fashion sense to move out in front with something daring that will be noticed. It is individualized and short-lived; the majority usually do not reach it.[3] *Fad* is like high fashion in being short-lived and risky, but is more frivolous and does not represent sure fashion sense. Rather, it is an adventure in which a person knows he is being a little risqué or silly even though "everybody is doing it" (as in goldfish swallowing, wearing miniskirts, Beatle haircuts). The point about fad is that it is a more or less conscious experiment in identity (which may be engaged in by a whole peer group), which looms larger than merely maintaining position or front. Finally, style may be called *pose* when it is used for an adventure in identity in which there is more risk than in fad, to claim identity that is more or less theatrical or illegitimate—far afield from what the individual or group is entitled to by upbringing and competence. Fad, high fashion, and pose are more interesting for our purpose of seeing where the identity search is going than is ordinary fashion (front).

Several things seem new (in degree, if not in kind) and especially significant among the fashion expressions of the 1960s:

(1) the sheer variety of "looks" (types) available to the common man;

(2) the explicitness of identity search (for the "real you");

(3) ego-screaming: the plea "look at me!";

(4) style rebellion (style used as a means of protest or defiance);

(5) theatricalism and masquerading on the street;

(6) pose as a way of getting to the social position one wants;

(7) dandyism: (living for style, turning away from the Horatio Alger (hard work, productivity) model of success;
(8) dandyism of the common man as well as of the aristocrat;
(9) pronounced escapism in many styles (such as those of beat-niks, hippies, surfers, and in language such as "cool" and "freak out");
(10) a new concept of the right to be whatever one pleases, re-gardless of what others think (the new romanticism);
(11) the breakdown of status symbols, the tendency of fashions to mix and obscure classes rather than differentiate them;
(12) the pursuit of status symbols reaching the dead end of a vi-cious circle breaking down meaning and making it harder to tell who is who.

These are some of the things I would like to call attention to in the following discussion of fashion's role in the modern identity search. We will discuss this under five main headings: "looks," "look at me!" (ego-screaming), style rebellion, poses (the urban mas-querade), and danger of stylelessness.

LOOKS

Are you a James Bond blonde?—cool, frosty-eyed, capable, the kind that Bond himself would go for? If so, keep your teeth white and gums pink. . . .
   Are you a Beatle baby? Got a crush on the Beatles? Heart go bingo for Ringo? Then you're swinging! For a ring-ding smile to match, try . . . Toothpaste . . . gives your teeth a gleam, tints your gums a "yeah yeah" pink.

(Advertisements in a London "tube," 1964.)

What does the well dressed millionairess wear for the occasion? The personal preference of this mink-and-diamonds girl is a Paisley silk playsuit in green and brown. . . . The *International Rich Look* is achieved by creamy raincoats and sun glasses, and a glossy scarf tied on the chin (for women). The sunglasses are worn out of habit, since the eyes are usually being shielded from the blazing sunshine of Greece, or Switzerland, or the South of France. . . . If you see yourself as a slender willowy type, look for the kind of suit Dior's girl wore. . . . Here is the *Tom Jones look* in all its delicious femininity. Shirt in the thinnest white linen, with long stock tie, yoke top and lavishly full sleeves, lavishly cuffed and frilled; worn with strictly tailored yellow pants. *Tom Jones* gave us more than a great film, it gave a great new look of romanticism and dash. . . . The *Modigliani girl* is the creation of William Loew, makeup director for Charles of the Ritz, who claims it is good for all ages, types, and colorings. It is elegantly lean without being cadaverous. The Modigliani face, almond-shaped eyes, and pale pink glow, is the latest status symbol in the world of beauty. . . . New Paris fashions symbolize *La Dolce Vita*. . . . At a new discotheque called The Daisy, she wears a hairpiece with bangs. Her best friends didn't recognize her. For a dinner at home, she piles up her own locks and achieves a *Scarlett O'Hara look*. A smart girl can have many pretty heads. . . . Chanel is rumored to have spent six months looking for the right and only way for women to wear pants. . . . American women, weary of *"butch" looks,* are turning to the *Chelsea look,* which itself is a combination of various *nostalgic looks:* Edwardian, Cossack, Guardsman. . . . "The *London look*—daring skirts above the knees, straight lines, vivid colors, and wild-looking stockings—is new here (New York). It seems very different from the American type. It is much more way out. It goes with pop art and the Beatles. . . . Blotta visualizes the fashionable woman as an Edwardian dandy. His *Dandy look* is so authentic you expect the models to be dipping into their snuff boxes. . . . Big girls become little girls for the summer with the *Sugar and Spice Look*. . . . Women's shoe styles now stress a *"little girl look"* at the same time teenage boys are taking to high heels, Beatle Boots. . . . Choose your *perfume type* and identify yourself with a special scent. Even if their backs are turned, their eyes glued to a book, and they're listening to the latest record being played full volume, they'll know you've come into a room, and they've got something to remember you by. . . . The *"Thirties Look"* features George Raft lapels, Bogart fedoras, Al Capone boutonnieres. . . . What I don't have is a folky look—you know, the *Joan Baez look*. Besides, what have I got to protest? The *skinny look* is likely to appeal to the younger set. . . . The new *leather look* is subtle in suede, brilliant in calf. . . . The *Cossack look* is furred, full-skirted, trimly booted, intensely feminine, that goes with Anna Karenina and all the romance of Old Russia. . . . One might say the fashion-makers are caste-ing about for a *new look*. Beneath their gauze turbans the models had whitened faces, and that red dot on the forehead was a caste mark. They wore *rajah* coats and rajah tunics. . . . The craze for second-hand clothes is more likely to survive in London than New York, because at the moment it's the only place where anybody can wear anything they like and get away with it. . . . A new awareness of Africa has taken hold, among whites and Negroes alike, reflected in the *African look*. . . . Every so once in a while, a new look comes along that makes what seemed good till that minute seem suddenly passé. Like the look of Sophia Loren in *Boy on a Dolphin:* All those *vivace,* pasta-posited curves had half the women in the audience feeling underweight, a bit squinchy. Loren, for a time, put bones out of business.

This collage of fashion advertising and comment is meant to illustrate the enormous variety of "looks" from different periods and cultures available to a person at one time as stylistic possibilities. Modern fashion seems to be ransacking every period and culture for new looks. It also illustrates the frank appeal of fashion advertising to finding oneself, the "real you":

Maybe the real you is a blonde. Every smart woman keeps searching for her identity—the inner woman she really is, and the outward expression of it. She looks for a special way to shape her mouth or tilt her chin, a new color, a fragrance that is her personal message to the world. When you see a woman who's found herself, you know it. There's a quiet excitement about her that says, "I like being me." Have you found the real you? Some women never do. In fact, many women never make the most exciting discovery of all: they should have been born blonde.

It seems evident, however, that in achieving looks a person is as likely to escape from his real self as find it. We note also that the aim of looks is not so much beauty or inherently desirable traits as theatrical effect: starkness, strikingness, even ugliness—color.

It is unfair and rather mean to imply that the pursuit of looks is only by women—that men do not also seek identities through fashion. Advertising to men has much the same emphasis on looks: the James Bond look (007), the "Trim Man," the Edwardian look, the surfer look, the "shaped look," the "natural shoulder look," the "conventional look." There is a new dandyism. The manager of a London men's boutique says:

Men are worse than women now—they drive us mad. They come in every week: What have you got that's new? Even the ones who haven't got money try to be original. They'll sew black patch pockets on a white jacket or something like that.

A male often seeks his look by his car or other vehicle, or by something he smokes:

Every time we buy a packet of cigarettes it gives us a certain . . . feeling of having made a purchase that says something about us, usually something rather nice. We seek out brands with attributes that we . . . feel "wash off" onto ourselves. Our favorite brands express our conceptions of ourselves, though not so much the selves we actually are as the selves we would like to be. . . .

Oldsmobile is a hot car. It stands for gay, lighthearted driving and speed. . . . Buick has the Big Car feeling . . . a Cadillac for the middle income group. . . . Mercury caters . . . to a rather flashy clientele that derives satisfaction from a plethora of chrome. Conveys the idea of brute power, indiscriminately used.[4]

Further comments from style observers and tailors leave little doubt about the male trend:

There can be no doubt that men are ready and eager for change in clothes, readier even than their better halves. . . . There have been far more changes in men's clothing in the last two and a half years (1964) than in women's. . . . What suits a woman today will suit a man tomorrow.[5]

The entire men's clothing business, from Saville Row to the ready-mades, is engaged in a wholesale plunder of ideas from a girl's world. . . . Young men's boutiques . . . are springing up all over the country. . . . There are more and more colored, frilly shirts . . . with stand-up collars or a frothy lace panel down the front with frilly cuffs to match. . . . Offered to young executives . . . are many familiar items from a girl's wardrobe . . . coats in seal skin and nutria, or in suede with linings of red fox, mink, opossum . . . the most shameless pinch from the girls' department is the arrival of coordinated separates for men.[6]

In the past few years the male cosmetics industry has burgeoned into a business which grosses annually some 350 million dollars and is still expanding. In 1963, for example, 151 different fragrances of all sorts were marketed for men. Last year (1964) that number jumped to 191. Hair sprays for men, wrinkle removers for men—much of the extensive catalog of female cosmetics is being adapted to the male.[7]

A specialist who opened a beauty salon for men in Paris said of his typical client: "He walks into my establishment, old, tired and worn—a few hours later he comes out a new man, Adonis, Apollo, an American Don Juan."[8]

For either sex, styles are a set of props for casting oneself in a character, rather than a means of expressing one's true self. An American woman views her body "as a craftsman views his raw material."[9]

> It may have been true ten years ago that only a few actors colored their hair. But since then a minor, and somewhat surprising, revolution has taken place. Today it is estimated that over 2,000,000 men from all walks of life have broken with tradition and have done something about their gray hair—bankers, farmers, longshoremen, teachers and police officers do it. Without blushing. They all have one thing in common: they don't want to look old before their time.[10]

The pursuit of looks, therefore, is a way that the conventional person can experiment with changing himself.

But for all the range of possibilities, they are mainly in "good taste," not too deviant. Fashion is conservative, square, approved by respectable people, identified with an elite class—the "in" set. Still, there are tendencies to extremes in fashion to which this conservatism does not apply.

"LOOK AT ME!"

There is in fashion a tendency to extremes that cannot be explained by the desire to identify oneself with an "in" set or even to achieve an interesting look. Indeed, about the time one concludes that fashion is conservative, governed by good taste, it contradicts that by breaking out in extremes that we call "high fashion" or "faddism." Such extremes are not accounted for by the desire of an elite class to differentiate itself from the masses, according to the classic theory of fashion (Simmel, Sapir). There is more going on here. There is in fashion a demand for attention too strong to be explained as desire for approval. It might be called ego-screaming ("look at me!"); it has "shock value."

Owners of boutiques in New York have discovered that what customers want is not only gorgeous clothes but individual attention. The manager of Fancy That states:

> It is specialization in merchandise and service in the form of attention and fashion guidance that brings customers into our store. . . . No de-

partment store is going to take half an hour to sell a six dollar pair of pants, but we do and we sell the customer the rest of the outfit at the same time.

Another manager says:

We are not and we don't want to be an everybody's store. Our things are just a little different because our designers work exclusively for us. Their look is our look and it's not everybody's look.

So the customer gets at the same time personal attention from clerks who fuss over him and gaudy gear to attract the eye of strangers. There is an almost pathetic need of many identity-deprived moderns—not to be dressed in good taste, not just to be identified with a class, but for clothes which almost plead, "Look at me!"

We doubt very much whether the following extremes—though "sexy"—can be explained by a desire for sex appeal.

Dress neckline takes new plunge. The House of . . . was first last season with the very decolleté late day and evening dresses that caused such a stir. This season he has more to show . . . more daringly decolleté, with deeply plunging Vs front and back and a jewel on the mid-riff.

At last week's collections the shaven model was greeted with cries of dismay. *The Bald Lady* looks stunned, possibly pretty (though it was hard to tell) and remained to all questions silent. "She's dumb," explained a guest, "She must be. Only a really dumb chick would let them do that to her."

Nokini. Paris.—With temperatures in the 90's, a 23-year-old English girl walked naked down the length of the crowded A. de l'Opera today. She was taken to a police station and later sent to a hospital for a psychiatric examination but pronounced quite sane.

Dior covers up. The House of Christian Dior will ignore the "topless" craze in its autumn-winter collection, and will raise necklines. Marc Bohan, Dior's designer, said yesterday that "the topless bathing suit has nothing to do with style. It will not last. It's not a fashion—it's a joke."

Two girls who went to a film premiere in Piccadilly in topless dresses had their appeals dismissed yesterday. They were conditionally discharged for twelve months for commiting an act of indecency to the annoyance of passengers in Piccadilly under a law of 1888.

Style show has "nude" look. The Molli Parnis "nude" is a short, stunning lace evening dress. It is made over nude net and worn with a nude slip.

So the nude look has eye-catching quality without risk.

Another fashion designer, Balenciaga, achieves what everyone wants, not by plunging necklines, bare midriff, or tantalizing nudity, but by severe understatement. A dress buyer says:

He's the master of understatement. Any woman who walks into a room in his clothes—however simply cold they look—must be noticed. She doesn't need added drama. She doesn't need a collar or cuffs. It's all there in the cut. His dresses have the simple secret that will make everyone notice a girl like this.

Shock value is what is aimed at—not for "sex appeal" but for audience interest. The comment is heard again and again from fashion experts, "They want to be looked at." "Daring" has little essentially to do with exposing the anatomy. It can be achieved by green wig or luminous lipstick. Women willingly sacrifice femininity (along with sex appeal) for flat chests, mannishness, wild shocks of hair, cadaverousness—anything to get themselves looked at. Males would probably be quick to testify that one does not find sex appeal in *Harper's Bazaar* or *Vogue*. That can be found in magazines for men. The prime motive of women's high fashion is to have a look that will get one attention, an audience—not a special audience that whistles.

Let us now consider an even more startling fashion development during 1964 to 1967: the tendency of males to look like females. In London in 1964 an odd doubt crept in the mind of observers of young men on the passing scene, "boy or girl?" Boys were looking more like girls and at the same time girls were looking more like boys; boy-girl look-alikes were common. Articles appeared in magazines with titles like "How to Tell a Boy from a Girl." Boys were willing to endure mockery for the right to look like girls.

I worked on a building site. I really enjoyed that while I was there. . . . I used to get ribbed at first about the hair, but it didn't last long. . . . They were comical but not malicious. If they liked someone, they liked someone. . . . The only thing worries me—when some people work up a vicious hate without knowing you. They must be bitter, to hate someone who just passes by. Otherwise, people just make a funny comment.[11]

The furor reached America when a woman called a hotel manager and complained, "There are four girls in the pool in topless bathing suits!" It was a group of entertainers—four boys with bleached platinum long hair, who looked so much like girls that one record distributor commented, "I didn't know whether to shake their hands or kiss them." Commentators began to despair over the loss of masculinity and the masculinization of women. The convergence was so bewildering that it was often almost impossible to distinguish the sexes even when they were placed together for comparison. In the United States by 1965 *Life* noted the influx of "teased, greased, tinted, sprayed and curled hairdos" among American males; the "mop top" was in and the "crew cut" was out; girls helped boys with their hairdos; mop-topped boys were dismissed from school because they refused to get haircuts. By 1966 long-haired "effeminate" boys were common in the United States—especially on college campuses and in urban centers where rock and roll music was played. It became a habit to refer to them as "beatniks," though they had little stylistically in common with the bearded types of the '50s. Even more startling, the miniskirted male appeared in Germany in late 1966.

Instead of dwelling on the sex theme, let us put all this into context with women's plunging necklines, "butch" looks, cadaverous looks, and ask whether it really has anything to do with sex? Is it not, rather, simply another version of the wish to be noticed, achieved by going to some colorful extreme? After all, a fully clothed dandy and a nude person both draw attention. When a boy who looks like a girl goes walking with a girl who looks like a boy they will get second looks from almost anybody—if only from the effort to solve the problem. The owner of one of New York's largest discotheques, which gives patrons a chance to cavort in any style they please, seminude or weirdly dressed from head to foot, stated the trend of fashion: "We recognize people's urge to be exhibitionist."

Our tentative conclusion is that we live in an era of ever freer identity experimentation and revision. The tendency to extremes in fad and fashion is one expression of a growing liberty to decide what one will be. This is generated by identify problems, prevalent in a mass society which frustrates the ego and makes it scream for attention. People are seeking audiences, trying to draw attention, rather like entertainers and celebrities.[12] They choose styles—cosmetics, hairdos, beards, sandals, wigs, eye patches, flamboyant costumes, much as would an actor choosing a costume in a dressing room—with an eye to its impact on audiences, to catching attention with startling effects, to "stealing the show." The choice of looks in fashion is so wide today that it is getting hard to say there is a correct class "uniform," definite styles which are in good taste. The bad taste of ego-screaming defeats the establishment of good taste. The disturbance of taste is so severe that even the lines between the sexes are becoming confused—not, I repeat, because of any change in sexuality but because of the need of egos to scream. So fashion today is becoming less and less a "uniform" of social class, less and less concerned with "correctness" (in the sense of Lord Chesterfield or the Duchess of Windsor or even Beau Brummel) or with maintaining class distinctions. The wish to set oneself apart is taking precedence over class, even peer group, identification; fashion is beginning to serve more for ego differentiation than class differentiation. So, now, probably high fashion is not distinguishing elite classes but merely those who scream from those who do not.[13] As is always true with noise, if too many scream, no one can hear the key.

But there is another aspect of this problem: style rebellion.

STYLE REBELLION

All over the world style rebellion is breaking out. In London, in Berlin, in Prague, in Stockholm, in Moscow, in Tokyo, in Bombay, we find unwashed, unkempt, barefooted and bearded, or flowing-haired and high-heeled men—and equally unattractive women—called "beatniks," "*gammler*," "*stiliagi*," or whatever name local idiom gives to them. The common theme is a pointed, grotesque rejection of what custom calls for people (even vagrants) to wear. Anita Ekberg, the actress, back in the United States from a European tour, asked:

What has happened—all these long-haired boys all over the place? The other day I saw a man with shoulder length hair carrying a baby. His wife was wearing a leather motorcycle jacket, boots and a crew cut. I would not be caught dead with a man with long hair.

The English, long inured to eccentricity, did their best to put up with styles flouting the nice appropriateness of costume that is the joy of genteel Englishmen. French police tried unsuccessfully to shoo them out of Paris. In West Berlin they were considered an insult to the image of neat, tidy, hard-working Germans. Chancellor Erhard said, "So long as I govern I shall do everything to destroy this pest."[14]

Not confined to beatniks, rebellion broke out among the well-dressed in "mod" styles. The English mods conscious of not only drawing attention by their gaudy gear but of criticizing and rejecting the second order and its style of life. A man said:

The clothes we wear are really a throwback to the Edwardian era, 1901–1910. Back then Edward VII was quite a king. He couldn't go along with his hypocrite of a mother, Queen Victoria. Old Edward really lived. He drank like a fish, ate like a swine, slept with anything he could get his hands on. Edward revolted against the hypocrisy of his times, and so are we.

A girl said:

A girl looks around at her Mum to see what life in England has done to her. And she doesn't like it. Least of all I don't. No central heating. No fridge. No conveniences of any sort. Way behind the times in everything. We still have the double sex standard here, and I don't buy it. I want a different world for me and my children. The adults won't give it to us, so we've got to make it for ourselves. That's what we are doing. We've got our own dress, our own music, our own heroes, our own standards—all of which you old people don't even try to understand. (Secretary, age 19.)[15]

Another mod said, "We want to stay smart forever. Not shoddy like our parents."

In music, likewise, style rebellion broke out. It was especially prominent in rock and roll of the 1950s, and in the Big Beat of the 1960s, which originated in the Mersey-side of the Liverpool docks, spread to America, and thence around the world. This music broke with almost every European musical tradition. It was abhorred by classicists and jazz fans alike. To all but teenage fans, it seemed an inexcusably barbarous caterwauling. Thunderous amplification of electrical guitars, with a tone of utmost stridency (even treble boosters used to increase the intensity of screaming), produced a sound that could be heard for miles around. Some communities revoked the licenses of dance halls featuring the music. A rebel radio station on a ship off the coast of England beamed the unwelcome music into the airwaves over the resistance of the BBC. Names of musical groups such as The Animals, The Wild Men, The Freaks, and The Things gave a hint of the wish to shock by repulsiveness and uncouthness. The groups were often negligent, dirty in appearance—like unwashed boys who had let themselves go, which is exactly what they were in many cases. I am quite willing to admit that my description of this music is not without prejudice; but I still say that anyone who forced himself to listen to it objectively would have to conclude that there was in it a stridency, an aggressiveness, an assault on the senses, a desire to shock beyond what was required by whatever esthetics the style might have—nor can it be explained by musical amateurishness. Just as you can tell when a child is banging on the piano to get on your nerves, so you can tell when a style of popular music has this aim. Especially when older people tried to suppress the music, there was a rebellious joy in rallying to "our own" music against "them," which gave a motive to it all which was distinctly unmusical.

The style rebel, however, feels that he is defending something—not just being nasty and obnoxious. So the beatnik explains why he keeps on wearing his beard even when he sees the boss frowning and knows that it threatens his job:

> Like, it isn't the beard, Larry, it's the pressure of conformity, it's Who says I *can't* have a beard if I want it? Or sandals if I want to wear them on the gig . . .? who the hell cares if I tote boxes and shipping crates with a beard? . . . So—I'm thinking—is it worth it, the gig, I mean? Or do I start trimming again . . .?

He explains how he originally started his beard conforming to the Jewish custom, the Seder. So it was conformity at first, not rebellion, which started it. But now it is for different values, a new kind of freedom against convention: "Beards are being worn by young people who reject the rewards of the goddam dog-eat-dog society." Beatnik style (pot, sex, jazz, and other kicks) is a pointed repudiation of square values.[16] So wearing a beard, long hair, or whatever the symbol may be, is not just deviation but public announcement of a way of life at variance with convention and assertion of a claim to the *right* to so live. The statement "It's *my* hair. I'll cut it as I please" might be translated as: (1) "I have a right to an identity"; and (2) "This includes the right to make myself what I please." The mere right to be a person is not new, of course: every society grants this, provided you take the identity it offers. Nor is the Jeffersonian concept of the right to pursue happiness in one's own way (so long as it does not interfere with the rights of others) new. Nor is the right to privacy, expressed in the phrase of Justice Brandeis as "the right to be let alone." What *is* new in modern style rebellion is the range of permissiveness. The style rebel of today goes beyond political and economic liberty to LSD trips, promiscuous sex, and crossing the lines between the sexes, claiming rights that neither Thomas Jefferson nor Horatio Alger ever heard of: the right to modify oneself arbitrarily in any way that one pleases; denial of obligation to stick to styles appropriate to one's class or station; the right to pose more or less deceptively as something else than what one is; the right to have kicks in any way that one pleases; the right to shock other people by being noisy, obstreperous, bad mannered, uncouth, and obscene in public; the right to maintain a style in private life which has no relation to the style of one's occupation (as the right of a judge to be a playboy in after hours). The enlargement of the concept of identity came from the psychoanalytic revolution of the twentieth century—and from the existentialist concept of realizing oneself by rebelling. I call this enlarged concept of the right to identity the new romanticism.

So style rebellion is more than the demand "Look at me!" It is a symbolic protest against the social order and its styles; a turning away, accompanied by an unmistakable element of aggression—whether a rallying cry for attack or the last sneer of one about to depart. But style rebellion is more than negative; it has a "cause." It asserts another way of life. It claims the right to be something that convention has heretofore said one has no right to be. It is by spiritual example, not political action, a bomb against the social order.

Style rebellion occurs in a typical battleground—the context of a war between youth and adults, the offbeat and the squares, outsiders and the Establishment. Such a war is reflected in the much-publicized legal battle for the custody of a little boy between his conservative grandparents and his beatnik father. The Iowa Supreme Court finally awarded the boy to his grandparents, ruling that the father's household was "unstable, unconventional, arty, bohemian and probably intellectually stimulating," adding that he was "either an agnostic or atheist and has no concern for formal religious training." The court awarded the boy to the grand-parents, describing them as "stable, conventional, middle-class," people who could "provide a solid foundation and secure atmosphere," observing that the grandfather "regularly teaches a Sunday school class." This result was widely hailed as a triumph for good sense. The rights of the father were considered less important than the right of the child to have a conventional upbringing.

Receiving so many symbolic insults from style rebels, it is understandable that squares take a righteous joy in putting down style rebellion when they get a legitimate opportunity—such as forcing beatniks to trim their locks and clean themselves up. In England, a boy who refused to cut his hair was put in a girl's class until he gave in. New York police, who arrested members of a motorcycle gang called the Aliens, reported with satisfaction that they gave them haircuts and shaves and forced them to take showers. A warden said:

> When we started to cut the hair of one of the gang members, we found that he was wearing a wig. That was pretty sad. We gave it back to him when he raised bail and left the jail today. One thing we noticed about them was that there was none of that tough guy stuff when they got here. They're different when you separate them. They always are.

Officials recalled, with missionary-like satisfaction, that one actually thanked them "for the haircut and the shave. Maybe I can get straightened out now."[17]

We can distinguish five common modes of style rebellion: (1) mockery, (2) dandyism, (3) negligence, (4) barbarism, and (5) puritanism.

Mockery is a natural response of one who has to stay around and put up with a situation he does not like. It is common among conscripts, students, and other captive populations. A rebel makes fun, whenever he gets a chance, even when conforming; thus he announces to the world he does not really "belong," has not "sold out." It can be seen in flippancy, the style of subtle disrespect, perhaps in the manner of saluting or in the snappy way of saying "Yes, sir!" It can be seen beneath the exaggerated "Uncle Tom" role of Negro menials in the United States. It can be seen in the lavishly embroidered scarlet letter *A* of Hester Prynne. Outright mockery in satire, burlesque, and slapstick, of course, make the whole thing clear. Mock heroism takes the exemplar of the rejected style—say Quixote or Hudibras—and makes a fool of him.[18] The mocker may find rebellion such fun that he stays around even when he is free to leave. Indeed, probably the greatest tragedy for a Moliére or a Swift would be a society that had nothing wrong with it.

Dandyism becomes a kind of rebellion, rather than merely high fashion, when the focus on style implies that nothing else is worth while. Then it may symbolize a turning away from important norms, such as morality or work and achievement. "Diamond Jim" Brady was a "fancy Dan," a real dandy, but not a style rebel. Nor would I so classify Barbey D'Aurevilly. The fanciness of his outfit was, like that of his contemporary Beau Brummell, an effort to stay on top of the high style set by aristocrats of his day.

> The most important event of his day was dressing and he spent several hours on it. Each day the hairdresser would come to wave his hair and to set it in curls round his forehead. Later he was to dye it and paint his face to disguise the ravages of time. His costume was composed of a tight-fitting frock coat, padded at chest and shoulders, with fluted skirts and a pinched in waist. To obtain the desired slimness, he wore what was virtually a corset, a broad belt stiffened with whale bone. With the frock coat he wore a waistcoat of bright green or bright blue velvet, a lace jabot and wide lace cuffs fastened by jeweled links, and tight fitting white trousers, with a stripe of blue, pink, or yellow running down the wide seams. Over this he donned a large cloak and a wide-brimmed black hat lined with red velvet; he also wore black gloves with gold stitching, and a dagger was stuck in his belt.[19]

An aristocrat may be, from the point of view of a workingman, worthless; but one cannot accuse him of being a rebel. The classic dandy was a conscious fashion leader, maintaining his place in a hierarchy; like the king, he is a lion of his social circle. He has a conservative stake in the fashions and aristocratic order of the day—"things as they are." It is rather another matter, however, when dandyism spreads to those who have little position to maintain as fashion leaders and no sense of stake in a social order. Sociologists have noted a kind of escapism in dandyism. Finestone described the hipster style of heroin "cats" as esthetically self-indulgent, private—marking a turning away from concern with achievement as defined by society-at-large.[20] A similar flamboyant self-indulgence could be seen in the zoot-suit styles of the 1940s.[21] Such flamboyance—perhaps as much as beatnik "bad taste"—announces rejection of prevailing norms, a certain gaiety like that of the Beatles, whose velvet-coated, long-haired Edwardian dandyism had a flippancy rather like a thumb-to-the-nose, saying "Ta, ta to you!" A mod male of 25 who says "I just live for my car and my clothes" is announcing that dandyism, for him, signifies quitting rather than joining the game of conventional society. Turning from achievement and productivity norms, focusing on style rather than success à la Horatio Alger, he is no longer an economic or a political man, except in the sense of being a conspicuous consumer. A mod girl explains the difficulties of being a dandy on 15 pounds per week:

> You need fifteen pounds a week to be a leader—most mods make between eight pounds and ten pounds a week and spend about four pounds on clothes. It's pure dress now . . . no gimmicks. Your handbag has to look expensive inside, it could never be plastic. A boy will carry trousers to a dance hall in a polythene bag so they won't get creased . . . they spend hours on their hair—they don't use any old blow drier, but one with a hood.[22]

A special report in *Life* asked whether the tasteless and shocking fads of Carnaby Street in "Mini-England" did not herald the economic and moral collapse of Britain? I am not sure style rebellion is as bad as all that, but such lower-class dandyism represents a turning away from serious practical values, an almost cultic preoccupation with esthetic kicks, a "living for today" reminiscent of the sectarian advice to take no thought for the morrow, "the lilies of the fields . . . toil not, neither do they spin." Such a turning away for the glories of personal style might be considered a part of anti-Establishment rebellion.

Negligence in styles say essentially, "Let me live my own life, you square!" They announce indifference and escape from prevailing norms (rather than trying to outshine them as in dandyism) expressed by calculated uncouthness—the style of the castaway, beachcomber, drifter, vagrant, outcast. The beatnik with his slovenly style, pursuing his life of kicks, represents such escapist negligence. It is also suggested by styles of American youth, such as blue jeans, ragged "tennies," T-shirts for all occasions. Long, stringy hair, beards, and the "folk singer" look can also symbolize escapism—the wandering bard—or nostalgia for a folkish or medieval past. Dark glasses are an especially important part of escapist style, symbolizing, "I can see you, but you can't see me," or "I am outside looking at you." Slang expressions of American youth, often combined with slovenly styles, suggest a hipster-like escape from the "square scene": "cool," "cool head," "cool it," "casual," "freak out," "it's a drag, let's cut out." So *Life* describes the spirit of youth at night on the Sunset Strip in Los Angeles:

> What you do on the Strip is simply go there and dig: each other, the sights and sounds, mostly yourself. Just go there—and feel it, man, freak out a little and see how beautiful it all can be. It's all so simple, so noncompetitive, so free from traumas of success or failure.[23]

So the hipster style combined with uncouthness is, like a sign saying "This way out," a symbolic escape hatch. In terms of identity, it is not just "getting away from it all" in the sense of obligations, but getting away from one's former self. The invitation to escape becomes more obvious when the beatnik becomes a guru, dispensing wisdom to college students,[24] or a prophet of LSD, advising them to "take trips," "turn on, drop out." Then the style rebel plays a part like the Pied Piper leading youth away from the village of the squares.

In this perspective, I think, one may examine the "surfer" style so popular in America after 1963. The mark of the surfer is a windswept, "castaway" look, ragged clothes, bare feet or tennies, and long blonde (often bleached) hair. The surfboard atop a car and the beach buggy are vehicles not only for athletic achievement but for getting away to a realm with no one except oneself and natural forces. The mystique of being "alone and on one's own" is strong in surfing devotees. Surfing is a carefree life, on the beach and on the water, a "world of its own," cut off from normal responsibilities; with it goes unconventional beatnik-like behavior which arouses the antagonism of beach residents toward surfers, as they call them "beach bums." It is no surprise that the surfing way of life dislocates many from school and career, temporarily or permanently.

Barbarism represents another direction of style rebellion, which instead of escaping comes back to shock and antagonize the squares. We find one of the best examples in those leather-jacketed motorcycle gangs with names like Hell's Angels, Hangmen, Gladiators, Maurauders, Satan's Slaves, Devil's Henchmen, El Diablos, and Outlaws who love to roar through communities disturbing residents and rallying at beaches and resorts for riots and wild parties. The insignia such groups use are significant: a death's head wearing a Nazi helmet and wings, swastikas, Luftwaffe insignia, the number 13, *M* (standing for marijuana), and bits of storm-trooper uniforms, added to a carefully ratty uniform—a typical basic ensemble being dark glasses, sawed-off jackets, Levis, and boots. Groups refer to these symbols as their "colors," to be displayed whenever in public. Many wear beards or let their hair grow in long, greasy locks. They call their motorcycles "hogs." A rider, wandering into a café where they were gathered, got the feeling from all this costume of being at a ludicrous children's party. A member explained their style:

> When you walk into a place where people can see you, you want to look as repulsive as possible. We're bastards to the world, and they're bastards to us.

Though they sleep like beatniks on dirty linens and live in "pads" with beer and oil cans scattered about the floor, this is not exactly individualism; the conformity under which they live, says writer William Murray, "would depress an executive trainee."[25] There is a definite, functional group style; and its purpose is plainly not just to identify members to one another as a uniform, but to create a barbarian image to defy and shock the squares. There is pride in this repulsive image (just as a dandy would be proud of his elegance, and as we may presume about the beatnik):

"We want to be what we are, and there ain't nobody going to change us." So here we have a kind of inverted dandyism, whose goal is repulsiveness rather than elegance; it has what Kenneth Burke would call the piety of vulgarity.[26]

From the standpoint of role-playing psychology, barbarian style has the same autosuggestive wisdom as that of the fashion model who says, "When I want to look beautiful I have to think I'm beautiful," or the society woman who says, "Whenever I want to pick myself up, I get a new dress, outfit, face, hairdo. I dress the way I wish to think of myself." Barbarian style, like Indian war paint, fits the role they want to play: crashing into communities on their "hogs" (like Western desperadoes shooting up a town). It makes them proud of their act and, suitably costumed, better able to carry it off.

Unlike fashion, uncouth and barbarian styles do not symbolize success and "in"-ness; do not announce to the world, "Look at me. I have made it." Rather, they announce "outsideness"[27]: "Everyone can see that we are failures"; and offbeatness: "Everyone can see we are not in step, and proud of it." Besides repelling the squares and announcing outsideness, such styles rally the outcasts with a sense of common war against the squares (a society which has "cheated" them), acting rather like a banner. The person of high fashion, though he may announce his "insideness," has no such rallying power or confidence in peers who will come to his aid.

"Fairy" and lesbian styles also have a flaunting quality, which shows an aim to shock. Male "queens" flounce and promenade in Times Square, New York, with hands on wiggling hips, feminine hairdos and manners, making faces, striking poses, and puckering their lips at cops and photographers. Plainly it is a "scene" for them. They do not come out in higher fashion only because of regulations against impersonating the opposite sex.[28] No doubt there is flaunting also, to some extent, in the "butch" style of women who wear men's suits, ties, flat-heeled shoes, short haircuts, no makeup, and walk with long strides, swinging arms, and hearty voices. Likewise streetwalkers doubtless would flaunt more were it not for legal sanctions. It would be a mistake to suppose that the purpose of flaunting is advertising of wares. Rather it is the statement of identity through the audacity of green stockings, scarlet gowns, net stockings, mascara—defiant acceptance of the image of the "bad girl": "This is me."[29] It is possible to solicit quite effectively without such display, which serves ego more than coquetry. In such displays by deviants, we may suppose there is a satisfaction in "coming out with it" that can never be found in covert activity, however successful. Some time or another, a person wants to "make the scene in all his glory." At the very least, such a display sets him off from ordinary conventional people, giving him an identity he can call his own.

Puritanism, finally, is a form of style rebellion which, instead of flaunting, sets oneself above ordinary people—who are now "sinners"—by moral reproach. Just as the stern uniform of the English puritans and American pilgrims was a reproach to the Cavaliers, so Mennonites today by their buggies and drab costumes reproach the hedonistic Christians in nearby towns. Black Muslim puritanism in America today reproaches both Negro and white styles. Members take Moorish names, and some men wear the fez; women cover their bodies completely with face powder the only cosmetic; they avoid smoking and drinking, listen to jazz without tapping their feet, and observe a long list of taboos. The result is to generate a new sense of self-respect among Negroes, greater by repudiating than copying white styles. The puritan style became an uplift to them and helped recruit new followers. A girl convert said: "I believed her because of the way she dressed, the way she acted and she was different from everyone else. Her way of life was different from what I knew."[30] Of course, the Black Muslim way of life is a more total revision of identity than could be accomplished by mere style rebellion without the support of a cultic group.

These various offbeat styles show people rejecting fashion as the style of conventional people, using costume to recast their identities outside the alternatives provided by the square structure. Rebellion in terms of flaunting and moral reproach is an important form of style creativeness. As Simmel long ago observed:

The fact that the demimonde is so frequently a pioneer in matters of fashion, is due to its peculiar uprooted form of life. The pariah existence to which society condemns the demimonde, produces an open or latent hatred against everything that has . . . sanction. . . . In . . . striving for new, previously unheard-of fashions . . . diametrically opposed to the existing one . . . lurks . . . the desire for destruction, which seems to be peculiar to all that lead this pariah-like existence. . . .[31]

Those who feel cheated enough to break with the square world will adopt startlingly different styles of life to express their emancipation, disprivilege, or lack of stake. Above all, it must reward them with identity. However, since their position is worse than that of the established classes, style has more of a job to do for them than merely announcing social position: it gives them a stronger sense of "I am I" and group cohesiveness. It is their psychological reward for paying the price of deviance. So, because it has more of a job to do, and not just because certain styles have been preempted by established groups, style rebellion searches for greater extremes, shops farther afield to exotic sources, and is more imaginatively theatrical. Such diverse styles show how costume can be used to recast identity outside the alternatives provided by the square structure. Rejecting models like the man-of-fashion, regular fellow, smoothie, and good Joe, outsiders set themselves apart and announce their alienation from the square world, whose opportunities they have rejected, or which have been closed to them.

THE URBAN MASQUERADE

Sitting on the Boulevard St. Michele in a sidewalk café, I watched the passing parade, as every good tourist does at least once. Everybody seemed to have turned out: Sorbonne students, office workers, tourists, fashion models, and "characters" of all kinds— artists, bohemians, intellectuals, folk singers, beatniks, impersonators of the opposite sex. Every "look" of fashion from the *haut couture* to the *bas couture* of London mods was there, and many following no recognizable fashion. All seemed to have turned out just to make the passing show more interesting. It was in some ways like the New York Easter Parade—except not as conventional. There was a feeling of being "on show"; people seemed to be watching each other out of the corners of their eyes as they do when they are before a television camera. Many seemed to be theatrically made up just for the occasion: in wigs, monocles, eye patches, beards, goatees, bleached and dyed hair, odd coiffures and transformations, white mascara, green fingernails, every cut and color of clothing. Indeed, it seemed as though a score of theaters had suddenly discharged their casts in full makeup upon the street.

I got a similar impression at a cocktail party, being surprised meeting a man whom I know fairly well. He had grown a full beard, very luxuriant, with ends waved and mustache waxed. Portly anyway, he was now indeed formidable; he moved in like a tank and people stood back from him. Being of English origin, he had the right, I supposed, to be somewhat exotic, perhaps a Schweppes colonel—but he seemed right off a movie set: a Prussian officer, a czar, a character from a Dostoevski novel or a James Bond movie. My thought was, *What got into Peter?* I did not know him well enough, however, to probe his motives with questions; I did know that he was on the whole conservative, stable, not in any sense a crackpot.

It occurred to me that this is an example of what is happening to a lot of people these days. They are feeling more free to revise themselves. There is a kind of theatricalism in the air. People are trying on various kinds of characters having little to do with their actual statuses. In Paris, Brooklyn, Los Angeles, Chicago, and London, a lot of people are tired of their lives and want to be somebody else, from somewhere more interesting.

Was that parade on the Boulevard St. Michele just commercialism for tourists, as when Dutch shopkeepers put on wooden shoes and stand outside for the benefit of customers passing? Doubtless commercial gain inspired some of the poses. An Oxford University student, for example, explained that he dressed like a folk singer, let his hair grow, and came to Paris summers to sing and play the guitar for tips outside restaurants and theaters; thus he made his school expenses for the year. A French engineering student played a role as folk-rock entertainer, called himself Antoine, and wore a shoulder-length coiffure, pastel-flowered Pucci shirts, and silky Courreges slacks. But such profit motivation hardly does for the majority of characters on the street, and closes the door to the perception that much personal extravagance today is uneconomic. (London clerks on 15 pounds per week may spend seven or eight pounds on mod styles from Carnaby Street boutiques).

A better explanation, I think, is that masquerading is becoming a very general, and fundamental, phenomenon, reflecting the mobility, identity problems, and identity search of people in mass society. It is true to some extent in any urban area, and startingly so in some—such as the Paris Left Bank, Greenwich Village, Times Square in New York, Soho in London, Haight Street in San Francisco, and the Sunset Strip or West Venice in Los Angeles. Here we see people trying on identity in ways that are distinctly theatrical. This leads to the parade of characters—theater-on-the-street.

Washington Square in Greenwich Village gives opportunities for all kinds of experiments in queer identity. Local residents sometimes complain to the New York Park Commissioner about the peculiar kinds of people and their obnoxious behavior:

> Groups have taken over large segments of the park, virtually making it their home . . . persistently engaging in offensive activity . . . noise . . . obscene language . . . drinking . . . staggering . . . littering . . . accosting . . . urinating . . . lying on benches . . . conspicuous love making . . . unsuitable for children.

Programs of games, square dances, and the like are conducted by a park director:

> "Okay, everybody," says a phys-ed type in sneakers, "let's do the hokey pokey."
> "Would you believe it," says a peroxided young man with face makeup. "Four of those girls are really guys in drag." He sashays off with his hand on his hip.[32]

As darkness falls and the square dancers and chess players go home, the real life of the park begins. Peculiar types soon take over, promenading or sitting in assigned locations, called "junkie's row," "faggot row," "dike row," and so forth. Among the types promenading and carrying on social life are both white and Negro faggots (male homosexuals), nymphs (promiscuous girls), downheads or nodheads (barbiturate addicts), upheads (benzedrine and dexedrine users), skels (alcoholics), vagrants, panhandlers, beatniks, beat musicians, pickpockets, jackrollers, petty racketeers, Hell's Angel types, and eccentric characters of every description—along with comparatively normal middle-class drunks sleeping off a binge and many teenagers. These types are all recognized and sorted in a practical way by the police—tolerated if they do not make too much trouble. A person with an identity problem "shopping" for a role that he cannot find in square society has only to "gravitate" (to use the term of A. K. Cohen) till he meets someone—whether an individual or a group—who can provide him with a style for meeting his unusual problem. It is not necessary to be accepted socially, for one can try out or copy almost any role in such a permissive atmosphere without committing or revealing oneself. A person need not dive out and swim for himself, need not make a radical break with his old identity; he can merely step from one established role to another; or, to change the metaphor, he can pick out his dish from a smorgasbord of available types. Such available roles place little demand on originality and inner resources. They are there, ready to be taken on, like costumes hanging in a dressing room. Training is available if needed.

Another kind of scene for trying on roles is the mod boutique-nightclub combination, which spread over the United States in 1966. This institution provided a sort of theatrical dressing room, where one could buy garish mod and other costumes, adjoining a scene where one could dance, flounce, flirt, flaunt, and lose oneself to one's heart's content. The boutique-nightclub was designed not for entertainment or for dancing as commonly understood, but as a scene for people to show off. It developed from the twist clubs like New York's Peppermint Lounge and discotheques, which marked the shift in emphasis from entertainers to guests, music becoming more and more a background for what guests themselves did. Then came the Cheetah in Manhattan, a ballroom designed as a Gargantuan circus for 2000 performing audience members. An 8000-foot dance floor provided plenty of room for guests to cavort in every dance step, monkeyshine or *bizarrerie* in getups of no-back vinyl, plunging neckline, disc dress, swinging mane, giraffe jump suit, barebacked ruffle, peekaboo midriff, coat-of-male, open network, striped prison suit. "We recognize people's urge to be exhibitionist," said the manager. Such an exhibitionist nightclub, in contrast with the almost puritanical restraint of a "bunny club," gets everybody into the act. Squares want a chance to pose, show off, be characters. The privilege of eccentricity is no longer for minorities.

A later improvement was the "psychedelic trip" or "total environment" nightclub, in 1967, which used audio-visual-olfactory devices, in addition to costume, dance, and music, to plunge actors into a whirlpool of sights, sounds, and odors, even using artificial fog machines to produce an eery atmosphere, disturb the sense of reality, and cause self-abandonment. In such a scene, people, resplendent in weird mod clothes, newly purchased from the adjoining boutique—hardly knowing themselves, let alone their partners—could let go in a fling that seemed at the time like being turned on in a psychedelic trip—a costumed adventure in identity in a fantasy world provided by the new theatricalism.

One might expect to meet five common kinds of poses in the urban masquerade, two of which are socially supported and three unsupported.

First is the *character* or, as we might call him, the honest eccentric. Raymond Duncan, for example, brother of the famous dancer Isadora, was often to be seen on the Left Bank of Paris or in the Louvre, dressed in ancient Roman costume—toga and sandals with a golden fillet about his head. Of all the Louvre patrons who admired the classic style, perhaps he was the only one with the courage of his convictions in the matter of dress. Likewise, Edith Sitwell admired the medieval style so much that she typically wore long gowns, marvelous hats, enormous rings, and a chain with a great gold Urim and Thummim ornament. She expressed her admiration of people who have the courage to choose and create their own unique roles in her book, *The English Eccentrics* (Boston: Houghton Mifflin, 1933). Such honest eccentrics are by no means any crazier than the rest of us, and it must be said that they provide and live in their own dramas and don't particularly care whether others join or not.

Second is the *deceptive independent poseur*; (or impostor) of which Fred Demara and "Prince" Mike Romanoff are famous examples. Such persons assume a role from the social structure to which they have no right, either to escape from psychological problems or for social prestige and gain. They take advantage of the looseness of the role structure—anonymity, impersonality, and poor screening procedures—and by means of considerable personal talent and charm pass themselves off. Modern society not only cannot weed out such impostors but probably encourages them—with its emphasis on front, its generation of identity problems, and its stimulation of people's hunger to be celebrities, which is partly caused by identity problems. "Prince" Mike himself, accepted in his imposture in Hollywood, made a significant comment: "There's nothing wrong with imposture in the world capital of make-believe." Asked what advice he would give to a young man who wanted to go into imposture, he said, "I would advise him to stay out of it. There's too much competition."[33]

Third is the *role vacationist*. Many people want to get far away from their old lives occasionally—farther away than is permissible under the rules of the role they usually play. To avoid conflict between their desired role and their usual one, they take a vacation from identity. An amusing example is found in the film starring Alec Guinness, *Captain's Paradise*, in which a ferryboat captain at Gibraltar shuttles back and forth between two very different lives— a model English husband with a demure wife on one side, a tireless nightclub-rounder and playboy on the other. Charles Chaplin's splurge at the Hotel Astor in New York is an example of the identity vacation in real life: While only a poor actor, he expended his meager savings for an elegant outfit and played the part of a rich gentleman for a few days. In the category of role vacationists also belong "weekend beatniks," who dress conventionally for the job and then go into the negligent style to escape. There are many curious examples of role vacationists in our society—such as a coed who dances as a topless go-go entertainer on the side, weekend nudists, or a medical doctor who plays as a jazz musician in nightclubs between hospital calls. Our kind of society seems to be encouraging more role vacations: leisure activities are richer and increasingly separated from occupation; the routine and emotional poverty of an alienated society doubtless dispose many to seek more interesting roles on the side; no one really knows what his neighbor does except at the moment of passage between automobile and front door.

These three types "go it alone"—though by different methods and for different reasons. So I call them unsupported poseurs.

Fourth is the theatrical *dandy* or fashion *darling*. A highly fashionable person is always verging on pose. In doing so, he is neither fraudulent nor eccentric but supported by a delighted, appreciative group; he is actually a leader whose poses inspire others. As an example we may choose a star of New York café society, "Edie" Warhol, who, in company with her artist husband Andy, became noted as an exemplar of avant-garde style. She left her formerly decorous position as a Social Registerite, great-grand-daughter of Endicott Peabody, to take on her role as a leader of café society. Her role seemed to be to show others what they might do with themselves artistically and sartorially. She characteristically appeared in startling outfits—such as leopardskin slacks—or with hair dyed silver, in transparent lilac pajamas with only a body stocking underneath. Her appearances were as sensational as those of a famous actress. People waited to see what she would wear next. For her flamboyance and vitality, so inspiring to others, general approval and envy were her rewards. She denied, however, that she was intentionally playing a role to a following:

> Who cares? I am not trying to create an image or a following. I act this way because that's the way I feel like acting. If people like it—fine. If they don't—that's their problem.[34]

But, try or not, she surely did help others to see what they could make of themselves.

Fifth is the *poseur supported by a deviant group*. By deviant group I mean any group which develops roles and values more or less in conflict with conventional or square society and is regarded as a problem by that society.[35] Such a group can offer dramatic props, tutelage, moral support, and scene partners to those who shop for a role not offered by conventional society. But there are layers of pose within pose; some are playing roles more authentically than others. For every original bohemian, for example, there are probably hundreds just playing the role, as conventionally as any fashion follower, and providing what might be called a supporting cast for him. Such a group not only gathers around an original stylist to copy his ways but exerts pressure upon him to play the leader, the lion, the guru. Sooner or later he may find his own refreshing individuality turned into a pose—another layer of pose. Like any other celebrity, he has an act and is expected to go into it whenever he is "on." So the bohemian Ernest Hemingway showed signs of pose, of playing to the crowd, in his later career.[36] And we see Allen Ginsberg, the "King of the Beat Poets," sitting Buddha-like holding audience with journalists wearing a gown that looks like a nightshirt; demonstrating Oriental breathing exercises, chants, and ritual; accompanying himself on a hand organ; giving his views on the state of the beatnik movement and effects of mind-changing drugs—with all the aplomb of a pundit.[37] Who will say where being oneself stops and playing a role to the public begins?

Indeed, among beatniks, we can find various levels of pose, most with some degree of group support. We can distinguish: (1) a leader beatnik, who plays a role to his following; (2) regular beatniks, whose style is as correctly beatnik as a society woman's is chic; (3) weekend beatniks, who have two styles supported by separate groups; (4) unsupported—one might call them cookbook—beatniks, who get their ideas about the role not from their fellows but from the copious literature; and (5) "fashionable" or "party" beatniks, for whom the style is merely a costume.

Different levels of pose can be illustrated in other groups, such as surfers, beachniks, skiniks (ski bums), whose ways of life on the fringes of society have distinctive styles which are objectionable to conventional people but serve as uniform for members. They may go to some effort to maintain the integrity of their type and to protect it from intruders and imitators. Surfers, for example, distinguish "true" surfers from phonies whom they call "hodads" and beginners whom they call "gremmies." A surfer look can be adopted by almost anyone who can afford the status symbols, such as a surfboard or peroxided hair, but the real surfer must measure up to group standards and undergo test and scrutiny; most of the self-styled true surfers are inclined to say that the beach is filled with hodads (poseurs). This suggests theater-on-the-beach. Many are quite satisfied just to imitate surfers:

> I like to go surfing with the others because it draws attention. When we drive down the street with some boards on top of the car people look at us and say, "There go some surfers," or "There go those rowdy surfers."

And going with surfers requires a considerable change of role:

> When Bruce associated with these new friends, many things began to change in his appearance. He began to let his hair grow and it became bleached from hours in the sun and surf. He began wearing the apparel of the crowd he now went with—he wore Bermudas, Levis, T-shirts, and no shoes or sandals. He was accepted fully by his new friends . . . and began to break off relationships with his old friends . . . he became very devoted to surfing and . . . never missed a day of surfing.

Such a role, pose or not, may be an identity *solution* for the one who takes it up, but from the standpoint of his old associates it is an identity *dislocation*. An individual may find it hard to go back to his old career or education, and feel ill at ease with associates who don't appreciate his role:

> Dave is a surfer and impresses the girls with his muscular build. He thrives on this to, as he says, "build up my ego." Obviously he is quite comfortable and in place at the beach; however, when Dave goes to work as an auditor for Civil Service, he feels "out of place." He said he feels this way because the men he works with are much older than he and the women are middle-aged and married, so he cannot impress either the men or the women.

Naturally, a person who feels maladjusted in society will gravitate to the groups who will support the image he wants to maintain for himself. Pose, individual or group-supported, is a steppingstone on this path.

An odd example of group-supported pose is found in a southern California gang called the Broadway Riders—motorcyclists *without motorcycles.* They affect the style of better-known motorcycle gangs such as the Hell's Angels—black leather jackets, tight pants, boots, long hair, unkempt beards, chains, buckles, sheath knives protruding from boots, slit ear and earring, and so on—but the makeup of this interesting group consists of youths who, for one reason or another (such as being in naval service on temporary station), cannot manage to obtain a vehicle. Yet they maintain their pose stoutly and do everything to convince the world that they are motorcyclists. The manager of a motorcycle shop, who knows them well, says:

> It gives them the position of being tough, to dress like them and be associated with their reputation; yet most aren't really tough at all. They hang around pizza parlors having nothing to do but discuss their exploits and their pseudo-motorcycles.

In such marginal groups as beatniks, surfers, beachniks, leather boys, and "gay" homosexuals, we have examples of pose, group-supported and group-created—a world in which roles can be played, supported by other players, different from those possible in the conventional world. Such a group pose is a model for members;

played to outsiders, it becomes a screen between them and society, a way of projecting an image and keeping outsiders at bay. To members, the role is not pose in the sense of fraudulence or screen, because its authenticity is tested by fellows who know.

No one knows in what numbers these and other types of poseurs are found in our society. But they go to make up the urban masquerade, which indicates, it seems to me, a growing desire to get away from oneself and become somebody else, by devices such as costume. A small number of posing individuals indicates individual problems such as psychopathy; but a large number indicates a socially generated identity problem. It also indicates the development of a kind of social organization that I have elsewhere called *pseudo-integration:*[38] a social fabric based heavily on front and pretense rather than on sincere role-playing. One has a society so hypocritical and pretending that people are not sure where they stand in relation to others; there is much anxiety, neurotic conflict, alienation, and a wish for something more genuine. From the standpoint of social structure, this means instability. You cannot build a society of Demaras or have real leadership by "Prince" Mikes. So, structurally speaking, a society with too many poseurs is like a house of cards.

But we are interested here in pose as an attempt to solve identity problems. It does, undoubtedly, offer many interesting histrionic opportunities to escape from and possibly remake oneself. A scene such as a Latin Quarter or a discotheque invites a person to try a new self, display himself, see himself as he would like to be—much as an art class invites a student to let himself go with paint or clay. Anonymity works like the freedom of a confessional booth, noted by Georg Simmel, allowing people to reveal themselves while screening themselves. The false faces of the urban masquerade not only hide identity, but no one would know who it was even if he peeked. For all these advertise themselves by wearing beards, wigs, or startling get-ups, there are those who just get lost through costume. This is especially so of dark glasses which, worn by day and even by night, cover up identity. Many delight in slipping about odd places in the urban masquerade without being recognized; it is for them a gateway to adventure. Some get it both ways: a *sensational* costume which *hides* identity permits them to have the satisfaction of being noticed—they may even pretend to be celebrities—without the responsibility of living up to a reputation. Perhaps there are more of these anonymous adventurers than self-advertisers. Such poseurs help make up the anonymous mass, the faceless crowd, of which many write. But is it so faceless really? Is it not rather false-faced, theatrical characters deliberately created, people choosing and acting the parts they want? Not, as in the Easter Parade, living up to social position by dress, but by pretending.

Such posing reflects the deep urge to show off, the thrust of the common man into the limelight, that is one of the distinguishing marks of the twentieth century. Because of it, fashion takes on a new function—not the conservative one of identifying a person with a class, but of setting him off as an individual, perhaps hiding his class. A new exhibitionism appears in sport, automobile driving, hobbies—everyone seems to want to be a splendid performer. So urban areas developed new kinds of institutions to meet such needs and we see misplaced theatricalism, theater on the street. In such institutions, which take place mostly by night, masquerade is "the thing"; eccentricity mixes with high fashion; people let themselves go with any fancy of themselves. In such places, the expectation prevails: Here is a place for characters, come out; let's see how interesting or weird you can be.

But there is still the question of how good posing really is as a solution to identity problems. People are getting away with it, obviously, but getting away with *what?* There are certain disadvantages to pose, even when group-supported, as in fashion, which suggests that it cannot be a true solution to identity problems. One price is anxiety, about carrying it off successfully or about being found out. (One sees rather grotesque examples of the precariousness of modern pose: a chic blonde in a miniskirt and patterned stockings in a coffee house sophisticatedly reading a copy of the French *Vogue* upside down.) But, even where no one sees through a masquerade, no one challenges it, and a group supports it, misplaced theatricalism still means that people are playing roles that are not their own—hence they have fragile, tentative, easily disturbed identities. This means role *consciousness*, which is perhaps the root of the identity problem: the inability to feel that one *is* one's role. There is also the question of what happens to identity when the entire scene becomes masquerade, when *everyone* is posing so successfully that the guidelines by which to tell what people really are are gone? What happens to identity when life becomes a masked ball?

DANGER OF STYLELESSNESS

When Eton schoolboys were given the choice of keeping or abandoning their traditional formal school uniforms with the long tails, stiff collars, and top hats, they chose to keep them. The easy explanation of a decision like this is that they were "conservative." I do not think this is the true reason, as anyone who has felt the currents stirring in Britain would probably agree. A better explanation is that they wanted to preserve a distinctive identity, rather than be blended with other English schoolboys, and were willing to put up with the discomforts of an archaic uniform for this sake. They saw a threat in keeping up with fashion.

There is now a reason to mistrust fashion as a way to identity. For the new romanticism, stressing the freedom to *be what one pleases*, contradicts the idea that one should dress suitably for one's station or profession and for the occasion. Were this right asserted simultaneously by most people, society would resemble a madhouse. But it *is* asserted often enough now to give a theatrical feeling to many areas of life; to allow people to escape social status, professional obligations, and demands of "respectability"; to intensify the fashion race for classes who were formerly outside fashion, creating new kinds of lower- and middle-class foppery; and to make us aware of the extent of style rebellion. This is Horatio Alger with a new twist: *self-made man* is taking on a special new meaning.

I propose to ask whether there is not danger of stylelessness in the midst of all this choice of styles, splendor of costume, and freedom to let oneself go? Let us see what such a danger consists of, considering fashions as symbols of the ego.

It is generally accepted that fashion is one of the main ways which a society provides for people to revise their own identities, within limits set by what is in vogue. The range of tolerance, from old-fashioned to fad and *haut couture*, gives individuals some leeway in making their own style. Though almost tyrannical at times in terms of their own control, fad and fashion are at the opposite pole from folkways;[39] they represent innovation and a loss of tradition. The fashion process is apparently speeding up today; this is partly due to the technical ease of imitating and merchandising status symbols. But it also seems plain that there is a new intensity in the wish for fashion, seen, for example, in dandyism in the lower classes, which shows not so much the desire for class status as the need for personal attention, growing due to identity problems at precisely the time when opportunities to be onstage are lessening. So one sees rather grotesque and frantic efforts to win the spotlight, such as people using billboards to publish personal sentiments (in Richmond, Indiana, a large one plastered with red hearts, saying "Happy Birthday, Sally. I love you, I love you, I love you") or a couple necking openly in the park while people pass by, with their radio playing loudly (for background music or to attract attention?). Success for the dandy is less a matter of making one's way à la Horatio Alger, and more a matter of making oneself stylistically and making or having a scene. Society seems obsessed with publicity, as Cleveland Amory has observed. As more people with identity problems are thus thrown on the market, there is sharper competition for fashion symbols and looks, a scraping of the bottom of the barrel for anything—domestic, exotic, new, old, fine, or vulgar (camp)—that will set one off and draw attention. This competition leads to proliferation of new types, offbeat and square.

Naturally, with all this going on, one may expect fashion to suffer a loss of center, due to individual improvisation and multiplying elites (models). Styles begin to come from anywhere. It is harder to find authority for *the* fashion; there is no wave of "right" style, only a variety of competing looks, more or less "in"—but in what? The "fashion hierarchy," which formerly "dictated" styles for much of the world, then feels threatened with collapse. A sign of what is happening was the "Chelsea invasion" of late 1964, which upset the orderly flow of fashion from the centers in London and Paris and brought in a rebellion called "Ye Ye" under the noses of Paris authorities. A former editor of *Vogue* said: a relative newcomer in design, Mary Quant,

> has changed the look . . . and opened the door for the host of young designers who are doing what would have seemed the impossible a few years ago—selling in Paris and in America, dressing princesses, prime ministers' wives, pop singers, and typists.[40]

Other commentators wrote:

A group of young English fashion designers, most of them girls in their early twenties, hitherto unheard of in the United States—have revolutionized New York fashion overnight. . . . While Fifth Avenue shops are vying with one another to boost the clothes of young designers, the Seventh Avenue wholesalers are busy copying the London look for mass production.[41]

Fashion in Paris used to come only from the world of hushed salons, discrete rendeuses, big names like Dior—and it cost a king's ransom. Now a handful of female talent is changing all that.[42]

It's all part of the Cult of the Young. If you want to sell to the young, then it follows that you need bright young designers with fresh, lively ideas, and the place to look for them is the art schools.[43]

Ye Ye is the French for Yeah Yeah . . . the guilded youth of Paris, whether singers, actresses or actors, are the Ye Yes. They dance in the Ye Ye discotheques . . . they wear the Ye Ye that young people throughout France copy. They buy them in the Ye Ye fashion houses, three of which showed their collections alongside the great and famous couturieres here in Paris last week.[44]

Who copies whom now: Haut Couture or the Pret-*à*-Porter, or does each go its own way? A year ago, two at the most, it would have been unthinkable to pose such a query. . . . Today the situation has changed. The Pret-*à*-Porter under the impetus of a small band of keen, clever young women designers like Christiane Bailly, Emmanuelle Khanh, and . . . Catherine Savoye, no longer seems to worry about the haut couture but has set out on a lone trail. . . . So totally different from the fragile, feminine, ladylike look of the haut couture that everyone concerned with fashion is agog to see what the old mistress will do about the challenge—for challenge it is.[45]

Indeed, for decades it has been realistic to speak of fashion as centerless and the idea of "dictatorship" as largely a myth. Stanley Marcus said:

Today we have no dictators in fashion who can sway the mode in one direction or another. . . . (The) leaders aren't the society leaders of yesterday; they aren't the ten best dressed women . . . the leaders are anonymous and their voices do not carry the authority of a Mrs. Belmont or a Mrs. Vanderbilt. Today these women of taste who are the leaders of fashion are in the colleges, in offices, in homes, among all classes.[46]

Thus it seems realistic to say that fashions do not trickle down in an orderly way from centers, but come from almost anywhere today; and to expect also that its pace is quickening in the stiff competition. Under such conditions we may expect styles to perish like ice cream.

Another apparent trend in fashion is the shift from status symbolism to ego symbolism. Fashion has always advertised the person and "costumed the ego," as Edward Sapir said; but the tendency to extremes (ego-screaming) and garishness and bad taste today suggest that it is doing more along these lines and less for its traditional function of class maintenance. Fashion is ceasing to be a hallmark by which classes can distinguish themselves and more a highly theatrical adventure in identity. From the standpoint of social rank, this is as though army privates were allowed to deck themselves in plumes, capes, visors, helmets, swords, facial tattoos—anything their fancy suggested. Then fashion would cease to be a uniform and become a costume.[47] Style would become like a Rorschach rather than a calling card—you might be able to diagnose a person's personality, but it would be harder to tell what he did or where he belonged socially.

Then, while it might be easier to make oneself interesting, it would be harder to proclaim, "I have made it." The lamentable result, indeed, would be that those who *had* made it by legitimate success would still need ego symbols. So they might go to extremes of expense or vulgarity (camp) to find ways to set themselves off from plebeians. Dame Fashion might be shopping in dime stores and flea markets to find something to set herself off from her maid or the hatcheck girl in the discotheque. And, as it became plain that the upper classes were not supplying the drumbeats of fashion anymore, attention would shift to show business, sporting life, playboys, the underworld, publi-ciety[48]—"where the action is." The result of all this striving for ego distinction would more likely be style outrage than conformity and good taste. Style outrage offends sensibilities and ultimately blunts them.

But a worse effect socially is that categories disintegrate. What I am anticipating is not just a blurring of class lines, but a debacle of social categories—youth-age, maleness-femaleness, occupation, except where set off by an official uniform. Life then might become like a "hard times" costume party where anything goes. Doubtless this would not be too hard on Americans, who are used to much informality; but it would be disastrous for what Edith Sitwell called "that peculiar and satisfactory knowledge of infallibility that is the hallmark and birthmark of the British nation."[49]

But beyond blurring social categories, as fashion becomes more ego-symbolizing, is a further question: What happens to ego itself, the supposed survivor? It seems plain that past a certain point, ego-screaming and pose stop serving functions of *identification* for the individual: however loud you scream or much you pose, you can't place yourself definitely. This would be so in a madhouse where everyone was screaming "Look at me!" by equally peculiar behavior, or in a masquerade where everyone was disguised. Is it so very different in the urban masquerade?

Along with increasing difficulty of identification is the more basic difficulty that fad and fashion are forms of copying, and that true identity cannot be attained by copying. A few fad leaders may have true originality—style for them is a unique signature; but the mass following them are simply draping a borrowed identity over whatever individuality they might have of their own; and, one might say, abdicating to taste-makers.[50] When faddism is not class-oriented, it does not increase individuality but just means that *types* are being copied rather than classes. And once the dogma of the new romanticism—that everyone has a right to be what he pleases—is generally accepted, it only aggravates imitativeness. The pace of style change and amount of ego-screaming increase, but few people are having more luck finding themselves. One sees absurdities like the woman who "went Chinese," furnished her entire home with Oriental rugs, jades, idols, dragons, and joss sticks—then, after a time, got rid of it lock, stock, and barrel and "went modern," the second style expressing her no better; her third try was Cape Cod. Or the lady who went from one coiffure and wig to another, trying to find her right color, type, and age. Such cases show the mistake of trying to find oneself by faddism followed by more faddism—the failure to recognize that true style is more than a badge or costume that one can put on. It is a statement of oneself. One cannot be a person without style; but it is easy to lose oneself by imitating style.

How, then, is it reasonable to suppose that by increasing the pace and variety of style that people will be more likely to find identity? Will they not more likely be in the predicament of the shopper at a rummage sale where goods are piled indiscriminately on the counters—having a poor chance of coming out with something that fits? Or, to change the metaphor, like the boy who is finally invited into a candy shop to help himself, and after a time comes out saying, "I thought chocolate was my favorite color, but now I'm not sure what I like." Even the elite are already confused; to quote Andy Warhol commenting on the perpetual partygoers of the discotheque set: "Those people don't know who they are. They don't even sleep—but, then, we don't either."[51]

As faddism, style rebellion, dandyism, and beatnikism increase, whole societies may undergo identity dislocation, people developing personalities less and less coherent and compatible with whatever social structure there is. By identity dislocation I mean those processes—whether deviant peer groups, hero worship, or eccentric ego symbolism—by which people become unfitted for the society within which they have been raised, its careers, occupations, educations—its opportunity structure." Nor is it to be expected that the confusion from faddism, style rebellion, ego-screaming, and masquerading will be confined to external symbols. Beliefs, opinions, tastes, and ethics will lose their power to declare and define the person.[52]

The irony of the loss of ego symbolism in classes where the whirl of faddism is increasing is that, whereas it is harder for a fashionable person to feel right about himself, those persons with cohesive groups—even deviant groups—which provide a definite uniform and style for them may get the best of it psychologically—that is, they know who *they* are, even if the member of café society or the jet set does not have the same assurance about himself. So declining fashion authority may throw the advantage in identity confirmation to deviant groups with rebel style and cohesiveness, such as the Hell's Angels or Black Muslims.

So we see the possibility that the pursuit of status symbols may become a vicious circle. As we know, Americans are concerned with getting such things as three-pen desk sets, wall-to-wall carpeting, silver water jugs in their offices, Cadillacs and Mustangs, and the new looks. But, it may be asked, does the pursuit of status symbols make it easier to establish identity or, past a point, does it not become the reverse? We can easily imagine the end of such a trend as like a play in which actors were allowed to costume themselves as they pleased. At such a point, where status symbols were freely interchanged and available, their value for fixing status would shrink to zero, like a debased currency. No one would know who anyone was anymore. Then the pursuit of status symbols would not only not be a solution to an identity problem, but it would *be* an identity problem and we would see the paradox that the pursuit of identity led to the loss of identity. When anybody can be anybody, nobody can be "somebody."

The basic reason why this must be so is that faddism and modernism, beyond a certain point, defeat the necessary conditions of symbolism. We can see how it would be with language, if words and meanings were changed monthly, seasonally. Why should it be different with the symbolism of the ego? Yet this is exactly what faddism, modernism, style rebellion, ego-screaming, and masquerading do: break down the basis by which a person can declare himself because symbols of identity become unreliable, the language of personal style becomes gibberish, the person becomes meaningless to others—and to himself.

Something like this has happened long ago in art, which provides us with a convenient example of the defeat of the conditions of symbolization. One of the most startling, and for our purposes significant, pieces of sculpture in recent years was the famous stuffed goat of Robert Rauschenberg, mounted with an old automobile tire about its middle, displayed in the exhibit "Ten Years of Modern Art," at the Tate Gallery, London, 1964. It easily stole the show as a conversation piece; but what, exactly, could one say about it? Interesting? Just for shock value? A joke? Some serious message? No one really knows. The fact is, Rauschenberg has created a *code* which successfully baffles communication; he has hidden his message, if any, by violating the principles of signification, the most elementary of which is that there must have been prior association between a sign and its referent. Where art has meaning, perhaps Sir Herbert Read's definition of what art tries to say will do:

The purpose of the artist is to use the natural object as a symbol for an inner state of mind or feeling, a personal and arbitrary emotion. The urge to the outward expression and definition of this feeling or emotion is the condition from which all art arises, whatever its medium and whatever species of imagery the artist may select as a medium of representation. Expression becomes a more complicated process when nature or a natural object is used as a symbol of human feeling or emotion. The artist may use a mountainous landscape to express feelings of terror, and so mountains are said to inspire feelings of terror. . . . It is . . . likely that there lurked in his unconscious and obscure feeling (nothing so definite as terror), to which this particular landscape corresponded. Nature is full of such "correspondences," as Baudelaire called them . . . as poets and painters we play a game of blind man's bluff and do not realize what we have caught until the bandage has been removed from our eyes. The act of creation is an unveiling of the inward eye.[53]

But if Rauschenberg expressed a correspondence and that was what made it a work of art, the question is whether anyone else sees the correspondence? It seems obvious that the artist must use preestablished symbols, for all the subjectivity of his message, if he wishes to communicate rather than present people with a problem of decipherment. Randomization produces codes; novelty is the enemy of symbolism. The most original stylist must somehow manage to use symbols when he wishes to tell people something.[54]

Now, applying this to style, it seems plain that faddism, ego-screaming, and much of what is called modernism are among the worst violators of semantic law, for they introduce randomization and approach gibberish. A person who lives relentlessly by fad and modernism is repeatedly shifting his ego symbols, laying on himself a veneer of weak symbols, or downright nonsymbols, in place of the identity he might be building. A whole community which lives by modernism, uprooting the symbols of the past in favor of new things, is like a lumber company cutting down the seed trees of a forest to produce a waste. Of course, most people innovate without thinking of the "forest" of symbols as a whole, assuming that *their* change occurs against a background of meanings which stay fixed. But what if everybody is getting out and hacking down symbols?

This is the fallacy of modernism: that one can introduce changes which uproot symbols indiscriminately, without regard for a forest of meanings, with concern only for practical aspects. Industrial, technological, and commercial uprooting of symbols are bad enough; faddism is the frivolous end of the spectrum. At the root of the problem is violation of the basic conditions for symbols—indeed, what seems an absolute limit which applies in every situation, and does not depend on taste: the rate at which symbols can be formed and invested with reliable memories, images, feelings, meanings. The inescapable fact seems to be that symbols form more slowly than utilities. You can learn to use a power lawnmower faster than you can learn the symbolism connected with, say, a scythe; you can learn the motor activities connected with jousting, jiu-jitsu, or folk dance faster than you can learn the traditional meaning of such activities; you can learn to use a comb faster than that comb can become an heirloom. So what happens to identity when a person surrounds himself with things that have come into existence yesterday or the day before that? The answer must be that since they cannot have much meaning, he cannot give himself much meaning by them.

Whatever is true here probably applies in some degree to any faddish class or modernizing country. It should apply *a fortiori* to America, which has been losing traditions at a faster rate for a longer time than any other country, though spectacular spurts of change have occurred in places like Japan and Turkey.

I have suggested in this chapter that a mass society generates a search for looks, ego-screaming, style rebellion, and masquerading to solve its identity problems. This causes the functions of fashion to shift from class maintenance by status symbols to identity seeking by ego symbols and, in the long run, the mass pursuit of identity by fad and fashion could become largely self-defeating. Already, in the waves of fashion today, the voyage of identity is losing its bearings, there are few shores of destination. Basically, there is violation of principles of symbolization, which mean loss of ability to find and define oneself. It is reasonable to predict that if rates of style change go up, our society is in danger of stylelessness. It is already true that one can go to many places outside America—even a primitive African village—and find more integrity of style than one can in New York City or Los Angeles. And moderns, desperate for style amid the fashion race and stainless steel gadgetry, travel everywhere looking for it—in ancient ruins, in the carved work of Eskimos, in the sound of flamenco. But playboys in their garish, swanky apartments do not live in style, if by style one means integrity; nor do beatniks and bohemians find it, but mostly pose instead. Style, as any artist knows, is a difficult achievement—perhaps more difficult today than in 400 B.C. Yet it grows naturally in villages and backwoods areas where *Look* and *Vogue* do not circulate. In our society too many things seem to be working against it—mainly violation of the laws by which symbols grow and exist.

It is to some extent true that the whole world is beginning to suffer from stylelessness amidst all its splendor of style. So people are looking to symbolic leaders to give them a style that their peers and the conditions of life around them lack. A changing society wants either a leader to move forward to or one to go. back to. A mass society, with its confusion of styles, especially needs symbolic leaders—hankers for them, sometimes screams when it sees them—though it cannot reasonably expect a mere leader, however astute, or cute, or hep, or conservative, to cure the style problem whose roots go deep in the violation of symbols with processes like acculturation, mobility, secularization, and indiscriminate modernization. So it often happens that mere celebrities—movie actors and the like—get the burden of supplying the mass with style, which they cannot possibly do with integrity, as I shall point out in a later chapter. So the search goes on, and its quarry is more elusive. It seems clear that modern societies are not gaining integrity of style by faddism, eclecticism, and the new romanticism; and, at the same time, traditional societies are casting away their styles with the eagerness of kids at a swimming hole, to plunge into modernism and the freedom to be what one pleases.

But there are ways to identity other than through pose and imitation. Modernists, who hanker for style, usually dislike ritual. But traditionalists are usually sentimental about it. Let us consider sentiment as a route to identity.

4 The Language of Ritual

The president of the class explained to the graduating seniors gathered in the Greek Bowl to rehearse their commencement that afternoon: "If you are willing to graduate without having your name called, it will save at least forty minutes in the hot sun." It had been the custom up to that time for each graduate to have his name called, cross the stage, and receive his diploma personally from the president of the college. But, as the class president explained, it was going to be warm that afternoon. After discussion, the class voted to speed up the ceremony by eliminating the calling of names.

At this point, a senior rose from one of the upper seats and pitched his folding chair down the steps into the arena where the orchestra was seated, narrowly missing the kettledrum. "I've waited four years for this," he said angrily, "and I'm damned if I'll graduate without having my name called!" Then he stalked out.

There was a moment of stunned silence. Then another motion came from the students, this time to have names called. It was passed unanimously.

A wave of feeling had made them realize that it was important to be honored personally at graduation, that this is what such ceremonies were for; they then agreed with the chair thrower (in principle, if not in style) that one had a *right* to this kind of satisfaction after four years of more or less anonymous drudgery. It was a victory for sentimentalists and traditionalists. A sociologist might add that graduation is one of the few remaining important rites of passage in modern society, wherein individuals can feel the significance of steps in status and get personal recognition before audiences. To eliminate name calling would be a blow.

But the following year name calling was abolished; whether by the administration or by majority consent was not clear. This time there was no objection, chair throwing or otherwise. Those who agreed were inclined to see getting a diploma as just a routine step to a job. Some were even willing to skip graduation altogether: "Give me my diploma by mail. I couldn't care less whether there is a graduation ceremony." A few lingering sentimentalists wistfully asked, "Why have one's name called if one's family won't be there, and nobody will know you even if your name is called?"

This is a case for our entire society regarding the use of ritual. In some institutions such as parades, funerals, churches, ritual would be missed if it were not there—it is the whole or at least a main point. Let us call these ritual institutions. In such institutions one would have a legitimate sense of being cheated if he did not get what he came for. In other institutions, especially those with rational rules and mechanized production, ritual seems out of place: it seems an intrusion, an interference with efficiency; at best, a dispensable luxury. Some businesses are reluctant even to take time for the ritual of the coffee break.

In which category is education—a mere step in getting a job, or an emotional experience of forming identity, of which ceremonies are an integral part? Obviously the trend of our bureaucratized mass society is toward the former; even college fraternities are abolishing ceremony.

In this light sentimentalists and traditionalists seem anachronistic in wishing to push not only education but much else back into ritualism, always asking, so to speak, for the *Whiffenpoof Song*. They argue the need to preserve the sense of the past and loyalty to institutions; and, especially sentimentalists, that life is not complete, the personality is starved without ceremonies that arouse feelings.

In writing this book, we side with the sentimentalists—not in exalting tradition for its own sake, or in calling for a return to the times of wassailing and jousting, or recommending knocking out teeth of young men in puberty rites, but in asserting the importance of mystiques and sentiments that can be adequately expressed only in ritual. We warn against the assumption that most—perhaps any—institutions can be stripped of ritual, streamlined to mechanical efficiency without doing harm both to the participants and society-at-large. We hold that what is needed is not less but more—at least better—ritual by which modern man can realize himself. Though all do not use it, and some cannot get it when they want it, it is still needed in a mass society. For ritual is the prime symbolic vehicle for experiencing emotions and mystiques together with others—including a *sense of oneself as sharing* such emotions, even when self-consciousness is, to some extent, lost in the sharing.

From this point of view, to cut ritual out of society is to rob the person of one aspect of the sense of himself. This aspect cannot be supplied by "efficient" bureaucratic procedure. A person whose identity is defined only by work and a license or employee number is entitled to feel like the bride who got only a city hall marriage after dreaming of a church wedding with all her friends there to see her and weep. And the fact that our society cannot decide whether to have ritual does not argue that it is not needed—only that some people fail to see the point of it. Why? Is it because ritual does nothing to earn its keep, or because some failure of communication prevents it from working as it should—a failure that perhaps could be remedied? We can make the best case for the importance of ritual by considering it as a language.

RITUAL AS LANGUAGE

If one thinks of ritual as some kind of rigmarole, magic, or pompous fanfare, then one belittles it; but if one thinks of it as a language, then one can easily argue its importance for society. Communication is obviously the nervous system of society, whose parts are coordinated through centers like the White House, the Pentagon, television, news, libraries, and schools. Human society is laced together by two kinds of language, discursive and nondiscursive.[1] Discursive is the easiest to discuss for the very good reason that it is the language we talk and think *with*. Words, grammars, mathematical symbols, codes, enable us to make literal statements, specify locations on maps, and things like that. This does not rule out poetic and mystical reference by even the same symbols. We are interested, however, in a kind of language especially adapted to things which are hard to talk about—illogical thoughts, vague allusions, nuances, mystiques, connotations—not normally or easily put into matter-of-fact statements. Nondiscursive language includes dance, pantomine, clowning,[2] sculpture, painting,[3] music, and, of course, ritual (on its nonverbal side). It also includes side effects of verbal language, such as body gesture and intonation.[4] What, for example, do the following gestures say: placing of the wedding ring ("Now you're mine forever"?); a public official's oath of office ("I'll try really hard, no kidding"?); the placing of a black cap on the head of a judge giving the death sentence ("This is more serious than you think"?); the clown's pratfall in circus burlesque ("It serves you right"?); a sand painting by a Navajo medicine man ("Get well"?)? We have no difficulty finding *some* literal sense in almost any ritual gesture; but it would be ludicrous to suppose that whatever we say does not leave something out, especially when the example comes from another culture. The Mass is more than its liturgy.[5] When the Australian aborigine is asked the meaning of certain paintings on the wall of a sacred cave, he *dances* his answer. So nondiscursive is not fully translatable into discursive language: the explanation of love is not love, of a joke is not funny, of music is not musical, of play is not fun, of theater is not drama, of poetry is not poetic, of mystery is not mystique, of sacredness is not the holy. Hence Anna Pavlova's famous statement when she was asked, "What do you say when you dance"—"If I could tell you, I wouldn't dance."

This is the "beyond" of semantics of which Langer writes.[6] The term I use for such a semantic beyond when it is important for people to refer to it though untranslatable into logical terms is *mystique*. This includes things like Zen satori, Voodoo influences, Balinese trance,[7] the meaning of Bartók, satisfaction from unpleasant ceremonies,[8] and Lévy-Bruhl's "primitive participation."

The mystique is the whole meaning that a person gets, usually without being able to fully describe it, from an experience like the following of a witness of the Anglican evensong and consecration of priests:

The long procession entered and we stood as the choir—decorous—dignified—beautifully spaced—passed to their places, followed by the canons in single file. There seemed no end of them—tall and short—old and young— . . . as they moved to their rightful stalls—the chapter clerk—the archdeacons—bishop suffragan—dean—and finally the tall figure of our bishop, taking his place under the canopy of the bishop's throne. . . . To me, the most moving moment of the . . . Ordering of Priests . . . was that in which not only the bishop but the semi-circle of priests around him all lay their hands on the new priest's head as the bishop utters these solemn words—"Receive thee Holy Ghost for the Office and Work of a Priest in the Church of God now committed unto thee by the Imposition of our hands." . . . One came away with a sense of more than ever "belonging" and also with the feeling of timelessness—of change and yet changelessness—in a centuries-old setting.

Mystiques need not be religious. Another example is that of the ancient, sentimental custom in Balmoral Castle for a bagpipe major to march into the Queen's dining room while the roast is being carved. He pipes three times around the table, then rests his foot on the royal chair while the Queen pours him a drink. No one seems able to explain all this, but guests have been reduced to tears by this age-old custom. Another example of mystique is quite modern: There is a curious, unspeakable bond among Volkswagen users that has been the subject of many jokes, even a literature.[9] It has something to do with the "bug" shape and is maintained by a joking relationship. It cannot be explained by the verbal reasons of American culture such as "economy" or "status symbol"; closer to the mystique is a statement like this from a woman, "I bought it because it needed me."

Nevertheless, though one cannot translate, it is possible to summarize, however inadequately, themes of ritual important in almost all groups, though the forms of expression vary. We might paraphrase some typical messages: (1) "You are not alone. We are all together"—the ritual of solidarity, fellowship, belongingness, *esprit de corps;*[10] (2) "Do not worry. Things will work out all right. Something you do not understand is working for you"—a language of reassurance, found often in white magic;[11] (3) "Congratulations, you made the grade"—the rites of status transition;[12] (4) "We hold this to be right and self-evident"—moral affirmation;[13] (5) "Crime does not pay"—the ill-doer gets what he deserves—dramatization of moral debt and punishment, the theme of morality plays, crime dramas, horse opera, court ceremony, and sorcery for law enforcement in primitive societies;[14] (6) "That is ridiculous. Don't be a jerk. Don't do it"—negative models and comic justice in clowning, burlesque, satire;[15] (7) "I owe you, you owe me"—the ritual of reciprocity;[16] (8) "We are like brothers"— the ritual of kinship extension;[17] (9) "Honestly, I'll really try. I'll never quit"—oaths and resolutions which bind a person to a path or obligation; (10) "Help us, Supreme Power, don't harm us"—the ritual of propitiation and penance; (11) "We are cleansed, redeemed, born again"—the ritual of purification;[18] (12) "Aren't we proud of ourselves!"—the ritual of pomp. Without presuming to exhaust them, I think we can see that such messages and mystiques are too much for mere verbal statement and too important to leave to chance. Groups take every opportunity to emphasize them by emotional ceremonies.

So I define ritual as a nondiscursive gestural language, institutionalized for regular occasions, to state sentiments and mystiques that a group values and needs.

Once seen as language, there is little argument about the general importance of ritual for society, since any language, even one which communicates only vague emotions, helps people to feel more together; and, if emotions are important, then ritual is at least *that* important. So solidarity and fullness of emotional life are two immediate consequences of communicating by ritual. To individuals this means feeling more intensely alive by shared sentiments and mystiques that an individual would not think of by himself; more sense of I as "we"; and cathartic expression of feelings such as anxiety, guilt, aggressiveness, horror, and pity, usually felt as pleasurable.[19] For groups, it means maintaining sentiments necessary for social structures, as explained by the theories of Durkheim and Radcliffe-Brown and illustrated by a large, mainly anthropological, literature.[20] So, for example, Firth analyzes the functions of a funeral in Tikopia. This case is curious because the body was missing: the son of a chief had been drowned at sea, but the people held his funeral anyway a year later. It shows clearly that funerals are symbols for *survivors*. For them the funeral did at least three things: (1) provided the bereaved with a role, a means of expressing their grief, and set a period to their mourning; (2) fulfilled the sequence of events, "maintained and reenforced the system of senti-ments" on which the social structure depended; and (3) mobilized a complex interchange of goods and services, which had not only ritual value of the gift but economic function of paying debts and getting commodities exchanged.[21] With such important transactions going on, it is easy to see why such a community could not afford to pass up a funeral—body or no body.

Another way of putting all this, instead of reenforcement of senti-ments, is to say that ritual helps maintain the consensus necessary for social equilibrium and order—especially the nonrational con-sensus. In this view,[22] agreement in feelings and values as well as thoughts is necessary for people to be able to live together and cooperate; societies are in a balance of tendencies causing people to draw together and form consensus or fly apart; every society needs rites to help maintain its supply of nonrational consensus. Should its activity support only rational consensus (science, information, legislation, practical reform), then its nonrational consensus (mores, sentiments, faiths) will become weak—nondiscursive communi-cation being the main vehicle for supporting this. Primary group interaction can supply much nonrational consensus without using ritual; but the rich development of ritual in primary groups shows how much such symbolism helps and is needed.

The family is a good place to illustrate the unifying effects of ritual on members of a group:

When Kay S. was three years old, her father held her on his lap and read to her on Christmas Eve Clement Moore's well known poem, "The Night Before Christmas." Each Christmas Eve thereafter this has been repeated. When Kay was five years old, her sister Jane was born, and during the succeeding years the reading of this poem on Christmas Eve became more and more of a ceremonial event. As the two daughters became older, they would sit on either side of their father on the family sofa, and mother and other relatives would be present. After the reading, refreshments came to be served, and talk would follow about Christmas celebrations of former years. As time went on, the ceremony became more and more elaborate. Candles were lit while other lights were extin-guished; the conversational aftermath lengthened. Nothing ever deterred Kay and Jane from being at home on Christmas Eve; dates with boys, even after their engagements had been announced, were not made; once Kay did not accept an invitation to a much desired trip so that she might be at home for "the reading." After Kay's marriage, she and her husband came to her parents' home on Christmas Eve in order to be present for the event. This practice has been continued down to the present time, both by Kay and her husband and by Jane and her husband. Last year, "father" read to both daughters, their husbands, three grandchildren and grandmother.[23]

The egg cups, pickle caster, and soup tureen figure in a family ceremonial. Mother is the high priestess of this rite. The dinner is served by candle light and the contents of the antique cabinet are emptied onto the table. We eat with the Family Silver off the soup plates my grandparents bought on their wedding day in 1881. We all love this. What is the value of this delightful family mumbo jumbo? It is to a closely knit family like ours what a wedding anniversary is to a couple who love one another very much. If the couple did not love one another the anniversary would be relatively meaningless; if they were divorced it would not be observed.[24]

This shows the warm identifying effects (in both senses: identifying people with one another and identifying oneself) and relevance of ritual to contemporary—not just savage—life.[25] Much the same could be shown for the sentimental, wacky, sometimes cruel, ceremonies of college fraternities and sororities; pep rallies and traditions for "school spirit"; singing around a campfire; or caroling in the community. When they work, they leave unforgettable memories which are the basis of identity and a nostalgic link with the group.

Our concern here, however, is more with what the ritual does for the individual than for society. Put positively, it gives a sense of emotional fullness and participation in mystiques, and for many people it is a high point of life, one more meaningful than mere matter-of-fact information. Cardinal Newman's statement illustrates how important ritual can be as a high point of life:

To me, nothing is so consoling, so piercing, so thrilling, so overcoming, as the Mass . . . I could attend Masses forever, and not be tired. It is not a mere form of words—it is a great action . . . it is . . . the evocation of the Eternal. He comes present on the altar in flesh and blood . . . that is the awful event which is the scope, and the interpretation, of every part of the solemnity.[26]

Put negatively, lack of ritual deprives an individual of messages of reassurance such as "You are not alone" and "Things will work out all right" (as we have inadequately tried to summarize some of the themes). William James wrote of the need for such "illusions"[27] in *The Will to Believe*. It is not necessary, however, to argue, as James did, that such messages and references are "true" in a scientific or philosophical sense. To the individual they mean, nevertheless, true feeling (existentially true): of realizing emotions, identifying with others and things beyond oneself, and identity in the sense of feeling oneself—"This is how I really feel." In this sense, any of the meanings of ritual, when experienced, might be said to bestow some kind of identity.

And ritual has the enormous, almost crushing, burden of preserving such fragile meanings—the most subtle, elusive, ineffable, precious—by relatively crude methods such as enactment and miming and cumbersome symbols such as ikons, candles, and costumes, while discursive language enjoys the advantages of grammar, syntax, logic, writing, print, formulas, graphs, and tables. Moreover, ritual, largely unwritten, has to fight against the tendency for things to drop out of consciousness—time the great thief—and of emotional habits to become routine. With such a struggle for awareness, it is all the more poignant to see ritual trying to perform its task in the face of determined resistance and efforts by some to get rid of it.

RESISTANCE TO RITUAL

In view of such important messages and functions, it seems rather odd that there should be resistance to use of the language of ritual. Alfred North Whitehead says modern men are ambivalent about ritual.

> Hard-headed men want facts and not symbols. A clear theoretic intellect . . . pushes aside symbols as mere make-believes. . . . Critics of the follies of humanity have performed notable service in clearing away the lumber of useless ceremony. . . .

But ritual keeps coming back because people want it:

> However you may endeavour to expel it, it ever returns. . . . However you reduce the functions of your government to their utmost simplicity, yet symbolism remains. It may be a healthier, manlier ceremonial, suggesting finer notions. But still it is symbolism. . . . It seems as though mankind must always be masquerading. . . . A social system is kept

together by . . . emotions clustered around habits and prejudices. . . .
There is an intricate expressed symbolism of language and of act which
is spread throughout the community. . . . The symbol evokes loyalties to
vaguely conceived notions, fundamental for our spiritual natures. . . .
Whereby the symbols acquire their power to organize the miscellaneous
crowd into a smoothly running community.[28]

So we have the paradox that society needs and must live by symbolism it despises intellectually.

From the point of view of a technological society, any method is
mistrusted whose processes and results are intangible, cannot be
physically measured, and are not repeatable in a way achieved by
precise instruments and machines. Likewise, bureaucracy, the great
human machine which organizes people according to rational rules,
looks askance at procedures employed for their own sake—that is,
for values such as esprit de corps and mystiques, rather than for
rational goals—seeing ritual, thinks of itself as afflicted by Parkin-
son's law. Sociologists usually treat ritualism as a type of inefficiency in bureaucracy.[29]

Another important source of resistance to ritual is the rationalism and positivism of a scientific society. Ritual is considered to
be in the domain of illogical and unscientific thought—its references
among the "meaningless" questions rejected by positivists such as
Alfred J. Ayer as beyond the range of serious inquiry. For those of
us who do not follow doctrinaire positivism, it is yet true that education prejudices us against ritual. Taught from elementary school
to place fact before feeling, to get "right" answers and give sound
reasons, modern man has been in a sense incapacitated for ritual
experience; he has been educated, in other words, to deny himself
the kind of identity he might find in suitable ritual. And even when
he admits it, there is a strong tendency to regard it as secondary,
inauthentic, rigmarole; he may condescend by calling it "ritualism"
pejoratively.[30]

Yet the need for the symbolism of myth and mystique has been
pointed out by thoughtful students, such as Langer, Ernst Cassirer,
Thurman Arnold,[31] and Kenneth Burke. Some writers point to the
price that man pays for excessive preoccupation with technology
and matter-of-fact methods and information.[32] Kenneth Burke says
the scientific attitude may run counter to the symbolic needs of society:

Many people with a naturalistic or positivist cast of mind look upon the ritual scapegoat as a mere "illusion." . . . Such people usually seem to feel that the cultivating of the scientific mind in general protects against susceptibility to the attempt to solve practical problems by the use of ritualistic (symbolic) victims . . . they seem to assume that the problem is solved by fragmentation. In effect, they would keep the devil on the run by making him legion. . . . But there is also a sense in which the condition of fragmentation itself might be felt to need an over-all cure. Fragmentation makes for triviality. . . . The whole aggregate of petty fragmentary victimage may thus require a "total" victim, if it in turn is to be cured.[33]

Burke does not categorically favor or disfavor ritual and mystification, but notes that "in a world wholly unmasked no social cohesion would be possible."

But, by such rather grudging concessions, the resistance to ritual in modern society is not reduced to a point where it can really work well. The fact is that even when used—conscientiously, reluctantly, or playfully—it often falls dead in the act and the utterance—like the sound of a chime dampened by velvet. The truth is that, not knowing what to do about ritual, whether to welcome it or cut it out, we botch it much of the time.

POVERTY OF RITUAL

With all this resistance and mistrust of ritual, it is no surprise that it has declined in amount and quality in our society and is, at best, a second-class activity.

Such poverty of ritual is seen in modern funerals, which have been bitterly criticized and satirized as a racket by writers such as Evelyn Waugh, *The Loved One*, and Jessica Mitford, *The American Way of Death*.[34] Modern funerals are becoming cold in efficiency or sickeningly falsely sentimentalized—the only reliable trend seems to be costliness. Traditional features such as services in church, eulogies to the dead, processions on foot, and gatherings at the graveside are disappearing. Efficiency—in terms of stainless-steel equipment, scientific embalming, leakproof caskets, smooth transfer to the cemetery, banks of flowers sent by people not attending—is increasing, without real attention or honor to the corpse. This trend was satirized by Waugh's suggestion to put bodies in a rocket and shoot them into outer space. Whimsical sentimentality, in terms of garish and peculiar arrangements, is also more available for those who can afford it (tradition no longer defines what is "appropriate"), epitomized by Forest Lawn Cemetery; but the community-at-large does not share in these sentiments, even regards them as queer. It seems plain that neither of these kinds of "improvements"—technical efficiency, peculiar sentimentality—gives a better ceremony by which to honor the dead, emphasize the importance of a status transition, or satisfy and console the bereaved. Indeed (cost quite aside), modern funerals represent a defeat to the bereaved, no contribution of meaning to the community, and small comfort to the dead.

Major festivals such as Easter and Christmas have become commercialized and secularized[35] to the point where many people are disappointed in them. A survey showed that many things were felt lacking in the modern spirit of Christmas; feelings of alienation were common about commercialization, innovations that spoil the spirit of Christmas (such as pink Christmas trees, plastic trees, mechanical revolving trees that play *Jingle Bells,* artificial wreaths, Santas in spaceships), loss of traditional features of Christmas (such as caroling), lack of real Christmas spirit, economic strain, and rush and crowds of Christmas shopping.[36]

Weddings are another area in which there is considerable cause for complaint—either because streamlined into a businesslike, minimal ceremony, made into a publicity stunt, or padded into a "schmaltzy," artificial, overcostly affair lacking in meaning. A clergyman comments:

> In cynical moods I have sometimes felt that as officiating clergyman I was accomplice in—or, at least, accessory to—two of the country's leading rackets: weddings and funerals. . . . Consider weddings . . . how what is in essence a simple ceremony can be built up into an elaborate, costly, and . . . nerve-wracking ceremonial. . . . A minister . . . stands by while they discuss the pros and cons of what is to him a holy place . . . as a theater for staging a show. It seems to him a desecration. . . . Once our organist, an austere man, a devotee of Bach, came to me in great perturbation. The groom . . . requested that the organist play "The Sweetheart of Sigma Chi." "Do I have to play that?" he asked wrathfully. "No," I answered, "we've got to make a stand somewhere. It may as well be here." . . . It is difficult to avoid a Hollywood atmosphere.

This can be heightened by playing with a rheostat so as to produce theatrical lighting effects and by the use of organ stops which produce what organists call "schmaltz" and privately designate as "corny." Such a buildup is incongruous with the simple, deeply reverent character of the wedding ritual itself, as any sensitive person must perceive.[37]

In the church itself, which should be a stronghold of ritual, there are many tendencies to eliminate, streamline, or modernize its forms. Some changes, such as elimination of archaic language, can probably be justified pragmatically as in the interest of reaching more people. Other features, however—images, ikons, and incense—are eliminated, reducing the impact of ritual on the senses—to what gain no one may be sure, for it has not been scientifically measured. Innovations to make the church "more contemporary" arouse interest in some and horror in others: the jazz Mass; electric guitars in church services; revolving altar stages permitting the church to be converted into a dance hall or theater; replacing sacramental wine and wafers with Wonder Bread and grape juice. One must admit that such trends produce in many a feeling that "something is missing," and in not a few an outrage to piety.

RITUAL AND SENTIMENT

Associated with such ritual poverty and failures is a poverty of sentiments; people's emotions now seem to be shallower than they were in bygone eras. While there is no exact way to measure how people felt in the past, I think that if a person will immerse himself in the literature and documents of America 50 or 100 years ago, he will conclude that more sentiments today are weaker and shallower than stronger and deeper. Plainly this is true of such things as family feeling (familism);[38] hometown nostalgia; "folk" feeling; neighborly spirit in urban areas; "school spirit" in universities and larger colleges; and feelings of the wrongness of certain kinds of misbehavior such as theft and sex outside marriage. A store manager comments:

> Kids caught stealing think it's a lark. We sure had a different attitude when I was a kid. If I'd been caught stealing, my parents probably would have taken me out of school. But parents today just don't seem to care. They are more interested in their child's side of the story. And the kids: their attitude is—so you caught me, so what?

One could make a good case that people care less intensely about things than they did fifty years ago. Fathers were more revered, homes and mothers more sentimentalized, ladies more respected. Modesty was more delicate, sex more dangerous and mysterious; shock, shame, guilt, and ruin more complete; wrongs wronger, anger more wrathful, punishment more deserved, villains blacker; virginity whiter, honor dearer, snobbery prouder; love more romantic, jealousy more possessive; vows and oaths more sacred; prayers more fervent, hell more vivid; patriotism more uncalculating, duty more compelling; and prejudices of all kinds stronger[39]—not a golden age, just one that felt more strongly. I am saying that whatever gains there may have been in the intensity of such sentiments as humanitarianism would not offset this. If social sentiments could be measured on some kind of meter, there would be less total voltage today—at least voltage that could be delivered in one current of common action.

One indication of this loss is the fact that so many perfectly respectable sentiments, which just happen to be old, are now regarded as "corny." Indeed, in the "cool" era, it is hard to find any sentiment which does not earn such a title. But the "cornball" has a perfect right to rise (from his grave, if need be), confront the modern generation, and ask, "All right. I am corny. What do *you* feel?"

I am not arguing for old-fashioned sentiments or against modern ones or recommending particular sentiments (it may be that some of those mentioned we can do without) or being in general a sentimentalist. I am arguing a more fundamental proposition: That a life full of sentiments is a fuller life in the sense of meaningfulness and happiness than one with weak sentiments; that there are probably countries which, in spite of material poverty, are happier places to live in than wealthy countries because they retain the fullness of social sentiments.[40]

For modern societies mass communication takes over some of the burden of sentimentality and ritual,[41] so they do not suffer as much as they would otherwise. The compensatory function of shows like musical comedies, "horse operas," and "soap operas" is not merely to provide fiction, but to fill in emotional emptiness. Were real life fuller, vicarious fulfillments would be proportionally less important as compensations (distinguished from entertainment). While all peoples use myth and fiction in some form, the mass audience has a special need, born of emptiness, so that fiction compensates in a way neither necessary nor possible in the folk society: we may distinguish between the impossible, miraculous feats of folk heroes, which everybody enjoys[42] and the very possible but, for many, unattainable emotional fulfillments of soap opera. Or take a hit like *The Sound of Music,* which was seen by over 35 million people in the first two years of its showing—repeatedly, some seeing it dozens of times, a hundred times, one lady 810 times— a "fantastic cult of followers showing no sign of waning."[43] Such humdrum fulfillments, if I may call them that—a happy life, cozy home, good husband, sweet wife, lovely children—become romantic only when there is a real lack in the lives of people, watching, possibly, family rituals which they do not have in their own homes. Only in an emotionally empty mass society could such things become as exciting as the deeds of folk heroes.

So, partly from these sops and compensations, our society is not aware of the true extent of its emotional poverty. It takes for granted that much of life is boring and meaningless, needing "escapes" for compensation. The cool, blasé, apathetic state is felt to be normal. This is rather like the state of a patient who suffers a vitamin or endocrine deficiency and has come to think that his normal state is to be tired and lacking in enthusiasm. Then the emotional nourishment mass communication provides may be likened to those refined white breads, cereals, and other foods which have had some of their food value removed; people eat, not knowing what they are missing.

But mass society occasionally awakens to its boredom, to its emotional undernourishment. Then it is an appropriate question to ask: What is the relation between unsatisfactory ritual and poverty of sentiments?

MISTAKEN RESPONSES TO FORMALISM

The easiest thing is to blame formalism. This takes us back to the problem of the college seniors; sociologists call it formalism: procedures which were originally worth while, rewarding, for what they achieved or for their own sake, become cold, mechanical, meaningless.[44] It is a symbolic malady, a blight on ritual, in which life goes out of forms which were once meaningful, or never enters forms which were intended to be meaningful. Who has not sat through long, drawn-out ceremonies—banquets, conventions, meetings, church services—wishing they were over? Every small boy knows formalism. Even Puritans probably felt it in their three-hour church services. When ritual is alive, however, people linger over it, enjoy it to the utmost—even when it is prolonged. But when a ceremony is felt to be acutely boring, the natural response is to shirk it or cut it out. Truants do one, reformers the other. So our college seniors decided to abolish name calling at graduation to shorten the ceremony. But, like amateur surgeons, they cut at the wrong place. It was a live nerve! This illustrates the characteristic failure of our society in dealing with the problem of ritual.

There are several kinds of mistaken responses to the problem of providing an adequate emotional language for social occasions. When a question comes up about ritual, the formalist says, "Go ahead, preserve appearances, no matter what people feel." The sentimentalist says, "Take a chance. Wear your heart on your sleeve. It may be catching." The hard-headed realist says, "Cut out the corn. People don't feel that way anymore. Let's get on with the business." Another approach is to make fun out of the ritual, "jazz it up," which usually destroys whatever meaning it may have had.

Let me try to describe these mistaken responses to formalism more systematically, in terms of what is done with symbols. There seem to be, basically, four. (1) One mistake is to cut ritual out, stop signaling when the message is not heard anyway. We can see this in traffic courts, city hall weddings, graduations by mail, where ceremony is dispensed with. The result is sheer poverty of ritual. Procedure becomes a barebones affair, devoid of courtesy or comfort. This might be called ritual nakedness. (2) A second mistake is to go on speaking the dead language and wearing the quaint costumes; persist in ritual which is formalistic, even when it alienates the audience. Here elaborate procedures disguise the fact nothing is said. This might be compared to the exchange of money which has lost its value, or wearing jewels which everyone knows are phony. (3) A third mistaken response is to introduce meaningless innovations. The new procedures and objects are nonsymbols (noise). This is illustrated by *pink* Christmas trees, or by nonobjective modern art in place of religious pictures in a church. Very often modernizing brings in designs which are functional but meaningless. The traditional square or folk dance may be replaced by rock and roll in a rural community. Here a genuine symbolic form, with functions for the family and community, is replaced by a type of music and dance which is probably about 90 percent sound and 10 percent meaning. Another example of meaningless innovation is sometimes seen in synthetic political pomp. Corps of press agents may try to create out of whatever materials are available "occasions," such as the visit of a U. S. President. But lack of a format of time-honored custom and hallowed symbols of pomp (such as the British have so much of) sometimes makes it difficult to produce more than mere publicity. For pomp, dignity, reverence, and authority depend on symbols; they cannot just be improvised by "arrangements." Such synthetic occasions, being meaningless, may suffer more from formalism than does authentic ritual, however pompous and prolonged. (4) Finally, one may introduce symbols which have inappropriate meaning, conflicting with the spirit of the occasion or making it into something else. This can be seen in weddings of celebrities—in swimming pools, airplanes, diving suits—which are plainly publicity stunts, destroying whatever sentiment a wedding is supposed to have, making it a joke. Another reason for introducing foreign symbols is to make an old form felt to be boring more fun— "pep it up," "jazz it up." Christmas carols may be "swung" or given a calypso or bossa nova beat. A "jazz Mass" is introduced into London Anglican churches. Such innovations either change the form into something else or produce conflicts between the tonality (secular nightclub associations) of jazz and the sentimental or sacred themes. Tampering with the symbols of Christmas has also been a rich source of discontent. People asked what they disliked about Christmas often complained about such things as "jazzed up" carols, spelling "Xmas" instead of "Christmas," metal or artificial trees of any kind, trees that do not have a piney odor, any color in the tree but green. Again, though there is less expressed dissatisfaction about it, commercial slogans and advertising may introduce a quite foreign note into such things as school games, float processions, and community festivals, though advertising is so prevalent in America it is sometimes hard to be aware of how intrusive it is. Yet another example of irrelevant symbolism which destroys the original meaning of ritual is "sick" humor in greeting cards which are expected to express affection, congratulation, or a wish that someone will get well. So people try to increase the psychological payoff by inappropriate symbols—the effect being rather like shooting off firecrackers in church.[45] It must be admitted that increasing the "fun" as a psychological payoff will draw audiences; but the specific meaning may be lost; and increasing "fun" makes no contribution to other sentiments which may be languishing because not adequately celebrated. So we see that this kind of response to formalism, introducing inconsistent symbols, either clashes with the regular meaning or changes it into something else. Those who favor modernization probably will argue that something else is exactly what is needed when ritual goes dead. But three questions must be faced: Is the something else a definite meaning or just a transient sensation? If a definite meaning, is it equivalent in value to what it replaces? And, for those who still want the *old* meaning, what is to carry it after the old symbol has been replaced?

Popular music, such an important bearer of sentiments in the mass society, illustrates many of these difficulties of unsatisfactory symbolism. As with fads, it violates some of the basic principles of symbolism: two of the most important being that a symbol cannot be shared unless its meaning is shared, and that a period of time is required for the meaning of a symbol to grow. Tunes come "in" for such a brief season that it is impossible for them to earn much meaning, however bright their sound; it is unlikely that a large number of people will share the same song in a way even approaching the role of folk music in a folk society. Romantic couples may remember "our" special tune—but each couple has a different one, and they don't have the same one as their children. Traditional music is vastly superior for stating old sentiments; yet even in seasons which call for the statement of old sentiments, the role of traditional music is secondary to pop. Indeed, the irony in mass society is that traditional music *is* pop—ancient tunes like *Greensleeves* come in as a "hit," dressed in new tonality and arrangement, then fade out, as though they deserved no better fate. The basic problem here is vanishing symbols. Doubtless many pop tunes would be as good as traditional ones, both musically and as bearers of sentiments—if only they would stay for awhile. Whatever causes songs to fade out and new ones no better to keep coming in, we have to admit that society is undercutting its symbols; and that these symbols are not adequate to bear the burden of the needed sentiments. So we see the nostalgia for "authentic" folk music, sung in the natural way by people raised in the tradition, as a hankering for genuine symbols and a reaction against the meaninglessness of pop.

The above four mistaken responses to formalism—cutting it out, keeping on with it, meaningless innovation, and inconsistent symbols—all result in sentiments weaker because not adequately celebrated. Such errors, when deliberately committed, usually come from mistaken notions about efficiency as speed, as need for "getting on with it"; from "fun" being more important than sentiment; from rationalistic objections to nondiscursive language and mystiques; or from ambivalent feelings about ritual leading to half-hearted, ineffective, and inconsistent use. It is plain that with all these troubles, we cannot rely on ritual to work naturally anymore. It is employed in hit-or-miss fashion; arbitrarily changed, "jazzed up," distorted in meaning; even when seriously tried, bungled, because people simply no longer know what they are doing. In things like pink "Xmas" trees, we have an example of a society bent on destroying its own symbols. The main point is the lack of recognition that ritual is a *language* that cannot be tampered with without danger of loss of meaning, and that it deserves the same protection as word language.

However, in noting that formalism means ritual is not working and in trying to describe mistaken responses to formalism, it seems to me that what we have much of the time is a *vicious circle*—A is affecting B and B affecting A, not just A causing B. The sequence of this vicious circle goes something like this: (1) People are not sure they want ritual in the first place, perhaps because of rationalistic education, or because sentiments are weak; (2) they use it half-heartedly, flippantly, or inconsistently; (3) it seems to fail, at least they think so; (4) now, sure they do not want it, they give up lip service, cut it out, or innovate recklessly; (5) the sentiments ritual serves weaken further—others may still want it but the voice of sentimentalists gets fainter; (6) now the cycle starts again, in the same or some other area. With this progressive weakening of sentiments and misconduct of ritual, soon it is "quaint," even "queer," to try to revive old ritual. A ritual may be said to be dead at the point where it is impossible to remember even intellectually what the sentiments "should be," used to be. Then what were formerly parts of ceremonies become "mere" dance, play, song, and so forth. They have no power to evoke sentiments because a generation has not learned to associate anything with them.

Such deterioration cannot be blamed on formalism nor does it prove that ritual does not work. It does show a vicious circle in which what we do, or fail to do, may make things worse than if we had left them alone. And the cycle is self-accelerating. How much of secularization is hastened by this kind of bungling, whereas doing nothing would avoid pushing the wheel of deterioration faster. We must face up to the problem that an emotional lack requires an adequate emotional medium of replacement—a language that will carry such meanings. Doubtless when such a language is properly used, it will have positive, not negative, effect. Though we cannot blame poverty of sentiments all on poverty of ritual, neither can we claim that sentiments would not be richer if they had more effective ritual.

What does one do about it? Once the problem is seen in these terms, as a malady of symbols, it becomes a matter not of weeping over dead ones but of saving and giving birth to live ones.[46] There is no direction but forward—"forward," however, not meaning "modernization" in an indiscriminate sweeping away of things like antique forms of expression and robes of office (whose value may lie in their oldness), but an enlightened effort to preserve, cultivate, and plant anew. Forward is between the horns of the dilemma of boredom with formalism, on the one hand, and the nakedness of no ritual at all on the other. Rational cultural revivalism[47] has a place when symbols which are fitting can be restored. In a society where "old" is almost equivalent to "obsolete," we need education for the appreciation of tradition. The drift to reckless innovation, at least, can be discouraged. Unfortunately, we have nothing corresponding to a dictionary to hold ritual language to proper use and keep it from abuse. Above all, recognizing the nature of the problem, greater effort should be made to understand and use the mysterious language of ritual. A charismatic solution has been the usual way by which society revitalizes itself;[48] but we need not wait for this. We can use science in the service of ritual rather than in opposition to it.

This implies a research program. One part would be investigating the nondiscursive meaning of ritual, both old and new: what people are trying to say, what they see in it. Mystiques can be analyzed empirically.[49] Another part of the investigation would be an inventory of areas and groups in which there is the most emotional and ritual poverty—"meaninglessness." It is easy to see some of these areas without an inventory; family life sometimes suffers from sheer thoughtlessness. Other areas, such as business, require a scientific appraisal—possibly tests or questionnaires—to measure the need for and value of ritual. A third part would be creative thinking to find forms of ritual appropriate to particular situations: alertness to old forms still viable or germinal rituals already present which could be expanded; brainstorming sessions for ideas, encouraging democratic participation in decisions; and use of theatrical, poetic, and artistic talents. A fourth part would be study of ritual as a dramatic technique. Ritual can fail or succeed in precisely the same ways as drama does. It can move people to tears or derisive laughter, it can grip audiences with suspense or cause them to sit back and criticize; actors can carry it off or fail through lack of poise and presence, or inept playing of parts. So ritual can be improved by taking heart that it is worthwhile and trying to do a better acting job. Fifth, experiments are needed to determine *which* form of ritual works, using controls and making comparisons by pretests and posttests. Some pretty wild experiments are possible— for example, using LSD in religious ceremonies. Finally, a new kind of "poverty program" might then be appropriate: to overcome emotional poverty, rebuild not slums but sentiments, restore the meaning of the relation of man-to-man and man-to-life—and balance the present overemphasis on material problems.

Such a program would, of course, be a coordinated effort of psychiatrists, psychologists, social workers, sociologists, public administrators, and other specialists, aiming to repair all aspects of emotional life—parent-child relationships, primary groups, school, church, community, mass communication, and so on—not just a concern with ritual. But the danger at present is not overemphasizing ritual but leaving it out of the equation. We should not be discouraged by rationalism into neglecting this essential aspect of life or intimidated by the bugaboo of *1984* (which showed ritual used to manipulate a totalitarian society) and so misled into the *non sequitur* that adequate ritual means a totalitarian society. It might be argued, indeed, that a liberal society needs ritual of its own to offset the lure of totalitarian solidarity.

Stimulating such research should be the looming age of leisure and the loss of meaning of work and identity from work. Ritual may prove one of the fillers of this vacuum, less difficult to provide than work in an automated society and more meaningful than mere play.

CONCLUSION

The purpose of this chapter was to further our study of the collective search for identity by pointing to the importance of mystiques, and to the need for and legitimacy of ritual as a nondiscursive language, even in a rationalistic society. We imply that to try to get rid of ritual as some kind of archaic barbarism is not helpful. Rather, its contribution to the fullness of emotional life should be stressed. Ritual is not only pleasant but absolutely necessary for giving people a full sense of themselves, of their place, of belonging; it fills the emotional void of mechanized and routinized life. Poverty of ritual is part of the reason for poverty of sentiment, which underlies the feeling that the system cheats—the alienation of beatniks and other rebels. No small part of the reason that life seems empty is that occasions like Easter and Christmas, as well as personal rites of passage, are empty events—or despairingly privatized (what a person feels in *his* life is only his private business); so the battery of social sentiments is not charged and grows weaker, in what I have described as a circular process. Nor do the pseudo-symbols, commercialized sentiment, and synthetic rituals of mass society prevent this.

The observation of poverty of ritual and of sentiment is here not so much an argument to study and repair ritual as an effort to describe the scene from which a collective search for identity gathers head. Lacking adequate ritual and warmth of sentiment in social life, we may expect people to grope, by cultic and other means, to find an emotional fullness that is so lacking in a formalistic mass society. Cults, then, are seen as new starts, new kernels of mystique and ritual, for those seeking to center their identities. In the next chapter we consider cultic movements from this point of view.

5 Cultic Movements

The School of Meditation teaches deep meditation, the results of which are immediate and practical. Inner happiness unfolds, tension and worry are relieved; the mind becomes clearer, the heart warmer and actions surer. The method is astonishingly simple and anyone may undertake it as part of the daily routine. To learn more, you are invited to a public lecture or private interview.

The School of Meditation.

Two ways of looking at life . . . are characteristic respectively of what we call the healthy-minded, who seek to be born only once, and of the sick souls, who must be twice-born in order to be happy. The result is two different conceptions of the universe of our experience. In the religion of the once-born, the world is a sort of rectilinear or one-storied affair. . . . In the religion of the twice-born, on the other hand, the world is a double-storied mystery. Peace cannot be reached by the simple addition of pluses and elimination of minuses from life. Natural good . . . can never be the thing intended for our lasting worship. It keeps us from our real good, rather; and renunciation and despair of it are our first step in the direction of the truth. There are two lives, the natural and the spiritual, and we must lose the one before we can participate in the other.

William James[2]

A man can be born again; the springs of life can be cleansed instantly. . . . If this is true of one, it can be true of any number. Thus, a nation can be born in a day if the ideals of the people can be changed.

William Jennings Bryan[3]

In the cultic movement, the identity search takes a particularly deep and serious form. More than just presenting external symbols, as in fad and pose, the cultist strives to recenter his life, devote his entire thought and being to "it." Costume and ornament, which may seem to the outsider faddish, have a part; but a life is called for by cult that goes far beyond the requirements of fad, both in length of time and depth of commitment. In the devotee's role, as we shall see, means are given for a much more sweeping revision of identity—which begins with the emotional experience of conversion, or realizing "it."

NUDISM RECONSIDERED

Along with spectacular science and technology, the twentieth century has witnessed a remarkable growth of interest in activities best described as cultic—such as mysticism, magic, astrology, charms, fortune telling, prophecies, spiritualism, ghosts, poltergeists, extrasensory perception, drugs for mystical experience, a vogue of Zen Buddhism, and new sects of all kinds. Jehovah's Witnesses, for example, grew from 60,000 to 950,000 in 20 years, claims congregations in 180 countries, and baptizes 7,000 by immersion on the same day in New York's Yankee Stadium. "Saints are back in fashion"; a writer notes that Rome, by 1954, had already canonized half again as many saints as did the nineteenth century.[4] There is a tremendous sale of religious and inspirational literature.[5] Billy Graham fills stadiums with over 30,000 "inquirers" at a time. Even the colleges surge with Youth For Christ, Moral Rearmament, and similar movements. Theologians greet the religious boom with misgivings, wondering if it is Christian, wondering if it is even religion.[6]

Indeed it is a problem, what is religion? It depends, in part, on whether one wants to consider such things as sports, hobbies, games, dances, fads, health activities, diets, regimens, educational methods, and therapies as having a cultic character. How can one decide whether people are more or less religious, unless one settles this? We are going to take a broad view of such matters and sidestep the question of religion by just considering cultic activities and their relation to the solution of identity problems. A large part of the mystique of any cult is what it does for identity. If cults are booming in the twentieth century, we presume it is because identity problems are also booming.

Let us, then, consider cultism as a kind of response to identity problems. Cults have much interest in clothes, vestments, and insignia which modify conventional appearance. Monastics cover themselves with robes and hoods, Masons come out in fezes and Arabic splendor. In modern England, the Druids are still a thriving movement, appearing before the public for dawn solstice ceremonies, at Stonehenge and other sites, parading in long white robes and hoods, under the watchful eye of the Ministry of Public Works, with police and barbed wire to keep back the crowds. One also sees a thriving movement of witches—of whom there are possibly 6000 in England—organized into covens of 13, headed by a priest or priestess, meeting for weird rites four times a year in remote country cottages and lonely moors. Such ceremonies are performed nude.

Why do people become witches and why do they take off their clothes? A member explains:

> We are just ordinary people. . . . We have doctors, teachers, businessmen, farmers, nurses, theatrical people, office workers and housewives among us. Most . . . have studied comparative religion. We do not try to convert others . . . we do not take everybody who wants to come in. . . .
>
> The interest appears to be growing. I think one reason is that people are failing to find a spiritual satisfaction they desire in organized religions.
>
> Why are we witches? The reason, I suppose, is that we know that this is the right path for us. The craft is a fertility cult: We worship the life source. . . .
>
> It is generally known that we are naked in our rites. This has given rise to disapproval. . . . Female witches always wear a necklace, a symbol of rebirth, and the priestess wears a wide silver bracelet with her witch name engraved upon it.[7]

The nudity, necklace, and witch names obviously have something to do with change of identity, symbolizing rebirth and the putting aside of wordly things which represent the old life. Witch cult, no less than saint cult, offers a new self. Likewise, we may presume, the costume, trappings, and pageantry of Free Masonry.

I think it is a mistake to look on nudism in Western society, when it occurs as a group practice, as a kind of sublimated peeping-Tomism. Whatever may be the motive of those who come to peer at the fence, it is not likely the motive of the members. So long as tampering with clothing (whether taking off or putting on) has dramatic significance, we should regard it as in the same class with actions like ablution, immersion, baptism, or burning with fire to destroy the past—as rituals for change in identity. I submit that the reasons for taking off one's clothes in a group activity are often precisely the same as those for putting on a costume: to dramatize oneself in a new way.

Nudists are at pains to explain that nudity has nothing to do with sex and much to do with health, well-being, and realizing oneself "naturally." Why should we be so reluctant to take them at their word? It is perfectly reasonable to suppose that nudism could symbolize for many a kind of return to innocence, a romping through the woods or playing in the water like babes. The comments of nudists themselves stress innocence and concern with remaking oneself, a more natural or better life: "Freedom of the sun hitting the whole body, freedom from clothes, self-expression"; "more an integral part of the universe"; "I don't have to impress anybody"; "I feel like myself all the time. I am expressing myself more honestly. I think I have become a better person"; "More relaxed, changed my approach to life, feel I have a better life"; "I feel natural. I have found people here more willing to be themselves, their real selves"; "It gives a sense of honesty with your fellow man. It doesn't make any difference if you are a professor or a truck driver . . . a truly democratic group of people"; "I don't want to be a conformist. I am a nonconformist." "I am getting to know more about myself—the sort of person I am"; Healthful . . . natural . . . I don't want my children growing up with fantasies . . . the body has to breathe." Sex interest is minimized: "It's no big thing after you've seen a thousand females. A woman looks more provocative in clothing." The attitude is wholesome, sometimes almost evangelical: "I wish my friends would come, and their families, and their families' friends." In short, I do not see how, after talking with nudists, one could come to any other conclusion than that they are remaking themselves by taking clothes off together.

What is a cultic group really up to? Once we dismiss the rather naive misunderstanding that nudists, witches, and Druids are up to some kind of naughty sex activity, we see the group as little different from any other association in wishing to pursue its interests undisturbed by gapers and interlopers. Even a country club builds a fence around its cherished putting greens. A cult, however, has a special need to exclude profane outsiders, whose attitude spoils the ritual and the spirit of fellowship. Its secrecy is no cause for alarm to the public, since it is not for conspiracy or misbehavior but only to do better together what they could not do if the group were too large or unsympathetic outsiders were present. There is a basic advantage in small, cohesive groups—for sharing feeling, interacting intensely, and supporting one another in perfect ritual. Even the profane rites of witches can be profaned. What all cults aim to produce in their members is identity change and realization of some kind of mystique.

Why should one want to get together for rigmarole and hocus-pocus that outsiders do not understand? I would say that cultic response is an answer to the banality of society: an effort to inject mystery and occultness into what otherwise would be prosaic routine. People use ritual to attain mystiques not available in humdrum daily living. Some life styles—such as Orthodox Hindu, Jewish, Moslem—have built-in mystique; but modern man lives in ritual nakedness. So, feeling the chill of the bareness of existence, he may wish to get together with others to do something that will give him a more intense feeling of himself and his relation to things. Mystique is essentially a feeling that there is something more, "beyond"—something better underneath the wrapping of the package, a box within a box, quite different from and more exciting than what we already know. It might be a messianic fantasy,[9] or a supernatural world scheme. In any case it is a beyond not realized by mere technical means, rather in conflict with rationality, and requiring the nondiscursive language of ritual. When people—nudists or anyone else—get together to use ritual to attain something they cannot easily explain to outsiders, their response is cultic. When it uses costume and make-believe, cult is more than mere play, masquerade, buffoonery; it is quite serious. Witch cult, for example, was genuine devotion and piety, expressed in prayers, vows, and renunciations; it was not just naughty frolicking by the light of the moon.[10] What people drink from in cult and what they seek when it is gone is not a type of pleasure but a *Grail*. In whatever form it occurs, it should not be discounted as a human activity; it is the zenith of the identity search—its highest mountain or deepest well.

By this kind of reasoning, there could be no widespread interest in new cults unless there were some emptiness or "sickness" of meaning in the existing order—not only churches but work, fun, and general values. I think the truth is that we have a boring social system. It is not that people are too "materialistic," but that materialistic hobbies as well as work have ceased to be deeply interesting. No longer engrossed, men turn to more "significant" activities. Thus *Time* reports a striking increase in applications to religious seminaries from men in their thirties and forties who *want to abandon successful careers*.[11] If materialistic activity were in itself interesting, there would be no need for cult—indeed, it would have its own cult. But there is something wrong with materialistic, bureaucratic, technological activity; it does not easily develop or achieve mystique. When work, play, fads are felt to be empty, people turn toward deeper solutions. What is the nature of the emptiness of modern society? It seems to be a disenchantment with "progress," a dissatisfaction with rationalism and bureaucracy, and an alienation and emotional impoverishment. It is well expressed in the following statement by Malcolm Muggeridge:

I disbelieve in progress, the pursuit of happiness, and all the concomitant notions and projects for creating a society in which human beings find ever greater contentment by being given in ever greater abundance the means to satisfy their material and bodily hopes and desires. In other words, I consider that the way of life in urbanized, rich countries as it exists today, and as it is likely to go on developing, is probably the most degraded and unillumined ever to come to pass on earth. . . . Nor, as far as I am concerned, is there any recompense in the so-called achievements of science. . . . This does not at all excite my mind, or even my curiosity. The atom has been split; the universe has been discovered, and will soon be explored. Neither achievement has any bearing on what alone interests me—which is why life exists, and what is the significance, if any, of my minute and so transitory part in it. All the world in a grain of sand; all the universe, too. If I could understand a grain of sand I should understand everything. Why, then, should going to the moon and Mars, or spending a holiday along the Milky Way, be expected to advance me further in my quest than going to Manchester and Liverpool, or spending a holiday in Brighton?

Education, the great mumbo-jumbo and fraud of the age, purports to equip us to live, and is prescribed as a universal remedy for everything from juvenile delinquency to premature senility. For the most part, it only serves to enlarge stupidity, inflate conceit, enhance credulity, and put those subjected to it at the mercy of brainwashers with printing presses, radio and television at their disposal. . . .

For as we abolish the ills and pains of the flesh we multiply those of the mind, so that by the time mankind are finally delivered from disease and decay—all pasteurised, their genes counted and rearranged, fitted with new replaceable plastic organs, able to eat, fornicate, and perform other physical functions innocuously and hygienically as and when desired—they will all be mad, and the world one huge psychiatric ward.[12]

When a person feels this way about the world, there are only two solutions. One is to turn away from the world, the other is to seek to be a new man in a new world. Cults are an especially effective means for the latter course since they are the only organizations that really focus on ritual rebirth.

It may be asked, Why do not existing churches meet the need for mystique and carry men to a new life in the new world? The answer seems obvious: they are part of the sickness; banality has crept into them, too; congregations are bored; they have become rationalistic, bureaucratic,[13] filled with the spirit of business; the mystery is gone, they really have no Grail. The general picture, in America at least, is of high recorded church membership, low attendance, and even lower interest. The majority of college students are dissatisfied with institutional religion.[14] New cults draw "shoppers" from among the dissatisfied members of established churches.[15] Of the over 250 recorded religious groups in the United States, 200 or so might be called small splinter groups—such fragmentation itself indicating dissatisfaction with institutional religion. By contrast, new cults offer new excitement and hope; as one member of a Church of God congregation said, "No ho-hum religion for us!" It must at least be said for the newer cults that they have the feeling they are going somewhere. In spite of their oddities, therefore, they arouse interest because all of us basically yearn for a better world and are curious to see their version.

In a society which suffers from banality, it is plain that fraternal organizations like the Shriners with their costume, trappings, pageantry, high jinks, and secret ritual have a buffering function to protect their members from the meaninglessness of society-at-large. Of these psychic compensations, a Shriner said:

> I am among other things a Noble of the Shrine, a member of the Council of Royal and Select Masters of the York Right, a Sublime Prince of the Royal Secret, a Knight of the East and West, a Knight of the Brazen Serpent and a Knight of the Sword. Sometimes when I go home late at night crocked and my wife raises hell, I tell her that's what I am, too.[16]

THESIS: CULTIC RESPONSE

My thesis, then, is that the cultic response is the natural result of the human need for meaning. I assume that man is a meaning-seeking animal; and that many, if not most, men are not content with "facts" in the positivistic sense of information which does not answer questions such as why man is here or what attitude to take toward existence. At the border of such facts is a world which is felt to be not only unknown but mysterious. A mystique supplies man with an orientation toward this mystery, represents in symbol and allegory what it is like—at least forces him to take account of it. Ritual, as pointed out in the last chapter, is the symbolic means for referring to such values that cannot be achieved by rational techniques or stated in discursive language. The function of cult is to state mystique and relate man to it by ritual; this I call the cultic response. When the need for meaning and mystique is defeated, the search for a new cultic response becomes urgent. This loss of mystique is part of the malady of symbols discussed in previous chapters. Thus the cultic response is an effort of man to rescue himself from banality and meaninglessness by creating new symbols capable of carrying mystiques.

Let us see now what a cult achieves in its symbols.

BROADER DEFINITION OF CULT

But if we are to give such dignity to cult as the rescuer of man from banality and the zenith of the search for identity, we must first rescue it from the abuse into which its name has fallen. We do wrong, I think, to use it in any way which implies that it is inferior to other kinds of activities—for example, to imply that it is a kind of superstition, or not as respectable as church, or to restrict it to oddball minority groups. Needless to say, this is common in popular usage, among certain religious writers, and, indeed, among sociologists, who have treated it as a religious subcategory at the opposite pole from a church or ecclesia—a small group, lacking organization and institutional structure, searching for mystical experience with the help of a charismatic leader, more radical than a sect.[17] On the other hand, anthropologists have included in cult a broad range of religious and magical activity, but their preoccupation with the primitive end of the spectrum has forced a faintly disparaging tone upon it—at least helping the average man to feel that cult connotes something savage.

What I propose is more in line with the usage of V. Ogden Vogt, who treats cult as a generic form of human activity on a par with education, indeed with culture.[18] Actually a great many writers of all sorts use the term in this way. If we are to be guided by this usage, there is almost no limit to what may be called cult. There is a cult of celibacy, a cult of sex, a cult of war, a cult of the dead, a cult of beauty, a cult of the sacred, a cult of the profane, a cult of reason, a cult of feelings, a cult of science, a cult of equality, a cult of women, a cult of nationalism, a cult of virginity, a cult of buffaloes, a cult of snakes, a cult of tea, a cult of peyote, a cult of alcohol, a cult of action, a cult of tranquility, a cult of this world and of the next. The overriding fact is that the world is full of seekers, devotees, and fanatics of many kinds. We need some generic word to designate this serious pursuit, amounting often to a kind of worship. Why, then, should not "religion" be the inclusive term for activities which represent the zenith of mystique and of man's search for identity? This suffers from the disadvantage of being too specific, too hard to extend to the whole range of phenomena—including such things as war and play and politics—in which men may find mystiques—sacred ones, too. In short, no other term than cult seems to serve so well to designate the kind of group that forms when people become devotees of some highest value and engage in ritual to achieve "it." The content of "it" may change—religion, magic, war, and so on—but as long as men are serious enough about it to become devotees and perform ritual, the general features of cultic experience and social organization are the same.[19] Why should not secular political organization—such as the enshrinement of Lenin's body in Moscow or the evangelism of the John Birch Society[20]—be called cult when it has such features?

But, if cult is so inclusive, where does one draw the line between it and other forms of activity? I would say that activity becomes cultic when it is raised to a high enough level of seriousness and fervor to center the life interest of participants and make them devotees rather than just workers or players. Even jest can become cult if people become serious enough about it. The reason people are so serious about cult is that not just "kicks" but identity is involved. If players begin to feel, "This isn't just sport, it's serious—the very meaning of life to us," then they should know that they are in the realm of cult rather than play. This involvement of identity and cult is the reason why psychotherapists so easily become cult leaders—because they tinker with and promise change of identity. It is the reason why religion and psychotherapy never quite get untangled—why ministers keep on performing psychotherapeutic functions and psychiatry, as Jung held, is basically religious. Six criteria, it seems to me, help us to decide whether an activity is cultic: (1) the quality of enthusiasm toward the central value—is it reverence, piety, devoutness, faith, loyalty, all-out commitment? (2) is there mystique—mysteries, esoteric knowledge—which only initiates or advanced disciples can share? (3) are such feelings and mystiques shared and celebrated by ritual? (4) the role of the devotee—centering of one's life by the regular performance of ritual; (5) emphasis on identity change or a redemption—satori, nirvana, enlightenment, salvation, rebirth, conversion; (6) solidarity of a fellowship or brotherhood. I would say that the more these qualities are developed, the more cult-like the group is.

We recognize the distinction between sacred and secular cult—that whose mystique has the quality of holiness and is profaned by contact with ordinary things[21]—and mystiques of the kind that one might find in magic, health foods, sports, or hero worship. In this chapter we are interested mostly in sacred cult, we shall reserve consideration of secular cult for the next chapter.

CENTERING FUNCTION OF CULT

Sacred sects provide the clearest example of what a cult is supposed to do, because in them the spirit is freshest and the work of conversion most plain. We can see, in examples such as the Self Realization Fellowship of Southern California, Jehovah's Witnesses, Father Divine's "Kingdom," or the Shakers of early New England that the sect is a cultic experiment, a fresh start on the road to redemption, trying to do for man spiritually what established religion, for some reason, has failed to do.[22] The task which any sect undertakes is to reform and redeem the individual from a formerly unsatisfactory life, by centering him completely on the highest good, through ritual (and consecrated work), thus to find the perfect life. However the means vary, the basic goals remain the same.

Though many sects have taken root in America since John Carver and William Bradford founded Plymouth colony in 1620, no truer example can be found than that of the Shakers. Their experiment represents one strand of the American pursuit of happiness, antedating by two years the secular pursuit announced by Jefferson in the Declaration of Independence. If happiness is the criterion, they were apparently more successful than the dour, anxious Puritans. They achieved a startling success in finding the perfect life, and in growing despite a zero birth rate. That they attained an unusual state of Grace is still evident from the records. And just as impressive is their integrity of style—evident to anyone who visits one of their colonies, such as Hancock, Massachusetts— something which all sects by no means achieve. They produced beautiful and distinctive art and furniture, a style known throughout the world, so marked that one could identify almost anything they made. Such a style is an important sign that they had collectively created an identity of their own as well as a material scheme of living. The fact that they dwindled, then, should not be held against them—certainly it is no proof of failure. What church could survive a birth rate like theirs? Indeed, considering their success in subduing the unruly impulse of sex, their ability to grow to some 6000 members by the 1850s, and do it with such evident signs of harmony and spiritual grace, must be accounted a notable success.

Their success was both practical and spiritual. On the economic side, their industry and craftsmanship produced a standard of living higher than that of the workers outside at the same time. As Andrews shows, the Shakers had no fear of want while city workers and ordinary farmers suffered from want; Shakers were clean and healthy while city workers were dirty and unhealthy; Shakers had welfare while city workers had practically no welfare; Shakers had excellent cattle and agriculture whereas people outside had inferior agriculture.[23] Moreover, the Shakers were progressive and made startling inventions. Also they proved, pardon me, that communism—as a brotherly love and sharing of all things—works. So one might say that they showed that Plato was right and Aristotle was wrong concerning the possibility of collectivism in small communities. It all came from the simple injunction of their leader, Ann Lee: "Put your hands to work and give your hearts to God."

But obviously it was not just an economic success. They had something going for them that secular communism lacks. Their cultic experiment was the real heart of their life. It is plain that they achieved ecstasy. Their religion was active and expressive, as one sees in the dances of primitive peoples or in the Kentucky revivals of the early 1800s. They showed their ecstasy by whirlings, quakings, and jerks; falling into trance; speaking in unknown tongues, spontaneous songs; and impulsive dances—all of which they looked on as spiritual messages and gifts. This spontaneous behavior became formalized into rituals, which were performed like parade maneuvers for audiences: the shuffling dance, the skipping dance, the ring dance, the square order shuffle, and the march with the precision of infantry. The high point of it all came in special ceremonies—pilgrimages and love feasts—in which there were hugging and kissing by groups of the same sex; drinking "spiritual wine" and then acting like "fools"; tub baths, giving each other good scrubbings; and spiritual feasts of imaginary food such as pomegranates, wine, and honey. During lengthy pilgrimages they felt no hunger for real food. It must have been pretty yeasty "spiritual cake" because after eating it they carried on as though they were intoxicated. As their own poem states:

There's something in the Shaker Cake
That does make souls contented here. . . . I will unveil this
mystery;

And tell them plainly how to make,
And feast upon the Shaker Cake.
'Tis called in Scripture "living bread,"
Because it quickens from the dead. . . .
No earthly substance we employ,
But just our inward peace and joy,
Nor is it any natural yeast
That gives us this continual feast. . . .
Those who do all sin forsake,
May freely feast on this good cake. . . .
It fills our souls with great delight,
Though 'tis to nature out of sight. . . .
Whene'er enquirers come to see,
This cake is set before them free,
And if they love it, surely, they
Will quit their sins and want to stay.[24]

They also maintained their spiritual purity by rituals such as periodic community-wide housecleaning with brooms and stamping around unbelievers to "chase out the devil."

What did they get out of all this? Plainly they were transported out of themselves into ecstatic experience, whether inspiration or folly. They were reborn and purified as persons, and given grace in the sense of new knowledge and virtue. Not only that, but they got physical cures for ailments ranging from canker sores to broken legs. They had fellowship, a sense of solidarity and security, sleeping as many as fourteen in one room. Everyone felt important—whether from skill as a craftsman, or being a singer or dancer or religious medium, or leader status as an elder. They got not only economic prosperity but freedom from war, crime, strife, and divorce. How much can you ask from a Utopia?

The Shakers were centered upon their rituals and the ecstasy induced by their "spiritual cake." No less do other cults center their members upon some experience of highest value which they feel gives them new life. So "Father" Divine advises his followers to think of him continually even when doing ordinary work:

The way to contact ME effectively is to LIVE the virtuous LIFE of CHRIST in every thought, word and deed. Failure to live herein is the cause of all failure to gain and regain life, liberty and the reality of happiness. . . . When Mr. Benning first contacted ME, he was in prison and because of his harmonious attitude towards ME and his faith in ME, he was freed and he received a parole . . . because he was released through the influence of MY SPIRIT and MY MIND, some of MY followers gave him a home and secured employment for him.

His followers testify to their new life attained by centering on "Father":

FATHER smiles in me and my eyes are bright.
FATHER talks in me and I am polite.
FATHER walks in me and my step is light.
For walking in HIS way, He keeps me right;
FATHER stays with me—and He holds me tight.
And all my battles He does fight.
As He whispers: "It is by faith and not by sight
And by MY spirit—not by power or might."[25]

Quakers achieve their centering not by active expression and dances, as did the Shakers, but by group meditation, sitting together in "the silence," waiting for guidance from the "inner light." Yogic cults, like the Vedanta Society and Self Realization Fellowship, use a more elaborate method of meditation, individual or group, helping themselves concentrate by breathing exercises, focusing attention on some object, reciting mantra, counting beads. The redeeming ecstasy sought here is called *samadhi,* or union with Brahman. All such examples—Shakers, Quakers, Father Divine, Vedanta, Self Realization Fellowship—show the effort of a cult, by whatever means, to achieve centering. This I would say is the fundamental cultic experience.

What happens in centering? No words have been found better than those of William James describing the shift in the "hot place" of consciousness:

Let us . . . in speaking of the hot place in a man's consciousness, the group of ideas to which he devotes himself, and from which he works, call it *the habitual center of his personal energy.* It makes a great difference to a man whether one set of his ideas, or another, be the center of his energy . . . to say that a man is "converted" means, in these terms, that religious ideas, previously peripheral in his consciousness, now take a central place, and that religious aims form the habitual center of his energy.[26]

Kenneth Burke describes this change as construction of a symbolic "altar" toward which ritual actions, "symbolic cleansing," are appropriate. Even a drug addict might "gradually organize his character about this outstanding 'altar' of his experience."[27] A Buddhist describes centering in these terms:

It depends . . . on . . . relinquishing his own small self as the subject of his search for a center. If he succeeds in doing this through conscious meditation . . . he will feel the rigidity in himself giving place to some new center. This new center is quite distinct from that other one, which in reality was nothing but the ego . . . he now experiences the center of his being as something far more than his own ego. . . . Everything is now centralized in perfect harmony with the systole and the diastole of the universe.[28]

So a person integrates himself by putting something highest (a *summum bonum*), a new consummation that gives him a feeling of new life, of rebirth. People become a cult when they do this together, using ritual means.

THE ACHIEVEMENT OF CENTERING

How is centering achieved? Looking at even a fraction of the more or less successful cults should convince us that a wide—almost a wild—variety of ritual means will work (though some, no doubt, work better than others, and this may be an important clue as to why cults fail). To work, a ritual must be capable of distributing the centering experience to some members—at least of the inner circle—of the cult. It might be by shouting, singing, dancing—such as was perfected by the Shakers and other expressive revivalists. It might be in the group silence of the Quakers. It might be in the solitary introspection of the Yogi, helped by various breathing exercises, repetition[29] of mantra, postures (asanas). It might be in the use of drugs or other chemicals which change the action of nerves (psilocybin, peyote, LSD—even alcohol).[30]

A Comanche once said, "The white man talks *about* Jesus; we talk *to* Jesus." . . . Peyote teaches in a variety of ways. One . . . is by heightening the sensibility . . . to one's self. . . . During the rite a good deal of time is spent in self-evaluation. Finally the individual engages in silent or vocal prayer to God, confessing his sins, redempting, and promising to follow the Peyote Road . . . if he has spiritual evil within him, peyote makes him vomit, thus purging him of sin.

Heightened sensibility to others manifests itself as what might be called mental telepathy. One either feels that he knows what others are thinking, or feels that he either influences, or is influenced by, the thoughts of others. . . .

A third way in which peyote teaches is by means of mystical experience. This is relatively uncommon. It is limited to peyotists of a certain personality type among the more knowledgeable members of the church . . . they have . . . a mystical temperament. . . . The mystical experience may be said to consist in the harmony of all immediate experience with whatever the individual conceives to be the highest good. Peyote has the remarkable property of helping one to have a mystical experience for an indefinite period of time, as opposed to most forms of mystical discipline under which the mystical experience commonly lasts for a matter of minutes.[31]

The centering experience might come from shamanistic techniques[32] or from the preaching of someone like Billy Graham; or merely from the image or presence of a charismatic individual or holy man.

After some conversation and tea drinking I was led into the presence of Sri Ramana himself. He was a small, thin man of about 70 with close cropped white hair and a stubby beard and mustache, an extremely kindly and intelligent face and a deeply tanned body, clad in a loin cloth. He reclined on a massive stone couch propped up with pillows. An American alarm clock ticked on a shelf behind him and a calendar hung from one of the posts that propped a canopy over his couch. An electric door lamp stood beside his head, a brazier full of hot coals burned in front of him and there was a stand full of burning incense to keep the flies away. He was holding darshan. His couch was flanked by a couple of privileged disciples in the yellow robes of the Hindu priesthood, and sitting cross-legged on the floor about him were two or three dozen people, all gazing rapturously at the master. From time to time a particularly fervent disciple would prostrate himself on the floor before the couch, methodically touching forehead, right ear and left ear to the flagstones. Occasionally one of the faithful would come forward with an offering of a banana or an orange, which Sri Ramana accepted with a benign smile. . . . Sri Ramana would have looked like a superior human being in any surroundings. He had the quietly assured look of a man who has experienced a great deal and thought everything through to a final, unshakable conclusion. Even an unbeliever could see that he possessed a sort of personal serenity that is rare even in the contemplative Orient. I mumbled a few words of greeting which I hoped were appropriate and was smilingly waved to a place on the floor. The Maharshi spoke very little . . . but that didn't seem to matter. "You can attain peace merely by being near him," the professor of English literature explained later. The Maharshi was presented with an old book of Tamil scriptures from which he read odd passages aloud, commenting on them in a leisurely tone of voice while his listeners gazed raptly. Finally he stopped talking altogether and simply smiled an endless warmhearted smile. After an hour or so he rose from his couch and, supporting himself with a long cane, was led by a disciple back to his living quarters.[33]

Centering might be achieved by self-starvation and ordeals, as in the American Indian vision quest.[34] It might be in a trance induced by rhythmical motion (as in the Jamaican "pocomania" or among Turkish whirling dervishes). It might be in a hypnotic trance, as in Voodooism or Balinese ceremony. It might be in a showing of relics or churinga to the faithful. It might be in a ceremonial procession or pilgrimage. Nothing more dramatically illustrates centering than to see 300,000 pilgrims gathering to pray at the Great Mosque enshrining the Kaaba, marking the center of Islam, all bending to the ground at once toward this holy object. It might be in a riotous dance followed by sexual orgy, as in the Russian peasant Khlysty sect.[36] Or, on the other hand, centering might be achieved by the simple device of eating some hot yams together, as Firth describes a Tikopian ritual meal. The men sit in the clan temple, cross-legged, each (except for the Chief) holding a large green leaf cupped in his hands, talking in whispers because of the sacredness of the occasion. There is an air of "tense expectancy" while the yams are being removed from an oven of hot stones. Suddenly, the sound of bare feet is heard outside, and through the doorway

bursts a man bearing in his arms a basket full of the steaming hot yam tubers. Passing swiftly along in front of the line of men, he gives a yam to each. He does not hand it politely; but hurls it to the recipient, who must catch it in the leaf. Immediately each man receives his tuber he bends over it and makes a bite at it. His first effort is a mumble, for the yam is piping hot. But in a short time one of the company has succeeded in nipping off a piece of the vegetable and swallowing it, while his comrades are still struggling in keen competition with the heat. As soon as the man has gulped down his bit of yam he gives a little whistle. This is the signal for everyone to stop. . . . There is a general relaxation of tension. The whistler is identified. People chaff him and one another at their ludicrous attempts to bite off and swallow the burning morsels. . . . When the yams have cooled, an ordinary meal takes place.

The Tikopia, says Firth, interpret this ceremony as a demonstration of devotion to their Supreme Deity, protector of the yams, a culture-hero who instituted it long ago. They snatch at the hot morsels because the first to swallow is believed to gain divine favor for the next season. "Moreover, the god himself is thought to be present to watch the performance. He descends to inhabit for a brief space the body of his representative the chief. It is his eyes which look out from the chief's countenance and observe the conduct of his people on the occasion." They believe the god is incarnate in the yam," at the sacramental moment it is the flesh of the god which is swallowed."[37]

All of these are ways in which a person enters cult experience, shares in its communion. From the variety of examples, it is plain that there is no single valid way to contact the cult value—but a variety of symbolic forms, all of which are capable of deeply changing and uplifting the individual.

CONVERSION

Conversion occurs, then, when a new member enters the "it" circle, shares in the communion, or feels the influence of the cultic value sufficiently to be changed by it. We distinguish here between adhesion—acceptance of membership in a religious group without taking a new way of life, keeping the old center—and conversion:

> By conversion we mean the reorientation of the soul of an individual, his deliberate turning from indifference or from an earlier piety to another, a turning which implies a consciousness that a great change is involved that the old was wrong and the new is right.[37]

Social psychologists believe that conversion occurs in the context of change in the groups with which one associates—disturbance in interpersonal relations, alienation from previous groups, finding new significant others who will support a new identity.[38] But I do not think it is justifiable at this point to conclude that a certain process of group interaction is necessary for conversion. Judging from accounts of those who have gone through such experiences, one can have it in the midst of a group exerting pressure (a Salvation Army setting); under the personal influence of a single teacher (guru); under the symbolic influence of a hero with whom one has not associated; even on one's own in a philosophical quest (as Nietzsche or St. Augustine); possibly even by chemosalvation (LSD). There must be some way for a receptive individual to experience the "it" value with sufficient impact, there being many possible symbols and forms of communication. Asked how they get their deepest religious experiences, people give a variety of answers:

I find my most religious feeling—when I feel closest to God—in individual meditation.

When I'm in church I usually feel quite near to God. Very often this happens at some time other than the Sunday Mass.

I feel most religious when I'm inside a church, usually before the service begins. This is the time when silent meditation seems to mean the most to me.

It makes me feel very holy when I read the Bible. I actually get the shivers sometimes and I wish I could have lived back in the time of Christ.

When reading the Bible or religious books such as *How to Believe* by Sockman, or *Power of Positive Thinking* by Peale, or *The Greatest Story Ever Told* by Oursler.

I experience a very religious feeling while saying my prayers at night in complete darkness and quiet.[39]

The common feeling of all converts is joy in sharing "it" and a sense of turning point and renewal. It is not a matter of doctrinal content, culture, or specific group setting—so far as one can judge. It seems plain that what Billy Graham does for one, Buddhism or LSD can do for another. In any convert there is an unmistakable emotional experience, a grateful realization of a new point of view, joy at finally seeing the truth, arriving "home."

Right there I made my decision for Christ. It was as simple as that—and as conclusive. Have you ever been outdoors on a dark day when the sun suddenly bursts through the clouds? Deep inside, that's how I felt. The next day everything—even the flowers and the leaves on the trees— looked different. I was finding out for the first time the sweetness and joy of God, of being truly born again.[40]

One night by mere accident I tuned my radio in on a broadcast by the Self Realization Fellowship. It was not convincing to me, but it did serve to arouse my interest. I attended a few meetings of the Yoga church. But they antagonized me. I was still interested, however, and then came the opportunity—the great moment—which instantly changed my life: I came face to face with The Master himself. When he looked into my eyes all my antagonism, all my doubts fell away and vanished. I realized that Paramhansa represented what I had long craved, what I had long sought—ultimate truth. I became a convert and his follower. I gave up my $500 a month job and came to the Golden World Colony to make my future home. I have found peace.[41]

(Question: What were the incidents leading up to your becoming a Jehovah's Witness?) Well, I had really been looking for the right faith, I went to almost every church I could find, they all talked and talked but something was always missing. I had just about given up hope until one day when a woman came to my door with a *Watchtower* magazine. (What was so special about the magazine, Mrs. K.?) Oh, it just had the truth! I can't really explain it but I felt it right away. All of a sudden it was there, I knew I had found what I was looking for. (Did you start taking Bible studies then?) No, I just waited every week for the magazine and I just shove my hand out the door and take the magazine and read it right away. I just couldn't wait for the next edition. It was all there, I just felt it, finally. I knew it was the truth. (How did you know it was the truth?) In my heart, not my head; but you have to be in the right spirit for God to talk to you.[42]

She says that since her conversion she has been really happy for the first time in her life. She now has direction and meaning for her existence. By following God's laws she can raise her children properly, have a good marriage, know exactly how to live every moment of her life—the methods are written in scripture. . . . Outwardly, she is a paragon of virtue or tries very hard to be. A model mother, wife and friend, she is always on hand to help. Of course, she is only trying to practice the teachings of Christ, but she is truly sincere and seems very contented and placid.[43]

Of twenty-two converts of the Free Methodist Church interviewed, nineteen said they were converted at a church service, usually of the evangelistic or revivalist type; three were converted at home. Seventeen mentioned joy as the emotion resulting from conversion; other common emotions were calmness, peace, and relief from sin. It seems to be the generic ability of all cult to offer such centering experiences and reorient the lives of their members. The convert, having entered the cultic circle and had such an experience, is convinced and returns for more. Elated by his discovery, he proselytizes, spreads the word, "This is IT!"[44]

RITUALS AND CULT

A cult forms when a new centering experience is found that allows people to organize rituals so that it can be repeated. Cults can form around various intense forms of experience—contact with a charismatic personality, inspired preaching, word of miracles (such as at Lourdes), impressive prophecy—so long as people are convinced that it offers the "it" experience and are willing to orient their lives toward it and the rituals necessary to repeat the message. Barnett describes how the Shaker cult grew up among the Indians of the Northwest from a hysterical trance, with "shaking," which gave a leader supposedly supernatural powers of healing and knowledge.[45] This is not greatly different from the origin of a cult among Christians in Chicago, from a psychological experience known as the "cracking of the jaw" which became a ritual for the group. These people were holding a "Jerusalem party" seeking an experience which they called "The Baptism of the Holy Spirit." One of the ladies attending, who was ignorant of religious methods, prayed for religious inspiration. She

> held out her hand and said, "Now, Lord, you know how ignorant I am, and you know how much I want this experience, and now I hold out my hand to receive it. Please give it to me." Immediately she felt a thrill of delight pass through her . . . as of a delightful electric shock all over her body. . . . She then said, "Now, Lord, I mean to go by Thy Guidance, and as I am so ignorant, please give me a tangible sign by which I shall always know what Thy will is." Immediately the Lord gave what she

believed to be the sign, which was that her lower jaw was cracked up against her upper jaw with a loud crack. . . . She understood . . . it . . . as the affirmative expression of the Lord's will.

She returned home and that night, at family prayers, she asked the Lord to show her where to read. As she ran her finger over the books of the Bible suddenly her jaw cracked; then as she ran her finger over the verses it cracked again.

She began to regulate her whole life by the cracking of her jaw. Very soon other people were attracted by this remarkable phenomenon, and began to come to her for guidance . . . a little community gathered around her, who all brought everything in their lives to be tested by the cracking of her jaw. They engaged or dismissed servants, arranged their households, transacted their business . . . entered into new businesses, formed friendships . . . dressed—did everything in fact by the guidance of this sign.

But, as the cracking of her jaw was very loud and annoyed her husband, this lady prayed considerately for another sign, which then came as a "drawing in" of her eyes as though pulled by a string from within.

The community in Chicago gradually increased. One after another was drawn into it, and they established a place of meeting a little out of Chicago, in a suburb, and met there on Sunday, when, among other things, the sign told them they were to use oranges for their communion service.

After this the lady began, by her sign, writing a new Bible with one of her party as scribe. After a series of bodily jerks, she would dictate in a slow, unnatural voice. None of her prophecies came true, but for several years her followers remained faithful. Then the group carried on with a new leader.[46]

This illustrates only one of the many kinds of peculiar experience which can acquire cultic value and form a group of devotees. It shows the development of a unique ritual, which made this cult possible. There is no way of telling which of such experiences have valid religious authority; but it is plain that a wide variety of thrills, emotions, and leaders can provide such authority. A crucial question is whether the group can organize to do something together—a ritual—by which to share the peculiar experience of the leader.

Once it solves this problem of ritualization, it can function as a cult, providing its members with a centering experience, in which they feel more involved with one another, more in contact with an emotional "reality" transcending ordinary life, and so—whether in hope or reality—transcending their old selves. This initial success, institutionalizing ritual that will reliably provide a centering experience, might be called "stabilizing the kick," to use an idiom that might be applied to a ritual such as passing the "joint" among marijuana smokers.

We can see, then, two basic patterns of cult. One is simply a circle of devotees, sharing a cultic experience by some ritual form such as breaking bread, passing a pipe, dancing with each other. The second is a more developed form, in which a priest administers a ritual to devotees, with a more or less complex, ultimately bureaucratic, machinery, along a line of development which has been explained by Max Weber.

Some groups, of which beatniks are an example, develop a primitive cultic style in pursuit of kicks ("Somewhere along the line I knew there'd be girls, visions, everything; somewhere along the line the pearl would be handed to me",[47] but fail to give their members the full measure of cultic experience because they do not sufficiently center and stabilize the kick. So Lawrence Lipton tries to develop the picture of beatniks as "holy barbarians." But another student of beatniks, Elwin H. Powell, shows the beat movement as an aimless one which, in its pursuit of kicks, is unable to center on a highest value. "The beatnik has failed to discover a belief system—a hierarchy of values—which would enable him to differentiate the trivial from the significant. . . . All things are equally sacred, equally profane."[48] So, beatniks have developed a cultic orientation and style, but have failed to develop true cult.

MAKING THE NEW MAN: ROLE OF THE DEVOTEE

A true cult not only gives its devotees the experience of "it" and centers their lives by performance of ritual, but perfects a role by which the cultic life can be more fully lived—perhaps requiring a break with ordinary life—and one's character perfected by days, weeks, years, a life organized in a schedule of cultic activities. This is the role of the devotee. To become a member of a cult, one must not only share the centering experience but assume the role of devotee.

The role of devotee is the efficient method which the cult has discovered for transforming the identities of its members—a more or less organized path of training and role models leading to perfection of the new life. Learning this role is like apprenticeship in a craft. The conversion experience brings a person within the "it" circle, but he still has a long way to go before he perfects himself as a new man.

Weber[49] distinguishes three main directions of the cultic path. First is the way of ritual devotion or worship, illustrated by the statement of this Catholic girl convert:

> I can hardly wait to go to church in the mornings and I visit almost daily in the evening to say my prayers. It's frightening to me to think of what I would be without Him but you know . . . God makes the weak strong and I feel strong—I am strong united with my God.

The second way is building up merit or karma by good works, as Jehovah's Witnesses try to earn salvation before Armageddon by preaching:

> Accept the help of Jehovah's Witnesses to speed your getting out of this doomed modern Sodom. . . . The safe course is clearly marked out before you. You are not alone, with no place to go. . . . God has built up his New World society on earth. . . . Regularly they study his Word, the Bible, and faithfully endeavor to live by it. You are welcome to study it with them. . . . Dedicate your life . . . and symbolize your dedication as Jesus did, by immersion in water. Then prove your dedication by undertaking His service . . . preaching "this good news of the kingdom" and declaring the "day of vengeance of our God." . . . Then YOU MAY SURVIVE ARMAGEDDON INTO GOD'S NEW WORLD.[50]

The third kind of cultic path is that of inward self-perfection or realization, illustrated by Bahais:

> Baha-u-llah constantly urges men to realize and give full expression to the perfections latent within them—the true inner self. . . . When a man becomes a Baha'i, God's Will becomes his will . . in the Path of God no errors can appall, no troubles dismay him. . . . Life is lifted to the heroic plain. . . . The real Baha'i will . . . love everyone . . . treat every man as

the gardener tends a rare and beautiful plant. . . . Severance from everything that is not of God, severance, that is, from all selfish and worldly . . . desires. . . . The practice of confession to priests and others is strictly forbidden . . . the sinner . . . must seek forgiveness from God alone.[51]

Whatever path he may take, the devotee's role is marked off from the life of the ordinary person by its sense of one-pointed centering, being twice-born, being set apart, and dedicated to the cultic path—whether as a regular core member who knows the creed and ritual by heart or the devoted disciple or amanuensis learning directly from a guru or perhaps the special role of the "lamp-trimmer-and-filler" who keeps the light burning, the flowers fresh, and performs other duties of the acolyte. It leads perhaps finally to the even more specialized role of priest, monk, or guru.

We are concerned here especially with those features of the devotee's role which specifically have to do with remaking the man. They include: (1) the cultic formula, (2) cultic instruction, (3) the service or liturgy, (4) cultic fellowship, (5) initiations, (6) witnessing and evangelism, and (7) the monastic path.

THE CULTIC FORMULA

Cults find it effective to get a convert started right away with a simple formula, which if he follows will advance him on the path. Perhaps it is a creed, catechism, koan, oath, affirmation, mantra, yoga technique, or votive prayer; it is to be repeated or recited daily or more often. Repetition is regarded as the key to success. Converts of the Self Realization Fellowship, for example, attest to the results of practicing a yogic method:

> I love to practice the concentration technique. I am supremely happy for the first time in my life. The SRF teaching is the saviour of the world—through the practice of SRF meditation techniques I am attaining a consciousness of inner peace never before known—I thoroughly study the *Praecepta,* and each day and each hour I endeavor to realize in life the wonderful lessons of Master Yogananda—the concentration technique is wonderful. I am getting fine results.

A convert to Buddhism might adopt a formula such as the following, recited by the monks of Southeast Asia: "I go to the Buddha as my refuge, I go to the doctrine (dharma) as my refuge, I go to the order (sangha) as my refuge. . . ." Other converts to Buddhism find the practice of "mindfulness" a formula for salvation:

> He ate, drank and slept Buddhism, until he eventually found he was actually practicing it, and what was more—it worked! So he became more methodical in his approach to the Dharma . . . he started examining his motives for doing things, to be mindful during his waking moments to his relationship with other people and his attitude to things, and he soon came to realize, in his own experience in everyday life, that here was a teaching that was true. In other words, he did not have to *believe* anything. All he was being asked to do was first, intellectually comprehend, then to practice . . . and see if it worked. . . . It did. . . . With his deepening understanding came correspondingly deeper experience. . . . The Dharma had become his life and life the Dharma.[52]

Those who apply to the Black Muslims for membership receive a letter saying:

> Enclosed is one of our small Muslim Daily Prayer Books. Learn the prayers by heart and pray five times daily facing the East. When you are free, you will be able to attend the Temple of Islam and be qualified as a Believer.[53]

The cultic formula may well be a ritual of penance or purification to wash a person clean of contamination, especially if it is one of what Marcus Bach calls the "conscience cults" (such as the Penitentes of New Mexico, Buchmanites or Moral Rearmament, or the Father Divine Movement) which so emphasize sin. The early success of the Buchmanites came from "house parties" in which each guest was given a chance to examine himself and seek out someone to whom to confess his sins, or to "come clean" before the entire group, thus to become a "washed clean soul." MRA also uses the formula of apology as an expression of Christian humility, producing such startling results as an Afrikaner Supreme Court Judge making headlines by apologizing to the Bantu for haughtiness. Father Divine's "secret weapon" was a formula of restitution by which a person could make good everything he had done that was wrong, after first taking pencil and paper and jotting down all his remembered misdeeds. Converts said, "If you want a clear conscience and a heart full of peace, seek Father."

Twenty years ago I stole a hundred dollars from the lady I worked for. She had died. I told Father. He said I had to give the hundred dollars away just the same. . . . I said I would give it to him. He refused. I looked around where to send it and thought there wasn't anybody who had done more for me than my country. So I sent the hundred dollars to the Treasurer of the United States. . . .[54]

Such formulas, unlike yoga or koan exercises which aim only at enlightenment, wash away sin as an obstacle in the devotee's path.

CULTIC INSTRUCTION

A convert cannot be self-sufficient, whatever the principle by which he has started or however sedulously he practices. Regular instruction in cultic values and ritual follows up the formula which began his life of devotion. Jehovah's Witnesses, for example, gather for weekly drill by question and answer on all aspects of their catechism and scriptures. A typical convert might study for over two years before being baptized. Since all are expected to be preachers, each must be fully prepared, including knowing a large part of the Bible by memory. Sunday school is not just for children. The Self Realization Fellowship puts its members through a correspondence course lasting over a year before they are fit to be initiated into the higher level of practice of kriya yoga. Catholicism, likewise, requires extensive instruction of laymen, though Protestantism varies greatly in the amount of instruction it requires, tending to regard the layman as more or less on his own in studying the Bible, even, as in the case of the Quakers, having so little explicit doctrine that there is nothing in the way of belief to teach. Yet most churches hold that lifelong learning, whether at the feet of a guru or at the foot of the pulpit, is necessary. Even Buddhism, which stresses that one must find out for himself and believes that the essence of Gautama's doctrine is contained in his silently holding up a lotus, has an enormous literature which must be learned before one gets far in the order.

All of this leads to a basic distinction between identity change by advancement in a hierarchy and identity change by participation in cultic life. Whereas instruction may get a person far in a hierarchy, there are definite limits to how much is needed for cultic "new life." Such limits are set by the fact that mystique cannot be really approached by intellectualizing. It is a commonplace of religion that theology and doctrine are useless without faith, that a child or peasant can be as close to heaven as an archbishop. Higher learning of intellectual doctrine has more to do with prestige and advancement in the status hierarchy than participation in cultic life, for which all that is functionally necessary is to share its mystique. So the only instruction that really matters for one who wants new life is that which helps success with cultic ritual.

THE SERVICE OR LITURGY

The heart of the cult is that symbolism which makes the highest value available to all members and keeps them centered as devotees. Instead of drawing examples from the better known religions, I shall describe a typical service of a smaller cult, the Self Realization Fellowship, to show how its liturgy focuses on change of identity. This church, a combination of Christianity and Hinduism, teaches "realization of the self" instead of salvation of the soul, as does Christianity. If one attends one of its services—perhaps in Hollywood, Encinitas, or San Diego, California—one comes into a dimly lit sanctuary with an ornate altar, displaying pictures of Christ, Buddha, Paramhansa Yogananda (their guru), and various other Hindu saints. People are sitting in absolute silence; no sound can be heard except an occasional rustle in a chair. After this meditation period, which might last from fifteen minutes to an hour, a monk appears. He is an American draped in a white robe, with the name "Brother————." The monk addresses a prayer to all the saints, including Jesus and Buddha; then he chants, playing on a small organ, with all following: "No birth, no death, no caste have I. Father, mother, have I none. I am He. I am He. . . ." (A chant by the Hindu sage Shankara.) Then he preaches on themes stressing tranquility, peace, health, diet, self-control, living sensibly, and practicing yoga meditation to find God.

The change of identity sought is best brought out by giving the argument of one of the sermons, which followed reading from Hindu and Christian scriptures, which included a parable about a lion cub who had been abandoned and raised among sheep, so that he thought he was a sheep. One day another lion attacked the flock and was first astonished, then indignant, to see a lion fleeing with the sheep in abject terror. He caught up with the lion, shook him roughly, rebuked him, and took him to a pool where he could see his head reflected in the water: "Thou art a lion, not a sheep. Open thine eyes and roar." This parable was then applied to the congregation: that everyone has a true identity which he does not realize unless he is awakened. The sermon taught that one's true identity is neither the physical body nor the mind with its thoughts and feelings nor the ego (which is only an image and activity of the mind), but an eternal and unchanging Self (atman) which is divine. This Self is, like the lion, the real king: *you are* the king. Wake up and realize who you are. The other things that you have mistakenly thought of as governing you are only the servants of the true self. "The whole purpose of religion is to re-identify ourselves. We are not the servants but the king." When these distractions—of mind, ego, physical sensations, and troubles—appear, "say, I am not that!" Then the monk offered the congregation the formula for realizing his message, a technique of yoga meditation which, practiced daily, would change one's life.

Group meditation then began, with the monk's remark that ten are stronger than one, with perhaps a healing period during meditation, in which one member after another came up front to bow to the saints and pray kneeling. Then the group stood and under the direction of the master all rubbed their palms together rapidly to feel the life force; then raised their palms outwardly to let this force flow to the rest of the world, while chanting "Om. Om. Om." A hymn and blessing terminated the service.

The result of all this is an unmistakable feeling of calm, peace, and a certain exaltation, which even an outsider who does not share the doctrine feels from the sheer effect of the group mood. Such calm and exaltation seem a promise to the newcomer of what might be achieved if the meditation practice were continued and perfected. The promise of the cult is that use of the formula (including yogic *asanas* and an esoteric meditation technique to be taught to worthy disciples after instruction) will result finally in ecstatic bliss *(samadhi)* with awareness at the same time of one's true self *(atman)* and union with God *(Brahman)*.

It may be noted how well adapted this teaching is to a person with *anomie* (lack of satisfactory relationship and support from others). It offers: (1) peace, happiness *within*—not in a society which disappoints you; (2) progress depending on *no one but your-self* (though the technique must be learned from them); (3) the world and its ambitions and frustrations and troubles are illusion *(maya)*; (4) the appeal to a person who is self-centered (as so many lonely ones are), that he can achieve "self-perfection" without necessarily relating himself to others in close fellowship. In this sense, the Self Realization Fellowship has what might be called an introverted appeal (Freudians might call it narcissistic).

THE CULTIC FELLOWSHIP

More commonly a cult offers not only an identity-redefining message but intense moral support and interaction within a fellowship in which all urge each other on the same path, as in the love feasts of Father Divine's followers, calling each other brothers and sisters and basking in the sense of overflowing love and magnetism of the "Father." A member of such a fellowship feels a tremendous sense of support. Says a Jehovah's Witness: "Somehow the brothers always seem to know when I need something. In Jehovah's Witnesses, we believe no one will ever go hungry—and no one ever does." But more important than support, perhaps, is the effect of total acceptance and perfect equality in fellowship, expressed in the Bahai ideal:

> The members . . . must be wholly free from estrangement and must manifest in themselves the Unity of God, for they are the waves of one sea, the drops of one river, the stars of one heaven, the rays of one sun, the trees of one orchard, the flowers of one garden.[55]

The members of such a fellowship draw together, associate more frequently with members than with outsiders—perhaps even their own families; they regard each other as brothers and sisters, use first names, and thus reenforce by close primary group interaction whatever is being achieved by ritual.

INITIATION OR BAPTISM

The crucial point of identity change is the rite of passage—initiation or baptism—in which the new member enters into full devotee status. Every sacred cult has some such ceremony. Often a new name is taken to emphasize the importance of the transition in identity. So, after completing his lessons and tests, the new Black Muslim drops his last name and middle initials ("slave names") and takes a new one, which may simply obliterate his old identity ("Charlie X.") or signify an African or Asiatic identity ("Brother Karriem Allah").[56]

WITNESSING

After initiation, the new member is expected to "witness" in some way—that is, proclaim his new identity, "stand up to be counted," and take part responsibly and visibly in the work of the movement. Witnessing is likely to be by public testimony and preaching the message or by service to the cult or the guru in a role such as that of acolyte. The Mormons require their youth to do missionary work for a period during their education. The Jehovah's Witnesses expect all able-bodied members to witness by preaching from door to door at least once a month. A lady Witness is 63 years old, but still feels the obligation to witness:

> I have a hard time getting around. So I usually go out once a month to preach the word. Most people are very insulting and they just won't listen.

Witnessing often involves a test or ordeal by which a person proves his commitment to his new identity. Witnessing also takes the form of devotional acts, contributions, perhaps an arduous mission or pilgrimage which marks the high point of the life of the devotee—as in the pilgrimage to Mecca which every good Moslem should make before he dies.

MONASTIC PATH

A basic choice which every sacred cult must make is whether to distinguish between those who wish to travel the cultic path with all speed, directly, and those who wish to combine it reasonably with the role of the householder and with the activities of ordinary life. The monastic role is the answer which so many religions have found to this question: as an optional path for those who wish to devote themselves wholly to cult activity, take the quick and necessarily steep ascent, leaving an easier and longer climb—possibly, as in the case of Hinduism, requiring more than one lifetime—for others. The monastic role, because it implies total centering and commitment, requires more strenuous witnessing—if not asceticism, at least renunciation of old habits and friends—and dramatic change of identity. The monastic breaks with the social obligations and values of his old life and undergoes depersonalization—drastic measures to wipe away his old identity.[57] We are all familiar with the systematic depersonalization undergone by a monastic in Catholicism: the arduous training in obedience and self-denial during the novitiate; the breaking of friendships and attachment to possessions (a novice nun commented, "Everything is designed to force you to live within yourself and not in others"); taking a new name; the final vows which end all connection with the old life (perhaps holding a candle as a symbol of intention to burn out one's life in the service of God). "I'm afraid," said one novice about to take her final vow, "it's such a big thing; like I'm going to the gas chamber tomorrow—dying tomorrow"—to which her Mother Superior answered, "No, no, dear, to be reborn."[58] Or, take the case of a young American, age twenty-one, from Brooklyn, who became a Buddhist monk in Ceylon: he was renamed Jinaloka (Light of Buddha); his head was carefully shaved; he received as his total possessions a begging bowl, three long yellow robes, a needle and some thread; his life then consisted of prayer and study within the Buddhist center in Ceylon, or begging from dawn till dark to obtain food to fill the bowls of his brethren. Likewise, the Self Realization Fellowship offers to those more serious students who wish to take the steep route, retreats and colonies where they may discard their street clothing, put on the vestments of a monk or nun, take on a Hindu name and title, and live a life of meditation, preaching, and voluntary service, renouncing normal roles within the community for the all-important goal of self-realization.

In these seven features—the cultic formula, instruction, ritual, fellowship, initiation, witnessing, and monastic path—we see some of the most important kinds of service a cult is able to offer to those who wish to dramatically change their identities and center themselves. We see the cult as the kind of a group which tries to change identity by such means, with the prime goal of ritual attainment of mystique. We see how the cult is able to overcome banality, giving its members a sense of significance and participation in something special they cannot usually get in the larger society. This has little to do, inherently, with economic well-being. The gain is in mystical identity not measurable in terms of the secular structure. So, as Wilson points out, the sect value cannot be looked on as a mere compensation for economic status deprivation. Christian Science, for example, is one of the wealthiest sects; its redemption has more to do with a self image of "perfection," especially for those who have physical handicaps. And even in sects like the Elim, a Pentecostal sect which recruits from the down-and-outers, the compensations are such things as the ability to get up, "speak in tongues," and be recognized for it, giving a feeling of significance to people who formerly had no claim to attention, now gratified by discovery of such mystical powers in themselves.[59]

THE PSYCHEDELIC MOVEMENT   *see cult. 147*

Such functions, of changing identity and adding mystique to the banality of life, are seen in the psychedelic movement, which swept into America, England, and Europe during the 1950s–1960s. Like an ironic fulfilment of Aldous Huxley's notion of a drug used by an entire society to make people happy (soma), a number of drugs were publicized (peyote, mescaline, psilocybin from sacred mushrooms, LSD–25) which had not only happiness-bringing but mind-transcending and sacramental properties. Huxley himself helped start the movement with his *Doors of Perception* (1954). Those like the Theosophists, yoga followers, and Zen Buddhists, who were already following mystical paths, were naturally much interested in medicines which promised to bring in the reward (samadhi, satori, nirvana, enlightenment) without the customary years of patient meditation, study, and work—which, after all, only a Puritan could want for its own sake. By the 1960s a substantial literature began to appear on the therapeutic and other values and side effects of the new drugs.[60] The American public became alarmed at the way psychedelic drug use was spreading among certain elements of the population—such as beatniks and college students. News articles and editorials appeared with captions like, LSD CAPTURING BEST YOUNG MINDS IN U.S. The student newspaper at San Francisco State College carried advertisements like the following:

THE PSYCHEDELIC CHAPEL presents: "Trip Through The Astral Plane" Featuring Recording Artist Ivan Ulz. Service Begins 8:30 p.m. Saturday, December 4, 110 Page Street. (Where the Jet Set Meets the Sin Crowd.)[61]

Many scholars would agree, I am sure, with Nevitt Sanford that by 1964:

We have in LSD use what amounts to a social movement. Those who accept the drug . . . have an ideology, one that accents the values of the inner life, of personal freedom, of mystical experience, and of love. . . . This ideology can be largely understood as a reaction against or, better, a withdrawal from major trends in contemporary society. More and more people "want out," and this includes . . . people who have been successful in the society and have received the rewards it promised them.[62]

This movement is of particular interest to us because it illustrates in the clearest possible way the essential features of cult: as a centering experience, as a withdrawal from a banal social order, and as an alternative to practical action. It is especially interesting because it is not a movement of down-and-outers, but of middle-class, educated, and "successful" people. So it shows the inadequacy of the merely material rewards of a prosperous society to realize people's needs.

This sect, like so many now reputable ones, experienced public opposition from the start. The analogy is marked between the misunderstandings and persecutions suffered by early Christianity, Islam, Lutheranism, Quakerism, Mormonism, and so on, and this new "religion"—except that the intolerance came from narcotic legislation and fear of drug addiction rather than religious prejudice. It was inevitable that when one of the pioneer experimenters, Dr. Timothy Leary, was arrested for illegal possession of marijuana in 1965, fined $30,000, and sentenced to 30 years (suspended), he should be hailed as a "prophet" and "martyr" as he carried on in spite of these "persecutions" to found the League for Spiritual Discovery (LSD). It was his evangelical mission to spread use of psychedelic drugs,[63] and he was willing to test by his own person in courts the constitutional right of people to use them for sacramental purposes in "shrines" in their own homes, under the principle of religious liberty.

Leary's apostolate actually began at Harvard University in 1960 when he and his associates, Dr. Ralph Metzner and Dr. Richard Alpert, did psychological experiments on volunteers with a variety of psychedelics—including morning glory seeds, nutmeg, marijuana, peyote, mescaline, psilocybin, and LSD. School officials soon became aware that more was going on than was usual in scientific laboratories; after some embarrassment—perhaps even feeling themselves in the role of pharisees—they "regretfully" dismissed Leary and Alpert in 1963.

Undaunted, Leary and Alpert formed a private research organization called International Foundation for International Freedom (IFIF); and, with some followers, made a hegira to found a study center which was to all effects a cultic colony in Zihuatanejo, a Mexican fishing village. This outpost drew all sorts of persons seeking spiritual fulfilment; they were swamped with over 5,000 applicants.[64] One of the most interesting institutions of this colony was a shrine-like tower, ten feet high, on the ocean beach in front of the hotel, which was known as the "soul" of the group. The practice was to keep one person in it, at all times, under the influence of LSD, a trance which might last from eight to twenty-four hours. While in the tower he had special status, rather like that of an American Indian on a vision quest: there was "high awareness of his presence"; his name was passed around and there were frequent inquiries as to his progress. To enter the tower was a much-sought-after privilege. It was a "dedicated ceremony," which the community watched with rather the same interest as one would watch the vows of a new nun or priest.[65]

A certain charismatic prestige attached to those who had successful experiences in the tower. The cult-like character of the movement was now quite plain to anyone who had doubted it while it was under the "experimental" auspices of Harvard. People became converts as they underwent LSD experience and began to proselytize; leaders with experience of many trips got the status of gurus. Mexican opinion, however, became increasingly unfavorable, and soon authorities interfered and demanded that they leave the country. Once again, the hegira resumed.

Help came to the movement at this point from a wealthy convert who turned over to Leary his 4000-acre estate in Millbrook, New York. This became not only an ashram for the prophet but a shrine and sanctuary for pilgrims from all over the world. However, peace did not last long; it was interrupted by a raid from the Dutchess County police who arrested four people, including Leary, for possession of marijuana.

Such "persecutions" did not deter Leary but seemed to confirm him in his role of "Prophet of LSD." He appeared in two widely publicized Senate Subcommittee Hearings in 1966 to urge the merits of psychedelic drugs and the religious right to use them under the Constitution. By then, Leary had fully adopted the role of a Hindu guru. He recited Hindu prayers with disciples in his Millbrook ashram; he gave sermons on lovingness and insights which come from "getting high."

> LSD is Western yoga. The aim of all Eastern religion, like the aim of LSD, is basically to get high: that is, to expand your consciousness and find ecstasy and revelation within.[66]

He commended the dropouts from society who, having heard the message of LSD, followed its call to "forsake all and follow."

> There *is* an LSD dropout problem, but it's nothing to worry about. It's something to cheer. The lesson I have . . . been passing on to others can be stated in six syllables: Turn on, tune in, drop out. . . . Drop out means to detach yourself from the tribal game. . . . American society is becoming an air-conditioned anthill.[67]

The results of this escapist rebellion, according to Leary, would not be passivity and shirking life but increased creativity and aliveness—new life. "I have not one shred of guilt about anything I have done in the last six years. . . . I'm the freest man in America."[68]

It is not necessary to belabor the psychedelic drug as the "communion wafer" or "spiritual cake" of this cult—its centering value.[69] Converts testified that it was a source of spiritual effects (ecstasy, euphoria, lovingness, insight) and viewed a trip as the doorway into a new life. Many serious students of religion concluded that among the effects of LSD were many which had a religious quality. Alan Watts reported:

> I was surprised and indeed embarrassed to find out, after two tries, that LSD would, in fact, produce for me a very, very powerful experience of cosmic consciousness. I thought . . . here's this thing that people have

been striving for for centuries—with yoga and *za-zen* . . . and after all it appears to be reasonably simple.[70]

Huston Smith performed an experiment in which 46 out of 69 judges were unable to tell the following account of a drug-induced from a "genuine" religious experience:

Suddenly I burst into a vast, new, indescribably wonderful universe . . . the thrill of the surprise and amazement, the awesomeness of the revelation, the engulfment in an overwhelming feeling-wave of gratitude and blessed wonderment, are as fresh . . . as if it had happened five minutes ago. . . . The sense of ultimate reality . . . knowledge . . . came instantaneously and with such force . . . that it was impossible . . . to doubt its validity.[71]

Controlled scientific studies showed that those who sought LSD experience felt more dissatisfaction with themselves and their lives than those who rejected it, and that users emphasized among its results "self-change" and "goal reduction."[72] Religious testimonies continued to pile up:

God is no longer only "out there" somewhere, but He is within you, and you are one with Him. No doubt of it even crosses one's awareness at this stage. . . . You not only see Truth, but you *are* truth. . . . Utilizing this inner Self . . . you realize fully that nothing can ever hurt you or bother you, not even death. It gives life a completely new meaning, and one which is indestructible . . . you no longer find yourself an outsider, separated from Nature and separated from God, and separated from your fellow beings.

I was blind before; all the things I did were only a desperate search for meaning to my life and trying to discover myself. I regret past errors, cruelties, lies, faithlessness, etc. But I have lived with self-loathing and guilt always and find it accomplishes nothing. I find I can forgive myself and not spend time weeping over spilt milk. What was done was done. I did them. I is over—I am reborn. I have punished myself enough. It is time to live—and do better in the light of what I have learned. . . . *I am God*. I am utterly shaken . . . the enormity is too much; sudden blazing joy, realization, humility, power. . . . Can I accept this? This, the Ultimate Reality. . . . I have a slight doubt as to my sanity—don't they lock you up for going around saying you are God? . . . Man is divine. Yes, of course. . . . I am God, the universe, Christ, all men, all everything—all exists within me. The Self is limitless, endless, eternal— it is all knowing, all aware, and at bottom good.[73]

Proper rituals were prescribed for administration of a trip, together with doctrine explaining its experiences.[74] Devices such as mandala (mystic designs) and drone sounds were used to help concentration. Once a person had been converted and reborn, he went on trips from time to time to renew his insight and further his development as a devotee. Veteran users, such as Leary, claimed to have had hundreds. Occasionally, a Trips Festival would be given, lasting perhaps three days and drawing as many as 10,000 people. Homes and other private locations were used for group ceremonies. Though members drew toward each other and away from those who disapproved of psychedelic drugs, and though sometimes the movement was forced underground by police action, it was not a secret cult with exclusive privileges and esoteric doctrines. Efforts were made to enlist anyone who was interested;[75] indeed the public became quite familiar with the LSD experience, as reported in magazine articles.

Increasingly stringent legislation was passed in the latter part of the decade, yet there was no reason to suppose it could be legally suppressed. The strong interest of middle-class people and of university students in it suggested it would present an enforcement problem rather like that of Prohibition—except that the "bottles" were infinitely harder to find. Another factor was continued strong interest of respectable scholars and clergymen in it (Walter Stace, Huston Smith, Alan Watts). Some indication of what may yet be in prospect for the movement was given by experimental religious services with drug-induced mysticism: at the Andover-Newton Theological Seminary, Boston University, in a private chapel with divinity students as volunteers, under the supervision of a psychiatrist.[76]

In short, the LSD movement, though drawing "oddballs" and subject to legal restriction, has as much right to be called a genuine religious movement as most other religious sects that have appeared in history. There is no justification for treating it as just a criminal conspiracy of drug addicts (noting that there are no signs of cult or religious claims of prophecy, enlightenment, or benefit to the world among real addicts, such as heroin-users).

The psychedelic movement serves for us as a "pure" case to illustrate the basic features of the elemental cult-making process. It shows the identity and mystique-giving function of cult as a response to the *banality* of society. For people drawn to LSD are not status-deprived or economically underprivileged—but bored. It illustrates how a mystique-giving experience draws a circle of devotees and a charismatic priesthood who, then, to explain their mystique cast about for ideology (drawing ideas from Hinduism, Buddhism, as well as modern psychology). The mystique itself, however, remains unintelligible to squares, who feel in its strangeness a threat to established values—which, indeed, it is. Their "misunderstanding" versus the zeal of cultists to evangelize produces conflict which turns the cult into a sect, more or less at war with conventional society.

The "war," however, is not a rebellion but a turning away from the values and a dropping out of the games of the Establishment. Its only real threat is dropping out itself as a loss of support and denial of obligation to "rational" values of the society—the possibility that large numbers of people might center their lives on cultic ritual and mystique. This is the eternal threat of sect to the social order.

The psychedelic movement also shows the difference between fad or fashion and cult as kinds of identity-defining movements. Cult represents a more profound turning away from established values than style rebellion (Chapter 3); and, in the role of the devotee, a more total commitment of the person than is possible in style imitation (faddism). It is in this sense a more successful identity-giving response.

Finally, the LSD movement seems to illustrate what is true of all cults: That it is impossible to appraise the validity of a mystique rationally, to translate it into common currency equally valid for members and nonmembers. Therefore, though it may be possible to judge effects of cult in conduct, regarding their mystique all cults deserve equal respect, those which seem sensible and those which seem weird. It is not for the outsider to judge the value of mystique.

CONCLUSIONS

We have looked at a variety of cultic and near-cultic movements—witchery, nudism, Druids, Masons, Shakers, Jehovah's Witnesses, Father Divine cult, Black Muslims, yoga, Self-Realization Fellowship, Buddhism, LSD. Movements become cultic to the extent that they (1) use costume (or no costume) to change identity, as in the case of witches, Druids, Masons, and some nudists—associations of whom are on the border of cult when they have a mystique about health, though ritual aside from "sun worship" may be lacking; (2) have a mystique (cultic value) not easily explainable in discursive language; (3) have ritual to attain: the mystique, centering of members on "it" as a *Summum Bonum,* or close fellowship approaching familism; and (4) use the role of the devotee to organize progress toward perfection (total integration) of cultic value in the life of the member—a perfect man (new man) in terms of ethics for living—and a path to enlightenment or salvation. We have noted various common devices cults employ to organize the role of the devotee: cultic formula, cultic instruction, the service, cultic fellowship, initiation or baptism, witnessing, and the monastic path. Because of such features I have treated cult in this chapter as the supreme form of identity-centered movement, a perfected way of making the new man. What cult supplies probably better than any other movement is centering, emotional richness, and mystique. But the variety of cultic movements suggests that not a particular kind of cultic content, not a particular mystique, but the stance of the devotee is what is important.

We have treated cult here as a type of movement that meets certain kinds of needs; that, in addition to factors favoring identity-seeking movements of all kinds, there are some which favor cultic activity especially. We accept the theory that strains give rise to various kinds of movements and outbursts.[77] For example, we consider the frustration ratio as part of revolutionary potential in Chapter 2. Among these strains which bring on identity-seeking movements (faddism, style rebellion, cultism, hero worship, crusading) are identity deprivation (anonymity, impersonality, mobility); status problems which make people marginal, "available," forcing them to seek compensatory status in other groups;[78] and the destruction of symbols, mentioned in Chapter 3 as leading to the danger of stylelessness. But certain types of strains seem especially to favor ritual and cultic responses. Stylelessness, for example, if felt as a lack of integrity, may force a person to seek centering by means more effective than faddism—such as cult. I see ritual and cult as specific answers to three kinds of strain: (1) emotional impoverishment, (2) banality, and (3) stylelessness. (I shall treat in Chapter 8 crusades, which also meet the need for centering.)

All of this may require us to look again at the formalism and banality of modern society, and the way it liberates people to search for cult. The modern city church, says Fichter, is like a filling station:

In the large urban parish . . . the great majority of lay persons seem to use the local church as a kind of "service station" for their religious needs: a place to go to Mass and Confession, get married, and have their children baptized and their old folks buried. Their communal "social" bond with the priest and other parishioners is analogous to that which an automobile owner has with the gas station manager and the latter's other customers. It is somewhat like the professional relationship between dentist and patients.[79]

So the smaller sects make fun of the established churches as dispensers of "ho-hum" religion. People also fail to react to patriotic ceremony. When English secondary school girls were polled on how they felt during the playing of the national anthem, the majority reported indifference.[80] If this is the way many people feel about the sacred ceremonies of their society, as well as about their work, it is no wonder that there is a cultic reaction in favor of things like LSD. Boredom is a liberating experience when it is a first step in the quest for something more significant. So the Taoist scripture notes that when ritual goes only skin-deep, it is a starting point for moral anarchy.[81] For, as old rituals lose their grip on a person, he is free to shop around, he becomes—if he has a spiritual need— "cult-prone."[82] Cult does not just remedy status problems; rather, it fills a void in spirituality. The cult provides more than fellowship and status; it supplies mystique. It supplies, as the Voodoo priest says, "the *gran mystère*" of sex in relation to everything from earth to eternity.[83] If fellowship and status were enough, then Voodoo could easily resemble a YMCA.

From the societal point of view, rather than that of the member or seeker, we see the function of cultic movements as helping maintain equilibrium, supplying or replenishing nonrational consensus by ritual, as explained in Chapter 4. The special contribution of cult is that it makes it possible for people to center more deeply on mystiques through the *role of the devotee* than they could just by work, discipline, or education, even when accompanied by ritual. No other institution does this job so well. Other institutions train and discipline their members and some have mystiques—but they lack a reliable way to get their members to share mystique. The reaction of the rationalist may be that we can do without devoutness and devotion. But the very cultic movements of modern society say that this is not so—that there is a failure of some kind in modern society and that new cults are an effort to repair the loss. If modern cultism seems centripetal and escapist, seems to steal loyalty from other institutions, it is because the center is lost and people are looking for a new one.

Let us compare cult with fad and other kinds of solutions. Fad seeks a solution through imitation, cult through the devotional role. The efforts of people to find style, meaning, and center may be likened to arrows shot at a target. Fads and style rebellion are arrows shot carelessly, most of them miss. Cults are arrows which hit the bull's-eye, supplying some people—if not the whole society—with a devotional center and an integrated style which is more than mere imitation. Fad means continual change of identity, cult is a resting place. Fad has a "fun" motivation, a lighthearted commitment; the cultist goes overboard, gets stuck in his decision. Yet there is this basic kinship between fad and cult: both are part of the search for style and integrity, both represent society in the making, and, though one is lighthearted and the other devout, I think it is safe to say that every faddist is a cultist at heart. Both are part of the societal search for nonrational consensus.

Such kinds of style search are not of the same stuff as political and economic measures. They do not seek to achieve material goals, but to fill a void in the spirit. They do not aim to work on the world, but to change the man. That they have little to do with political and economic measures is shown by the fact that cultic and style movements thrive in countries and among classes where political and economic problems have largely been solved. After you already make $12,000 a year, have two cars, and a new home, you may still have a cultic and a style problem. On the other hand, a person making $4,000 a year may have solved his cultic and style problem. So we see cultism and style rebellion, among the upper and middle as well as lower classes, as quitting the "game" of society, losing interest in economics and politics. Popular inspirational literature is largely apolitical,[84] reflecting, I think, not ignorance of political means but an awareness of their irrelevance. Likewise, the middle-class psychedelic movement seems anarchistic with its recommendation to drop out. So I pick up the theme of Chapter 2, "rebellion with no place to go," that style rebellion and cultic movements are efforts to find solutions to which political and economic measures—indeed, science too—are not even relevant answers—unless they take the form of fad, which makes them trivial, or that of cult, which makes them rather ominous.[85] For, after all the work, you are still left with questions: Do you have a meaningful life? Are you a better person? So it seems safe to predict that, regardless of what economic and political measures are used, unless solutions are found for psychospiritual problems like emotional emptiness, we may expect more cultism and style rebellion.

But there are other forms of response to the problems which cultism and faddism try to solve—which, indeed, are more or less cultic, though in a disguised form. Let us consider such things as play, therapy, hero worship, and crusades.

6 Secular Cult

To those of us who have been raised on the puritan hard-work ethic, the presumption is dear that people who are at leisure for too long a time will deteriorate or get into trouble. So, on the island of Moorea, a writer notes (not without satisfaction) that it takes an American about two months of unspoiled, paradisaical leisure before life begins to seem pointless, he feels he is "going to pot," and longs to get back to the "rat race" he so eagerly left. Equally satisfying to the puritan spirit is to see people playing so hard it is no longer fun—as with golfers whose eighteen holes are as arduous as a climb of the Matterhorn, ulcers within equaling the blisters outside. But to the philosopher who wants people to live well in leisure, neither horn of this dilemma is very satisfying: meaningless play versus meaningless (joyless) work. There must be something better for modern man. Anthropologists help by pointing out that there is no absolute need for disjunction of play from work—or, for that matter, play from religion, religion from sex, business from welfare—since other cultures have managed to combine these things. It is possible to work religiously, play religiously, work playfully, use sex religiously, and so on.

Our concern here is with the question: What sort of future is there, in the age of widespread leisure which experts assure us is upon us, for the meaningfulness of life when a secular society is denied "work" and, shall we say, condemned to "play"? It would be a gloomy outlook, indeed, if there were no alternative to work but triviality, if things had to go as they do for Americans on Moorea. But if it is possible for leisure to increase greatly in significance without making it into work, then all might go well. How could this be?

It seems to me that a trend is already evident which may suggest the answer of the future: a search for deeper meaning in "fun" which is basically cultic. Such a trend is also apparent in other sectors of rational, technical activity, such as education and therapy. Thus our secular society is already trying to find outside of sacred cult the answer to its meaning problem—that labels such as "fun," "education," and "therapy" often disguise a secular cultic quest. I would say this is because once the elements of deeper meaning (ecstasy, mystique, and identity finding) enter any activity, the conventional distinctions between play, work, art, religion, education, therapy, and welfare break down. So long as the thread of identity search runs through them, it is impossible to draw a sharp line between them; they are, as it were, sectors on the same front.[1] So we note a markedly cultic aspect of recreation when it takes the form of what Alan Watts calls "the new ecstatics"—the emerging quest for ecstasy through such things as pop art, psychedelics, sexual mysticism, mantra chanting, and folk rock.[2]

"FUN"

THE NEW ROMANTICISM

It is not necessary to wait for the day of leisure to reach high noon to see that already people are playing harder than ever, longer than ever, and in new ways. Fun is breaking out all over. There is a search for sensations in ever new kinds of amusement: from skin diving and surfing to antique car racing and beer-and-banjo fun; from mountain climbing to parachute jumping; to camping with lounge chairs and colored tents. Business executives come home with broken legs from skiing, while we have full-dress English-style hunts in Indiana and group safaris for polar bears in Norway and elephants in Kenya. Tourists regard the world as an oyster which they will open with their cameras. Remote vacation spots like Majorca, Puerto Vallarta, and Tahiti are being overrun by tourists as magazines like *Holiday* and *Sunset* publicize one spot after another.

Such things seem a preview of what will happen when we undergo the crisis of automation and leisure becomes a full-time career. While the fun may not be expensive, there is no reason to believe that it will not be novel and energetic. Yet, so far, the bursting out of fun has not brought the rejoicing that might have been expected; experts on leisure have taken a dim, if not melancholy, view of the problem of the devil finding work for idle hands, of the pointlessness of the pursuit of thrills, of the meaninglessness of organized recreation, of the prospect that people will be enervated equally by audience experience (spectatoritis) and activities which do not satisfy.[3]

Yet there is no question that "fun" is becoming a new focal point of mass interest and the playboy has risen as a hero of the ideal of "living it up," the "swinging life." For more and more people, with puritanism declining, he stands as a model, not of how to *waste* one's life, but of how to live it *more fully*. One sees, for example, Hugh Hefner (who to playboys stands for what Timothy Leary stands for to the psychedelic movement) in his lush bachelor apartment, with "acres of hi-fi," gorgeous decor, ankle-deep carpets, ornate bar, basement swimming pool, and a "nook" adjoining the pool where a playboy can retire with his girl friend (with a hole in the floor above for guests to peek through). Here the founder of *Playboy* magazine lives in all his glory as a style model for millions of other playboys and "bunny club" members. Television and cinema show him in his office, riffling through the pages of his magazine—girls, clothes, boats, girls, guns, humor, girls; "vrooming" from his office to his apartment in his white supercharged Jaguar; spending a night of riotous celebration, drinking, twisting, diving in the pool—men walking about in under-shorts, glass in hand, and girls in every sort of costume and noncostume. Hefner comments on what made him such a success—"I guess I'm about the luckiest guy in the whole world." He also guesses he is a "genius" to be a trend-setter for a whole generation, to bring in a new concept of living. His co-workers, speaking of their "gratitude" to him, sound almost like a cult; one says, "He's become a sort of guide for millions of other guys exactly like himself." Indeed, Hefner consciously conceives himself as the prophet of a new era in which people have plenty of money and leisure, in which old styles and morality no longer hold; he publishes an apparently endless series of definitive statements of "The Playboy Philosophy" on the right to freedom in prostitution, promiscuity, and things like that. So, with Hefner, the long tradition of the playboy rises to the dignity of a philosophy—even a "bill of rights."

The enthronement of the playboy and of his queen, the playgirl, has had its effect even on those hard-working puritans, the businessmen. The bunny clubs were, I think, an answer to the wish of businessmen—"We have a right to fun too"—an effort to harmonize the style of the playboy with that of the hard worker, a place where one might go, possibly with a client, to feel like a playboy vicariously for awhile, buy drinks at a dollar and a half apiece, look at the girls ("but you mustn't touch")—all without risk to reputation or fear that the wife will be mad. I see the bunny clubs, therefore, as an offshoot of the playboy ideal, an effort to provide some of the style to "expense-account aristocrats," a compromise for those who are making enough money to want some of the fun but who are not free to take up the playboy life.

This is just one of the changes we may expect in a new era of leisure when people seek identities that cannot be based on work or which deny the importance of work. It is a good question at what point a social type that was originally a model of something not to be becomes a prophet, a serious exemplar of a new identity for modern man. The "swinging life" is already here; so its heroes will claim their place in the pantheon along with the self-made men, strong men, patriots, culture heroes, martyrs, and saints. Moreover, loss of prestige in the work role—loss perhaps of even the opportunity to work—means that the identity search must find new avenues in recreation; the number of play identities will increase, work (boring, anyway) will take more and more a back seat to hobbies. Then, will more words that originally signified a wasted or worthless life—philanderer, adventurer, idler, beatnik, beach rat, beachcomber, tennis bum, ski bum—come to have a heroic significance? An indignant newspaper editorial treats the large number of traveling "students" who have become "scroungers," adept at tricks for getting free meals and lodgings that used to be the expertise of hoboes. At least, there can be little doubt that as people play harder more of the time, there will be an increase in the number of "nonworking" models for identity.

Such a change in roles is not to be expected without a change in ethos, a change in the sense of what is right. It will be right to have kinds of fun formerly considered wrong. Movies such as *Tom Jones, Zorba the Greek, Never On Sunday,* and *Goldfinger* (James Bond) clearly state the philosophy that "sex is fun." But there is more to this than appears on the surface, more than the idea that sex is right or that fun is right.[4] It is a deeper mystique behind the notion of a right to have kicks. It is the right to find oneself, to realize oneself, through fun as "peak experience."[5] Hedonism receives new validation as the search for and affirmation of identity: the *right to* identity. This I call the new romanticism. The older romanticism was a cult which asserted the primacy of emotion, intuition, and energy over reason—the heart over the head.[6] The new romanticism asserts the right to a self; fun is legitimized as a way of fulfilling oneself, not just because it is part of one's right to happiness. The kick has a new validity based on one's right to a self. This isn't saying that if you aren't having fun you are missing something in life; it is saying that if you aren't having fun you aren't really there. This is Rousseau improved by Camus. To say "I'm doing it for myself" sounds selfish, but to say "I'm doing it for my identity" makes it a basic right with which no one can argue. So the new romanticism extends even to the really obscene attitude exhibited by those such as Norman Mailer that any feeling is as valid as any other—even a murderous one, a depraved one— so long as one realizes oneself by it. Hence, the writer's artistic obligation to turn his insides out to the public. I hope I have managed to explain that this romanticism is not just the old one of Quixote or Rousseau. The new romanticism is not necessarily poetic or chivalrous or beautiful. Its only claim is that something shall be real for me. This makes it superior to everything else in a world of shams and clichés. A feeling which does something for my identity is right because I have a right to an identity. But when everyone in the mass begins to assert this right, according to his own ideas, it begins to look like the rebellion that so alarmed Ortega y Gasset. One can assert this right by going back to nature and discarding civilized forms; one can assert it on the beach, at a wild party, by perversion, crime, or rebellion. There is really no point at which the authority can look the rebel in the eye and say, "You have no right to develop your identity in this way."

So a society which becomes pleasure seeking in this way is more than just hedonistic. It has a deeply serious intent, a mystique, by which to try to protect itself from the meaninglessness of *La Dolce Vita*.

When play acquires this mystique it becomes cultic. Such a mystique is seen in "nature camps" established at remote and beautiful sites like Cefalu (Sicily) and Corfu (Greece) in Tahitian style with bamboo huts, sarongs, and bikinis, devoted to "*la formule: la desintoxication mentale et physique*. . . . Joy revives essential truths. The individual rediscovers and remodels himself."[7]

CULTIC TENDENCY IN PLAY

Many sports today are beginning to develop mystiques and add a cultic burden which goes beyond what used to be called a character-developing value of sport. Devotees become centered in new ways and develop mystiques which even sportsmen in neighboring fields cannot understand. Their devotion goes beyond mere amusement, even beyond professionalism, to a kind of zealous piety. Sports then provide an "it" experience which is somewhat more than the joy of the game. This is perhaps especially true of daring and thrilling activities which set a person apart by a kind of charisma.

Examples of such mystique can be found among dare-devils, mountain climbers, parachute jumpers,[8] balloonists, high-wire performers, high steel workers, karate enthusiasts, and surfers. Statements by mountain climbers indicate such mystiques:

> Life is at its best when risked. . . . Mysterious impulses which cause men to peer into the unknown. . . . Like all profound experiences it is a paradox: both challenge and escape. There is certainly an element of escapism in most climbers. I climb partly to get away, for a time, from the life of the city and some of the values of contemporary living. But there is the reality even in the escape. You climb to discover things about yourself. To be on your own, to be with yourself, facing yourself in situations of stress and danger. . . . This is the . . . compulsion towards self-discovery. Once you've tasted it you forever feel the urge to see where your limit lies.[9]

A sky-diver tries to explain his mystique:

We're a closely knit group, we sky-divers. . . . It's a mental thing, jumping out without a chute. You've got one thing on your mind—you've got to convince yourself it can be done and then you do it. When you jump out at around 15,000 feet it's two degrees above zero out there. Very cool, very beautiful. Sky-diving is the best fun there is. People ask me what do you feel up there, going down. Well, it's a feeling of its own. You don't feel like you're going down in an elevator. You feel—well, free. Sometimes another sky-diver and I, we'll play catch with oranges. The real fun is the free fall—that's the whole turkey. The parachute part is just a matter of getting down safely.[10]

Surfers try to explain their mystique:

The bigger the wave, the bigger the challenge, all alone, you blend for a moment with immense power. You feel close to God.[11]

Surfing has become a state of mind, a wild, uninhibited existence that revolves around the sun, the surf, and the sand. The first time you stand on a surfboard, you'll know why surfing will never die out. Plummeting down a hill of water sometimes as high as a four story building and being able to move your board to the right or left side and to somewhat control its speed, brings about a feeling similar to flying. Not only are you moving but the force you've harnessed is also moving. That is, until you take a wipeout. Surfers will attempt to surf any large body of ocean that seems surfable, and if it is not surfable they will attempt to ride it anyway in an exhausting effort to get their "charge" (optimum level of adventure). The life of the surfer has a definite rhythm and beat to it. This is the beat of the surf and the beat of the wild driving music he listens to when he is not at the beach surfing. Personally, this music plays a very important part of my life.[12]

Such statements approach cultism when they convey an idea of a special experience that is the best there is—higher than ordinary life, setting a person apart but closer to those who share the mystique, doing something important to change his conception of himself and center his life. Overcoming fear and weakness by an ordeal is often part of the mystique. Most daring and thrilling sports provide at least three important payoffs to identity: (1) intense encounter with "reality"; (2) discovery, proof, transcendence of self; and (3) an audience before whom to shine, not the least of which is a circle of devoted hero worshipers. Is it any surprise, then, that cults easily grow up in sports which provide such identity payoffs? Saul Bellow expresses the mystique of dangerous sport when he forces his hero Henderson into an encounter with a lioness. "She will make consciousness to shine. She will burnish you. She will force the present moment upon you. . . . When the fear yields, a beauty is disclosed in its place.[13]

Some sports help identity change by the theatrical device of costume. So English devotees of the art of kendo dress in full Samurai armor including long side trousers, jacket, breastplate, and an apron with five flaps, surmounted with a mask, to encounter one another in ceremonial combat shouting fierce war cries. Devotees say that kendo is not just a combat technique, a sport, or an art, but a creed, the final aim of which is "self-control, and the balance of a trained body, mind and intellect."[14] The costume aspect of play takes us into theater as an adventure in identity.

Likewise, intensity of sensation in rhythmic music is capable of giving people a sense of identity change and a cultic attitude. It is well known that jazz has a mystique as an "it" experience. A promoter of jazz festivals said:

It is something quite special, you know, these jazz festivals. It's an event, a happening; it's more than a series of continuous concerts. And it really changes people's lives. I know of an attorney who was really from Squaresville, a Lawrence Welk fan. He got inveigled one year into going to the Monterey Jazz Festival . . . and, lo and behold, he became a Dizzy Gillespie fan.

Hoagy Carmichel comments on Bix Beiderbecke in the manner of one who has contacted a religious prophet:

When Bix opened his soul to me that day, I learned and experienced one of life's innermost secrets to happiness—pleasure that it had taken a whole lifetime of living and conduct to achieve in full.

Another jazz artist, Mezz Mezzrow, brings out even more clearly the cultic implications:

When you're a kid and your first millennium falls on you, when you get in a groove that you know is *right* for you, find a way of expressing something deep down and know it is *your* way—it makes you bubble inside. But it's hard to tell outsiders about it. It's all locked up . . . then, once in a million years, somebody like Bix comes along and you know the same millennium is upon him too . . . that gives you the courage of your convictions—all of a sudden you know you aren't plodding around in circles in a wilderness.[15]

The appreciator as well as the performer of jazz shares in the cultic experience:

> The tenorman *had it* and everybody knew he had it. Dean was clutching his head in the crowd, and it was a mad crowd. They were all urging that tenorman to hold it and keep it with cries and wild eyes. . . .
>
> "Now, man, that alto man last night had IT—he held it once he found it. . . ." I wanted to know what "IT" meant. "Ah, well"—Dean laughed—"now you're asking me impon-de-rables. . . . All of a sudden somewhere in the middle of the chorus he *gets it*—everybody looks up and knows; they listen; he picks it up and carries. Time stops. He's filling empty space with the substance of our lives. . . . It's not the tune that counts but IT"—Dean could go no farther. . . .

Two hipsters venerate George Shearing as a divinity of jazz:

> "There he is! That's him! Old God Shearing!" . . . Shearing rose from the piano, dripping with sweat; those were his great 1949 days before he became cool and commercial. When he was gone Dean pointed to the empty piano seat. "God's empty chair," he said. . . . I suddenly realized it was only the tea we were smoking . . . it made me think that everything was about to arrive—a moment when you know all and everything is decided forever.[16]

Another testimony from a hipster about how jazz integrates (centers) his life:

> Jazz music gives forms to my mind, forms in sound, and I feel it's better than any psychoanalyst, because art is a healer . . . it's a connected universe, just like the words we formed out of the grunts and hollers, it organizes my universe for me. . . .[17]

Some of the redemption in jazz comes from the liberation of creative energy within oneself; but, doubtless, much comes from something which jazz shares with primitive music and shamanism, the magic of a hypnotic beat.[18] Some of this hypnotism can be seen in the rock and roll of teenagers:

> It was difficult to tell whether the boys and girls were dancing with each other or as singles. They never touched each other and there was no obvious leading and following. There was no laughter, no conversation, only the blank faces of youngsters who worked in unison, like labor

gangs in the deep south. Most of the tables at the vacant booths had mugs of beer on them, occasionally a highball, but scarcely anyone came back to drink them. Hour after hour, they just kept flapping and bouncing, under the spell of the guitars and drums to the point one of my companions said, "They seem almost mesmerized."

Hip artists such as Robert Rauschenberg, Larry Rivers, and Andy Warhol sometimes paint while listening to rock and roll music. Warhol explains: "It makes me mindless, and I paint better." As dancers enter the hypnotic beat, they are transported out of themselves, their inhibitions fade, eyes glaze over, and they have the feeling of swimming alone in a sea of sound. A girl college student says: "I give everything that is in me. And when I get going, I'm gone. It's the only time I feel whole." Thus it is possible for people to have redeeming experiences in the ecstasy intense stimulation produces as in the Big Beat.

Sheer preoccupation and interest—as in art or hobby— sometimes seem to approach worship. It is often said that the attitude of Americans toward automobiles is more than utilitarian, that there is a car cult, with various orders centering their devotion on sports cars, hotrods, antique cars, racing cars, and dune buggies and jeeps. Above it all looms the apotheosis of cars, the wonder car that can do everything, as seen in the machinegun-equipped sports car that 007 used to follow Goldfinger, which could trace people, baffle pursuers with smoke screens, and flatten enemy tires. Ian Fleming, creator of James Bond, has caught the spirit of the car cult in the following passage:

> She was beautiful . . . from the rows and rows of gleaming knobs on the dashboard to the brand-new, dark-red leather upholstery; from the cream-colored, collapsible roof to the fine new tires; from the glistening silver of the huge exhaust pipes snaking away from holes in the bright green hood to the glittering license plates. . . .
>
> Silently they climbed in through the low doors that opened and shut with the most delicious clicks. . . . Commander Pott put the big car into gear and slowly they rumbled and roared . . . up the lane towards the highway, and the springs were soft as silk and always this delicious rumble came out behind from the huge fishtail exhausts. . . .
>
> Well, I can tell you that the huge, long, gleaming green car almost flew. With a click of the big central gear lever, Commander Pott got out of the first gear into second at forty miles per hour, with another click at

seventy miles per hour he was in third, and as they touched *one hundred miles an hour,* he put the huge car into top gear and there they were passing the black beetle cars almost as if they were standing still. . . .[19]

Hobbies often become cultic when individuals invest themselves by effort and seek perfection in equipment or in themselves. This point, at which interest becomes devotion, is indicated by words like "fan," "bug," and "fanatic," applied to enthusiasts. One can see it in classical guitarists, who practice zealously, attend concerts more faithfully than churchgoers, and enshrine certain performers as heroes (Segovia, Julian Bream, John Williams); they meet in clubs and workshops to play, compare, discuss, and exchange information, are always on the lookout for a better instrument, a quest of perfection; they make their own instruments with devoted craftsmanship and have sectarian contempt for the heathen, especially those who play electrical amplified guitars, or with picks. Spouses often complain of such devotion to a hobby (he's "fallen in love" with a guitar, "married to golf") because they recognize a rival. Such an enthusiast has found a meaning in life in his hobby; he lights a candle to his cult regularly. While such devotion cannot be called worship in the religious sense (prayer, propitiation, sacredness), it is too serious to be dismissed as play, and is cultic in features such as centering, hero worship, and mystique not evident to the uninitiated. Any activity can be cultic at the point when a person not only does it but lives for it.

Spectators also help make cult by assuming the role of devoted fans. Again, there is a point at which an admiring audience becomes a worshiping congregation. This can be seen in many followings of entertainers and sports stars. Some people queued for over 24 hours in bad weather for the Wimbledon tennis finals. How serious can you get as a spectator? Baseball is at least one sport in America which maintains annual celebrations for its heroes, such as Babe Ruth Day, and has a formal shrine—Baseball's Hall of Fame—to immortalize the heroes and relics of the game.[20]

A curious athletic institution at Santa Monica, California, called Muscle Beach, shows many features of cult. On this mile or so of sand can be found probably the largest concentration of beautiful torsos in the world. Devotees of the Body Beautiful come from miles around to display themselves at Santa Monica, many others to watch or ogle: weight lifters with barbells, 200 pounds at a hoist; beautiful females in leopard skins, thrown from one burly adagio dancer to another; pyramids of acrobats; and youths of all sizes, boys and girls, energetically copying. Here the gods come to life—Hercules and Venus in countless incarnations. A beautifully proportioned body is the main goal, and visual display the high feast. For devotees, this activity is a way of life; the same people come week after week to work out faithfully or lounge and loaf on the beach. How seriously do they take all this? Is it worship? It must be admitted that the onlooking crowds are casual. But the participants are dedicated and work out piously; they have a mystique too—health and beauty and self-perfection through exercise and sun. There is no afterlife, it is all in the present; nearby, religious preachers on soapboxes call for repentance for sins. It is a secular piety, a worldly enthusiasm, comparable to true religion. They are devotees, dedicated, subordinating themselves to a value (which does not require celibacy) and their performance is ritual— a repeated rigmarole of a consummatory (nondiscursively meaningful) payoff, for themselves as performers and audience as congregation.

When a sport or hobby combines such features, we can see in it at least three centering factors which work reciprocally to help it become cultic: (1) "I love this sport" (the dedication of the actor); (2) "They like my performance—me" (the actor feeling the appreciation and hero worship of the audience); and (3) "I owe it to the sport and my audience to please them and dedicate myself." Thus we see understandable factors working to make a performing art or sport a pious obligation.

Finally, we find what might be called a high point of secular cult in activities—whether games, dances, audience experiences, or club activities—in which the purpose is self-abandonment. A dance craze called La Bostella, which exploded out of Paris in 1965, was described as "part psychotherapy, part wrestling match and part whoopee," consisting of a flamenco hand clap, then writhing and moans as dancers pile on the floor in a heap.[21] Some of this letting go can be seen in "Go-Go" dancing; a participant describes it as follows:

As you walk into the room the music hits you like a wall. Almost unconsciously a person will find himself tapping his foot to the deep throbbing "beat." It seems to charge the air with excitement. A person gets the feeling that he wants to do something. All of a sudden the floor is full of writhing, twisting bodies. A high percentage of people at this Go-Go dance hall were college students. Most expressed a desire to "lose themselves" and get away from all the tensions and frustrations of studying, tests, and term papers.

Orchestras playing the Big Beat aim consciously at self-abandonment. A musician said:

> That's all we ask from an audience—frenzy. That's the only sign of real acceptance. . . . We were mobbed. . . . They just went mad at the sight of us. That was frenzy.

Discotheques became established institutions where one could let oneself go with Go-Go, Frug, Swim, Surf, Watusi, Hully Gully, Wobble, Slop, and Jerk. A teacher said:

> You can't *not* dance in a discotheque. First, the dances are too easy not to dance. Second, they're too sexy not to dance. Third, that pack of people on the floor is having too much fun not to join them.[22]

Letting oneself go in a discotheque, however, is not just loss of self but a new form of self-experience. As a *habitué* explained it: "The object is not to get hung up on feeling the music but to concentrate on feeling your own presence." The discotheque grew rapidly during the middle 1960s into a more effective institution for self-abandonment, the "total environment" nightclub, which was designed to break contact with ordinary life and disorient a person by sensory experience. The prototype was the Cheetah in New York City, which invited dancers to gyrate madly in out-of-this world costumes—red vinyl space-age outfits, aluminum wigs, fluorescent clothing, silver motorcycle jackets with purple crepe pants—in the midst of flashing, changing colored lights, artificial smoke, and the deafening sound of rock and roll orchestras. The idea of "psychedelic art" was quickly incorporated, whose purpose was to take a person out of himself on a trip simulating LSD experience, to "explode his mind" by a shattering assault upon the senses and bewildering effects such as 21 movies at the same time. Artificial fog machines helped create an eerie atmosphere in which a person was not sure where he was or who was with him. These nightclubs had a boutique adjoining where participants could outfit themselves with identity-transcending costumes before entering the "wiggy scene." A manager of one of these clubs, The Lightworks in New York City, explained the purpose of it all: "An inter-media performance . . . should create inner tranquility, happiness, a sense of floating and being joyously out-of-self."[23]

Audience-participation sports also have some of this function. At roller derbies fights and furious action provoke similar responses in spectators. An enthusiast said:

> People do things at the roller games that they normally wouldn't do. I personally know a lady who is very quiet and reserved. When she attends Roller Derby she is, well, you might say someone else. She hits the people next to her; I've seen her grab the person in front of her and shake and pull at him. Other people in the crowd do the same things. I saw one girl crying because her hero was in a fight. At the El Monte Arena there was a riot. Some women even took off their high heel shoes and were fighting with the players. (To the question, do you block or hit the people around you?) All the people I asked said they did except one person. But I had been watching this person during the game and several times I saw her knock the person next to her. At the Roller Games we find people acting outside of themselves in search of excitement missing from their lives.

Nude parties staged by the Sexual Freedom Leagues of the San Francisco area show another dimension of self-abandonment. Twenty or so couples, married and unmarried, gather in apartments, remove their clothes, darken the room, play phonograph records, drink wine, and engage in an orgy. The promoters of nude parties contend that their purpose is intellectual and not merely sensual—to realize the ideal of freedom: "Man will only become free when he can overcome his own guilt and when society stops trying to manage his sex life for him." The philosophy of sexual freedom is based on two principles: "Do you want to? Does it *not* hurt anyone else?" A girl member said, derisive of nudists, "We don't need that health and sunshine jazz to justify removing clothes. Our attitude is frankly sensual." Doubtless, as with any sport, participants range from those whose attitude is merely sensual to those with a mystique about realizing themselves. As a means of identity change, the orgy permits one to affirm new identity by sensual experience not ordinarily permitted and to escape from old identity in the anonymity. Orgy is the extreme of the dimension of seeking new identity through intense experience. Its frequency in primitive fertility cults shows that mankind has long known about its cultic power. Orgy does not, of course, guarantee a religious experience, but it does provide experiences which can easily become cultic: sensual contact with "reality" about which mystique can be developed; centering on an ecstatic high point; and loss of old self.

We have tried to consider how activities which are play or "fun" can become cult-like. We have noted certain factors which especially favor identity change and fulfilment: (1) ordeals by which one finds new capacities within oneself; (2) fellowship with an elect who have a mystique not shared with outsiders; (3) vestment change; (4) intensity of stimulation leading to ecstasy; (5) interest so strong that one invests oneself; (6) spectators' vicarious excitement; (7) audience hero worship; and (8) self-abandonment in orgy.

The point, then, is that various kinds of experiences can give one the feeling that this is the highest, the best there is. They need not be sacred to develop mystique and cultic devotion. I would hold that all such kicks or ecstasies are associated with changes of identity—a sign that something is happening. Such experiences with feelings of ultimate validity, legitimize themselves as the right to identity—what I call the new romanticism—which opens the way to the exploration of offbeat experience for even higher identity, to try to understand the psychological "triggers" and more efficient methods of self-realization.[24] We have no way of knowing how high a kick can go, or how far man can go in realizing himself, by experiences both sacred and secular, cultic and otherwise. It seems safe to say, however, that there will be more efforts to penetrate the sensory horizon, and that many of them will be in the form of offbeat secular cult. It also seems plain that it is wrong to develop a mystique, as D. H. Lawrence did, about one particular kind of experience, such as sex, being the highest form of realization. All the indications from the variety of cults, both secular and sacred, are that awakening (satori) can come from a variety of experiences—perhaps even a knock on the head. Nor is there anything irreligious about this observation, because who could presume to say how God would choose to reveal himself? All that man can do is continue his search for supreme moments.

CULTIC TENDENCY AND SIGNATORY STYLE IN ART

Art is naturally cultic in tendency because it is naturally self-ful-filling. It is well known that almost every major artist forms a circle of devotees and imitators, to whom he is hero (as example) or guru (as teacher); that artists form "schools" with orthodoxies as firm and heresies as bitter as any in religion; that art, almost by defini-tion, has a mystique, because it does not speak discursively (even poetry despite its use of words), may shun representation or objec-tivity, and often leaves in mystery the author's intention; that art to its devotees is a sacred calling to which they devote their lives with monastic austerity; and that art is an important part—technique—of ritual.

There is no need to enlarge upon these familiar facts, but I would like to note a trend in modern art which seems to express the new romanticism and have much in common with the identity finding that one sees in play. It is a trend to personal statement, parallel to ego-screaming in fashion and the search for offbeat kicks in play. The poet John Ciardi describes the emergence of signatory style:

> It was, I believe, André Malraux . . . who observed that Van Gogh had carried personal style to the point at which he could paint (as he did) a simple chair with such individuality that he made of it as much a sig-nature as an object represented. I am moved to generalize further that one mark of every artist we call "modern" may be found in his impulse to achieve not "style" but "a style." By "style" I mean the way the medium is used to forward what used to be called "the subject" and is now generally called "the esthetic experience." By "a style" I mean the way the medium is used to forward the author's individuality. Nor need it be understood that one of these impulses can exist in a work of art without the other: I am after a matter of emphasis. "Style" is, at root, representational (whether of outward appearances or of inner-response-to), whereas "a style" is signatory. . . . It is worth asking if contem-porary taste has not gone too far in enshrining "a voice" at the expense of "voice."[25]

We see this tendency in both fine art and pop art, including jazz and popular music. It explains much of the caterwauling and in-comprehensibility—the pursuit of "sounds" and "effects" ever more weird and strident. It is the new romanticism, I think—the idea that whatever one does for one's identity is right—that gives a license to these forms of expression that otherwise would not be esthetically tolerated. The audience holds back its judgment, saying to itself implicitly, I don't like it, it's ugly, but it's *his* style and he is expressing himself." The artist, on the other hand, imbued with the new romanticism, thinks, *I am not especially concerned with whether you like it. My right to style takes precedence over your enjoyment or understanding of art.* He may even avoid producing something simply pleasant or beautiful, because he wants a signatory style all his own. The final corruption comes when audiences themselves become so concerned with identity, so imbued with the new romanticism, that they prize signatory style more than esthetics. Then they reward the artist simply for being different. The tribute "he has character, individuality" then outweighs the fact that no one is getting any actual enjoyment from his art. This trend, I think, is symptomatic of the identity problems of modern society; it would not occur where there were not widespread identity problems. In such case, art becomes preoccupied with personal statement, a search for any means—style, clothing, play, speech, art, religion—by which to say something distinctive, leave one's footprint on the sand, however soon it might be washed away. Art becomes idiosyncratic and personal, like a monogram—better yet, a private cipher. The artist signs himself all over the paintings in his show, but it is often not a check that either he or others can cash.

DEVIATION AND NONSQUARE "FUN"

How is all this search for identity in kicks and self-realization acting on the structure of our society? It seems to me it is opening an ever wider door through which one can pass outside the square world. The argument would be that once the new romanticism (having my kicks is a right) is established, it is impossible to confine it to approved or conventional channels. For one thing, it is a natural right which, like Martin Luther's conscience, takes precedence over ordinary social rules. These rules are inauthentic clichés, in existentialist jargon. So that if a person finds that school or work or conventional play does not offer him an authentic identity, he has a perfect right to look for it where he can find it. Moreover, once the quest for identity is seen to lie in the direction of sensations, it is impossible to confine it to moderate ones, for it tends to extremes to overcome the effects of jading.

So there is a built-in tendency to deviation in the new romanticism. It legitimizes offbeat adventures outside one's social position, class, religion—even beyond the pale of morality itself. In existentialist literature, as in the writing of Camus and Sartre, it becomes a right to realize oneself by radically choosing danger, rebellion, violence, even killing somebody: if such experiences allow the individual to find himself, they are in their view justified—however hard they may be on somebody else. So in Norman Mailer's novel, *An American Dream,* we see the hero, after murdering his wife, attaining the nirvana of danger walking around the 12-inch-wide parapet of a 32-story building:

> I kept going down the third leg; and the wall came nearer to me; my limbs came alive again; each step I took something good was coming in, I could do this, I knew I could do it now. There was the hint of when I would finally be done—some bliss from infancy moved through the lock of my lungs.

The new romanticism gives the perverse kind of right to violent gangs, rioting for fun, and those leather-jacketed motorcyclists who roar through towns drinking and terrorizing people like bandits in the Old West. Especially for the down-and-outers and the alienated ones who feel cheated, such ways of realizing oneself seem open and legitimate. The best experiences seem outside the square world.

> I walked . . . wishing I were a Negro, feeling that the best the white world had offered was not ecstasy for me, not enough life, joy, kicks, darkness, music, not enough night. . . . I wished I were a Denver Mexican, or even a poor overworked Jap, anything but what I was so drearily, a "white man" disillusioned.[26]

> Pot is like, well, it makes you aware, aware of the *present,* you come *alive,* you got eyes for the scene, man, and ears to hear with . . . most of the time we're listening but we're not *hearing,* man.[27]

"Turn on, tune in, drop out."

Violence and public law-flouting give much the same emotional payoffs to identity for the nonsquare, as daring and thrilling sports do for the square: intense encounter with "reality," discovery and proof of self through ordeals, the mystique of the new romanticism, and an audience before whom to shine and be recognized—though perhaps also punished.

Those who have found a satisfactory identity in conventional society and have a large stake in it can only recoil in distaste—if not horror—from such carryings-on as LSD "festivals," riots for "fun," or the "parties" of the Sexual Freedom League, which reject the established values of hard work, prudence, morality, and wholesome fun. They cannot see the identity needs that have inspired the new romanticism. Yet they feel defensive because they see the growing trend—even among their own children—toward offbeat kicks. They feel out-of-date and somehow a need to justify being square. Senator Margaret Chase Smith said:

> Many years ago, the word square was one of the most honored words in our vocabulary. The square deal was an honest deal. A square meal was a full and good meal. It was the square shooter rather than the sharp shooter who was admired. What is a square today? He's the fellow who never learned to get away with it, who gets choked up when the flag unfurls. There has been too much glorification of the angle players, the corner cutters, and the goof offs. One of America's greatest needs is for more people who are square.[28]

So there is this dividing line, this lack of understanding, between the squares and the new romantics. But it is harder to specify this line—and small consolation to those who wish to defend it—for even within the square domain kicks are getting more violent and unusual. In such places as discotheques, lines of propriety are becoming so blurred one does not quite know what is conventional and when one has gone too far. One does not quite know what is proper conduct for youth, as when wealthy young men invited to a debutante's coming-out party in New York tore up a mansion and described their activity as "having a ball." Nor can we be sure that people want to stay in the middle-of-the-road when an automobile manufacturer says:

> People don't want to be told that a car is safe. It gives an image of the humdrum and the ordinary, so it makes them feel that they're ordinary

people. They want a car to lift them out of their ordinary lives—they
want to feel power at their command. A good advertisement is one that
creates excitement about the car.

Likewise, crowds gather most heavily at the curves of the race-
track where there is the most danger not only for racers but for
themselves. And the public shows great interest in bizarre "horror"
movies and in all kinds of abnormality on the screen. Some odd
things are going on in legitimate theater these days, too—plays like
*Who's Afraid of Virginia Woolf, The Entertaining Mr. Sloane,
Poor Bitos,* and *Afore Night Comes,* which could only by a stretch
of the imagination be called fun. The audience reels out, stunned by
the sheer cruelty of what has been presented under the guise of entertainment. One cannot classify legitimate theater-goers into
squares and nonsquares; but some walk out, and some remain to
try to realize existential values by going beyond the pale, beyond
what is proper and decent, stripping away the poses by which ordinary people pretend that life is not really so bad after all. So not
only for alienated ones, but even for squares, contact with "reality"
outside conventional experience is coming to be preferred to
"fun"—and some of it, though violent and painful, is called "fun."
Who can say that pain and violence do not contain dimensions of
identity realization for squares as well as nonsquares?[29]
Once "fun" stops being what people do for amusement or relaxation from work and becomes part of a search for identity, it provides a basis for a theory of why people deviate. The stress is not so
much the failure of social control (anomie) or rebellion at the frustrating opportunity structure, but, rather, just what people do who
are bored, want to have more meaning in their lives, and make
certain choices in their leisure. This search for meaningful fun, for
"kicks," leads from banal forms of amusement to realizing ones; it
takes the seeker to offbeat experiences, cults, poses, and bizarre
drama. The movement is essentially an esthetic and a moral one; it
is one of alienation, of moving toward what may be real. Every
"pot" smoker, every rebellious adolescent, and every beatnik feels
he is making an esthetic—and in terms of the new romanticism a
moral—choice. But the square does not see why all the good roads
should not lead to Rome. He condemns those who travel the by-
ways, defines them as deviant,[30] punishes them and so contributes
to the career of the delinquent.

My hypothesis, in brief, is that squares have firm identity and are satisfied with the opportunities of the status quo; therefore they do not need, do not understand, and are likely to condemn the offbeat adventures in identity which one sees in cultism, style rebellion, avante-garde drama, "sick" humor, and the entire philosophy of kicks. Those with identity problems, on the other hand, feel cheated by the status quo, disdainful of its opportunities, and search for new identity along the "trail of kicks." Nonsquares do not feel these directions are wrong because they have a small stake in the conventional order, an urgent need for identity, and the support of the new romanticism. "If these dead cats are going to blow it up, then the hell with it, man. I mean, I'll get my kicks while I can. Life gets shorter every day, I mean, man, the only worthwhile thing is in myself. Anything else is a drag."[31]

So the beatnik way of life, as that of the hipster, may be looked on as a positive search rather than merely a negative escape or rebellion. So I saw a beatnik come bounding, not shambling, into a London park. He dove over a hedge with a somersault and landed, neatly, legs crossed. He sat gazing at the sun, his eyes blinking. His companion, also, leaped across the bushes, a little less impetuously, and then the two set forth across the green, the leader bushy, unkempt, shuffling, his arms dangling with palms backward like an ape. The spectators gazed at the two with some curiosity—not without irritation—at the impropriety introduced into what was otherwise a proper English morning. Yet they seemed a little envious of the freshness of their intrusion. I could not help wondering what that beatnik was thinking about while he was blinking and smiling at the sun. Was it joy at getting out of a dark and dirty room? Or was it something like, "I follow my light wherever it may lead me. Too bad for these benighted squares who have no such light and no such search." Those who find their kicks within the respectable order of family, church, school, and business need not sympathize with this search; but they must put aside their point of view long enough to realize that important, even legitimate, values may lie outside the status quo.

How far and where may one go in the legitimate search for kicks? Obviously, some people make pathetic mistakes in their search for realizing experiences. The attitude of the heroin "cat," says Finestone, was "sacred, almost mystical," it was "more important to him than eating." It was second only to *the* kick.

Heroin . . . was the ultimate "kick" . . . an activity completely beyond the comprehension of the "square." No other "kick" offered such an instantaneous intensification of the immediate moment of experience and set it apart from everyday experience in such spectacular fashion. . . . It was the "greatest kick of them all."[32]

Addicts say of their drug kicks:

I realized that here was something I'd been looking for all my life, and the last piece of the jigsaw puzzle fell into place.[33]

It made me very relaxed, very high. I grooved with it. I dig junk. I won't kid anybody. I dig the high, the whole bit. I like the feeling. I like the feeling of *not* feeling. . . . I could never be a square. . . . I was once, but once I took that first shot, that shattered the whole bit—because then I knew. I knew what it was to be high. I knew what it was to groove with junk.[34]

Such statements indicate that some addicts get a feeling of having attained the *summum bonum*, which to them seems equivalent (however mistaken they may be) to the religious ecstasy of the peyote ceremony or the illumination of the mystic. The important thing to see is that much of what we call deviance is essentially a cultic quest to find highest experience and new identity among those who feel cheated. The search for identity occurs along a wide front, only some of which is rationalized by the new romanticism of the right to kicks—crowd behavior, the urban masquerade, vicarious identity voyages in drama and fiction, identity vacations in recreation, adulation of popular heroes, play and games—topped by those experiences, square or nonsquare, which provide a sense of contact with ultimate values and rebirth of self.

In short, the kick is for an identity-seeking deviate what conversion is for the cultist. It is the point at which the "trail of kicks" stops with some kind of commitment.[35] Wherever such commitment occurs, it is no surprise to find devotees forming defensive, cohesive groups to preserve their mystique and make it into what may someday be a new conservatism. Then the group will have certain strategic choices of relationship as a *modus vivendi* with an unfriendly society: evangelism, separatism, rebellion, or parasitism. But, in any case, the deviate who has a highest kick is likely to define himself rather as does a sectarian, seeing the outside society as enemies of the true, the good, and the real, philistines who are trying to rob him of his *summum bonum*. The motivation and the organization for deviation are similar to those of a religious sectarian group—but its cultic value is less sacred. The kicks philosophy does provide an *authority*, not just a motive, for deviation, which is at least charismatic and may approach religion.

Yet for those who feel cheated, or are insufficiently paid off, by the conventional games of society, there is still a choice between two broad sectors of search: the square and the nonsquare. In the former category I would put much that is called "fun," even when it gets a little extreme; fad and fashion; identity voyages in drama and fiction; role vacations in recreation; crowd enthusiams; hero worship; and therapy. These I would call the "safe" routes of identity adventure; though some may be physically dangerous, none require a break with respectable identity or encountering the animosity of the squares. The nonsquare sector of identity search— which is where the "trail of kicks" usually leads one—consists of such things as style rebellions, extreme faddism, violent sensations, cultic devotion to play which goes to great extremes, deviant kicks, rebellion, and minority crusades, which we have yet to treat. The nonsquare sector is risky to status and respectability—it may be hard for a person to return to old identity—and usually requires some invocation of the new romanticism for justification.

Therapy is one of the square directions of identity search which, like play, tends to become cultic when it offers identity change.

CULTIC TENDENCY IN HEALTH AND KNOWLEDGE SEEKING

There is no risk to reputation in a visit to a doctor (unless, perhaps, if he is a psychiatrist), or in undertaking a course of study, if the curriculum is not too exotic. But there is a point at which research acquires a mystique and the dispenser of knowledge becomes a guru—a point at which the patient becomes a disciple and the doctor a medicine man. A Grail quest underlies much of what we call education and health seeking. One can see it in vogues of ideas which promise to help man or reveal something to him—psychoanalysis, dianetics, semantics, cybernetics, existentialism, Zen, yoga, sensitivity training—perhaps even science itself when it takes the form of a positivism like that of George Lundberg's *Can Science*

Save Us? While inquiry can take a person into some very exotic areas, education and health seeking tend to have more of a fence-mending character, bringing a person back into what society defines as "normal" rather than releasing him into identity adventures. Education, therapy, and play are respectable forms under which a search for identity (even for kicks) can be hidden; but once they begin to dramatically succeed, they become cultic, and the secret is out.

I do not propose to cover this field but merely to point up a few examples of health and knowledge seeking in which identity search and cultic features are clear.

We may refer again to the institution of Muscle Beach, which can be classified either as play or health seeking—and in either case is a cultic activity. Then there are those so-called health spas which, though ostensibly resorts for health and beauty, have an extraordinary mystique and offer such things as monastic regimen, wonder-working foods and cosmetics, and yoga rituals to their clients. People who participate in these regimens come out with more than a sense of healthful well-being; they feel renovated as persons. A woman said:

> I looked at everyone, my doe-eyed self included . . . in our pink suits with our hair scooped back and our faces scrubbed clean with our Golden Door Soap Drops. I'm thinner and healthier, and my skin is clearer and it does quite glow, just as they said it would, and I have pink polish on my toenails. I was delighted with myself. . . .[36]

There is concern not only with physical health but such things as peace of mind, nirvana, releasing spiritual forces, the cleansing effect of a "Holy Ganges ritual." There is a mystique about the Spartan discipline and the bullying of a calisthenics director that is almost penitential. People find it difficult to say what has happened to them at such resorts; but the exercises, cosmetics, diets, waters, and treatments seem to have a panacea quality, and the cultic atmosphere is unmistakable. There is a point at which exercise and dieting for the body become ritual and penance for the soul.

Nor is there reason to doubt that individual diet control and food faddism often assume a cultic quality: when there is a mystique about the value of foods; a pious grinding of seeds and sprouting of beans according to ritual formulas; vegetarian diets conform to the taboos of Hinduism; books such as *Let's Cook It Right,* by Adele Davis, become bibles for large followings. We suspect, in other words, that there is a point at which diet becomes moral austerity and nutrition becomes regeneration—that behind all the yogurt and blackstrap molasses are Grail symbols.

When we turn to the more serious business of getting well for a person who is ill, we recognize a powerful cultic tendency in therapy which has been plain since the time of Esculapius. Striking or mysterious successes, such as that of Sister Kenny,[37] are especially likely to develop cultic movements. Mental healing is prone to become cultic because its cures are a restoration not of the body but of the self, and because it draws people with identity problems amenable to solution by conversion. Wheelis notes the tendency of mental patients to demand magical formulas and push the doctor into the role of medicine man.[38] The sectarian orthodoxies and rivalries of psychoanalysis are also well known. Allan Watts says:

> It has become increasingly obvious that psychoanalysis is a system of creed, code and cult—in short, a religion, complete with apostolic succession, ritual, meditation practices, warring sects, heresies and heresiarchs.[39]

Some psychotherapists, such as Carl Jung or Georg Groddeck, take a frankly cultic stance toward the forces with which they are dealing—the "unconscious" or "it"—treating them as another name for God.[40] Sociologists perceive something like conversion in the "moral career" of the mental patient and other deviants who are treated therapeutically.[41]

Group therapy is especially interesting along these lines because it not only may put the leader in a guru-like position but generates dynamics resembling religious groups—togetherness similar to cultic fellowship, confessional techniques, and change of identity which has the earmarks of conversion. In such ways, group dynamics, by developing novel techniques to help people find themselves[42] and increase their sensitivity to others, might be said to converge with religion. Nor have ministers and priests been slow to see the relevance of group therapy and use it in their work.[43] Of course, evangelists have long used the dynamics of the crowd. So group therapy draws much the same audience as do the sects—people seeking to unburden and find themselves.

A group therapist may try to avoid the role of guru and adhere conscientiously to nondirective methods, perhaps shrinking into the position of a mere chairman, yet the cards are stacked against him by the very nature of the confessional and self-finding (redemptive) process and the needs of the clients who are, after all, seekers. Carl Rogers is outstanding among therapists who reject the "God-like" position of judging or directing a patient's life. Yet, during a "Weekend with Carl Rogers" in southern California, after a speech by Rogers in which he disclaimed any wish to have a guiding role in a therapy in which people are supposed to direct themselves, a participant arose and answered, "But Dr. Rogers, we are your disciples."

Synanon, the celebrated group therapy for drug addicts in southern California, seems to have accepted cultic features—at least it owes much of its success to them. Its members act like converts: witness, evangelize; addicts who have "stayed clean" testify publicly about their "new life." The movement was started by Charles Dederich, a man of pronounced charismatic qualities, who found a technique that seemed to work remarkably well with alcoholics, addicts, criminals, and homosexuals, with the same generality that evangelism is supposed to work on "lost souls." It is not preaching but an aggressively interactive technique which leads to confessional results, with "smashing" or "attack therapy," in which converts (all former offenders) interact vigorously with the newcomer, give him a "haircut" by ridicule, sarcasm, and verbal abuse to break down the old image of himself with which he has "conned" his way through society. They offer him a chance, after "coming clean" and "staying clean," to lead a new life in a brotherly-sisterly atmosphere of "TLC" (tender loving care) provided by their fellowship. "Kicking" the addiction "cold turkey," "sweating it out" without substitutive drugs, is part of the ordeal, in the midst of TLC, out of which comes a "new man." Smashing produces not just solidarity but a change within which makes him want to stay clean, take responsibility for himself, speak honestly, abandon his cynicism, take care of the other guy, and, most surprising, have a sense of mission toward a world he had formerly regarded with enmity.

This conversion, like any mystical experience, was originally hard to explain; but soon the movement developed an ideology—theology, if you prefer—making use of ideas such as Abraham

Maslow's theory of self-actualization.[44] The convert went forth to preach but did not leave the cult; rather, he was supported by it, centered by the value of the Synanon "games" (the "communion"), and kept the status his work in the group conferred. Should he feel himself slipping, or see another member doing so, there was always more attack therapy to help him confess and restore him to good standing—and the reward of TLC. There was also a threat, rather like excommunication, should a member fail to stay clean. The fact that hundreds of members did stay clean spoke eloquently for the genuineness of the conversion.

One could not expect anything so good to be confined to down-and-outers. The movement soon spread to "normal" middle-class people who were neither sick nor down-and-out, but had enough of an identity problem to feel they might get something out of Synanon "Square Games." Synanon "Game Clubs" appealed not just to lonely people but to many extroverts with a high rate of interaction who felt that, in spite of their many "friends," they were not getting through to people or achieving awareness of themselves. They gladly endured attack therapy for something more real than good-Joemanship. So the idea of group therapy for well and successful people spread; as journalists were quick to point out, by the middle of the 1960s California was on a "group therapy binge."

In no sense do I derogate Synanon, or any other form of group therapy, by noting its resemblance to the Salvation Army or Jehovah's Witnesses in making new men and saving sinners. Though the "theology" is that of Maslow rather than that of Billy Graham, the cultic features are too plain to ignore. Rather, I say that the success of group therapy may well be partly due to cultic features, and it is to be credited for giving evangelism a new cutting edge by improved techniques of interaction. I think that the paths of scientific therapy and cultic conversion converge in making the new man, though the ideologies are different; what a Christian means by "new life" is not fundamentally different from what a psychotherapist means. However, though the paths are parallel and group dynamics may one day go farther ahead, it still seems to me that success is more with the cults.

The techniques of "brainwashing" also show convergence with cultic methods, especially the Chinese "thought reforms." While the Russian methods stress isolation (what might be called artificially induced anomie), both Chinese and Russians use old-fashioned cultic methods, such as self-examination, group confession, forgiveness, close fellowship, and the pressure of a unanimous group to bring about psychic self-abandonment.[45] Despite certain well-publicized exceptions, there seems to be little in ordinary brainwashing that is insidiously clever or greatly different from what one cult or another has done in the past few thousand years.

When cult does—as it often does—prove more successful than therapy, group or individual, as a means of changing people, it is presumably because it is better organized in such things as group fellowship and support, ritual for dramatizing identity change, cultic formula, the role of the devotee as a life pattern (rather than just a temporary therapy), and deeper centering by faith and feeling about ultimate values. Whereas therapies, especially when they try to avoid cultic features, are likely to leave the patient on his own after a brief period of support, with no fraternal fellowship, no ritual to center his life, no devotee's career, no evangelical calling, no contact with Higher Reality—except what communion one can get out of a tranquilizer.

Finally, in our view of the main directions of secular cult, we should not overlook "research" that is really a quest for self-realization rather than just one for knowledge. In some degree, this applies to philosophy, literature, art, psychology, psychiatry, sociology—practically all of human relations study—if one can detect the point at which the quest for mystique and self-realization looms larger than that for objective knowledge. While there is always room for dispute in any branch of inquiry—for example, whether mathematics has a mystique—it seems more clear in that kind of research called psychical, occultism, or parapsychology.[46] Aside from outright churches devoted to spiritualism, theosophy, and such, numerous societies investigate in more or less scientific spirit phenomena outside conventional science (which views them with suspicion) from ESP to stigmata, mysticism, and poltergeists. The Society for Psychical Research, founded in 1882 in London, has branches in America; and the Parapsychology Foundation has members all over the United States. Important in the activities of such societies are charismatic individuals with mediumistic, mind-reading, or other extraordinary powers—such as Peter Hurkos, who claims 85 percent accuracy in divining facts from an object given as clue, and who has helped police in many countries. While parapsychological organizations usually deny religious character (even rejecting the tax advantages of calling their organizations churches), they do many things that look cultic and would be very appropriate to an organization whose central problem was attaining mystique and realizing or saving the man. These include lectures on spiritual subjects, courses to develop psychic powers, self training to conquer tension, yoga, self-hypnosis, prayer therapy, and experiments with astral projection led by a minister. Can one call such studies merely scientific, when they seem so clearly efforts to penetrate mystery and find something to be devoted to? Should one call the goal of such inquiry facts or a mystique to give meaning to man?

CONCLUSION

We have looked at a subdued, more or less disguised, thread of cultism running through activities labeled "fun," on the one hand, and education, therapy, and knowledge seeking, on the other. Somewhere beyond these respectable activities is, as I see it, a cultic search for offbeat kicks that squares regard as dangerous, deviant, even criminal. To call such things cultic brings out the thread of identity search, the quest for the new life of the new man, which is the goal of religious cult and the very meaning of conversion. Why should not the more intense forms of play, therapy, education, inquiry, and misbehavior be aiming at the same thing? It seems to me that they all become cultic when they develop mystiques, gurus, devotee roles, "in" fellowship, centered on some value which might be called a Grail because it is outside the ordinary sphere or a *summum bonum* because it is the highest point of existence.

If there is resistance to using the label "cult" in such a broad way, perhaps we should ask how much of it is due to the rationalism of a system which produces "one-dimensional men" and minute specialization in subjects that have no centering value, while pushing "religion" into an ever-narrowing sphere. Is such rationalism on a firm foundation, considering the conclusions of Freud and Pareto and the growing number of intellectuals who have left the laboratory and "gone East" in search of mystical solutions? We should consider, at least, that if "cultic" is not the best word then neither are play, education, therapy, or intellectual inquiry very good words for this kind of activity.

The secular cultic trend is becoming more urgent because of certain tensions of self-defeat within the modern age of leisure. Leisure invites a man to find himself, and the new romanticism proclaims that he has a right to do so. So he purchases all of the equipment for art, play, sports, health, education, and self-improvement that advertisers tell him he needs for self-expression. Then he arrives, thus laden, on the beach, the playing field, the school, the art museum, the natural preserve, the discotheque, to find a million others equipped, dressed, and yearning just like himself. Thus expectations of self-fulfilment are arising precisely when features of modern mass society and bureaucracy must defeat them; bureaucracy shutting the door on self-realization in work; technology closing the door on work itself; mass society filled with the faceless crowd and the audience watching celebrities achieving identities (or so they imagine) not possible for the man on the street, who hankers for a place in the limelight but never gets there. One can see something like this mutual mass defeat, on a small scale, when a group of teenagers all get guitars with amplifiers and other noisemaking musical equipment. Suddenly it becomes apparent that, though each may think he is "expressing" himself, no one can hear his own sound in the hubbub. Thus a competition of claims and equipment for supposedly realizing these claims have grown faster than the opportunities for realizing oneself in interactive situations—for example, the amplifying equipment that might enable one to realize oneself before an audience has not multiplied the number of audiences. So the average person, lost in the great crowd of people supposedly realizing themselves, actually has less chance of realizing himself.

Let us turn, however, to one of the most important avenues of mass identity search, vicarious experience of the hero or celebrity, to see what kind of voyage of identity he offers and the destination for which he seems headed.

7 Heroes and Celebrities

People look to me for something away from their everyday lives. I guess you'd call it a fantasy.

Marilyn Monroe[1]

Men have always lived through heroes—to sustain them with ideals and to help them in times of trouble. But their functions and types are not the same today. We propose to describe in this chapter how people use heroes, individually and collectively, for voyages of identity (vicarious experiences through the hero's role). *Hero worship* is a yearning relationship in which a person, in a sense, gets away from himself by wishing or imagining himself to be like someone else whom he admires. But all voyages of identity do not lead in the same direction—either for the individual, who has many choices, or for society, which is mainly interested in directing the choices toward certain approved models.

As far as the social order is concerned, there are three main directions in which people can move in relation to social structure by means of heroes; these I have labeled reinforcement, seduction, and transcendence. Today we have many new types of heroes who would not have been recognized—let alone admired—in the time of Theodore Roosevelt, even of Franklin Delano. These types are embraced by the term "celebrities," which covers a multitude of variations in achievement and style.

There are many questions about such figures and their roles in our life. For one thing, many are not in any special way "heroic"; they are not the kind of people one can with real justification admire. But they are nonetheless admired; indeed, the cult of celebrities is becoming more characteristic of and prominent in our society. The question, then, is where do these celebrities take us, what kinds of identity voyages do they provide? It seems plain that many do not support tribal or other collective identity, but are individualized (you have yours and I have mine). Many do not reinforce role structure or traditional values and virtues, as do "great men" and legendary figures like Beowulf. The "Mitty" function is conspicuous in the mass use of celebrities—compensating people for what they cannot do themselves (always, then, symbolizing a certain amount of frustration, even in vicarious gratification.) Also, many heroes are so ordinary today that there is a question, even if one did achieve what they did, or become what they were, whether one would have gone anyplace. Are celebrities taking us where we really want to go? At any rate, what is the impact of the celebrity cult on the quality and style of modern life?

We propose to consider here, first, how heroes are used psychologically, drawing upon people's statements about themselves; second, types of identity voyage in relation to the social structure; third, the behavior of mass, or collective, hero worship; and, finally, the cult of celebrities—an effort to evaluate where it is taking us. These are essential questions which we must answer if we are to know the part heroes play in the collective search for identity.

THE USES OF HEROES

It is useful to distinguish right away between the individual hero, standing for what a person wants for himself, and the group superself, standing for what people want for themselves collectively. Every society supplies both, though there are times, as in crisis, when a group superself is especially needed. For example, modernizing societies often go through a "strong man" era, when emerging leaders symbolize a national identity taking shape as tribal and ethnic traditions weaken—as Ataturk, Bolívar, Benito Juarez, Nasser, Kenyata, Sukarno, Mao Tse-tung. Likewise, modern societies—many advanced in identity crisis—many try to reassert group identity by reversion, or nostalgic reference, to good or strong men such as de Gaulle, Churchill, Hitler, and Mussolini, who provide a style and flatter the national ego—if only for a moment, perhaps, before the dream bursts into military defeat, despotism, *La Dolce Vita,* or "mini-England." Perhaps for America

Lindbergh and John F. Kennedy had much of this significance: an advanced society (with problems of corruption and identity) turning to an image of youth, vigor, and idealism (the "fine, clean young man" who would symbolize an integrity not always evident in everyday affairs): a group superself. But advanced modern societies always have the problem of heroes like James Bond to put alongside their Lindberghs and Churchills, their Washingtons and Nelsons. They are embarrassed by the riches and by the shoddy products of mass communication. Therefore they cannot entirely claim the integrity a de Gaulle figure implies when they do put him up as a strong man. Such a figure is much more a statement of what people feel they ought to be than what they are; there is no going back, the clock has moved. So the group superself may or may not reflect what people are doing and seeking: it is doubtful if Frenchmen have sought in de Gaulle the way to act in their *own lives,* as they might have in someone like Jean Gabin or Jean-Paul Belmondo. De Gaulle, as an oversized Frenchman, was right for a national role, but would have been uncomfortable in a bistro or a boudoir.

As distinguished from group superselves, celebrities are used today by the mass for individual dream realizations, supplying a type of psychic mobility. Their function is not so much to play the big role, but to supply fulfilments of great significance to "nobodies" who live vicariously in these celebrities (themselves former nobodies) as playboys, great lovers, love queens, sports stars, singers, rock and roll musicians, successful writers, disc jockeys, TV stars, and so on. Thus the celebrity has, one might say, a kind of office to perform, to supply success to those who cannot make it (epitomized, perhaps, by the way Sammy Davis, Jr., exploited his disadvantage: "handicap? Talk about handicap—I'm a one-eyed Negro Jew.").[2] In such use of celebrities, the "Mitty" function predominates. This is because the odds against success are very high, so the identity problems modern life accentuates are compensated by heroes. From dreams of realization one wakes to a different, or more limited, reality. When identity problems are prevalent, there is perhaps more of a leaning on what the hero does and less on what a man does himself.

In any case, whether individual hero or group superself, the function of the hero is to supply a vicarious voyage through what he does himself. This need not be an important deed nor the doer a great man. Sometimes a trivial, if colorful, exploit is all that is needed. The essential quality of the vicarious voyage is illustrated by the sailing across the Atlantic of a tiny $13^1/2$-foot-boat, the *Tinkerbelle,* by Robert Manry, from Falmouth, Massachusetts, to Falmouth, England, in 1965. This Mitty-like exploit by a middle-aged news copy editor awakened momentary dreams in thousands of white-collar workers—that they, too, might sail away some morning to an improbable destination to return in glory, as Lindbergh did, now Manry!, perhaps never to return. The essential quality for a vicarious voyage, however, is not merely an adventure but an exciting movement or change of status: finding oneself in a new situation revealing unexpected resources—perhaps some version of the ugly duckling theme. In terms of the theory of this book, we define the hero, not as someone who is especially good, but who realizes dreams for people that they cannot do for themselves, a kind of person in which we lose or find ourselves. Essentially he is a vehicle for psychic mobility—whether in mass media, fiction, or everyday life—and identification is the psychic mechanism on which one "rides." Some of these identity voyages actually help a person to get where he wants to go: for example, a young musician watching a concert performer. Others are merely compensatory; they do not help a person to get there but he feels better for having lived the role vicariously. In any case, a hero who provides such vicarious voyages is likely to be surrounded by a circle, or following, of "fans," who are the part of the public staking their identities on the ride he provides.

People of all ages use heroes in some way, but teenagers give us the sharpest, most sincere picture of the hero voyage of identity, because this is the age at which idealization is freshest and most impetuous—as parents are ceasing to be primary models[3] and career choices have to be made and many grown-up roles adopted in a hurry from the models available. A few statements by persons of various ages will illustrate the kinds of things that heroes are acknowledged to do for identity.

President John F. Kennedy had an impact on my life. I practically worshiped him. His charm, grace, and simplicity made me aware of the essential qualities. I cherished his words and wisdom and complete ab-

sence of flaws. I have hoped in my own mind that the man I end up with
will resemble the image I hold of Kennedy. (College freshman girl, age
18).

At the time that Sandra Dee was popular I thoroughly believed that
"it's true blondes have more fun" (I'm a brunette). I guess that could be
one of the predominant reasons why I chose to identify with someone
who was blonde. However, I believe at that time I had an unconscious
idea of the kind of image I would like to be like and Sandra Dee filled
the bill perfectly. She was what I hoped to be like—a darling girl, a
perfect figure, pretty smile and dimples, all the clothes in the world, and
many boyfriends—plus an outstanding personality. The first movie I
saw her in was "Gidget" and after that I saw all the films she made and
read all the articles in the movie magazines on her. Of course, the light
dawned on me later and I saw that she was not as perfect as I believed
she was and I became contented to be myself. (Freshman girl, age 18).[4]

I've had dozens of heroes, and they have all fallen by the wayside.
One of my heroes in grammar school was an only child. At nine years,
his mother forced him to wear long curls and starched collars to school.
He had to fight his way through. I sure admired that guy, his courage.
Whole gangs used to pick on him at once. And he cleaned them up. I
can see those fights today. The whole school used to turn out to see
them. Finally his mother let him cut his hair but he remained eccentric,
aloof. I became friends with him. Another of my heroes was in our high
school gym class. There were four teams competing in an intra-class
contest, a long relay race. Our team was losing. An unknown boy (I
didn't know his name at the time) came from behind with an amazing
burst of speed to win the race. He came from so far back it seemed impossible for our team to win. Boy, we just jumped up and down. He
became my hero. I fairly worshiped the guy. (Man, 30, recalling
boyhood heroes.)

This guy (my teacher) had quite an effect on me. He convinced me
that I should be an intellectual. Brother George was an extra energetic
teacher. He would write notes to himself in shorthand on the black-
board. He impressed me as being wonderful. He spoke Spanish, French,
and English, and would say the same thing in all three languages. His
wisecracks also impressed me. He came from California, and would tell
stories of mountains and movie stars. He talked of meeting them, and
about the different tricks used in movie filming. The thing which impressed me most was his fund of stimulating remarks, and the fact that

he treated the boys as equals, never stood on dignity. I remember one case where a fellow in class said, "I bet I can beat you in Indian wrestling." He let the kid pull him over and then cracked his arms like a whip and with ease threw him. He acted as a leveller, put kids in their place. One was a well built star football player. Brother George had to "whittle him down." Kids accepted his leadership. He could arrange teams and appoint captains. We felt that he was the best brother in the whole damn school. . . . At that time I had a pretty large inferiority complex. I was undersize for my age and pretty well excluded from everything. He did a lot for me. He roughed me up, made me think I was a little better than I thought I was before, that I was just as good as the other fellow. I wanted to be like him. He gave me the idea of being a teacher. I got the idea that teachers could be almost as good as baseball players. (Male, 29, recalling experience in a parochial school.)

The first hero I ever fastened on for any length of time was Greta Garbo. She was glamorous, beautiful, sophisticated—all the things that I wanted to be at that time. I wanted to be like her very much. I thought she was wonderful. I was hungry for any scrap of information I could get, any movie magazine which told what she was like, how she dressed. I wanted to familiarize myself as completely as possible with her life. I found out that she was a sad person, and I affected a sad attitude although I was by nature an exuberant person. I let the corners of my mouth turn down and my hair hang straight. I thought she was lonely and sad, and I felt lonely and sad. I was in that confused, adolescent state of mind, trying to grow up, insecure, wanting something to be like. I didn't necessarily want to be like my mother. I think I wanted to be more glamorous. Greta Garbo gave me a role to act by. I used to think, "How would Greta Garbo act, what would she do?" and then I would try to do the same thing. My mother wanted me to be a good housekeeper and I was revolting against that. I didn't want to scrub floors. Greta seemed so successful, glamorous, and beautiful, so much like a fairy story. I collected pictures of her, all I could get. I kept a scrapbook. I used to dream of writing her a letter, and out of all the hundreds of letters I would be singled out by her. My letter would appeal to her, and I would be taken out of my life. I daydreamed about her, and kept a diary in which I wrote of her and how similar we were. I remember years later reading it, and being so disgusted that I burnt the thing up. I think she had quite an influence on me for a short time: all my actions and dress were motivated by her image. During the time I admired her, she was absolutely perfect. Even now I find it hard to find defects in her, even though I don't feel strongly about her. (Question:

What was it about her that appealed strongly to you?) Her loneliness. Everything I read about her said she was lonely and solitary, and I was lonely. And I liked her nationality. She was Swedish and I was Swedish. She was tall and lanky and gawky and so was I. And then she was a success. I thought that I could be like her, we were so much alike. I saw myself as an actress and thought I could act. I liked the idea of her big beautiful home with a wall around it where I could be aloof. I never tried acting, but I always felt I could be right up there with her, that I had the talent for acting. I remember finding one of her photographs, on which I had written "Can I be like her?" What mostly intrigued me was that she was a poor girl and made good and was successful, and the fact that we were so much alike. There was hope for me. (Woman, 50, recalling teenage heroine.)

These examples, from younger and older persons, show the poignancy, wistfulness, and deep impact of hero worship as an orientation, helping a person to find, and in a sense to make, himself. They show how he uses a hero, sharing in his role vicariously, borrowing from him, imitating, sometimes using him as a fulcrum for rebellion against a parental model. A major hero like Garbo, Valentino, or Monroe may have an impact on a whole generation.

Such accounts justify our concern with hero worship as a character-building and identity-finding agency, and suggest that we shall never know what education is accomplishing, so long as the content of hero worship is ignored or is discounted as merely a passing phase of youth. They show below the level of rational education the nonrational choice and loyalty to heroes, and a yearning that can act as an emotional force in society, perhaps shift a nation's self image or engage people in movements—a wind that is always blowing, and the question is, where?

DIRECTIONS OF IDENTITY VOYAGES

What are the main directions of the voyages of identity through heroes? Our society offers what might be called a cafeteria selection—indeed, a smorgasbord—of choices probably wider than that of any other society or previous generation (which is probably not unassociated with our identity problems). We cannot describe all of the possible psychological journeys, as indicated by the social types of American society[5] (perhaps a function of the number of types of heroes multiplied by the kinds of personality among fans); but we can at least offer a simple, yet basic, classification of journeys in terms of relationship to the social structure—where a hero's role takes one in relation to one's own position and perspective in society. While all heroes provide some contribution to identity, it would be a mistake to suppose that all support the social order. In this regard, we can distinguish two main directions of identity voyage: an "educational" tour of role possibilities within, and largely approved by, the social order; or a kind of exit door for experiments in self-revision, and a fulcrum for leverage for rebellion or unsupported poses by which an individual can resist pressure to conformity and perhaps escape the social structure. This breaks down into three broad alternatives: (1) a journey which keeps a person within the social structure and takes him toward goals it approves; (2) a journey which keeps a person within the perspective of the structure but shows him how, or tempts him, to break its rules, leading him to feel bad about it afterward because he still judges himself by the old rules; and (3) a journey which takes him outside his social structure to a point where he relinquishes its perspective and his former self image, feels new experiences, glimpses new identities, and begins to judge himself with new rules. Let us call these routes reinforcement, seduction, and transcendence.

To illustrate, we might compare the possible effects of reading three kinds of writing. Suppose a person is reading the autobiography of Benjamin Franklin and admires his industry, thrift, and sturdy Protestant self-reliance; he is impressed by his moral progress, checklist of virtues, and reckoning of minutes in the day; and he is inspired to try to make something of himself by the same model. This would be a fair case, I daresay, of reinforcement of a role and a goal institutionalized in American society. On the other hand, suppose this gentleman is reading another kind of success story, Fred Pasley's biography of *Al Capone, The Story of a Self Made Man.* He is reading how Capone built up a hundred-million-dollar racket behind the front of a secondhand furniture store, admiring the cleverness with which he managed his farflung operations, the ruthlessness with which he wiped out rivals in the St. Valentine's Day Massacre, and the style with which he played the role of the "big shot," and he may even think of him as a kind of Neapolitan Robin Hood. He concludes that every business is a racket and therefore one ought to try to be like Capone—only smarter. I do not suppose it would be going too far to say that this "hero's" life is seducing this admirer to break the rules of his own society and incur its punishment though he has no real ability to justify himself by a different set of rules. If, on the other hand, a person is deeply impressed by the life of Henry David Thoreau, and moved by the argument of *On Civil Disobedience* to break a tax law, because of a new viewpoint as an ethical anarchist, I suppose it would be proper to say that he is emancipated by the example of his hero, rather than seduced into committing a common crime without a redeeming point of view that transcends the old norms. For a person who has truly transcended norms, feels liberation, not guilt, in violating them—perhaps even feeling "washed clean" like a religious convert, or "proven" with the mystique of a martyr, or prophetic with the conviction of a Nietzsche.

REINFORCEMENT BY HEROES

To reinforce a person in social roles—encourage him to play those which are highly valued—and to maintain the image of the group superself are presumably the classic functions of heroes in all societies. This is the unconscious conspiracy of storytellers, ballad writers, and poets. So Plato deplored Homer's license in showing the foibles of those such as Achilles, who were to serve as models for the young. So figures like Joan of Arc, Lincoln, Edison, and various saints are institutionalized to stack the cards in favor of a certain ethic or role. Society says "Be like that," and builds educational disciplines and shrines around it. A Japanese recalls with pride the hara-kiri of his father:

> My father called me, and told me that he felt under compulsion to join the spirit of General Nogi, and that he wished me to assist him in the act of hara-kiri—if assistance became necessary through his failure to perform it efficiently. I was to stand beside him, slightly to his rear, with his great two-handed sword upraised, and strike off his head if all did not go well. I remonstrated with him, because he was yet a comparatively young man, only 51. But he said that he had followed General Nogi through many years of fierce battle and he was resolved to follow

him in death. I watched him bathe, put on his white kimono and prepare the place of his ending. Then he took up his gold-hilted *waha-zashi,* the short sword, and wrapped a snow white cloth about its hilt and the upper part of the blade. Slowly he thrust the blade deep into his abdomen on the left side, and then cut across to the right side, turned the blade and cut upwards, His face was very white and tense, and his eyes closed as he pushed the blade home. I watched closely for any signs of weakness, for that would have been the signal for me to decapitate him, but there was none. He was a great warrior and a true samurai.[6]

So the son preserves with pride the heroic image of his father; and, doubtless, sees to it that his son does so in turn. And so societies use heroes as a character-building force to establish traits that help a person play expected or admired roles.

But the individual does not usually see a conspiracy by society to coerce him into certain roles. The beauty of heroes as a character-building force is that the individual, daydreaming, *chooses for himself,* within the opportunities the available models provide—which, fortunately for the social order, usually "just happen to be" more supporting than erosive or subversive. (Yet this ratio between supporting and subversive roles presented by heroes is crucial and should be of constant concern to a changing society.) Pride in hero-ism and the pleasure of hero worship sweeten the choice of good by what Freud would call "narcissistic gratifications" to overcome resistance to culture[7]—such as reluctance to make sacrifices ac-cording to models like the saint and the martyr.

I imagined myself as a famous football, baseball, or basketball star or even as an Olympic star; I imagined myself a "brain"—a scientist or something like that; with the arrival of the jet and rocket age, I imagined myself another Alan Shepard or John Glenn landing on the moon; I seriously considered myself a priest helping save souls; I imagined myself as a social worker or the like helping others. (Male, 18, college freshman.)

I identified with the role of the college student. I knew that some day I wanted to be one, so I worked for this goal insofar as school goes. I did my best to identify with my sex and stay in tune with the crowd so far as dress, hair styles, popular songs and movies went. Aside from the roles I actually played, there were those that I imagined myself in. I did this mostly through daydreaming. At one time I would imagine myself with an exciting job in Europe, a movie star at another, even the wife of the President (Kennedy) at times. Each of the roles I imagined myself playing seemed beyond attainment. (Female, 19, college freshman.)

My hero in my youth was Arrowsmith, in the picture starring Ronald Colman. When I first saw it, it nearly bowled me over. I saw it again and again, about six times. I read Sinclair Lewis's novel. I daydreamed, picturing myself as a heroic scientist fighting plague, making brilliant discoveries, and marrying a beautiful girl like Helen Hayes. I became a fan of Ronald Colman, following him in other pictures, hoping to again see the same heroic personage—which I never did quite. I resolved at this time (in high school) to become a doctor. I took up microscopy as a hobby, cultivated bacteria, and pictured myself as Arrowsmith in his laboratory. I took premedical studies in college, for about two years, before I gave up my idea of becoming a doctor after witnessing and smelling an autopsy, which woke me up from dreams and made me realize that for me medicine had been a romance rather than a profession that I really wanted. (Male, 49, college professor.)

These examples show normal identifications of teenagers, with supportive roles predominating. Heroes are steppingstones for trials of identity. They greatly extend the identity voyage by stimulating exciting daydreams beyond where an individual might go under his own power. Yet for all its romance, it is roaming on a short tether, for most heroes glamorize a role or career that society wants, therefore leading the horse from a romp in the pasture back to the barn.

Although a person may be attracted to a hero by his personality, one usually finds that a *role* is the main thing. Often people choose heroes quite different from themselves in personality because they admire their roles. So long as the role is satisfactory, it is quite possible for a hero to have traits different from those of the admirer, even traits the admirer does not like. The relationship to a hero is not a personal one, as with a friend, but an effort to use his role imaginatively.

I guess I idolized Elvis Presley for several reasons. I thought he was good looking and I really feel he has a good voice. However, what I idolized most was the fact that he came from a poorer family, and was able to shoot up in popularity so very fast. Almost overnight he became a millionaire. Then, once he had achieved this new status, he did what he hoped he would, he bought for his family a new home, cars, and all the nice things which they previously hadn't had. This made him even more of an idol in my eyes. (Female, 18, college freshman.)

I *do not like* Bob Hope personally, but I have a great deal of admiration for him because he gives of himself to make others happy (such as his Christmas tour each year). (Female, 18, college freshman.)

Scarlett O'Hara's spirit and determination impressed me most. She would never admit defeat, though she experienced heartbreak and saw the utter decline of a civilization she had been brought up in. I never felt pity for Scarlett, but I did admire her very much. Her courage and practicality and individuality in an age when these qualities in a woman were considered inappropriate made me feel proud of her. I often wished I had a larger dose of these qualities in my own personal makeup. She was courageous, headstrong, intelligent, practical, as well as domineering, determined, and sometimes quite cruel. Scarlett wasn't an altogether likeable person; in fact sometimes I disliked her very much! But her generous helping of good qualities outweighed her bad ones. (Female, 19, college freshman.)

I could empathize with Scarlett because, like her, I feel that land is a prized possession and part of one's self. The land seems to offer a little security which most everyone seems to be searching for. The most significant part of *Gone With the Wind* is Scarlett's love for the land. She goes to almost any extreme to save the property, as when she married her sister's beau in order to pay some debts so that the land would not be lost by her family. Although it may seem that Scarlett was a cold, cruel person, at times she showed herself to be kind, gentle, and loving, as at the end of the war when she and others helped the tired, beaten, hungry soldiers on their way home. Scarlett's acts seemed cruel at times. Although I disapproved of some of her actions, I admired her much because she had the courage to act. Her goal was to obtain something substantial, the land. When she was sure of her security, as at the end of the war, she was able to open up and give of herself to make others less miserable. This generous person is how I wish to think of Scarlett O'Hara. (Female, 18, college freshman.)

Here we see the admirer picking out what he wishes from the hero's roles and traits according to the requirements of his own vicarious journey.

A hero of one's own sex is most likely to meet these requirements, and is usually chosen,[8] though in some roles it may not matter (as in the military role of Joan of Arc). Where it matters most, of course, is where the hero is a "heart throb," perfect lover, or ideal mate, used as a model for daydreaming and romantic choice.

> For many years my idol, like many other teenage girls, was Elvis. When he went into the Army, however, I quickly found a new heart throb, Fabian. Elvis was referred to as sexy. Fabian was cute. I think that the main reason I had these types of idols was that I was expected to and would have been regarded as different if I did not. Idolizing a person such as the President or other leading statesmen was regarded as "square." (Female, 19, college freshman.)

> I liked Frankie Avalon, not so much as a singer, but because of his handsome face, golden tan, and body build. He is a type of person I had thought of marrying. Bob Anderson was the boy that I liked in high school. He reminded me of Frankie Avalon, and I will never forget the night of the school dance when he asked me to dance with him. I said to myself, "Imagine, just an ordinary girl like me dancing with a good looking boy." (Female, 18, college freshman.)

Yet it is important to distinguish this rather special use of a hero as a lover or heart throb from other uses of his role—especially in learning how to do things—in matters such as personal style, and skills for hobbies or careers.

> I bought most of Ricky Nelson's records, and I liked to sing along with him, and you can hardly notice my singing, for our voices blend so nicely. (Male, 18, college freshman.)

> At one time or another I identified with all the members of the Dave Brubeck Quartet. Since I could play each of the instruments and was a jazz fan, I naturally identified with each member of the group. I used to sit and listen to their records and then try to play the parts on each individual instrument. (Male, 19, college sophomore.)

Besides skills, perhaps more important, the teenager gains emotional support from the hero for his roles.

> I admired Doris Hart throughout the book (*Tennis With Hart,* a story of how a girl stricken with a disease of the legs, recovered from an operation and became a tennis champion at Wimbledon) because of the simple fact that she never gave up striving to win her goal. Doris wanted to become a champion at tennis—and she did! In spite of her handicap, Doris practiced day by day to achieve that which meant so much to her.

I played tennis in high school, and, I must admit, I became very discouraged at times. But, after reading *Tennis With Hart* and seeing the drive that Doris had toward her goal, I realized that I should have that want of tennis too, and—I ran on the courts in high spirit again! I liked Doris Hart very much simply because she wanted to become good in tennis just as I would like also. She was a determined person, just as I like to think of myself. Doris worked hard at achieving her main desire, and she made me realize how important it is that I work hard too. (Female, 18, college freshman.)

I liked older men, who were graying around the temples. One was a speech teacher in 9th grade. He brought me out of my shyness. He had a very soft-spoken voice and beautiful blue eyes, a wide smile and dimples. He could get the shy people to get up in front of the class and participate in skits and plays. He just had a way about him that made you want to work. Half the school had a crush on him. I think it was because at times he could look and act shy, yet he did all these outstanding things—so why couldn't we? (Female, 20, college junior.)

I found it easy to identify with the heroine in *Sweet Bird of Youth*, starring Paul Newman. Not only were we similar in appearance (blonde, blue eyes, approximately the same height and build) but, more important, had both been waiting for what seemed like such a terribly long time to see "the" man once again. Through her, it seemed that I was not alone in my boredom and loneliness. The movie did affect me to such a degree that I returned the following night to see it again. (Female, 18, college freshman.)

At the time I saw this movie (a story of the break-up of a love affair because the boy's father insisted that he attend college and study a certain profession) I identified very strongly with the girl and felt her situation to be almost identical with mine. I felt my boyfriend's parents were discouraging our relationship, since they were of a higher social class than my family, and because I might distract their son from school. I was terribly afraid of losing Bert and of how the loss would affect me. I saw the girl's nervous breakdown as my eventual course of action. I cried for over fifteen minutes at the end of the movie and could not stop thinking about the story for several weeks. (Female, 18, college freshman.)

I identified with Montgomery Clift (movie *Red River*, with John Wayne). He was young, handsome, a good horseman, and knew cattle and how to run them. I can fit into three of these very easily. Clift was emotional with his dad more than any other person. (This fits.) In fact, he and his dad had a fight. Well, last summer dad and I unfortunately had a fight, and dad knocked me out. In the picture, Wayne and son were always bickering. This fits me like a tight rein. The whole picture was just a mirror of my experiences last summer. We have a ranch in British Columbia. At the picture's end Clift and Wayne realized their faults and all ended well. Last summer's end was almost the exact duplicate as Dad and I were faced with our first prolonged separation and realized it was far better to face the future with each other's support than separately. (Male, 18, college freshman.)

The following examples show the moralizing effect of the hero as a "good guy":

I identified myself with James Stewart in *Mr. Smith Goes to Washington* (story about a man elected to the United States Senate, who becomes involved in a scandal and makes a single-handed fight to preserve his reputation) in the scenes in which he has been implicated in the scandal. He decides he can't let his boys down, so with the help of his secretary he filibusters. Thus, Jeff Smith (James Stewart), an ordinary person who is still awed by his new surroundings, stands before the U.S. Senate ready to fight the state machine with only a moral cause as a weapon. The feeling I got as he stands there, hoarse, barely able to remain on his feet, is a feeling of great loss or sympathy which really chokes one up, almost to the point of tears, moreover, there is the feeling of hatred for the forces which would leave such a good person in such a difficult situation. I identified myself as such a crusader who fights seemingly insurmountable odds for a just cause. I liked Jeff Smith because he had the courage to fight for his just cause. (Male, 18, college freshman.)

(Film *The Cardinal*, story of a young priest, Steven Fermoyle.) His sister was found dying from excess bleeding caused by an unsuccessful abortion. After rushing her to the hospital, the doctor came out and told Steven that there was only one choice, to save his sister whom he loved a great deal, or save the life of a child who was not yet born and of whom he knew nothing. Being a Catholic, he knew that there was only one choice, and that was to save the child. His decision to many might seem wrong, but it was what he believed in, and what he knew he had to do, even though she was his sister. I liked the character of Steven Fermoyle because of his strong character, standing up for what he knew he had to do even though he did not want to. I feel he was a sincere person, though ambitious. Someday I hope I can stand up for half as many of my Catholic principles as he did when I am faced with them. (Female, 19, college freshman.)

It isn't very hard at all to identify with Jack Lemmon (film *The Days of Wine and Roses*, about a married couple and their bout with alcoholism). You feel his frustration throughout the story, that he can be helped yet his wife will not accept help. Approaching the end of the story, you really feel some of the pain and helplessness that Lemmon feels as he sees the results of his actions, his agony knowing that he has led his wife into this life and can't help her out. What brought the point home is that Lemmon is very, very normal; and what happened is very like real life. Perhaps this is why it had such an impact on me. Friends I run around with have been drinking for years. It is such a short step to what the movie portrays that it gets to be a bit frightening. I know that my consumption of liquor has decreased, and this movie had something to do with it. (Male, 22, college junior.)

These examples illustrate reinforcement of roles, skills, and attitudes desired or needed by the social order by means of heroes. They represent what I would call the short tether, a romp in the pasture of vicarious experience, but most of the paths leading back to the barn of adjustment to the role structure. The teenager is not naïve enough to accept models that are too obviously didactic and "corny" (even John F. Kennedy was regarded by some as square); on the whole, he makes constructive and wholesome choices.

But in the smorgasbord modern mass media offer—ranging from crusaders to gangsters, saints to sexpots, self-made men to playboys—obviously all the models are not supporting the social structure. Let us consider a second major possibility.

SEDUCTIVE EXPERIENCE

This is that the hero will provide a voyage of identity like a romp in a fenced-off pasture, taking a person into roles forbidden or defined as "bad" by his culture. The hero is in many ways a "good guy" but—because of his greater daring, impulsiveness, talent, luck (or bad luck), or charm—breaks the rules in such a glamorous way that he does not become an ordinary criminal or villain. His success, near success, or romantic failure (perhaps martyrdom) teaches a lesson quite different from the didactic one of the villain, whose punishment is proof that breaking the rules does not pay.

The lesson is, rather, that it is possible, permissible, even admirable, to romp in the forbidden pasture.

This has been amply pointed out by comments about such mass media heroes as Mickey Spillane's Mike Hammer and Ian Fleming's James Bond.[8] The license to kill, brutality, sensuality, materialism, and egoism make them surprisingly similar to villains, except that they are cast in the good guy—even the law enforcer—role and avoid some of the more blackhearted and contemptible traits, such as treachery, cowardice, and small-mindedness. Gallantry, a certain largeness of soul expressed as courage or generosity, enables heroes to get away with many things that ordinary men cannot. This I call the seductive power of the hero; he looks like a good guy but does many of the things that the bad guy does.

How does the normal person react to a seductive hero? If he imitates the good qualities of a role which is defined technically as bad, there may be little harm.

> I identified with Bernardo, the leader of the Puerto Rican gang (in *West Side Story*) mainly because of his attitude. He seemed the type to be very cool and calm in any situation. He was what one would call "cool." He acted in a superior manner, which was one of the reasons that he was probably chosen leader of the gang. He was courageous, and he commanded the respect and admiration of all the members of his gang as well as members of the other gang. I tried to look and act like him. (Male, 19, college sophomore.)

On the other hand, the hero may lead his admirer into roles which he later regrets and feels guilty about.

> My Navy friend was the epitome of a California "cat." He was everything I pretended to be. He came from San Pedro, smoked marijuana, knew all the "sayings," rolled drunks, stole money from "farmers" (sailors from Oklahoma, Nebraska, Kansas, etc.). I liked him because he was as rotten as I wanted to be and between the two of us we broke every rule and regulation of the Navy (of society too) that we could without getting caught (almost). We each got caught once. (Male, 30, college junior.)

The seductive effect of the hero may not be to outright crime, but merely to a style which favors violation of social rules.

In the movies, I have always liked the big, brutal type, that always gets the girl in the end. (Robert Mitchum, Kirk Douglas, Sean Connery as James Bond.) I like these characters because of the roles they play. They are the big, tall, strong men. They always end up with the beautiful girl. They are the heroes. (Male, 18, college freshman.)

I found James Dean (in *Giant*) to be very dynamic and full of vigor, a violent type of person. I liked him because he seemed so real in life. (Male, 18, college freshman.)

I used to see all of Elizabeth Taylor's movies, and envy her because she had such a lovely face. Another thing I liked about her was her divorce from Eddie Fisher and marrying Richard Burton. I thought that was interesting because she kept going from one man to another. (Female, 18, college freshman.)

Though one may enjoy vicarious experience of a seductive hero with little conscious shame or guilt, doubtless a moral strain of some kind (some psychologists call it "cognitive dissonance") is produced in the superego—if only a need for casuistry or a worry about consequences. The death of the hero (as with the outlaws Robin Hood, Jesse James, and John Dillinger) helps to palliate such moral strain. But morality waits patiently for most of the corrupting heroes of mass media to get their just deserts. Except for the grossest pornography—and this applies hardly at all to violence—they go on romping without rebuke.

From an intellectual point of view, the main shortcoming of the seductive hero as teacher is that he leads a person into experience felt traditionally to be wrong, but does not redefine and recreate standards by which experience is to be judged. He eludes and confuses morality, but makes little contribution to it in terms of insight. His excursion into the realm outside mores has done little for him or anyone else philosophically. He is not a new man but an old one who was punished, or who got away with it.

The third alternative of a hero's possible influence is more creative.

TRANSCENDING EXPERIENCE

This more creative possibility is that the hero not only helps the horse to escape into the forbidden pasture but helps him to get a new conception of himself, the pasture, and the barn. Let us call this kind of effect transcending or liberating. Transcending experience, instead of giving a person a rather smirking feeling of having gotten away with something naughty, produces a fresh point of view, a feeling of integrity, and makes a new man. Doubtless this is what Nietzsche meant by the "transvaluation of all values," an experience having some of the impact of a religious conversion, of Jesus upon Saul, in helping a person to see the world with new eyes. Such a hero provides a new "generalized other" (in G. H. Mead's terminology) or "superego" (in Freud's), more than the viewpoint of an outlaw peer group, by which a person can judge himself in terms he feels are superior to those of his forefathers and peers. It may be that the former associates cannot tell the difference between this new man and an old man ruined, but the new man himself feels raised, not fallen.

So *Life* magazine finds a curious mystique of American college youth about Jean-Paul Belmondo whose "sexy, cool, ugly-handsome, heroically nonheroic, utterly irrepressible ... non-conformist" style "has given youth a new image of itself." How do devotees in Belmondo enclaves on college campuses describe this impact?

> It's the only justified hero worship there is right now.—He's free and separate and not petty. He has wings.—Students are wary of the organization man. The opposite is the disorganization man, and that's what Belmondo is. But he is self-sufficient. We admire many of his traits.— Belmondo's the coolest guy there is. One guy in our dorm didn't like Belmondo. We ostracized him.—He's always got a little hidden smile, humor that other actors just don't have. That's cool, that's today, that's what the kids dig. He's the center of hepsville.—His biggest attraction is that he doesn't have any goals or objectives in his films. He's sort of a modern Western man who doesn't have to think.—He's the epitome of what I'd like to be. Know yourself and own yourself.[9]

Thus these college students feel this hero has given them a new conception of themselves, through his disengaged, individualistic style, which is more than the idea that "I can get away with something" that traditional morality frowns upon; rather, it is a sense of liberation into a new perspective which has a sense of ethical right— mystique though it may be. By transcendence I mean a person gets new eyes to look at the world and a sense of new self, which is more than license to an old self.

Three stages in liberation through the role of a hero can be distinguished. First is awakening to new values, new experience which enriches a person's perception of values outside the old perspective. Sometimes this is called "escape." A student describes her reading of an adventure story about an explorer in the Amazon jungle:

> I often found myself changing places with the author. My long desire to break away from the everyday world seemed to transfer me to Leonard's side. The brave actions that the author did were some that I had often daydreamed about. His bravery, especially with snakes, influenced me, because I have always been deathly afraid of them and hoped that I could overcome this fear. The beauty and tranquility of the jungle are something I have always looked for, but never found. Leonard Clark saw the beauty and strange serenity of the jungle. He realized that gold was not actually what he was looking for but, instead, the wealth of understanding and being aware of the world around him. At times Leonard Clark was a very confused man, not knowing which path to take or what advice to follow. Because I often found myself confused and unknowing which way to go, and because I love the out of doors, I associated myself with the author. (Female, 19, college sophomore.)

Another student describes the influence of reading *The Razor's Edge* by W. Somerset Maugham:

> One of the characters, Larry, wasn't like anyone I have ever met. He sought for happiness, but not through the normal channels. He sought for happiness in his mind, the world over. He learned the discipline of mysticism, and that the world is a manifestation of the eternal nature. He lived in India for five years in an ashrama with the yogis and meditated with them. Larry described the yogi and the word I remember most was saintliness. From this experience Larry gained peace and true happiness. He wasn't influenced by what the world demanded of him but was only interested in finding an inner peace and complete understanding of himself and others. To me this is absolutely wonderful. If I could achieve this, I would feel as if I had accomplished something. To feel at peace with myself is the most important thing in the world. When I read this book I felt that if I could only stop the world for awhile and be left alone to think, everything would fall into place, my purpose and my life. For some time I had been searching for this but I had not found a book, or a person, who could answer this for me. After reading the

novel, I realized that Mr. Maugham was trying to say, "You must find your place in life *yourself,* and you can find this place through meditation and deep thought." I have read and been influenced by many books and authors, from Thoreau to T. S. Eliot, but I feel this is by far the most important in my life. (Female, 18, college freshman.)

Another gained a sense of freedom from Ayn Rand's novel, *The Fountainhead,* by identifying with the hero, Howard Roark:

This story was very much like my real life. I've always been independent and I don't like to do what everyone is doing or wear what everyone is wearing. I don't like phoney people. People must be able to live with themselves before they can really get along with others. Roark had a real power of resistance to be admired. This was not put on just to be different, for he had a tough battle with the public. He believed it wasn't always necessary to follow the will of the majority. This to me is freedom and self-satisfaction. This book was not the type to be put down and forgotten. It strikes close to home at a few "sacred cows." (Female, 18, college freshman.)

These cases show a shift of perception away from the conventional perspective and a sense of emancipation, an ability to "go it alone," from identification with the hero.

Second is alienation from the perspective of the old group, a sense that one cannot "go home again"[10] because the hero's perspective has led one to turn a stranger's eye on one's own group. Such a result is reported from reading *The Catcher in the Rye* by J. D. Salinger:

After Holden Caulfield flunked out of school, he spent three days and nights underground in New York. He is confused amidst the milieu by the dishonesty and cheapness he sees around him. The story was about a boy's quest for truth and innocence in modern society. He didn't like school, because it is full of phonies and everybody studies so you can learn enough to be smart enough to buy a Cadillac, and you have to pretend to care when the football team loses, and everybody sticks together in dirty little cliques. I think that every person who is honestly searching for the meaning of truth in our so-called advanced civilization identifies with Holden, because he is trying to see people as they really are. Because he was so sensitive and young, he was deeply affected by the cheapness and ruthlessness that he saw. In the end he had a nervous breakdown. It could not ruin him, but only made him stronger, older and wiser. I liked Holden because he struggled like all teenagers do. He was sensitive, honestly inquisitive, and, like most teenagers, discontented, confused, and observant about society. (Female, 18, college freshman.)

Another reports alienation from the world on reading a story by Franz Kafka:

Gregor, an unimportant nobody, a person who is merely ordinary, not deserving any fate extraordinary, awoke one morning to find he was an immense, hard, shiny roach-like bug. He lived like that, with his family trying to keep him hidden, until he finally dried up and died. He never knew the cause of his metamorphosis and never changed back. I identified quite strongly with poor Gregor. I could feel the sense of futility pervading the work. I read the book taking barely a breath, because I had to find out the reason for the man's pitiful condition. When it finally began to be apparent that there *was* no reason, I felt a slow rising anger against a world that would let such a thing happen. To me, the real cause of Gregor's plight was the insufferable blindness of all humanity. How such a man could have been left in his condition by those who should have tried most to help him is beyond me. I couldn't help but feel that Kafka's symbolism stood for each man's nature, and that that nature was one of non-communication, each one with his own views, unwilling to accept those of any other. I think that this view of human nature would appeal strongly to teenagers, for they are trying to assert their own humanity, and society seems to incessantly reject it. (Female, 19, college sophomore.)

A third student is alienated by Hawthorne's *The Scarlet Letter*, applying the indictment of Puritanism to society as a whole:

I read this twice. Man's inhumanity to man is dominant all the way through the novel. Hester Prynne had committed the worst sin of Puritan society. She was given the punishment of standing on a scaffold before the people of Boston, and also forced to wear a scarlet letter "A" on the breast of her dress for the rest of her life. Society itself is probably the most evil institution in our world. It has the power to ruin an individual's life. The Puritan society was harsh in its beliefs. Any deviate was severely punished. I felt strong sympathy for Hester and sheer hatred of the society itself and Roger Chillingworth (the revengeful husband). Most people forgive and forget, but never would the Puritan New England society let Hester forget her sin. As I said, I came to thoroughly hate the Puritan society. This book had great impact on my thoughts. I began to compare our society today with the Puritan society. In many ways they are quite similar. Society, from its beginnings, has inflicted selfish cruelty on undeserving individuals. (Female, 19, college freshman.)

Identification with a hero who has suffered from society, or who is himself alienated, helps to disenchant a person with his own society.

Beyond alienation is a third stage, which we might designate as identity dislocation, development of an identity which does not fit into the old role structure. This involves an image of oneself as no longer fitting, as belonging somewhere else; and a break with old identity, roles, friends, associates, culture. The following extract shows a person exploring an identity ordinarily forbidden to him through the role of a hero who crossed racial lines, and developing a conception of himself which transcended his former prejudices:

John Howard Griffin, in *Black Like Me,* darkened his skin in order to appear like a Negro, and traveled in the deep South in 1959. The book is a journal of his experiences as a Negro in the South. In Griffin's words, "The real story is the universal one of men who destroy the souls and bodies of other men (and in the process destroy themselves, for reasons neither really understand)." I identified with the author throughout the book. With him I felt the fear of changing to a different and strange identity, crossing class and caste lines into an existential quicksand from which he may not return easily. I, too, felt with him, the free floating anxiety characterizing his new role; he had to guard himself and recognize the nuances of behavior required of him in his new role. There was nothing to shield him from realities of raw experience. I felt his every emotion as he described: his sense of injustice, his alienation from "the other" caste of people, his feeling of helplessness, his fear in the presence of potentially hostile others, his compassion for the people of both races, his hatred of hatred and ignorance. Both before and after I read this novel, I have found that I define myself as *man,* white, American, college student, etc. This book has helped me to recognize this. The first part of life is that I am alive on this earth as a human being. I am a bit of insignificant protoplasm creeping around on a rather hostile planet. In this situation, the only things I can communicate with are other human beings, the only essence outside my own that I can feel anything for is the essence of my fellow man. Only fools lose their "human-ness." And, if I am to understand myself, I must learn to understand "my other selves," regardless of how they define themselves or how I define myself. Griffin was a courageous man dropping a self-imposed definition of himself to confront the world with naked existence sans the props that hold up most people. The only way I want to define myself is as an alive person (as opposed to a dead person). (Male, 20, college sophomore.)

Another account of the effect of reading *The Catcher in the Rye* shows change in self-conception and maladjustment with former associates:

I sympathized strongly with Holden Caulfield, and read the novel three times, twice in high school and again within the last month. His extremely sensitive view of our society was a magnification of my own views. I felt very alone and was able to pick fault with everyone I met. Since I did not have as acute an awareness of society as Holden Caulfield, he was able to express for me the many things I couldn't think or say clearly myself. I definitely identified with him, and was affected for many months after my first encounter with the novel. As Holden described the things in his world, I began to apply them to the things that confronted me each day, and share his feelings and opinions. Along with his outlook on life, I also picked up his vulgar language and found myself much too descriptive in speech. Sometimes this offended others. (Female, 18, college freshman.)

A movie (*Gidget,* starring Sandra Dee) offers a springboard by which a girl can vicariously leap from femininity into a role usually reserved for boys:

Sandra Dee was trying to be a surfer and she wanted to be accepted by a group of male surfers, who lived in a shack on the beach—as one of them or at least as a good surfer. These boys only laughed. In one scene I wanted to cheer her on when she ran by a group of silly, giggling girls in bikinis and stuck her tongue out at them because the surfers weren't impressed by their playing with a beach ball. In another scene, Sandra was practicing her surfing on her bed, and she was getting a little discouraged. I felt sorry for her and wanted to tell her to keep trying. Gidget was different and she stood up for what she believed. She thought it was silly to giggle and throw a beach ball around to impress the boys. Gidget wanted to show the boys that she could be just as good as they were, and even though she was laughed at, she kept up the struggle for a long time. (Female, 18, college freshman.)

I am not implying that identification with an unusual hero is sufficient to cause identity dislocation, without motivation by a personality problem. The hero serves only as a cue and guide; if a springboard, one must want to jump. But potential rebels, needing only something to fight for or against and an image of how to do it, can find their leverage in literary characters such as Antigone, Dorothea Brooke (Eliot's *Middlemarch*), Carol Kennicott (Lewis' *Main Street*), or Howard Roark. The following extracts show how heroes play their part in dislocating identities:

Not long ago I met a boy. We discovered we both liked folk music, so on this foundation we started going out together. I was a senior in high school then and Steve had just dropped out in the second semester of his senior year. He told me that it wasn't because he had been expelled that he had left school but because the administration had considered him a dangerous influence in school. I couldn't tell at that time what the administration could have meant but little by little I began to see things about Steve that made him seem one of the strangest persons I had met We both liked to read and I had just finished reading Ayn Rand's *We the Living*. I didn't know Ayn Rand's philosophy, so probably didn't get the message from it she intended ("con" altruism, don't let anything or anyone interfere with your ego, the futility of trying to be altruistic). Steve proceeded to explain this philosophy and told me that his idol was Ayn Rand and that he wanted to become her protégé. After I read *The Fountainhead,* I was amazed to see parts of Steve's character in practically all the characters of that book. Although he said he didn't agree entirely with Rand's philosophy, the very fact that he was becoming her characters proved to me that he was patterning his life after them. Steve thought he was superior to everyone else. He wanted to become a writer, but school interfered with that, so when the opportunity arose, he quit. One of the major complaints he had about school was that his teachers didn't understand his writing. I read some of his short stories and understood them quite well. Every one of them tore down some established institution, not only American but even basic universal institutions. Steve hated organizations, institutions, rules, anything that stepped in his path to discover himself. He cared for no one; if he ever did anything for anyone, it was only to gain personal pleasure or satisfy his own egoistic needs. Since his defiance of order through writing was never published, he tried to find every way in daily life he could to express his contempt. He got traffic tickets every week—speeding, drinking while driving, and just about any illegal thing he could think of to do. He ditched the draft, somehow. He even door to door campaigned any "way out" thing he could think of. Some of the things he protested were: public schools, a national army, government, the draft, the family, policemen or any law enforcing officers, all taxes, any obligations to the state or country or religion or God. I couldn't explain what he was *for*, because even when he used to tell me he would contradict his former views time and again. For instance, he believed in some sort of socialistic or communistic society, and yet to my mind a society such as this would destroy his concept of the individual finding himself and not permitting anyone or anything to prevent him from doing exactly what he wanted. I have never met anyone who seemed a stereotype of the characters in a book before. (Female, 18, college freshman.)

I first noted Adolf Hitler in 1928. Journalists regarded him as a fad, but I immediately thought of him as important. His was the only political movement that ever appealed to me much. It promised to rid the world of its woes. He was like Napoleon. He did things I would have liked to have done. He had the right way of solving the problems of the world. He was a man of action. He succeeded. Maybe it was his idealism—the strength of his ideology. He pretty well to my mind exemplified the hero of the Nordic mind, archetype of German conqueror. I admired him, looked upon him as a sort of an iconoclast who would overthrow conservative dogmatism. I had an affection for him, saw him as a sort of saviour of Western culture. I had loyalty and would defend him; got into a number of arguments, which almost cost me my job. He was a definite factor in my life. He offered hope. I somehow saw a new means of achieving results along the lines I had been thinking of but saw no chance of achieving. I wore an Iron Cross, had swastikas and pictures of him. I read *Mein Kampf* and a number of articles about him. Did a little private propagandizing. Thought about him. I desired to share him with others, would welcome fellow admirers. It was hard for me to see why there was so much opposition to him. He had a more effective way of remaking the world than kindness. The things that impressed me most about him were his eloquence and decisive action. He reminded me of Hannibal, Caesar, Napoleon, Genghis Khan. His jubilation at the capitulation of France and signing the armistice in the coach the first armistice was signed in. His personal actions during the purge of 1934 or 1935 in which he personally led storm troopers and carried out the purge at considerable risk to himself. His self-sacrifice during the last days of the defense of Berlin. He stayed in the bunker to defend the city against the Russians. His personal appearances to troops. His unfailing belief in success. His defense of a cause that was losing but will never be lost. His mistakes were of a sort that heroes make. (Male, 50, businessman.)

These examples—ranging from trivial to politically significant—show how heroes are used by suitably motivated people as springboards for identity dislocation. Lack of a springboard does not prevent an act, nor does a springboard cause it: it only helps a person to jump a little farther.

Such examples—of reinforcing, seductive, and transcending heroes—show three kinds of identity voyages possible in a society with a smorgasbord of models like ours. We see seduction and transcendence working against reinforcement. Identity dislocation occurs if a person grows away from the reinforced role models of his society—with the help of seducing or transcending heroes—to the point where he no longer fits in, feels that he belongs somewhere else, and tends to break with his old life, roles, friends, associates. Such an effect might be caused by direct peer group influence (what sociologists call "differential association"), religious or ideological conversion, or by hero worship not directly supported by a peer group. The effect of dislocating heroes is, of course, precisely opposite to that of institutionalized models (such as "Truthful George," "Honest Abe," Florence Nightingale). It seems plain that models such as the beatnik, folk singer, jacket boy, Hell's Angel, rock and roll musician, hipster, skinik, beachnik, surfer, and playboy are more or less dislocating to American youth. There is no reason to suppose that identity dislocation through heroes is restricted to any age group. It is reasonable to expect that identity dislocation for all kinds of people will increase with social mobility—whether personal or psychic through fiction, biography, news, history, or other vicarious media.

I have tried here to outline three of the main directions of identity voyage that heroes make possible: (1) reinforcement, shaping character for roles in one's own society; (2) seduction, offering an experience which violates social rules and puts a person into moral and social strain; and (3) transcendence, attaining a viewpoint that cannot be gotten within the group, that must be attained outside, or through the eyes of an outsider, which enables a person to redefine himself more favorably than "bad".

The sociological importance of the hero is that he can be an outsider, coming from almost anywhere, who offers the leverage of his own image as a significant other to put against and resist the pressures and models of peer group, fathers, and forefathers. He is, therefore, especially significant in acculturation as an emancipator. While hero worship normally acts in conjunction with peer, family, religious, and general cultural influence, it is quite capable of acting contrary to, and of withstanding, them.

Much of this is not visible; it is going on *within* a man who does nothing visibly. This is the "Mitty function," the compensation of unfulfilled dreams and identity. So the smorgasbord of role choices does not necessarily mean greater opportunity for fulfilment of self. Rather it may go along with the considerable frustration of unrealized identity: the unfulfilled person may harbor many dreams of what he might be from psychic mobility; he is sophisticated beyond his lot in life.

It seems to me, then, that there is a shift away from reinforcing to other kinds of functions for the heroes of modern and modernizing societies. From Homer to Joyce and Kazantzakis, from Beowulf to James Bond, from Reynard to Mickey Mouse, the hero goes on in one form or another. But we can note apparent shifts of emphasis and function from traditional to modern socieites. One is in the medium in which we encounter heroes: a traditional society's heroes are in oral tradition (folklore, legend, ritual drama), while a modern society's are in mass media (print, picture, radio, cinema, television—relatively "hot" media).[11] Second, a traditional society's heroes are experienced in a context of social control—group storytelling or ritual—whereas modern heroes are experienced more privately (even when "alone in a crowd"). Third, traditional heroes are a few approved models representing what society wants; while modern heroes are numerous, diverse, novel, fictitious, or real persons, often not "heroic," possibly antiheroes, not necessarily approved or what society wants but representing what individuals in a mass want. Fourth, traditional heroes have predominantly reinforcing functions, while in modern heroes there seems to be a shift to nonsupportive (seductive or transcending) models. Fifth, traditional heroes are more likely to function as group superselves and represent strong tribal or other collective identity than those of modern society. Finally, modern heroes are more likely than traditional heroes to have a strong compensatory function—to make up for frustrations, to supply vicariously perhaps the only interesting identity a person has in a society of many people with identity problems.

MASS HERO WORSHIP AND THE CULT OF CELEBRITIES

Such things may help us to understand why hero worship in the mass is frenzied and the cult of celebrities is so important in modern society. The enthusiasm for heroes comes in part from the identity problems of people who are "available," to use Kornhauser's phrase,[12] together with the fun of the vicarious voyages—hitchhiking made possible by the mass media. Mass hero worship means masses of people enthusiastically "going someplace" vicariously, using celebrities of their choice as vehicles, with communication facilities projecting images to large numbers of people.

Mass hero worship is not just the convergence of individual lines of choice; at some point it becomes a shared experience. An obvious example is when innumerable "fans" find themselves in a crowd sharing enthusiasm for the same favorite. Soon they become aware of a fellowship. This sense of fellowship strengthens hero worship in several ways. It gives it a sanction: it is right, even glorious and noble, to feel this way about the same person together. A role is recognized, named, organized, and governed by rules, concerning how a devotee, fan, buff, *aficionado* should act and what his rights are. Fellowship in hero worship may give rise to clubs, organizations, and institutions devoted to the hero. The basic tendency of the behavior toward celebrities, as I conceive it, is cultic; it is one of the most important forms of secular cult in modern society.

Most of the curious forms of behavior toward celebrities make sense when viewed as a collective effort to put someone into a cultic status, where he can be efficiently used by devotees. There must be opportunities for psychic contact with the hero, symbolic devices which enable devotees to identify with him closely, and a continual supply of information about the heroes that they can use for inspirational purposes. *Inspiration* means more than mere enjoyment or appreciation; it means investment of one's personality in a relationship of communication that arouses enthusiasm because it is doing something for one's own idenity. The devotee literally is nourished psychologically by his hero. Every moment of contact, every source of information, every anecdote, every memento—even, perhaps, a cigarette butt—is precious. So one is not surprised to read that when a musical group called The Rolling Stones played for teenage fans, they threw chewing-gum wrappers as souvenirs to the crowd, and the fans struggled and crawled on the floor to pick them up.

Likewise, a touch is a precious memento to a hero worshiper. "I touched him! I touched him!" is the familiar cry that every celebrity hears when he is buffeted and bruised by crowds (the Duke of Windsor reminisced, "If I were out of reach, a blow on my head with a folded newspaper appeared to satisfy the impulse"). Since souvenirs are what is wanted, something more than a mere touch is highly desirable. The celebrity is likely to have his clothing torn off and pieces taken as souvenirs. This is not theft but expression of an attitude which is almost proprietary. Along with it goes an intense curiosity, a hunger for information. Jack Dempsey recalled, "They want to look at your eyes and your ears to see how badly you have been injured. They want to pick up a word here or a gesture there which, later on, they can relay, magnified, to their own little public." Albert Einstein remarked wryly, "I often feel among crowds like a prostitute who is under constant police surveillance." A respectable-looking woman of middle age tried to peek into Charles Lindbergh's mouth while he was having dinner at a New York hotel to see whether he was eating "green beans or green peas." So Kahn describes how fans kept watch over Frank Sinatra, invaded his privacy, and chased him in packs:

> They pin club buttons not only over their hearts but also on their socks . . . inscribe his name on sweaters and coats. A girl whose arm he had accidentally brushed while trying to escape from a pack of fans wore a bandage over the spot for two weeks, to prevent anybody from brushing against it. Another became the envy of her gang, when, after Sinatra had checked out of a hotel room, she got into it before the maids did and escaped with a precious cigarette butt and a half used packet of matches, both of which she assumed her idol had touched. . . . Whenever Sinatra emerges from his hotel and hops into one of the limousines he engages while in any town, any girls who are lucky enough to be near a vacant taxi swarm into it and take off after him. Others light out on foot,

but . . . lose track of his car after a block or so. Then, breathing heavily, they try to guess where he is eating or—since he almost always goes to the theater after dinner—which of the shows is on his agenda.[13]

Such "nonsense" makes more sense when one sees it as a kind of hunger for identity and a form of cultic devotion which reaches a competitive frenzy.

Other features of mass society having to do with the organization of communication about celebrities also make more sense when viewed in this light—for example, the institution known as celebrity watching. The function of many restaurants, nightclubs, and discotheques known as "celebrity hangouts" is not to provide food or entertainment but to allow people to watch celebrities (who, themselves, may be subsidized for their patronage). Celebrity watching is a major preoccupation of a mass society with countless people nourishing themselves vicariously by watching the famous. This can dominate the tone of some localities. *Time* comments:

When it comes to celebrity watching, the town of Beverly Hills, California (population 33,500), is the capital of the world. "We're all voyeurs here," says screen writer Peter Stone, who just escalated a notch toward celebrityhood himself by winning an Oscar for the year's best script, *Father Goose*. "When we pull up to a red light we all look over at the next car to see who's in it."[14]

Likewise, television quiz shows, "guest appearances," and so on are thinly disguised forms of celebrity cult—institutions to feed celebrity hunger. Occasionally a feast—one might say a debauch—of celebrities occurs, fascinating the entire nation, as, for example, the famous masked ball of Truman Capote at New York's Hotel Plaza in 1966. It brought together persons such as Marianne Moore, Frank Sinatra, Alice Roosevelt Longworth, Andy Warhol, Henry Ford, Norman Mailer, McGeorge Bundy, Douglas Fairbanks, Walter Lippmann, William Buckley, Lynda Bird Johnson, and Princess Luciana Pignatelli—all in masks, with, as Capote said, people "practically committing suicide because they didn't get invitations." But most of the time fan magazines, gossip columns, fan mail, and a farflung organization of fan clubs provide the pipeline of information about celebrities.

The fan club, even when commercially inspired, is not a mere association but basically a form of hero cult.[15] Such a cult is not imposed from above, but grows from zeal and fervor below. Because of this fervor, it will tolerate all kinds of "nonsense" from the hero—for example, the following from Muhammad Ali (Cassius Clay), World's Heavyweight Boxing Champion, to his fans about his obligation to serve them as a hero:

> To my friends who are interested in joining my International Fan Club I want you to know some of the unique privileges and qualifications which go with it. First of all you should know that every member of the International Fan Club automatically becomes one of "THE GREATEST." Just as I am KING of the boxing world you become "KING" among your friends and in your neighborhood. Here is what an International Fan Club member receives: a wallet size I.F.C. identification card with a picture of Muhammad Ali (me), World's Heavyweight Champion on it; a five inch by seven inch membership award certificate, suitable for framing and hanging on you wall; an IFC membership button with gold printed IFC emblem and my picture on it; you will be kept informed by letter of all my activities: what I'm doing . . . where I travel. . . . Members may purchase my photo album . . . for the reduced membership price. . . . (All fans should have one.) Remember . . . that . . . you will have club buddies all over the world. This is why you'll be one of "THE GREATEST" when you join my club! . . . Thank you for writing me. I'm always happy to hear from my fans. Sincerely, World's Heavyweight Boxing Champion.[16]

We get a good picture of what the fan club is doing for the personalities of its members from the Frank Sinatra Fan Club, said to be the oldest permanently established fan club in the Western world. A female Sinatra fan for over two decades tells what the members do to maintain a vicarious but nonetheless active relationship with the hero. They collect his recordings, see all his films, read everything printed about him, write him applauding his successes and thanking him, treasure his autographed pictures and especially letters, and send him get-well cards—even potted plants—when he is ill. As an organization they put out a bulletin, "Speaking Frankly," to keep members up-to-date, also pictures and sometimes mirrors and pins with Frank's picture on them. They work as a pressure group to thank publications which praise him; and defend him, even trying to boycott or have banned publications which criticize him. "We are proud of him and wouldn't want him changed for anything. It makes you feel good to know you have a real friend whom you can depend on. . . . Frank is a wonderful person, sincere, loyal and understanding." Thus they maintain an idealized image which gives them inspiration and comfort. "It is hard to put in words just what Frank means to us. He has been so wonderful and we love him. There is an understanding between us that can't be described." Though this devotee has never met Sinatra, she has received an autographed picture and recordings from him over years, from this gaining a feeling of a bond of mutual solicitude. Once when she was worried and depressed a package came in the mail containing one of his albums, inscribed, "To ****, best wishes, Frank Sinatra." This made her feel better, as "he knew" it would.[16]

These examples show how the fan club serves its members. It brings celebrity watching to perfection: not just occasional treasured glimpses but a constant pipeline of information and communication to devotees; and psychological support through the feeling of relationship with the hero—sometimes, in fact, mutual; in any case, fellowship among devotees sharing a mystique of "loyalty."

The supreme consummation of any cult is personal contact with its central value—in this case the hero, who appears to the faithful to validate the ikons (pictures, souvenirs, relics) which represent him symbolically. The thrill of such personification can hardly be much less than that of Pygmalion seeing his statue come to life. So Alexander King describes a meeting of the Joan Crawford Fan Club when the "goddess" herself appeared—in a style so amusing that I cannot forbear quoting at length:

When we arrived at the theater, around eight-fifteen, the meeting of the Manhattan chapter of the Joan Crawford Fan Club was already in full session. The fans were all gathered in the lounge, which, in such movie houses, is just the dimly lit antechamber to the powder room and the ball room. Between these two comfort stations about fifty collapsible chairs had been set up by the accommodating management, and seated on those chairs was the surprise of my life.

You see, I'd always associated autograph collecting with a lot of dizzy kids with bad teeth and bad skin who had dandruff on their eyelashes. But here, assembled in this deadly anteroom. . . were a lot of sober-looking middle-aged and even quite elderly people. There were about a dozen and a half youngsters around, too, but, by and large, the group seemed like a cross section of any part of any middle-class American neighborhood.

It floored me. They weren't particularly well dressed or anything, but they certainly weren't on the bum, either. Very few people in America ever are, for long. Some of the women wore sweaters, but quite a few of them had hats on; not Lilly Daché or Mr. John type hats, but a least they wore head-pieces, instead of just hair nets. The men were the usual vacant-faced city dwellers who haven't any handicraft or other specialized occupation sufficiently differentiated to put its stamp on them.

When I finally began to pay a little more attention to the chair, it became quite obvious that the leading spirit of this organization was the officiating president, an unusually homely girl called Vera Zimmerman. Vera's hair seemed to have the exact texture of Brillo, and, although she couldn't have been more than fifteen, she already had the beginnings of a very promising mustache. Her other accomplishments I'm going to skip for the moment.

After the reading of the minutes, Vera cleared her throat so thoroughly that it took quite a sizable batch of Kleenex to take care of this transaction; then after she'd downed two paper cups full of water, she made a truly stupendous announcement.

"I want to tell you confidentially," she said, "that Miss Joan Crawford is in town, right now. She is here incognito, so none of us is supposed to know anything about it."

I don't have to tell you that the room absolutely simmered with suppressed excitement. Joan Crawford enthusiasts of all sizes and ages had stopped fidgeting and scratching themselves and now looked at each other sideways in wild surmise. It was a tense moment in our lives.

"I just want to tell you," Vera continued, "that, because Miss Crawford is such a close friend of mine, and I kept begging her and begging her for about an hour—as I said, because she's such a close friend, she agreed to drop in on this meeting for a few minutes tonight."

The audience sat frozen in an absolute ecstasy of delight and stupefied anticipation. I could hear the horns growing all around me.

"She's going to the theater tonight," said Vera, "and I expect she'll be by here in about ten minutes from now. She's planning to just drop by, like any other member of our chapter, see? She'll go to the back of the room and participate in the meeting, like any other member, and she made me promise, on my solemn word, that everybody will just go on with the business of this meeting, just as if she wasn't here at all. Remember, she's anonymous! And I gave my solemn word to her, or she wouldn't drop in at all. Now, it's up to us to act like it was just an ordinary Thursday night and nobody special had dropped in at all."

Well, you can just imagine that the meeting was a complete shambles after that. Elderly matrons started tittering like schoolgirls; the younger people had to relieve their feelings by going, en masse, to the toilets; the blower shifted his dog to the other arm, and the secretary, whose name was Weaver Killian, once more began to read the minutes of the last meeting.

But it was all right by me, because now it looked as if we might get some real pictures. Meanwhile, everybody in that crazy room was shaking with acute autograph jitters. It was certainly tough for them to just go on living until their idol could really, finally, appear among them in the flesh.

Funny, I thought to myself, nothing ever changes very much in the human character. The gods of the Greek Areopagus came down from Olympus and visited, and sometimes even cohabited with, ordinary mortals. And now Joan Crawford was about to descend from her heights to shed a moment's beneficent luster on common mankind.

"How about some pictures?" my photographer asked me.

"Well," I said, "we can't take any without permission. It's a ticklish situation right at this moment. We're liable to queer Vera and all the rest of them, because it will look as if she'd notified us. So hold it for a little while. Who knows what the hell is liable to happen."

Well, the next thing that happened was that Joan Crawford's golden evening slippers appeared at the top of the staircase, to be instantly followed by a white cascade of snarling foxes. A few seconds later, the staring, wild mask of her face became visible, and let me confess that even I had grown quite excited in the atmosphere of frantic suspense that pervaded the premises.

She looked surprisingly like a badly animated puppet, and, as she was covered from her ears to her ankles by dozens of limp skins, the impression of lifelessness was almost complete. She was accompanied by a tall, frozen-jawed Englishman, whose type was very much in vogue as an escort during that particular season.

Well, Joan and her Johnnie walked, or rather, drifted to the back of the room and sat down on the two folding chairs that had obviously been prepared especially for them. My photographer and I happened to be sitting almost alongside them, and I tell you that it seemed to me that Joan was, for some mysterious reason, almost as excited at that moment as everybody else in the place. She had a tough time breathing with any sort of regularity, and I finally even noticed a handful of bloody fingernails come out of that bundle of fur and settle convulsively in the general region of her heart.

Down front, the officers of the club attempted to proceed about their business with some semblance of purpose and order. Weaver Killian read the minutes of last week's meeting for the third time. When he had finished, there was a moment of indecisive silence, and it was during this moment that I was suddenly assailed by the eeriest feeling. It seemed to me that I was witnessing some sort of staggering biological phenomenon, something like an atavistic reversion on an unprecedented scale. You see, I was convinced that the people sitting there in front of me were all starting to grow eyes in the backs of their heads.

They were so feverishly, intensely alert, that I could see the blood clearly pulsating in their ears, and I felt with growing certainty that all this suppressed tension was bound to end in some sort of explosion. I tell you, it was beginning to get insupportable.

And then Vera Zimmerman spoke up. She talked very strangely, like someone under a strong hypnotic compulsion, and it was clear to me that the words were absolutely wrung out of her, almost as if against her own real wishes.

"I gave my solemn word," she said. "I gave my solemn word to Miss Crawford—to Joan, I mean, she's asked me to call her Joan—and I just want to say that I told everybody here that she's here incognito. But, now that Miss Crawford, Joan, is really here amongst us, I hope she'll forgive me if I ask her to address just a few words to this meeting."

Poor Vera raised her stricken face and looked towards the back of the room so appealingly, that I was just on the verge of saying, "Hear! hear!" when Joan Crawford slowly got up and, in a trancelike condition just like Vera's, started to float down to the small dais.

And now that they were all officially absolved by their chairman's breach of contract, everyone in the place automatically swiveled in the direction of Joan's progress. The poor bewildered Englishman had also gotten to his feet, of course, and glided aimlessly in her wake toward the front end of the room.

Joan at last very abstractedly stepped onto the platform and looked down at the lot of us, as she were suffering from an acute attack of amnesia. I'm telling you, she looked as if she was positively bewildered by all those goddamned staring faces in front of her.

It made no sense. After all, she was certainly used to mass adulation, wasn't she? So what the hell had suddenly gotten into the dame?

And then her arms slowly emerged out of that fur tent and she opened them wide, in a conventional gesture of the religious revivalist who is asking for volunteers to come up to the penitents' bench. She stood like that, silently, for about thirty seconds, and then, suddenly, unbelievably, she lowered her head and started to cry. But I mean *cry!* She bawled like a six-year-old kid whose first Didy-Doll has just dropped into the family well. She simply leaked with sorrow and shook with shameless, uncontrollable sobs. And then, when she started to wipe her face, she smeared mascara all over her white fox furs, all over her arms and hands, and believe me, she certainly didn't give the slightest damn what she looked like at that moment.

The Englishman kept fluttering around her, like a torn kite that's been cought in an updraft, but, despite his ineffectual appearance, he somehow managed to slip her a handkerchief, and he finally even got her down off that platform. In an emergency he turned out to be a real man, after all. In the end, I saw him firmly putting his arm around her shoulders and purposefully piloting her up the stairs, out into the night again.

But the rest of us remained. I'm wondering if anybody is really fit to describe the condition of that audience, which had been so completely stunned out of its not too abundant wits and now sat openmouthed and perspiring in the dim light of that gruesome meeting room.

A goddess had wept; had wept completely, and shamelessly, as any heartbroken human drab might weep. No wonder all their eyes were cast down, and not a single voice was to be heard; for the room had certainly been hexed and turned suddenly into a dwelling place of unnamable sorrow and ambiguous contrition.

As I looked at that assembly of white-faced, frightened people, it came to me that they were like a conclave of innocent communicants who had just been accused of activities terribly dangerous to the public safety. I watched them move slowly and reluctantly toward the exit, as if they expected an enormous police wagon to cart them all off to some unimaginable place of grim retribution. Let me tell you, it was a bitter Thursday night.

"What the hell was this all about?" said my photographer. "What the hell was wrong with the daffy doll, anyway?"

"It's obvious," I said.

Of course there was nothing obvious about it at all.

"She's a dame who was awful poor once herself," I said, "and I suppose, when she stood up there and looked at all those adoring schlemiels staring worshipfully up at her, it suddenly hit her, that there, but for the grace of God, was herself. Maybe it's been quite a long time since she's been face to face, and that close up to her own boring, mediocre past; it suddenly must have walloped her where it hurt her pretty bad."

I was making up this whole rigmarole, just for the benefit of a younger man who liked to have neat answers to everything. He was never satisfied merely to see Vesuvius erupting and covering the whole neighborhood with boiling water and hot ashes; he wanted to hear all the appropriate statistics relating to such an outburst, and, also, to know the meaning of the thermal-dynamics involved and to have it all properly arranged and classified for future reference. So, I had just quickly improvised the sort of answer that would send him home peaceably and in a state of reasonable contentment. Still, when I finally got home, I couldn't help but wonder whether I hadn't, by the merest accident, just happened to hit on the only right and sensible solution.

For, after all, why in hell did she suddenly burst out bawling the way she did?[18]

Contempt is not quite fair for this scene, as only the devotee can know what he gets from his communion. Without doubt, what fans get from a hero is important for them. Such behavior as celebrity watching, the touching mania, fan clubs, and the personal appearance arousing ecstasy in followers shows that the role of the hero is, in a sense, psychologically nutritional—people hanker for him, he provides for them a kind of feast—and that his service to the mass is vehicular, in that he allows a lot of people to take an identity voyage all at once—not in a canoe but in an ocean liner, not on a motorcycle but on a bus.

How can popular worship of heroes be compared with religion? While it does not offer contact with a sacred reality beyond the ordinary world, there are important similarities. Fans do not pray to a popular hero as one might to a saint for intercession, but there is a kind of prayer in the wish, "Can I be like that?" There is no supernatural salvation, but a very real spiritual realization made possible by the hero as a model. There is no approved doctrine, scripture, or ethical lesson; but some message there is, if one can only read it. In main, I think that hero worship has this in common with religion: a profound concern with identity (both group and individual); and an ability to elevate, ennoble, realize, give mystique. The realization of this function—whether in individuals cherishing souvenirs of entertainment stars or crowds such as those lining up to venerate the body of Lenin in Red Square—is capable of making it as important as the church. It is easy, therefore, for a hero cult to compete with, if not displace, religion as the institution having the most impact on character.

CULT OF CELEBRITIES—WHERE IS IT TAKING US?

The most significant feature in the history of an epoch is the manner it has of welcoming a Great Man.

Thomas Carlyle

If we try to appraise the cult of celebrities from the point of view of Carlyle, as an institution of *heroes* to build character and uphold the values of society, some shortcomings are immediately apparent. It does not work, for example, like a saint cult, to organize a community by veneration, name days, and holy days. It does not hold up a common ideal for all, support morality, courage, or any of the recognized virtues. It has little common focus, its idols representing diverse and conflicting ideals and working at cross purposes. The churches, with their task of upholding ideals, have found much cause for complaint in celebrity cult.[19] If Carlyle were alive today, he probably would, above all, lament the fact that the cult of celebrities seems to pick out and prefer ordinary over great men.

For it is obvious that those receiving the most popular homage, fan mail by the sack, are not, as a rule, the most important and meritorious men in our country. Persons doing the real work—in business, politics, education, science, technology, religion, social welfare—receive little attention unless they hit the public eye in a very special way which generally has little to do with their practical contribution. Popular interest is in celebrities—mostly in the entertainment and communication fields—who have a talent for capturing audiences, managing publicity, and showmanship tactics. So the white knight of the flashbulb not only steals the show from those who are doing the real work but displaces from the pedestal traditional great men—George Washington, for example, is not half so interesting as any of a dozen singers, playboys, athletes, movie stars. Even the success story—of making good by hard work—has lost much of its glamour since success is so often epitomized by celebrities who have made good the easy way by showmanship or entertainment gimmicks, and who present a shoddy image of living it up rather than the comparatively rare one of service and ethics as seen in a figure like Albert Schweitzer. It was

Carlyle who, over a century ago, first noted and lamented this trend, now aggravated by mass communication.

Well, then, the problem is, Where are modern celebrities taking us? What kinds of identity voyages do they offer to the masses? If, by tradition, a hero should elevate and reinforce ideals, what about celebrities who are not heroic?

If we take the view of Carlyle that heroes should be great men, then the prospect is depressing. While it is hard to find a historical baseline by which to prove that there has been a deterioration of heroes (did the Puritan of Hawthorne's time have higher models, on the whole, than the white-collar worker of today?), it is fairly easy to convince oneself of the mediocrity of current celebrities just by taking a good look at them—any collection, in the newspapers or on television, will do. Indeed, it is not implausible to suppose that if a hundred celebrities were chosen at random from the *Celebrity Register,* or from persons drawing the largest crowds or getting most space in popular magazines or time on television, they would prove no better (by any defensible criterion, whether of real achievement or personal, moral, or intellectual merit) than one hundred persons taken at random off the street. If reliable ways could be found for measuring merit—wisdom, virtue, even plain honesty—it could probably be shown that most celebrities are just what they often admit they are: the boy or girl next door—with a little luck.[20] The "luck" might be no more than the "sound" of a voice, a fortunate film vehicle, a good press agent, or a dimple in the right place.

A hint of what is happening to heroism today is given by the furor over the award by Queen Elizabeth of the decoration of the Order of the British Empire (MBE) in 1965, to the Beatles, whose huge dollar earnings had been of benefit to British trade. As a result of this ceremony, six English war veterans turned in their MBEs, one commenting indignantly, "English royalty wants to put me on the same level as those vulgar nincompoops." Another said, "There is nothing brave about yapping at a howling mob of teenagers with a million in the bank."[21] In other words, people of genuine merit felt degraded by comparison with these new celebrities. Does not their indignation express a feeling of many that standards of merit have slipped, that luck in capturing audiences is put on a par with virtues like courage, service, and self-sacrifice?

The celebrity himself is often rather apologetic, the first to accept what Walter Winchell calls the "roulette" philosophy of success, whose proponents include Perry Como, Frank Sinatra, Bing Crosby, and William Holden who says:

> My success is just luck. I'm the kind of guy, I guess, that any other man can identify himself with. If Holden can do it, the man in the audience thinks, then I can do it too—slug the villain, get the girl, anything.[22]

He is often the first to recognize that "imperfection" is an important part of his popular appeal—because of the filip it gives to the imagination of the average man to say to himself, "If he, who is so ordinary, then why not I?" This is leveling down rather than measuring up.

Public relations experts themselves sustain this picture by promoting the impression of their power to build anybody into a celebrity. Statements by participants—an entertainer and his manager Bob Marcucci, creator of Fabian, Frankie Avalon, and John Andrea—show the shoddiness of the buildup process, which blows up an image like cotton candy from the most ordinary materials. The creature (John Andrea) tells how he has changed under the coaching of his manager: his name is shortened from D'Andrea to Andrea; he walks differently, with toes turned in and less slouch; his speech is improved by "pestering and nagging" and the help of a vocabulary-building book; he feels a new man. The creator comments:

> John, he's starting to bloom. It's a slow, tough process. . . . When I first saw him, it was in a crumby club in Atlantic City. . . . He was doing a number and I suddenly realized—he had the look. You can't define the look. Fabian had the look and Frankie Avalon. John had the look. But he needed to be groomed. He had no poise, no savez-faire (sic), is that the word? and he was a very introverted kid, didn't enjoy himself with people, and you could see the way he was performing. That had to be changed so he could become big. . . . So there were diction lessons and drama lessons and music lessons and publicity and tours, wardrobe, the works. I figure I got $50,000 tied up in this kid before he makes a penny. . . . I feel like I'm really creating something here that's exciting. You may not believe this, but when I was just a kid I once saw *Pygmalion* with Leslie Howard. That picture hit me like a bullet. I really dug it. I said to myself in that crumby theatre in South Philadelphia,

"Marcucci, you're going to do that Pygmalion bit. You're going to change things. You're going to create.[23]

A whole profession of specialists calling themselves "image makers" has grown up; and, if they are half so powerful as they think they are, one shudders to think of the creations that will come from their pygmy-pygmalion brains.

After being built up, or succeeding by sheer luck, we find the celebrity living it up according to the popular image of success, again with the help of a public relations agent, who coaches him and disseminates releases like "Success overtakes Patti Chandler":

> For 20-year-old Patti Chandler, the glittery world of Hollywood has become wonderfully real. Patti is about to succeed in movies, and the rewards are already at hand. She has a contract calling for five pictures this year. She has a gloriously rich boyfriend and time as well for the less serious young actors who work with her. Instead of making her own clothes and bikinis, she buys them now in expensive shops, and she has turned in her little black car for a brighter, sportier one, in which she can air her friends' dogs (fancy poodles). People have always turned to look as Patti walked by. But she is excited because today many are fans who recognize her from her pictures.[24]

So the celebrity is seen to be of ordinary stuff; and the knowledge of the buildup and image behind his success do little to encourage the idea that fame is based on merit, or that popular interest is focused on merit that makes "heroes" superior to ordinary men.

If we adhere to the view of Carlyle, then modern celebrity worship is a debased hero cult, whose orientation is horizontal, if not downward, directed mostly toward persons at the farthest remove from Emerson's great men, Foxe's martyrs, Plutarch's Lives. To the extent that it is focused on persons who are not heroes, it becomes a voyage of identity from nowhere to nowhere. Does a "personality" like Bardot, Sean Connery (James Bond), "Liz" Taylor, Frank Sinatra, Dean Martin—even Mary Martin— really add anything to what you had before? Is there any reason for an ordinary person to give up the style he now has in favor of such models? Is it only a matter of fads in styles, sounds, looks? Is the self-made man story improved by being seen as a buildup? To the extent that these questions apply, the image of the hero and his success as a voyage of identity is a train which really does not go anywhere but brings people back to the same place—or, just possibly, leaves them off someplace they had not intended to go, worse off than before.

Viewing it as one would if saints were being canonized from the ranks of unreformed pickpockets, we would say that there is a fault in the selective process, an absence of effective screening. No rigorous test is put in the way of those who enter the winner's circle, which guarantees that they will in fact have some superiority of character, talent, wit, or wisdom—even sincerity or mere toughness—above the ordinary. The truth is that almost *any kind of person* can become a popular hero today. This is largely because modern communication has made it so easy for the ordinary man to seize the spotlight. One cannot rule out a Bobby Baker, even an Al Capone. Were the merit badges really to the good, the race to the swift, and the battle to the brave and strong, the common man might feel envious, but he would not feel so much *common ground* with his heroes. Nor would the lesson be that any kind of person can be a hero. But if the style of the playboy, the cabaret performer, the pseudohillbilly, the sexpot, the tosspot is good enough, then why should a person try to live up to a higher standard—if all he wants is success? Perhaps the most painful thing of all, from a Carlylean point of view, is that people no longer expect heroes to be extraordinary.

Another aspect of the problem is that the *range* of models available is probably wider than ever before in history. One can stay within a charmed circle ranging from Tarzan to Einstein, James Bond to Dr. Murphy, Henry V to Henry VIII, Hugh Hefner to Albert Schweitzer, Joan of Arc to Joan Baez. Psychic mobility is doubtless increasing in terms of available voyages of identity, the ability to imaginatively revise oneself. One can get about anything one wants in a hero today; this means loss of consensus about heroes. Under such conditions, one cannot guarantee that people from a new generation will want the same things as their parents, or that they will agree among themselves on values.

The question calling for research, then, is twofold: (1) Which are the most frequent and influential mass choices of identity? (2) What is the proportion, or balance, of identity voyages of various types? Not much is known about either of these questions. Not only is there doubt that celebrities of today are better than the people who admire them, but there is an uncomfortable possibility that the proportion of reinforcing to seducing and transcending models has shifted to a critical point of imbalance—that more "heroes" are tearing down consensus than building it up. Sorting out identity voyages into categories such as reinforcing, seducing, and transcending has yet to be done. Still, the difficulty of such subjective evaluations is no excuse for not making them; after all, everything that matters is subjective. To repeat, the question that needs investigation is whether the proportion of "bad (seducing) and transcending models to "good" (reinforcing) models has shifted dangerously to where a balance supporting mores cannot be maintained—as suggested by Robert C. Angell. The widespread dire pronouncements about rising crime rates and the malaise of modern society must also be considered.

It is apparent, at least, that many celebrities are feeding the dropout trend. This refers to types like James Dean and other rebels without a cause; Joan Baez, Bob Dylan, other folk singers of protest and style rebellion; Lenny Bruce and other "sick" humorists; the Beatles, Rolling Stones, and other such musical style rebels; Hugh Hefner and the playboys; Jean-Paul Belmondo as the disengaged hero; Lawrence Lipton, Jack Kerouac, Allen Ginsberg, and the beatniks; and Timothy Leary and the hippies and LSD cultists.

Another question is whether the increasing range of heroes and psychic mobility are increasing frustration. (the "Mitty syndrome") For example, is the teenager happier after seeing the worldwide antics of the Beatles or the jet-set style of Julie Christie in *Darling?* There is an unsettled ratio between the satisfactions of vicarious experience which compensate people for what they are not, and the frustration of unrealized selves and too many inappropriate models.

At any rate, it seems plain that the mass is engaging in identity voyages that would have astounded and shocked the previous generation—some of them inconceivable to a square like Teddy Roosevelt, and certainly depressing to Carlyle. And every country that undergoes the "transistor revolution" is embarking upon such voyages.

When seductive and transcending models outweigh reinforcing ones, I presume one has an alienated society in which square models are rejected in favor of dropout types. Such models are used, rather, for escape and groping toward new styles. Though they may ultimately lead to something constructive, at the time they serve dispersion more than social integration.

But the Carlylean perspective is bound to be disappointing. It is like trying to weigh shrimps in a scale designed for tuna fish. It may be asked, what right have we to expect the mass heroes of today to measure up to the great man? Most of them are little people like ourselves, whose attempts to find a life style, whose little victories, whose dramatically simulated emotions or interesting looks have caught the imagination or warmed the heart of people, many of whose lives are so much poorer that these seem rich.

Once we abandon the Carlylean perspective, the celebrities of today stop being merely disappointing and become interesting in a new way—as persons who become famous as beatniks, folk singers, hippies, playboys, playgirls, sexpots, good Joes, smart operators, charmers, personality kids, splendid performers, jacket boys, surfers, hipsters, pundits, mystics, dandies, characters, daredevils, rebels, super athletes, disk jockeys, and comedians—as experiments in identity, some pathetic, some brave. Like fads, they are efforts to find an exciting and victorious way of living under modern conditions of bureaucracy, impersonality, and pushbutton comfort, which work so powerfully to defeat the heroic spirit.

If these triumphs are largely compensatory and vicarious rather than real for the mass, amid obstacles to heroism so great, why should we depreciate them in a world which is relatively poor in identity? It is rather like complaining about a candle when there is no electricity.

Moreover, viewed within the same theoretical perspective as fads, the majority of heroes are *bound* to be failures because they are competing in a societal selection which must have its failures to find its successes. Nor can one say with confidence that any popular hero, however ludicrous—say, the hippie—will not be the progenitor of a new way of life.

Society actually has no better way at present of finding new life styles than the experiments in identity which in this book we have treated under topics like fad, fashion, style rebellion, poses, cultism, and popular heroes.

In the next chapter we turn from the dreams made possible by heroes to the course of action which has the greatest power for changing identity—the crusade.

8 Crusades

Heroes take people on vicarious journeys, but crusades take them on real ones. If one starts acting like a hero, he may become a crusader. A crusade may require him to act like a hero. A crusade is a type of movement that rises above ordinary life because it requires one to leave business-as-usual and commit himself earnestly to something he belives in deeply. It is, therefore, capable of producing powerful effects, both on society and on one's conception of oneself. It is, to use various metaphors, a game in which the stakes are high, a plunge, a path from which there is no return. It requires faith in something good enough to justify the trouble and risk. A statement of one of the original crusaders is not foreign to the spirit of all crusaders: "I am marching with a goodly band, and we have placed ourselves entirely in the hands of God, for we go forth as His servants to accomplish His will."[1] Because of such spirit, one may say a crusade is a movement which carries both a cross and a sword. The sword signifies attack on wrong, defense of right, and cutting the bonds of ordinary concern. The cross signifies commitment to higher ideals, mystiques—indeed, every crusade has a cultic aspect, whatever its practical goals, because it needs and uses ritual and achieves redemption of identity along with its practical work. So I would treat crusading as a prime route of identity transformation, one of the few kinds of movement besides cult that does for its members internally as much as it does to society at large.

This is far from implying that a crusade must be a religious movement; rather, I propose to treat it as a generic kind of movement that might arise in any era—though more likely in some than in others. History *does* repeat itself, if one can ignore enough particulars. Many historians will support such a contention: Crane Brinton, searching for recurring patterns of revolution; or Richard Hofstadter, noting that the propaganda appeals of fascist demagogues of the 1940s resembled those of Populism in America in the 1880s: "There seemed to be certain persistent themes in popular agitation of this sort that transcend particular historical eras."[2]

Which is exactly my point. Doubtless there were movements like crusades before Christianity began. The mentality can be found in other cultural contexts: the *Koran* says, "Those who believe do battle for the cause of Allah; and those who disbelieve do battle for the cause of idols. So fight the minions of the devil." Crusading is generic, I think, because it lies, not in a particular set of beliefs about salvation, but in elements of human nature such as the melodramatic conception of conflict between good guys and bad guys, the righteousness of authority, and the sense of shock to mores or social structure (anomie) which doubtless all societies experience.

Americans rather like crusades. Hofstadter says:

Americans do not abide very quietly the evils of life. We are forever restlessly pitting ourselves against them, demanding changes, improvements, remedies. . . . There is a wide and pervasive tendency to believe . . . that there is some great but essentially very simple struggle going on, at the heart of which there lies some single conspiratorial force, whether it be the force represented by the "gold bugs," the Catholic Church, big business, corrupt politicians, the liquor interests and the saloons, or the Communist Party, and that this evil is something that must be not merely limited, checked and controlled but rather extripated root and branch. . . .

So we go off on periodic psychic sprees that purport to be moral crusades: liberate the people once and for all from the gold bugs, restore absolute popular democracy or completely honest competition in business, wipe out the saloon and liquor forever from the nation's life, destroy the political machines and put an end to corruption, or achieve absolute, total, and final security against war, espionage, and the affairs of the external world. The people who attach themselves to these several absolutisms are not always the same people, but they do create for each other a common climate of absolutist enthusiasm.[3]

While we may regret the results of some crusades, such a mentality, in itself, is neither good nor bad; but it *is* righteous; and if you are on its side it is "right." From its rightness comes its power to mobilize and change people and its courage—or presumption— to change society. Without crusading, I daresay, social change would be a rather lukewarm affair of trying to build a better world by piecemeal improvements and pragmatic methods, with minimum disturbance to the status quo. There would be little sense of moral conflict between groups. Major changes would be slow, except where innovations were obviously sensible (as in the improvements of auto design) or "fun" (as in the case of fads and fashions). No one would become famous for stirring up things in the manner of a Margaret Sanger, Carry Nation, or Gandhi. But, because it is so human to crusade, we do not really know whether society could get what it wanted without such activity for whenever we have large changes—as from modernism and acculturation—we have usually had crusading in some form. We do not know whether changes like the Reformation or English Revolution could have occurred without people being thrown in jail and having their heads bashed. But, though we do not know exactly what crusading accomplishes, there is little doubt that our society would be less exciting if there were no people with zeal for causes.

These aspects of the question I propose to consider here: the kind of mentality that gives men the courage to upset and try to improve society; the pattern of collective action in crusades; and, especially, the cultic function, whether explicit in a movement like Cromwell's or implicit in a movement like anticommunism in the United States.

This is the main reason for discussing crusades in this book: their redemptive possibilities, their power to snatch a person from a humdrum life and offer him a chance to define himself by engagement.

THE CRUSADER AS A SOCIAL TYPE

What kind of person is a crusader and what is his role? If we are to go beyond a mere dictionary definition (one who undertakes a "remedial enterprise with zeal and enthusiasm"), it might be by considering people such as Harriet Beecher Stowe, William Lloyd Garrison, Margaret Sanger, and William Booth, often called crusaders by historians and biographers; or persons most often though of as crusaders—Billy Graham, Martin Luther King, Carry Nation, George Lincoln Rockwell, Adolf Hitler, Susan B. Anthony, Gandhi, Jesus Christ, Richard the Lion-Hearted, Martin Luther, Dorothea Dix, and Mario Savio.[4] It is plain that Americans do not automatically consider crusading good or bad, but feel that various people of whom one approves or disapproves can play the role. The commonest things said in describing crusaders were: works or fights for a cause in which he believes, effectiveness in rallying people, and rebel or pioneer who broke new ground. The range of personal traits—from Carry Nation to Mario Savio, from Martin Luther King to George Lincoln Rockwell—is great; we seek, therefore, something that might be shared by diverse persons, such as a stereotypical image, a role, and perhaps a mentality or outlook which different kinds of people could share. This is what I mean by saying that a crusader is a social type rather than a personality type.[5]

The most stereotypic example of the crusading mentality and role is probably Carry Nation and her hatchet, which are symbols of good versus evil, clearing the way for the new order, or defending the threatened values of the old order. This hatchet probably goes back in an unbroken line of symbolism to Don Quixote's lance and Richard I's two-handed sword—indeed, to Excalibur, for all I know the first mythical hero in the distant past who came in time of need to strike a blow for the good. This is the militant spirit of someone who knows he is right and intends to do something about it—stir people up, even brave society's wrath if necessary. It is expressed in a speech by the slavery abolitionist William Lloyd Garrison:

> I determined, at every hazard, to lift up the standard of emancipation in the eyes of the nation, *within sight of Bunker Hill and the birthplace of liberty*. That standard is now unfurled; and long may it float . . . till every chain be broken, and every bondsman set free! Let Southern oppressors tremble—let their secret abettors tremble—let their Northern apologists tremble—let all the enemies of the persecuted blacks tremble. . . . Assenting to the "self-evident truth" maintained in the

American Declaration of Independence, "that all men are created equal, and endowed by their Creator with certain inalienable rights—among which are life, liberty and the pursuit of happiness," I shall strenuously contend for the immediate enfranchisement of our slave population. . . . I am aware, that many object to the severity of my language; but is there not cause for severity? I *will* be as harsh as truth, and as uncompromising as justice. On this subject, I do not wish to think, or speak, or write, with moderation. No! No! Tell a man whose house is on fire, to give a moderate alarm; tell him to moderately rescue his wife from the hands of the ravisher; tell the mother to gradually extricate her babe from the fire into which it has fallen;—but urge me not to use moderation in a cause like the present. I am in earnest—I will not equivocate—I will not excuse—I will not retreat a single inch—*and I will be heard*. The apathy of the people is enough to make every statue leap from its pedestal, and to hasten the resurrection of the dead. . . . Posterity will bear testimony that I was right. I desire to thank God, that he enables me to disregard "the fear of man which bringeth a snare," and to speak his truth in its simplicity and power.[6]

Another abolitionist, Benjamin Lundy, expresses the crusader's spirit:

My humble exertions shall be directed to the one great end—my whole self shall be devoted to the holy work—my march shall be *steadily onward*—and neither sectarian pride, party zeal, nor even persecution itself, from the "Powers that be" or that may be, shall turn me to the right hand or the left.[7]

So the Civil War soldier takes the spirit of the crusader in his song:

> Let the hero born of woman
> Crush the serpent with his heel,
> Since God is marching on.

And the modern crusader speaks in the sermons of Billy Graham:

The world is waiting tonight for a young man riding a white charger to say to the world: "Follow me! Let's clean up the world."

Teddy Roosevelt was not an ideal crusader in his work, yet he stated the viewpoint—especially the sense of moral conflict—as well as many who played the role better:

There are, in the body politic, economic, and social, many and grave evils, and there is urgent necessity for the sternest war upon them. There should be relentless exposure of an attack upon every evil man, whether politician or businessman, every evil practice, whether in politics, in business, or in social life. I hail as a benefactor every writer or speaker, every man who, on the platform, or in book, magazine, or newspaper, with merciless severity makes such attack, provided always that . . . the attack is of use only if it is absolutely truthful. . . . (There is) a kind of moral color blindness; and people affected by it come to the conclusion that no man is really black, and no man really white, but that all are gray. In other words, they believe neither in the truth of the attack, nor in the honesty of the man who is attacked; they grow as suspicious of the accusation as of the offense; it becomes well nigh hopeless to stir them either to wrath against wrongdoing or to enthusiasm for what is right; and such a mental attitude in the public gives hope to every knave, and is the despair of all honest men.[8]

The crusader's sense of wrong-to-be-righted requires him to picture the evil in terms which seem vivid and overheated, if not paranoid, to others who do not share his viewpoint. So the interviewer asks the Jehovah's Witness, "How do you know you are doing the right thing, do you ever doubt your faith?" And she answers:

Oh I know but if I ever doubt or do something wrong it is because of the devil. Satan is still on the loose you see, he is always working against the Lord and trying to win people to his side. We Witnesses have to always guard against him. Still he gets some of us. Those he does are excommunicated. Satan poisons people's minds. Most other churches follow Satan; that's why they have become so corrupt. We are always working against him.

Seeing such evil, the crusader regards his role as an alarm to wake up the world from complacency before it is too late. It is the spirit of Paul Revere. Says the Liberty Bell Press:

Help awaken others! Give *None Dare Call It Treason* to friends, relatives, neighbors, clergymen, school teachers, libraries. . . . Do we face a hopeless battle? Has time run out for America? The answer is up to *you*. . . . What can you do? . . . Enlist others. . . . Take action. . . . Get into politics. . . . J. Edgar Hoover said, "The basic answer to communism is moral. The fight is economic, social, psychological, diplomatic, strategic—but above all it is spiritual." . . . It is not necessary to form your own organization. Thousands have already been formed. The Liberty Bell Press recommends the American Legion, John Birch Society, Daughters of the American Revolution, Cardinal Mindszenty Foundation, Christian Anti-Communism Crusade, Christian Crusade of Tulsa, Oklahoma; America's Future; Church League of America; Circuit Riders Incorporated; Americans For Constitutional Action; Foundation For Economic Education, among others. . . . A program for victory . . . cannot be achieved until Americans elect a President and a Congress with the will to win *and* the courage to "cleanse" the policy-making agencies of government of those who, for one reason or another, have aided the communists down through the years.[9]

The radical no less than the conservative feels the crusader's zeal to save the world:

> But deep in the heart of his hungry soul,
> Though the smug world casts him out,
> There burns like the flames of a glowing coal,
> The fires of love devout.
>
> Of a world in which all may live,
> And prosperity be for all,
> Where no slave shall bow to a parasite's greed,
> Or answer a master's call.[10]

In any case, the moral militance and sense of alarm and need for action is a rebuke to those who sit around and will not join the fight; it is the rebuke of Quixote to Sancho Panza.

Within these outlines, the range of action of crusading spirit is wide. We can distinguish some of the main types: *censorial,* puritanical crusaders who want to suppress vice or expel evil from the social system, of whom the paragon is Anthony Comstock, or some of the temperance leaders;[11] *rights and welfare* fighters to improve the status of underprivileged groups, such as child welfare crusaders, feminists, abolitionists, Civil Liberties Union, and civil rights workers in the South;[12] *revolutionary,* who want to stir people to disobedience and rebellion aimed at overthrowing the political status quo, such as Thomas Paine or Nikolai Lenin; *evangelistic,* who fight to spread messages not primarily demanding political action but saving the world spiritually, such as Billy Graham; *reactionary,* countercrusaders against reformers and radicals, who view other crusaders as villains—for example, the Ku Klux Klan role against civil rights workers in the South; and *national and military,* who conceive the state and its military forces as having a moral role to save the world—many militarists and conquerors provide examples. War propaganda, of course, uses the crusade theme.

Whether we like a crusader or approve of his program or not, it is possible to agree, I think, that he shares certain basic characteristics with other crusaders. One of these is vigorous, militant activism with a sense of mission. Margaret Sanger remarked, "I would not contain my ideas, I wanted to get on with what I had to do in the world."[13] Second is determination to go ahead in spite of lack of public support, even with public opposition. Comstock said,

> I am resolved that I will not in God's strength yield to other people's opinion, but will, if I feel and believe I am right, stand firm. Jesus was never moved from the path of duty, however hard, by public opinion, why should I?[14]

Susan Anthony on her deathbed, at the age of 86, said:

> Just think of it, I have been striving for over sixty years for a little bit of justice no bigger than that, and yet I must die without obtaining it. Oh it seems so cruel.[15]

Third is a sense of alarum to wake up the world, a sense of duty to fight an evil which others do not perceive or are complacent about. Fourth is taking oneself seriously: a lack of humor or ironic detachment toward one's role; a sense of noble purpose versus a complacent or ignoble world; a kind of high-mindedness or moralism which easily seems arrogant or foolish. This is the basic split between the crusader and most of us—between Quixote and Sancho Panza, between Galahad and Lancelot. In taking himself so seriously, the crusader is utterly committed or, to use a sociologist's term, lacks role distance.[16] The rest of us, not so high-minded, may look askance at him, possibly may fear him.

Such traits of the crusader can be seen in Woodrow Wilson, whose seriousness and high-mindedness caused him to endure ordeals that others would have avoided. He insisted on seeing the role of the United States as fighting without a single selfish interest, without rancor, for democracy, for the right of those who submit to authority to have a voice in their own governments, for the rights and liberties of small nations, for a universal dominion of right by such a concert of free peoples as shall bring peace and safety to all nations and make the world itself at last free.[17]

Herbert Hoover said of him:

He was a man of staunch morals. He was more than just an idealist, he was the personification of the heritage of idealism of the American people. He brought spiritual concepts to the peace table. He was a born crusader. . . . His mind ran to "moral principles," "justice," and "right." In them he had deep convictions. In some phases of character he partook of the original Presbyterians, what they concluded was right, was therefore right against all comers.[18]

Though not strictly a martyr, in a real sense he did die for his cause. Shortly before his death he said, "I am ready to fight from now until all the fight has been taken out of me by death to redeem the faith and promises of the United States." He carried on like a true crusader, even when warned that he might not survive his campaign to win popular support. He said, "Even though . . . it might mean the giving up of my life, I shall gladly make the sacrifice to save the Treaty."[19] But it was on his mission to negotiate the Treaty of Versailles that he most clearly displayed the high-mindedness that makes a crusader. William A. White describes his role:

Down the gangplank walked this Yankee knight errant followed by a desperate crew of college professors in horn-rimmed glasses, carrying textbooks, encyclopedias, maps, charts, graphs, statistics, and all sorts of literary crowbars with which to pry up the boundaries of Europe and move them around in the interest of justice, as seen through the Fourteen Points. Of course, these invaders were trying to implant an ideal. At the bottom of the ideal was an attempt to institutionalize the Golden Rule—a big job.[20]

Who, by contrast, is *not* a crusader? Among good men and important leaders in America, there are many who do not fit the role. Abraham Lincoln, for example, who, as historians describe him, when he signed the Emancipation Proclamation, did so rather late in a manner that might be described as footdragging and opportunistic.[21] Nor was Lincoln Steffens a very good crusader, for all his muckraking. Unlike most reformers, Steffens mistrusted "righteous" people. He thought the world could be saved by intelligence—even intelligent dishonesty—whereas self-righteous men suffered from a blindness to the dishonesty built into middle-class culture—for example, the patronage system. (When Steffens pointed out to Theodore Roosevelt that patronage was "legitimate" bribery, Roosevelt became furious.) It was essential to Steffens to distinguish between man and system: to admit that a good man might have to do bad things; to see that the system needed reform even while one was playing by its crooked rules. He liked technocracy because of its scientific promise, but mistrusted the Russian revolutionaries (even while he approved of the Revolution) because they were "righteous."[22] Nor does Franklin Delano Roosevelt qualify as a crusader, despite his historic achievements. Historians, such as Arthur Schlesinger, Jr., call him a pragmatist—a supreme one—and contrast him with the idealist Henry Wallace, and with Wilson. Roosevelt was, says R. G. Tugwell, "a supreme practitioner of the art of compromise."[23] He lacked fixed direction and sense of righteous purpose, followed public opinion intuitively, and experimented freely, even recklessly, by "month-to-month improvisation." "Flexibility was both his strength and his weakness".[24] If one had to arrange the American Presidents here mentioned in order of crusading spirit, Wilson would probably lead, with Theodore Roosevelt, for all his vigor, a poor second. Franklin Roosevelt and Lincoln—great reformers though they were—would fight for a very poor third. All this, despite the fact that Wilson's major crusades—to end war and to establish a world court—were both practical failures.

It may be generally said that politicians do not make good crusaders; they reject the crusading role almost instinctively. If they must speak high-mindedly to satisfy public opinion, they nevertheless try to act practically. They see the crusader by his high-mindedness going out on a limb and burning his bridges behind him. They see that, although the crusader may occasionally win startling successes when he appeals to the masses, the price of his role is high: the risk and sacrifice make it a game with high ante and large bets. The pragmatist asks, in contrast, how can I get some of what I want with least expenditure? Politics is the "art of the possible"—or, "where are the centers of power?" Politicians prefer influence and manipulation to an all-out attack from which there is no retreat. Even when they employ the "crusade" theme in propaganda, it is unlikely that they act this way themselves. So we do not usually find the crusader as a prominent leader in power structures, but mainly as agitator, outsider, troublemaker to others who feel less strongly about the morality of a cause, or act for it more practically. The career of Vice-President Henry Wallace provides a good example: he was dropped from candidacy for a second term by Franklin Roosevelt when his advocacy of "Globaloney" and "a quart of milk for every Hottentot" became embarrassing to the New Deal.

In justice to pragmatists, let us admit the unsuitability of the crusading spirit in day-to-day work. One would not use it to rally secretaries, bureaucrats, mechanics to action. Nor is it applicable to judges or legislators—except, perhaps, in an emergency such as a declaration of war. Crusading appeals are called for only when the job is so difficult and extraordinary that *heroic* energies must be mobilized, and when there is a *moral* issue. Military men sometimes like to think of themselves as "professionals" doing a job; but, since their calling is inherently self-sacrificial, based on moral duty rather than excellent pay, it is natural for them to use the crusading theme to rally others and explain what they are doing. So the moralistic, noble tone of General Eisenhower's Victory Order of the Day after the German surrender, Berlin, May 9, 1945:

> The route you have traveled through hundreds of miles is marked by the graves of former comrades. Each of the fallen died as a member of the team to which you belong, bound together by a common love of liberty and a refusal to submit to enslavement. Our common problems of the immediate and distant future can be best solved in the same conceptions of cooperation and devotion to the cause of human freedom as have made this Expeditionary Force such a mighty engine of righteous destruction.[25]

I have tried here to define the crusader as a distinct social type— not in terms of personality but in terms of a "man-of-action" role with a moralistic mentality and a militant program of action symbolized by the cross and the sword. The crusader is neither a businessman nor a politician nor a philosopher (for all his ideals), nor a social worker (for all his good deeds). Yet Gandhi shows the prac-

tical mixture—a crusader with a peculiar blend of political pragmatism and sacrificial saintliness. The closer we get to a real
crusader, the closer we get to Don Quixote or Sir Galahad. The
basic quality that makes his role possible is that he takes himself
and his own view of the world more seriously than others do—so
seriously, in fact, that he is likely to be a big bore to those playfully
inclined because he cannot laugh at himself. He will not compromise and may even put those who disagree with him in jail. His
seriousness essentially comes from the fact that he sees a mortal
struggle of good against evil—no laughing matter. This struggle is
so serious that he wants all effort, even art and play, to serve his
mission. He tends to be rather a puritan. As a man of action, his
measures are militant, though not necessarily military. He believes
in the sword, figuratively, because of his sense of war for good
against evil; evil, he feels, requires stern measures.

But the man of the world looks askance at this serious, determined crusader. He regards him as a fool, or as a dangerous bigot
or persecutor. So Samuel Butler describes "Sir Hudibras." And, in
doing so, Butler represents all the anticrusaders—who probably
outnumber crusaders—including those whose outlook is so rationalistic that they have no mystique of higher good or good versus evil,
hence see no need for heroic action; those so satisfied with the
status quo that they can find nothing to fight for; and those so alienated that they find it difficult to rally to righteous struggle and
do not care for causes of any kind. These make up the audience to
whom the crusader preaches, or the majority against whom he acts.

CRUSADE AS A MOVEMENT

You cannot have a crusade by yourself. Like any collective
process—a social party, a game, a conversation, a fight, a crowd, a
culture—the whole is prior to the part. A crusade comes into being,
then forms its members—their disposition, mentalities, and roles—
according to its requirements. We have described the crusader as a
type; individuals such as William Booth or Harriet Beecher Stowe
are perfect—even stereotypic—examples. Still, it is fairly obvious
that many more people enter a crusade and *acquire* its mentality
and role than have it to begin with. Even those who lead become
transformed from mere idealists, intellectuals, and reformers into

eloquent speakers and battle-hardened veterans. Those who enter later become transformed not only by the struggle itself but by the models of the leaders and martyrs who went before. All acquire a certain aura of heroism. So, from the point of view of the recruit, the crusade is a role opportunity: to form oneself according to a pattern not ordinarily available, to rise to a higher level of input (commitment) and output (heroism), to test oneself by mortal encounter and engagement; above all, then, to find a new conception of oneself.

For this reason, then, we wish to examine a crusade as a collective process: the kind of self-finding opportunity it affords. We are especially interested in features which seem to mark the crusade off from ordinary movements—such as militance, righteousness, sense of uphill struggle, and image of evil. While all activities called crusades do not equally have such features, one might say that those which do approach the ideal type of the perfect crusade and thereby gain power to transform their members and generate *esprit de corps*. Take, for example, three crusades announced in the newspapers in the same town at the same time: (1) a "United Crusade" to raise funds for community welfare, which started its drive with these words: "Let's roll up our sleeves and get to work"; (2) a "Stamp Out Crime" crusade inaugurated by the Independent Insurance Agents Association to honor individuals who come to the aid of the police; and (3) a "Christian Anti-Communism Crusade" led by Dr. Fred Schwarz, which began its meetings with the national anthem, a flag salute, and a prayer that we may be "stirred" tonight for the "cause of freedom," concluding its program of anticommunist songs and a speech by Schwarz with the statement "We have tried to survey the evil forces loose in the world."

There is little doubt which of these is really most crusade-like in spirit. So one might arrange activities called crusades on a scale of moral elevation and intensity, with the "United Crusade" at one end and Garrison fighting slavery at the other. The point is that people do not really care about many worthy social programs, but they *do* care about a real crusade. Moral intensity and elevation seem to describe two of these dimensions of caring: the feeling of rightness and the sense of being called upon to work for a higher purpose, performance beyond the requirements of ordinary duty. In general, bureaucracy has no crusading spirit. Military operations may or may not have it. Zeal, or caring beyond matter-of-fact job requirements, is the beginning of a crusading spirit. Fanaticism is its end point.

Let us, therefore, look at features of an ideal crusade, trying to understand how it develops *esprit de corps,* high commitment, and an opportunity to escape from ordinary life into heroism. The main features, which make a movement crusade-like are: (1) militance, (2) righteousness, (3) sense of uphill struggle, (4) image of evil, (5) unwillingness to compromise, and (6) implied evangelism.

MILITANCE

The announced goals of the Schwarz Anti-Communism Crusade in 1966 were: the formation of 1000 study groups, an educational program on the pathology of communism, special schools of anti-communism, supplying every serviceman in Vietnam with a copy of the book *You Can Trust the Communists,* televised schools of anti-communism, and maintenance of "our work" within the United States and in twenty-one other countries. "The Lord loveth a cheerful giver. With Christian love, Fred Schwarz, President." While crusades may operate within the context of education or social welfare work, they are nonetheless conflict groups[26] with a sense of drive, of taking up the sword for and against something; they have rallying slogans such as "Save——," "Capture——," "V for Victory," "We shall overcome." Even a Cancer Fund crusade uses the symbol of a sword. Crusades draw fighters and encourage a spirit like that of this socialist:

> I fought on the kerbside, at the factory gate, in strike committees, in a militant march from Stepney to Trafalgar Square. I have walked with an ashplant in my hand confident, even hopeful, that the police would be forced to break up our demonstration and give the Party its martyrs. But if this sounds a little cynical to you, be assured that much of what I fought for as a Communist I fight for still as a Socialist. It has taken me eighteen years to realize that I have been carrying the wrong banner in the right fight.[27]

As vigorous, concerted actions of fighters, crusades have thrust—a spear-like or spearhead quality. It may be a peaceful thrust, as in the Peace Corps as a "peace army," a "moral equivalent of war";[28] but all true crusades have an agonistic, striving motivation at the opposite pole from Buddhism, Taoism, and other quietistic philoso-phies—though, it may be regretted, not from Christianity. Even for pacifism, even for love, a crusade is militant—hence the paradox of the "Christian soldier." In one year, 1882, in England, 669 members of the Salvation Army were knocked down or brutally assaulted, sixty buildings were virtually wrecked by mobs. The Sal-vation Army toughened its members at the baptism of children with these words: "You must be willing that the child should spend all its life in The Salvation Army, wherever God should choose to send it, that it should be despised, hated, cursed, beaten, kicked, impris-oned or killed for Christ's sake."[29] Evangelists see their life as a fight:

> This evening, in a quiet hotel room, Team members and wives gathered for prayer. Holy Communion was served. Billy told us, "I want with all my heart to lay my life on the line for Jesus Christ. I'm not even sure I know how, but I want to." . . . This evening Billy "took his lumps" on BBC television. With only two minutes notice he was confronted by two rough opponents in a grueling dialogue; but God was with him.[30]

> The clergy of Greenland have been opposed to the people's getting an accurate knowledge of the Bible. They have at times encouraged parents to send their children to heckle and pester the missionaries . . . when the missionaries would pitch their tent, the clergy would see to it that large groups of juveniles would be on hand to mock them. Often the children threw dirt and stones at the tent, or loosened the ropes and pegs, while the adults stood by and laughed. (A Jehovah's Witness describes his evangelical work in Greenland.)

The crusader knows that even with a relatively innocuous message, the course of his work is likely to be stormy; so the crusade calls for valor and excludes or rebukes the cowardly. The reason for this storminess is that the crusade rejects things-as-they-are and works without a consensus for which it must fight; it always threatens somebody's peace of mind. At the heart of conflict is not merely a practical but a moral issue—an impasse which usually cannot be solved by merely rational methods of persuasion and education be-cause it is a value conflict. Unable to persuade and negotiate suc-cessfully, the movement takes up arms for a fight, physically or symbolically. So the "sexual freedom" movement in America became a crusade at the moment when, beyond merely violating mores, it maintained a propaganda table at the University of California at Berkeley, distributing buttons saying "take it off," "I'm willing if you are"; a leader of the movement waded nude with two girls into the ocean at San Francisco and got himself jailed—clearly in the role of the crusader, not just a law violator. But were the values of this movement acceptable to the public, or demonstrable by mere argument, then it would have no motive to become a crusade.

RIGHTEOUSNESS

Although a crusade requires a fight in some sense, every fight is not a crusade. A strike or a feud is no more a crusade than is a fight of two bears for a salmon, unless justifying the militance is a sense of the absolute rightness and worthiness of the cause. This sense of right keeps the crusader from conceiving himself—even when he creates serious disturbances—as a mere troublemaker or criminal. The sense of right must be absolute enough to withstand contradiction and challenge, and make the fighter unwilling to compromise. A crusade is not pragmatic in spirit, so opportunism and Machiavellianism are inappropriate to it. Likewise, self-interest always endangers the crusading spirit, which is noble in self-conception, sacrificial, grateful for the chance to labor, wanting to do good. A self-interested person is not comfortable with the crusader label.

> When I requested information from John regarding his role as a crusader in Alcoholics Anonymous, he had misgivings concerning the terminology, crusader. He felt that he was in A.A. for what he personally received in benefits and not for what his "cure" could do for others. He stated to me, "I'm in this for myself."

The goal of the crusade is noble, not merely good. Bread-and-butter values are not enough for a crusade—in an abundant society, at least. Grander purposes must be stated in abstractions to justify sacrifices; that is, the crusade draws on resources of idealism, not just on animal energy. This ideal makes possible the crusader's noble conception of his own role—as saviour, defender, knight, fighter for the right; it makes him, as Howard S. Becker says, a "moral entrepreneur"[31] who wants to revise morality to a higher level. So crusading spirit, whenever it enters, inevitably introduces morality into politics. It produces differences serious enough to fight over, hard not to fight over. It brings in not merely reformers, but puritans, idealists, utopians, saints, and martyrs. It aims at not merely victory but a triumph of right, a new scheme of life where men can be better. In short, a crusade—whatever its practical aims—is a moral battle, an effort to change the social order morally. So the crusader is a cousin of the evangelist: the cultist carries his message, but the crusader carries battle for his message.

SENSE OF UPHILL STRUGGLE

Unlike mainstream movements, a crusade has a sense of an uphill fight against odds—a minority group outlook. Typically there is a righteous minority versus a recalcitrant or complacent majority. However right abolitionists, feminists, prohibitionists, civil rights fighters, anticommunists, or World Federalists may feel, they also feel it is natural to suffer misunderstanding, opposition and ridicule, even go to jail, for what they believe. Even when a crusade is numerically a majority and the battle is practically won, it still keeps alive the feeling that there is a tough job ahead. This is rather a paradox in that, though a crusade starts from a righteous moral base which gives it a claim to represent the majority interest—and perhaps it does represent the majority interest—it is in the psychological position of thinking of itself as a moral minority trying to awaken, rally, rebuke, and force its will on a reluctant majority. The crusade benefits from its sense of uphill struggle and does not want to give it up. It has the morale of determination; its will is hardened and it is ready for prolonged struggle for victory— if not today or tomorrow, then the day after tomorrow. Without this dramatic sense, a crusade would deteriorate into a mere practical movement. Thus crusades are unlikely to arise within the mainstream of society or in the achievement of goals that are so practicable or easy that they do not require struggle. In this sense, a certain short-run despair is part of the mystique of a crusade, helping to stimulate its spirit. In this sense, too, a crusade is inherently radical, even when its symbolism is conservative; it thrusts against the majority and benefits from the tension, whether its direction is progressive to a "new era" or back to a "golden age"—in either case, a status quo which we do not have now, which will take some doing to achieve.

IMAGE OF EVIL

The goal of a crusade is to defeat an evil, not merely to solve a problem. This gives it the sense of righteousness, of nobility, of the good sword, and of an unfair fight; thus the crusader may think of himself as a hero and define his opponents as villains. Indeed, the crusade classifies as a kind of vilifying movement.[32] A crusade without a villain would be as unlikely as a murder mystery without a corpse. Even nonviolent and pacifistic movements have a hard time avoiding hating people they fight so hard, picturing them as aggressors or persecutors. How much easier it is for those who have no objection to making villains to see those who oppose their sacred cause as devils. So William Jennings Bryan, in his famous attack on Darwinism, did not criticize it as a scientific idea but condemned it as an evil and called for a kind of war on it:

> There is that in each human life that corresponds to the mainspring of a watch—that which is absolutely necessary if the life is to be what it should be, a real life and not a mere existence. That necessary thing is *a belief in God*. . . . If there is at work in the world today anything that tends to break this mainspring, it is the duty of the moral, as well as the Christian, world to combat this influence in every possible way. I believe there is such a menace to fundamental morality. The hypothesis to which the name of Darwin has been given—the hypothesis that links man to the lower forms of life and makes him a lineal descendent of the brute—is obscuring God and weakening all the virtues that rest upon the religious tie between God and man. . . . Taxpayers should prevent the teaching in the public schools of atheism, agnosticism, Darwinism, or any other hypothesis that links man in blood relationship with the brutes.[33]

With a very different perspective, Mario Savio, leader of the Berkeley "free speech" movement, defines his enemy as bureaucracy:

> In our free speech fight at the University of California, we have come up against what may emerge as the greatest problem of our nation—depersonalized, unresponsive bureaucracy. We have encountered the organized status quo in Mississippi, but it is the same in Berkeley. . . . In Mississippi an autocratic and powerful minority rules, through or-

ganized violence . . . in California, the privileged minority manipulates the University bureaucracy to suppress the students' political expression. That "respectable" bureaucracy masks the financial plutocrats; that impersonal bureaucracy is the efficient enemy in a "Brave New World."[34]

It is also true that, whether or not one feels a moral need for the image of the villain, it helps a crusade to "sell" its program to the public. For example, much of the effectiveness of the propaganda of the Anti-Saloon League, says Odegard, came from making a villain out of the saloon:

The League directed its propaganda not so much *for* prohibition as *against* the saloon and its evils. This was an effective device because even drinkers who balked at the idea of absolute prohibition were willing to admit that the American saloon had become a noisome thing. . . . (According to the League's publications) "The saloon is the storm center of crime; the devil's headquarters on earth; the schoolmaster of a broken decalogue; the defiler of youth; the enemy of the home; the foe of peace; the deceiver of nations; the beast of sensuality; the past master of intrigue; the vagabond of poverty; the social vulture; the rendezvous of demagogues; the enlisting office of sin; the serpent of Eden; a ponderous second edition of hell, revised, enlarged and illuminated."[35]

Beneath this "sales value" of villains is a social function: that the morale of a crusade is based upon the hope that the trouble can be simplified to one root that can be lopped off or eradicated. In other words, a purgative function is part of the mystique of a crusade. Were it not for this hope of finally defeating an oversized villain, there would be little dramatic interest in a crusade and little climax when its practical goal was achieved.[36] It may be that the villain draws more people to a cause than those who lead and suffer for it.

UNWILLINGNESS TO COMPROMISE

The above characteristics—militance, righteousness, determination to win an uphill struggle, and the image of evil—make the crusade unwilling to compromise and give it a tendency to go to extremes. The crusader's attitude is illustrated by the intemperance of Garrison's statement, previously cited ("I am aware, that many object to the severity of my language . . . I will be . . . harsh . . . and . . . uncompromising . . . I do not wish to think, or speak, or write, with moderation."). The crusader tends to view half measures and concessions as treason to the cause, and to penalize those who wish to bargain. This may be called fanaticism or sincerity, depending on how one likes the goals. With all this contributing to the head of steam, it is easy to see why crusades develop an overdrive which carries them past set objectives to actions they did not contemplate—as did the original Crusaders, as did Cromwell, as did Robespierre, as did Fidel Castro and other revolutionists. It just seems you cannot fight so hard for so long for anything so "good" against anything so "bad" without some tendency to extremes when the ball finally gets into your hands. How can you set limits on something that is good, or stop fighting something that is bad? A crusader really does not know where he will stop. He drives as far as he can go. So William Booth, in building the Salvation Army, was not satisfied with success in England, but took the world for his parish, personally traveling by ocean liner, motorcade, even bullock cart—he never stopped trying to reach people with his message. In 60 years he traveled 5 million miles and preached 60,000 sermons.[37] A good soldier, a real crusader, just because he did not know when to stop!

IMPLIED EVANGELISM EVEN WHEN GOALS ARE PRACTICAL

All these elements give the crusade an implied evangelism even when its goals are practical. William Booth had a doctrine to help make him a missionary; yet even when there is no explicit doctrine, as in the work of CORE and SNCC for civil rights in the South, the fervor and symbolism keep the issues from being mere "bread and butter" or political rights issues. The implicit evangelism of civil rights can be seen in the mystic fervor of a slogan like "We shall overcome"; it can also be seen in the sacrifices of the martyrs. This implicit evangelism is the crusade's mystique. At the same time its message to outsiders and emotional payoff to participants go beyond the practical results—and, indeed, practical results may be a mere fringe benefit, since the real reason a fighter is in the movement is for what it does for him personally, in terms of emotional intensification, moral confirmation, proof of manhood, and so on. A crusade is like a cult in having a mystique, beyond a practical program, consisting of those things outsiders do not readily see and appreciate (beliefs, assumptions, sacred values, meanings, sanctifications, redemptions, visions of millennium or Armageddon, devils, myths,[38] Grail symbols, prophecies, perhaps cures and magic) which provide an emotional payoff for members.

In this light we should view such things as: the satisfaction Woodrow Wilson got from sacrificing himself for the "lost cause" of the Versailles Treaty and World Court; the notion of "manifest destiny" that inspired the American wars with Spain and Mexico; the chivalric imagery by which Winston Churchill thrilled the English in their fight against Germany; and Hitler's turgid fantasies about the Jewish conspiracy, the purity of the "Aryan" race, and his own Siegfried-like infallibility. Marxism, also, is full of cultic mystique, with its confidence in iron laws of history, "withering away" of the state, and the classless society.

With such things going for the members, it is no surprise that crusades carry on even when their practical efforts are temporarily a failure. From the mystique comes not only the motivation to carry on but to sacrifice beyond what real, day-to-day results justify. With Grail symbols, salvation, image of evil or demonic threats, and millennium reached or golden age restored in the reckoning, it is quite impossible to say when a movement has failed from purely practical considerations. Its goal is more exciting and dramatic than anything that can be reduced to mere programs of social welfare, higher wages, minority rights, military victory, or restored capitalism—nothing less than a realization and purification of self and society, a purgation of basic evil from the world, and institution of some eternal and absolute form of good. Thus, it is quite possible for a temperance fighter to carry on while the rest of the world guzzles liquor and puffs cigarettes.

In this section I have tried to explain how a crusade is different from a movement aiming at only practical results and in what sense a crusade is a movement which carries both a cross and a sword. When a movement develops moral fervor from a mystique which offers something to get excited about and sacrifice for, it tends to become a crusade. Reform and welfare movements become crusades when they begin to aim at some absolute good or sweeping away of evil rather than merely a gain in the balance between good and bad in human society. Likewise, political control movements become crusades when, beyond passing a law or changing an administration, they promise to "save" society. Finally, any movement becomes a crusade when in a conflict for what it wants to achieve, it begins to demand personal commitment like that of a cult, or to ask a person to take risks beyond what immediately tangible rewards justify, or to change himself as a person. The crusade offers a person the opportunity to change himself by fighting for a good cause.

CRUSADING SPIRIT IN AMERICA TODAY

If these are the characteristics of a crusade, then we can infer some of the social conditions which allow such a movement to thrive. One would be a supply of morally righteous people whose strong consciences (superegos) can provide thrust and backbone to the effort. This implies strength of tradition or depth of social sentiments from which people can draw a sense of righteousness. For example, if a crusade is religious, then a reservoir of piety is needed, at least in core members; if a crusade is nationalistic or militaristic and calls for voluntary enlistment and contributions, then a plentiful supply of grass roots patriotism is needed. Such zealous people may be viewed as "idealists" or "cornballs" by the slacker part of the population; but this is not a disadvantage (it may be an advantage in giving minority feeling) so long as a subculture supplies the moral base—a stock of sincere ideals, beliefs, mores—to serve as a launching pad for the crusade. Moreover, these righteous people must be determined enough—which often means rigid or authoritarian enough—to fight for and refuse to compromise their beliefs, to wish to *impose* these ideals upon a complacent or unwilling society. In other words, they must have some of the spirit of Carry Nation.

Conversely, they cannot be so other-directed or conciliatory and consensus-seeking that they bargain away their principles pragmatically or lose them in appeasement. This might be called the risk of the missionary who stays too long: that he bargains with the doctrinal enemy, takes his point of view, and begins to lose his own. In other words, crusading thrives when there is a reform temper in which people are other-directed enough to be concerned about crusading, but not so psychically mobile that they shift their point of view from empathy with others.[39]

Another condition favoring crusades is deepening moral conflict or crisis—a social strain[40] sufficient to stir righteous people to vigorous, even desperate action. It might be a trend—such as immigration, entrance of women and children into the labor force, acculturation and increasing communication and literacy bringing about a revolution of expectations—or a status revolution which comes to a head as a crisis, the point at which strain becomes intolerable, visible, and people feel something must be done.

Such an issue is likely to have been defined and dramatized by a symbolic leader[41] who "nailed the theses to the door" so that other people could see the issue and be rallied to the cause. Such symbolic leaders usually come from an intelligentsia sufficiently informed and psychically mobile to see the need first, and educated enough to communicate it effectively to the people. Therefore, in traditional societies, among the conducive factors for crusades are sufficiently high levels of literacy and urbanization.[42]

Fourth, a crusade needs opposition—whether supplied by an enemy outside, a countermovement, recalcitrant people, or the sheer toughness of sin—to have something to fight against and generate minority feeling. Countercrusades (such as the Ku Klux Klan versus the civil rights movement) probably reinforce each other. Therefore, generally speaking, crusades need a pluralistic society, in which there are groups with strong moral consensus and sufficient disagreement to pit them against one another on issues hard to resolve by practical methods.

From such considerations, it is easy to see that America no longer maximizes conditions favorable to crusading: she is not able to generate large numbers of "do-gooders" with the "backbone" for crusading. If there ever was a golden age for crusading in the United States, it was probably the century before World War II, in which there were several peaks of reform and moralistic public action. Bode describes the temper of 1840-1861 as:

> one of the great reform periods in the United States. In sharp contrast to the cynical post-war era . . . (it was) the heyday of crusades . . . for the insane, the poor, the disabled, for women's rights, for the 10 hour day for workmen, and above all for the abolition of Negro slavery. If we had to pick out any single example . . . of this crusading zeal, it would be Harriet Beecher Stowe's . . . *Uncle Tom's Cabin*.[43]

Following the post-Civil War cynicism came the period referred to by Hofstadter as the age of reform—from the Populism of the 1890s, the Bryan campaign of 1896, the Progressive movements and muckraking of 1900–1914, to the New Deal.[44] These upsurges of reform were connected with trends and strains such as: the chaotic growth of cities; infloodings of immigrants; rampant industrialism, investment, and economic exploitation; women and children in the labor force; the rise of the urban boss (muckrakers' "devil"); increasing conflict between rural, native, white Protestants and immigrant Catholics; a status revolution displacing Mugwumps; and growth of a reading public with a taste for yellow journalism.[45]

Filler well describes the crusading zeal of the muckrakers of these times—how, for example, Theodore Roosevelt arose as "a shining young knight in the habiliments of chivalry" from the ranks of the machine politicians—and the many muckraking campaigns, such as exposés of meatpacking (Upton Sinclair), the "shame of the cities" (Lincoln Steffens), the Standard Oil trust (Ida Tarbell), the "poison trust" and impure food (Dr. H. W. Wiley), the "white slave" traffic, and so on. A guiding faith of the liberal crusaders was that the cure for the evils of democracy was more democracy.[46] This was our heyday of do-goodism and stop-badism. There was a keen sense of injustice and wanting to do something about it. And the moral conscience was still strong in the face of strains defined as evil, not merely "problems." There was conflict between cultures— not only immigrant but Protestant versus Catholic and rural versus urban. The intelligentsia were aroused and disturbed by status problems. And the awareness of issues was helped by the growth of a reading public and mass journalism.

World War I put an end to the golden age of crusading in the United States. Moralism in politics went out of style from that time on. Anyone who has studied documentary films or popular songs of the World War I era can hardly fail to be struck by the naïveté and chauvinism of popular spirit—how different from the spirit, say, of 1929, surely of 1939! World War I ended the muckraking era, says Filler, because it brought the liberals into "strange alliances" with people such as munitions makers and paid propagandists. "An age set in which held reform lightly."[47] After Wilson, moral idealism suffered a kind of bankruptcy.[48] The Prohibition Amendment was not the zenith but the last gasp of puritan spirit in national politics. The Yankee conscience, though still troubled by social problems, sank into the sentiment that "everyone was in some very serious sense responsible for everything"; unable to drain off its own guilt, moral indignation turned into self-accusation.[49]

The New Deal was not a reform crusade but a pragmatic and opportunistic program with an antimoralistic temper.[50] The repeal of the 18th Amendment was a symbolic defeat for moralism in politics. The antimoralistic temper of the New Deal was expressed by Thurman Arnold's view of "trustbusting" as ritual, not practical, politics. Various intellectual trends were weakening the absolutism on which crusading spirit depends—for example, secularization, decline of belief in hell and sin, defeat of religious fundamentalism (Darrow), popularity of psychoanalysis, relativism in morality, environmental determinism, and the rise of humanism, hedonism, and the live-for-now outlook. World War II, though a desperate conflict (calling itself "crusade in Europe"), had little of the "make-the-world-safe-for-democracy" fervor of World War I—note, for example, the cynicism of the term "liberating" employed by American troops during the reconquest of Europe.

During the 1950s came a quiescent, silent period, so well described by sociologists as an exhaustion of ideology, a drying up of radicalism, and a turning of concern toward culture and status rather than politics.[51] This was a poor scene for a crusader. Other-directedness and bland conformity seemed to dominate. Though disturbed by status anxieties and outbursts of moralism in politics such as McCarthyism, Eisenhower seemed a more representative symbol. "Alienation" began to be a favorite term to describe the temper of both the vociferously discontented and the "silent" members of the American mass public.

It was not surprising, then, that entering the sixties "old fighters" remembering the "good old days" should find cause to lament that things were not the same—there were no causes to lance for anymore. Kenneth Rexroth, the "Grand Old Man" of bohemianism, remarked that the socialist faith had run out on him.

The moral content of the old radical movement has vanished . . . the classics of socialist and anarchistic literature seem at mid-century to speak a foolish and naive language.[52]

Ben Hecht, a great fighter against censorship and puritanism, complained that there was nothing to crusade for anymore.

> When I first launched myself . . . as a writer, there was one great enemy. He was called morality, Victorianism, hypocrisy. Censors were strangling literature, strangling theater, ripping "September Morn" out of the window because she was nude. We all fought against Victorianism, morality and hypocrisy as if this was the greatest enemy of mankind. Well, I've lived to see that enemy laid by the heels. . . . I was arrested . . . a long time ago, for writing a book that was supposed to be lewd, obscene, lascivious. The book could be printed in a ladies' magazine today. In fact, it might not be accepted because it's so gentle and sweet. The disappearance of the censor has really rattled me—I no longer know which side I'm on. . . I hear things in the theater in New York that literally shock me, and I'm not easy to shock. They're the same words I heard in brothels. . . . The new playwrights are so busy with dirty words you'd think they'd discovered a new plot. But, as I say, I don't know which side I'm on—we fought for this freedom and we got it.[53]

J. Allen Smith is quoted by Eric Goldman as having said:

> The real trouble with us reformers is that we made reform a crusade against standards. Well, we smashed them all and now neither we nor anybody else have anything left.[54]

"Nothing left" refers not so much to an absence of rules (we still have plenty) but to a lack of those categorical imperatives that put fire in the eye of a crusader. This is what I would call a "wet tinder" situation—a shortage of ignitable materials such as moral idealism, absolutism, ideology or utopia, and patriotic zeal. Crusading elements remain relatively small minority groups labeled "cornball" or "extremist" by the majority. This does not hurt their spirit, but it does their prospects. They are unable to "sell." Their wave does not spread to the majority because beneath apathy is a pervasive alienation which keeps many people from joining things or counting on each other, from hoping that "right" will prevail, or from focusing on one symbol of supreme good versus evil, and which fosters escapism in not a few. With distrust of ideology so widespread, even crusaders become tainted with Machiavellianism or manipulated by it: Galahad gets rust on his shield. In such an adverse climate of opinion, a crusade, if it starts at all, is like a wave that is breaking against an outgoing tide.

Then, about the time Americans had concluded they were a "silent generation," new bursts of crusading spirit exploded: the civil rights movement in the South; "free speech" demonstrations on college campuses;[55] peace and anti-Vietnam war protests;[56] and the beard (stimulated by beatnikism and Castroism) coming to symbolize protest against the Establishment. The crusading spirit of much of this was unmistakable.

INTERNATIONAL DAYS OF PROTEST . . . TEACH-IN . . . PROTEST WALK. We will meet in front of the Draft Board Office . . . the walk will proceed to the Army Recruiting Office and thence to the offices of our Congressmen. Next we will walk to the Copley Press, and finally to the Eleventh Naval Headquarters, where the walk will end. . . . YOUR PARTICIPATION IS ESSENTIAL. . . . WE CANNOT BE SILENT ACCOMPLICES TO THE UNNECESSARY KILLING OF AMERICANS AND VIETNAMESE. WE MUST NOT ACQUIESCE IN THE FACE OF PENTAGON-DIRECTED GENOCIDE. WE DARE NOT QUIETLY ACCEPT THE CONTINUING ESCALATION, WHICH CAN ONLY LEAD TO NUCLEAR WAR. . . . JOIN US.

Along with such protest came a surge of more practical idealism in Peace Corps and Vista[57] volunteering on college campuses. Sparking all of this was probably the bus boycott led by Martin Luther King in Montgomery, Alabama, leading to a Supreme Court decision of October 1956 that segregated seating in municipal buses was illegal; this gave rise to major new forms of militant nonviolent action, such as the CORE sit-ins which began in February 1960 and the "freedom rides" initiated by James Farmer.[58] Likewise, from the radical right[59] came crusades against communism viewed by many liberals as a resurgence of McCarthyism; and countercrusades against civil rights fighters by white racist extremists, who were willing to attack crowds of women and children with clubs, hoses, and dogs—when tried for violent acts in Southern courts, they carried confederate flags and received standing ovations when acquitted. It became clear that, on both sides of the civil rights question, a real crusade was on, for which people were willing to die.

They ask me—do you believe in violence? If it takes violence to defend our Constitution, the answer is yes!!! I love this Republic and I love this country and I love the very principles down to the Constitution, but this bunch of gangsters in Washington has violated it, has committed every act, from the top level of treason right on down, against the white people, against God, against this nation. Remember the words of Jesus Christ, who said, "You can't love two masters! You love the one and HATE the other."[60]

By an understandable dialectic, Negro revolt became more extreme and sectarian. Extremist groups such as CORE, SNCC,[61] the Black Muslims, and the New York Black Panther Party threatened the leadership of NAACP and the Urban League, urging "black power" and rejecting moderation as "Uncle Tomism."

Allah will help us get . . . freedom, justice . . . we must have some of this earth that we can call our own. . . . HURRY AND JOIN UNTO YOUR OWN KIND! THE TIME OF THIS WORLD IS NOW AT HAND.[62]

So the silent fifties seemed to have been followed by the erupting sixties.

But, as it proved, the new radicalism, for all its vehemence and alarming promise, did not become politically more than a "police problem." The activists on college campuses remained a small minority. No ideology emanated from it to reach a larger public—either radical left or radical right. (The "radicalism" of the right was based on the doctrine of laissez-faire, two centuries old; and that of the civil rights movement was collecting the last installment on the Emancipation Proclamation, over a hundred years old.) Esoteric doctrines like objectivism proclaimed by followers of Ayn Rand had little appeal to the man on the street. Indeed, the new radicalism was more mystique than ideology—a faith in action and involvement, combined with mistrust of theory, that made it ambiguous about goals. As one member of the "indignant generation" put it:

The student movement is based on very general principles for rights, justice and so on. Many, of us are for things that no political party has come out for—most of us are for banning the bomb. We just work on a broad set of principles, and as issues come up, we decide how to act. We approach all the problems without the strict theory that older people are so fond of.[63]

Forced to find a label, one might say that whatever ideology or idealism there was in the new left could best be described as a kind of humanism that went beyond loyalty to particular mores, tradition, faith, or nation. "People to people," "people everywhere" were the slogans—which, rather than sympathy for communism, perhaps explains why so much crusading took unpatriotic forms such as burning draft cards, interfering with munitions shipments, or sending humanitarian aid to the "enemy." A statement by a teenager is typical: "I would give blood to the Viet Cong anytime. The important thing is people, not political systems."[64] This humanism, though it was compassionate, quite lacked the sentimental self-righteousness of crusaders like Carry Nation or Harriet Beecher Stowe. It had no illusions about revising society by political methods to make everything right. One of the principal spokesmen of the new left, Edward M. Keating, said:

> The "New Left" does not fit within the political spectrum. If anything, it belongs to the social spectrum. The end sought is not a new system, since systems—whether the current one in this country, those in communist countries, or, for that matter, any system of the past—are irrelevant. What *is* relevant is justice. Whereas the "Old Left" sought economic justice, the "New Left" has a far broader concern that encompasses social, economic, and political justice. Its ultimate goal is peace—domestic and international—and peace is impossible without justice. . . . We will have to let go of traditional rhetoric, stereotyped thought, preconceptions, and everything else that inhibits man from fulfilling himself.[64]

However, while the new left wanted change, it felt no great inspiration to crusade for economic and welfare legislation—Medicare, public housing, civil rights laws, minimum wage laws, revision of the Taft-Hartley Law, antipoverty programs, extension of Social Security benefits, and federal aid to schools—of kinds already being achieved by the middle class; nor on the other hand, could it see in them the menace of "creeping socialism," as did the right. Thus a polarization grew between two factions in the United States which saw things in different terms—not the old issues, but different world views—the humanism of man-is-one versus the melodrama of some-men-are-good-and-some-are-bad. To the new left: mankind is one, even if it does not feel that way; human rights are more important than property rights or even national interest; communism is only one evil (as a form of totalitarianism), of which there are many, even in our society; war is bankrupt as a method of international relations so some other means must be found. To the extreme right: mankind is divided between communism and the free enterprise system; private property and the nation must be defended at all costs and to fail to do so is treason; communism as a world conspiracy is the single greatest enemy; war is justified to defend the nation and property, therefore to fight communism.

Such an opposition, however, was not the kind one could readily settle by political methods. Indeed, the new radicalism, though it believed in "activism"—especially in protest—was, as Christopher Lasch said, more concerned with morals and culture than politics in the practical sense.[66] Thus it was no surprise to see *Newsweek* observe, by mid-1966, that student participation in the civil rights movement was waning; the "big exodus to the South" seemed to be over, one reason being diversion of interest to the Vietnam war, another that civil rights were becoming law, so that the movement lost some of its dramatic appeal. A student said:

> It's still dangerous, but it's not a political act anymore. It's a wholesome, goody-goody thing because papa LBJ is behind you.[67]

And, by the end of 1966, *Time* observed:

> The old fire to hit the streets has largely faded. A new desire to work pragmatically to tutor Negro kids and help out in slums is rising. . . . (At Berkeley) the students once aflame with political causes are drifting toward the introspective life of psychedelic drugs and the beat life. It is what Chancellor Assistant John Searle calls "a move from the political culture to the hipster world."[68]

For the vast majority, even among university students, crusading for the left did not generate a wave; activists probably did not number more than 2 percent.

By the late 1960s, the big thing on the college radical scene was psychedelic drugs and other forms of hipsterism and style rebellion, implying a shift from politics to life style as a means of expression (as we have described in Chapter 2). The old word ideology and political methods seemed irrelevant. Flamboyant costume, long hair, and campaigning to legalize "pot" seemed as significant as civil rights. The new humanism of the left seemed to make more of such things meaningful than could be justified within any practical political program. They were "rebels without cause" if one tries to define them by specific action programs. But moral protest and rejection of prevailing American style there were aplenty. One reason that style rebellion makes sense even when political action does not is that it has a different ethical base. Militant political action requires a certain righteousness and confidence in programs; but, even when such things dry up, one still has personal taste and, perhaps, the romantic notion of the right to be what one pleases, which do not require the same validation by consensus with others.

Though the 1960s faded from their original promise of widespread crusading activism in the white sector, the fact remains that there was in this decade a greater upsurgence of crusading spirit than the silence of the fifties would have led one to expect. Notable expressions were the effort of students to take over Columbia University in April 1968 and the Poor People's March on Washington, D.C., in the summer of 1968. Such events seem to indicate that crusading cannot be permanently dried up, but that it is a spring which runs ever fresh even when conditions are unfavorable—like hero worship, it is a generic tendency whose sources are in human nature. Yet a social milieu which lacks adequate moral base and belief in ideology is like wet tinder and cannot sustain enough crusading spirit for a long enough time to make much of a difference in the course of history—except perhaps to symbolize minority group feeling. Which is a good thing, pragmatists would say, since they do no like crusading.

With the trends of hipsterism and style rebellion weakening the ranks of the left, it seems that a stronger political potential for crusading remains on the right, with its firm moral base, its feeling of defending morality from evil, and its residual puritanism, exacerbated by seeing "corruption" (such as style rebellion) all around. It wishes to bring back the good old days of laissez-faire and feels a growing sense of frustration as it sees time recede while the mainstream flows toward the left.[69]

RESULTS AND FUNCTIONS OF CRUSADES

Having considered the characteristics of crusades, the mentality and moral base they need, and our doubts that the American climate of opinion is as favorable to them as it used to be, let us now ask what this form of social action does for those who *do* choose it? In other words, do crusades accomplish anything that ordinary pragmatic efforts do not?

PRACTICAL RESULTS OF CRUSADES

It seems plain that history owes much to crusades. Most of the major political revolutions were crusades or had this kind of spirit in a determined minority. Famous heroes of history, such as Bolívar in Latin America or Joan of Arc in France, have played this kind of role. It is only necessary to mention names such as Margaret Sanger, Jane Addams, Peter Cooper, William Booth, Florence Nightingale, and martyred Martin Luther King to show that crusading has resulted in legislation and new institutions for social welfare—not only in America but throughout the world. And even if such changes would have come in due time without crusading, one may argue that they would not have moved so fast without a determined minority willing to fight and sacrifice for them.

In such cases of success, what was the contribution of crusading spirit? It gave people a certain kind of morale, the "backbone" to persist in a cause that otherwise might have died on the vine. It gave people the courage and energy to challenge the inertia of the status quo: mores, conservatism, vested interests, reaction. Above all, as its proponents would argue, it made possible radical change quickly, instead of gradually. Thus crusading has made sense both to the impatient and to the exasperated.

Yet movements have failed as crusades or had to abandon their crusading spirit along the way in order to succeed with less ideal-istic aims. A case in point is the transformation of the United States labor movement after 1886 from a reform crusade to a bread-and-butter organization—the parting of the ways between the Knights of Labor and the American Federation of Labor. The two con-flicting organizations drew up a "treaty" by which the labor movement was divided into two separate and distinct compartments. The Knights of Labor, on the one hand, were to continue their efforts to abolish the wage system, educate the working class, and reform society radically; the national unions, on the other hand, were to be mere trade unions, paramount in the economic field, their business to settle questions of wages, hours, and working conditions through the process of collective bargaining.[70] There is little doubt, now, which of these two organizations succeeded, and which line of action was the best for American labor. The bread-and-butter goals of Samuel Gompers paid off pragmatically.

Prohibition, of course, is another example of the failure of crusading. We all know the lamentable consequences of Prohibition: a harvest of antipuritanical style rebellion, alcoholism, and the evil fruits of racketeering and organized crime. Likewise, in England the Cromwell regime brought in unpopular and impermanent austerities. Also, countercrusades can impede what the majority regards as progress: as the campaigns against vivisection for medical research and fluoridation of drinking water, and of the KKK against civil rights, or of the white minorities in Rhodesia and South Africa.

Perhaps it is the crusading spirit of the reaction that provides the best justification for crusading spirit in the reform movement. At any rate, on the crusader rests the burden of proof that what he wants can only be obtained by the strenuous methods and high costs of conflict—that a large payoff makes up for immediate sacrifices and risks. This question is well illustrated by the controversy within the American civil rights movement in 1966 to 1967 between the extremists of the Black Power bloc, such as CORE and SNCC, who wanted to move fast toward their goals, regardless of what violence might erupt; and the more prudent position of NAACP and Martin Luther King, that gains were being made by moderate methods, that violence was too great a price to pay for doubtful additional gains from aggressiveness, that the Gandhian concept of nonviolent "mass power" worked best. Crusade was still in King's conception, though nonviolent action emphasized pragmatic methods and small, step-by-step gains which the more militant crusaders disdained as "Uncle Tomism" and "turn-the-other-cheekism."

The evidence of history does not seem to settle this question of whether the long-shot risk of crusading—immediate sacrifices for a possibly larger future payoff—is justified. But, perhaps, both from results like Prohibition and the hopes of both black and white extremists, we can reach the conclusion that, if crusading minorities get what they want by militant methods it will probably be something that the rest of us do not want, such as oligarchy or puritanism. For there is a real threat to democracy from any militant crusading element. This was illustrated by the way the Anti-Saloon League used pressure politics to impose its will upon the American people.[71] It was illustrated in 1964 by the way the Goldwaterites "captured" the Republican Party convention with tactics which shocked liberals like Rockefeller, Scranton, and Romney. Even in victory, they did not have a true majority of Republicans; it was a tail wagging the dog, as the election showed. Though crusaders usually think of themselves as Paul Reveres saving society, the majority may view them as would-be despots.

Whether or not we agree with their goals, we probably must agree that certain dangers to democracy are inherent in crusading. One is that every crusade tends, by the very difficulty of its struggle and the fervor of its hope, to develop overdrive—a determination that may go too far. The veterans of the fight, after victory, may be reluctant to give way to sensible administrators.[72] Purges and terrorism may be necessary to finish the business because, as we have noted, crusade goals are not merely practical but purgative. The absolute morality of a crusade, also, leads easily to authoritarianism; indeed, the ideal crusader is close to a fanatic.[73] Because a crusade is authoritarian and oligarchic, it generates illegal movements, including crusades in reaction—whether civil disobedience, black markets and bootlegging, or insurgency and underground resistance, none of which are unqualified gains for society. A crusading movement is basically a political sect. As sociologist Robert E. Park has pointed out, political sects "are determined that such heavens as they hope for will be achieved presently, on this earth, and, as far as possible, here and now."[74] Their tendency, therefore, is totalitarian, though they may not always insist upon having their way. It is interesting—and not irrelevant, I think—to speculate what St. Paul's followers would have done if they had a power bloc in the United States Senate? Would they, in their zeal to create a good society, pass laws that we would today regard as totalitarian? Because the political sect combines cultic fervor with zeal to remake the secular world, it is likely to be very disturbing to whatever is going on at the time and have a splintering effect upon society—even if there is no victory.

If these are potentialities of a crusading movement, then we may conclude that although crusades *do* achieve much and may be necessary for radical reforms, and that their practical effectiveness does result from their unusual morale, they are very "strong medicine" for democracy and, like any strong medicine, can kill or cure. They should be used only after weaker prescriptions have been tried and found insufficient.

Having noted the possible dangers of crusading to democracy, I do not propose to settle the practical question of when such methods should be used; our interest is psychological. In this regard, we return to the fact that, although crusades "fail" practically, they carry on; they have a remarkable power of persistence. So a historian describes the moral fervor of the women's temperance crusade. Women, by prayer meetings in and outside saloons, managed to close some of them—even all of them in one town for an entire winter. They kept up their effort with unflagging spirit year after year, in spite of the "disgraceful and humiliating fact" that there were more places where liquor was sold than before the crusade.[75] Is there, then, some other payoff even when practical results are discouraging? Common sense suggests that there can be emotional rewards. We now turn to this aspect of the crusade.

DRAMATIC RITUAL FUNCTIONS

The other side of the question is that, regardless of what the crusade does to society or how it rewards its members materially, there is an emotional payoff in terms of personal meaningfulness and symbolic rewards to the movement and to society-at-large—for example, from the martyr's role. Of many a lost crusade it is possible to say, "It was a great fight while it lasted" and posterity can gain satisfaction from the examples of those who gave up their lives, as it seemed at the time, fruitlessly.

So Thurman Arnold, in his *Foklore of Capitalism* and *Symbols of Government,* distinguished two domains of political action: the practical and the ritual. What politicians do, in a more or less Machiavellian manner, to get things done; and the ceremonial role of the dramatists, moralists, reformers, and crusaders, whose function is to represent to people how they like to think of themselves and the way their government works. Arnold's implication was that this division of functions was permanent, especially in a changing society—that the ideal and the real would never come together. It seemed to disdain reformers, to throw doubt on whether they would ever be able to do what they claimed to do; yet Arnold's analysis actually showed reformers to be useful in new ways, as *dramatists* of society's purpose and values. Now ritual was recognized as having a *raison d'etre*, a function. Even if trust-busting did not bust any trusts, it might be contributing to the morale and moral balance of a working democratic society.

Applying this to crusades, might there not be important dramatic results even when a movement is practically useless, even in some ways harmful? Here Gusfield's study of the American temperance movement supplies a definite answer. He shows that the real goals were not just to reduce the amount of alcohol drinking, but to satisfy the feelings and serve the status of self-conception of certain groups—that the temperance movement was dramatizing the moral ideals of fundamentalists and helping the relative status of rural Protestants versus urban Catholics:

> Prohibition had become a symbol of cultural domination or loss. If the Prohibitionists won, it was also a victory of the rural, Protestant American over the secular, urban, and non-Protestant immigrant. It was the triumph of respectability over its opposite. It quieted the fear that the abstainer's culture was not really the criterion by which respectability was judged in the dominant areas of the total society. . . . To see that government, as do other institutions, is a prestige granting agency is to recognize that status politics is neither extraordinary nor an irrational force in American history. Seymour Lipset appears to be quite mistaken when he writes, "Where there are status anxieties, there is little or nothing which a government can do." Governments can constantly affect the status order. During the 1930's the Democratic Party won many votes by increasing the number of Jews and Catholics appointed to state and federal judgeships. Such jobs did little to increase the total number of jobs open to these ethnic and religious groups. They did constitute a greater representation and through this a greater recognition of the worth of these groups. In this sense they were rituals of prestige enhancements, just as Andrew Jackson's inauguration symbolized the advent of the "common man" to power and prestige by the fact that rough men

in boots strode across the floors of the White House. It is just this consequence of the Temperance movement for the public designation of respectability that we have seen throughout this study.[76]

The Goldwater movement in 1964 was another example of this status-asserting moral symbolism. One might say it was an effort to affirm the self image and style of a self-reliant entrepreneur (Goldwater himself affected a cowboy hip-shooter style); the atmosphere of the Goldwater campaign was emotional, one might even say revivalistic. Did not his candidacy help some of the 25 percent of the electorate who voted for him define themselves more clearly and get a sense of mission, even though he did not win? For, from a functional point of view, it may be with a crusade as with a cult, that not the destination but the journey is important: though you do not get there, you may have experienced something along the way that is significant.

As I have implied in Chapter 4, the need for dramatic ritual functions in modern society—therefore in this aspect for crusades—may be more rather than less. Not only bureaucratic organizations but, notes Hobsbawm, "Modern social movements are surprisingly lacking in deliberately contrived ritual. Officially, what binds their members together is content and not form." So a worker may be able to tell only by his union card that he is committed to certain activities and solidarity with his fellows. Even a Communist Party member commits himself to duties as demanding as those of any church "with no greater ceremony than the taking of a piece of paste-board of purely utilitarian design on which stamps are periodically stuck." But ritual has a tendency to grow back spontaneously in trade unions and political parties.[77] Does this not suggest that the crusade and the secret brotherhood, as well as the cult, may be especially important for putting the cloak-and-dagger element[78]—the feeling and mystique—back into life after they have been conscientiously banished by rationalism and bureaucracy?

The crusade is precisely that kind of movement which blends the ritual and mystique of cult with practical goals of work and struggle for something. Unlike cult, however, it focuses primarily not on emotional centering but on the job it has to do. But, because it takes one away from a hundred trivial tasks to one supreme task, it is a wonderful opportunity to redefine oneself by action and center oneself on the supreme good; and, for this purpose, the more evangelistic it becomes the better.

For example, some anticommunist groups in the United States—as Billy James Hargis' Christian Anti-Communist Crusade, Fred Schwarz's group, and the John Birch Society—are doing something other than helping the FBI detect threats to the Constitution. They add nothing to the amount of available information, but do much to stir up emotion about things we already know, and, regarding domestic communism at least, arouse a vigilance far out of proportion to the actual size of a party estimated to have about 20,000 members, which the FBI feels fully able to handle. This evangelism not only does not inform but interferes in many ways with liberal education, furthering a climate of fear among educators—not of the communists but of the anticommunists! What, then, is it achieving? If we assume that a crusade, like a cult, is doing something at the dramatic-ritual level for its members—possibly for society-at-large—that a matter-of-fact movement or police action could not, then it may be earning its keep for many Americans in giving them roles as modern Paul Reveres.

Such dramatic-ritual functions have two main aspects: cultic (internal) emotional payoff to members, and dramatic (external) to society-at-large.

Cultic (Internal Ritual) Functions   A visit to a John Birch Society meeting shows clearly enough what crusading does for its members. We see Robert Welch giving a speech to about 500 members in a packed convention room in a California hotel. An over-life-size photograph of John Birch is displayed on the platform beside the American flag. The meeting begins with a flag salute and prayer invocation. Then, after some business, Welch begins. He is obviously the "big moment" the crowd has been waiting for. He apologizes at the beginning because he "doesn't want to talk too long." A member in the audience calls out, "Go ahead and talk for five hours! We'll listen." Indeed, he does give a long speech. The crowd hangs on his words, drinking them up as though it cannot get enough. His speech is a ranting, rather bad-tempered, but not humorless, tirade against the whole of American society as an "insane asylum" going to pot morally. He gives vivid examples of corruption and bad behavior. Americans are insane because they cannot see the communist menace in all this. Drastic measures are needed, but no one does anything. The implication is that *we* are the ones who are sane and right. In his talk, Welch makes no specific action proposals, reminding his audience that the John Birch Society is not a political party—indeed is nonpolitical as an organization though members as individuals may be political. The crowd enjoys the tone and the feeling of his speech, as one would a sermon that makes one feel good; they are not disappointed that specific action proposals are not made. On this occasion, at least, evangelism is enough. Welch has been spelling out in his words and living presence a role model for them. The meeting ends with discussion and testimonials from the floor; a man rises to tell how his life has become more meaningful since he joined the Society: "I'm a new man since joining, life has started over for me." Unlike an evangelical meeting, however, nobody comes forward to be saved; most were apparently already converts. But the emotional ritual of such proceedings shows that its function is like that of a church service for the faithful. They come away confirmed and uplifted, feeling that life has more significance.

Little different, basically, is a meeting of World War I veterans, which also has a crusade-like quality. The National Commander warns them of the Red menace and asks them to stay alert to subversion:

> While our sons and grandsons are fighting them in the jungles of Viet Nam, they are busy here at home seeking to undermine . . . our government. . . . Schools and colleges . . . labor disputes . . . racial demonstrations. . . . Veterans of World War I must stay alert to cope with this subversive element . . . we must be very careful not to be drawn into their net and by association, contribute to their cause.

Of course they know all this. They get together to stir each other, arouse the "good old" feelings, and strengthen the sense of togetherness in a fight (whether or not they do anything about it practically).

Yet another crusading group, the Black Muslims, provide their own evangelism, designed to confirm and uplift the Negro in his pride in blackness by stressing puritan values—a real moral gain— and building the hate image of the white man, so unifying themselves emotionally (supplemented possibly by karate drills) and stirring themselves by the apocalyptic view of a coming struggle, which is rather like that of Armageddon for the Jehovah's Witnesses (though there is no sign of an actual plan for a militant uprising—the political objectives of the Black Muslims are surprisingly ambiguous). In such settings it is difficult to· distinguish crusading spirit from emotional evangelism.[79]

It seems fair to put such activities, even though they may have a political orientation, in the cultic category along with the Salvation Army, Jehovah's Witnesses, and Billy Graham's crusade, where religious salvation is paramount. Members come away from such revivalistic meetings feeling good because they have experienced emotional relief, uplift, and confirmation in their outlook on life; romance has been brought into a perhaps otherwise drab existence. There is also the sense of comradely support among crusaders:

> If you belong, everybody helps everybody else out. I never had anybody to help me before when I was sick; but they did it without ever being asked. You always go out (to preach) with someone else, and even when people aren't very nice it makes you feel good inside to do something for the Witnesses. We are taught not to get mad no matter what people say to us, and it isn't so hard anymore; even in school, there are about ten other Witnesses in Bobby's class, so when they don't salute the flag it isn't so hard. When we go to assemblies, it is a real good feeling to be with so many people that are just like us and it makes me feel real strong. Since we have been in the Witnesses things are a lot better, we know a lot of people and when we have trouble there is always someone to help, and we help others too. It's made a big difference in the way I feel, I'm not scared or worried so much, and that's a good feeling.[80]

But beyond the general values of emotional revivalism, we wish to consider more specifically how the crusading *role* contributes to identity. What is it that it gives that workaday life usually does not? I wish to point out there the contribution to identity of: (1) the feeling of return home; (2) the test by which to prove oneself; (3) the break with normal life; (4) reorientation of life; (5) the opportunity for a heroic role; (6) the purgative function of the image of evil; and (7) the vision of the good.

1. The first thing to note is that the crusader role has an unusual capacity for giving the feeling of "rightness"—more so, even, than rational certification procedures, such as court decisions, licensing,

conferring of diplomas, or professional promotions. The crusade's power of conferring rightness resembles that of a cult in giving a deep moral, rather than a merely technical, sense of rightness, and in making life more exciting. An "urban populist" tells how he got involved in a movement:

> I got involved in raising money for the International Brigade, for the sharecroppers down south, helping stop the evictions of city people who couldn't pay rent, fighting for public housing. Wherever you turned you saw injustice. The issues stuck out as clearly as they did in a prison. You knew what was good and what was evil. Life was very exciting. . . .[81]

A civil rights crusader tells how his sense of rightness was strengthened:

> At first, when I joined CORE, it was really to get away from home and be somebody on my own, I guess; but when I saw how things were I really got interested. When you go through someplace like Mississippi, you really feel identification with the Negroes and you get so mad at the way things are you really don't believe it can really be like that. After being exposed to the way things are in the South, my self interests took a back seat. When I got back I had joined SNCC because it was more personal than CORE, and I felt that I wanted to be right in there where something was being done and not so organized. I felt a lot older and more sure of myself when I got back. I don't have any religious reasons for what I'm doing. I just feel that if you think something is right, you have to do something and not just talk. I get discouraged at the apathy about civil rights sometimes, everything is so slow. Now, even if the organization should fall apart, I would keep on working somehow or another. I have learned a lot, I feel more aware and intellectually alert. But I am frustrated by the so-called intellectual approach to civil rights. Emotion is a part of any movement and I am very emotionally involved in civil rights.[82]

A housewife, crusader for a different kind of cause, says:

> When I heard that they would not let the kids pray in school anymore, I said that's terrible; here we are a Christian country and the kids can't even say grace or anything! We go to a Baptist church, and the next Sunday I talked to the minister and he told me that some people were getting together to do something. I went to the meeting and lots of people felt just like I did. My husband said, "For God's sake, why don't you mind your own business. Stay home, why don't you!" He never wants me to do anything, but I kept on anyhow. So I went to the

meetings and they gave me some papers and I talked to a lot of people on our block. Some of them were real interested and some of them wouldn't listen at all. But I do it all the time now, talk I mean, to everybody I can and I think the law should be changed. I'm going to keep right on until it is. I meet a lot of other people I never knew before and it feels good to hear people that feel just like you do. I get my house cleaned up after the kids go to school, and it's kind of exciting to have this other thing to do. Besides this is a very important thing, if the kids can't pray in school, the communists will be able to get in anywhere. So this is a big thing we are doing.[83]

It may be that something in early life sensitizes a crusader to "wrongness" which makes him want to respond to make things right. A SNCC crusader says:

In early life I saw great injustice in my own home. My grandparents on my father's side dominated my mother and made her very unhappy. My mother took me and left when I was eight years old. Ever since, any injustice or domination of people that can't fight back makes me angry. We moved to Virginia, and I was aware of Jim Crow laws but didn't pay much attention at the time. Then I entered college, I became interested in civil rights through reading and listening to the professors. I admired Dr.——— and this has a lot to do with it too.[84]

Malcolm X tells of the wrongs he experienced as a child, culminating in the murder of his father by white men, which prepared him to be an antiwhite crusader.[85] The straight-laced upbringing of Harriet Beecher Stowe doubtless sensitized her moral indignation and helped prepare her for the role of crusader. She had a keen sense of wrong and esteemed moral indignation chief among the virtues.[86] But, however the leader acquires the "overactive superego" which helps him to see wrong, he, in turn, helps stir the sensitivity of others by the situations he provokes and the example of his role. The crusader, by participation, gets a satisfying sense of his own rightness:

I think anyone, even a student, who sees the injustice of the South's segregation system cannot help but realize what is wrong and act. . . . I can't stand it. I feel I must do something about it. People in civil rights groups are not interested in football, dances or school spirit. These are games and lots of us don't want to play them. We want to deal with life and reality. In a time when loads of people are uncertain about nearly everything, we can identify with the Negro cause and know it is right.[87]

The sense of rightness that a crusade gives might, I think, be summarized by the following statement: "After all the things that I have done in my life, many of which I was not particularly proud of, *this is right!*" This is what I mean by the feeling of a return home morally. A person may live much of his life with programs, institutions, ideas, and people he has no heart for; he is not even sure they are moral. The crusade allows him to return home. Bandages, scars, and jail time can further signify the sense of right, what Cameron calls "status-through-militancy."[88]

2. The crusade offers not merely a freshened perception of right, but the kind of thing one can *do* to actualize that feeling and prove oneself. Actions vary greatly in their power to confer rightness. A public demonstration or testimony is likely to do more than a private resolution or deed. A Christian crusader who had for the first time professed his faith publicly said, "Through this experience (of witnessing) I now find a joy. I went with real fear in my heart. Now, my life has taken on new meaning." Donating blood is symbolically more significant than money to buy the same amount of blood; somehow it gives an "in" feeling, bridging the alienation of man from man in a mysterious way. Work "beyond the call of duty" gives one a sense of right by its sacrificial element (whereas much modern work not only gives no sense of rightness but actually makes a man feel wrong, as in "deals" or sales in which he has to compromise morality). A fight involving risk and sacrifice has the mystique of the donation of blood, multiplied by the gravity of the danger. A crusade offers some kind of test by which a person can prove himself morally, a moment to "stand up and be counted"—an occasion that may never have come before, especially unlikely in a bureaucracy. The commonest forms of this test are, perhaps, the "baptism of fire," an ordeal with risk in which one conquers fear. A Negro girl member of SNCC said: "Now I've been down there (the South) I'm not scared. I really don't mind if they kill me." Another member of SNCC said:

> I felt that I had to do something to help, so when the student Y sponsored the trip to Virginia I went along. At first I felt guilty about that, because there really was no danger there and I really felt like I was making no sacrifices. The second trip, to Atlanta, was better because I really felt that we were helping and it was dangerous. We stayed at a Negro college, and even though there were only four Negroes out of

twenty students, we seemed to get a sense of identification—at least when I was in a white area. Even when I was alone, I had the funny feeling of being afraid and careful as if I were Negro; it was so real I could feel it in my skin.[89]

Getting arrested for the cause had double significance, as personal test and message to the public:

Sure, we want to get arrested when we demonstrate. We want to make it clear to the public that we are serious. And we want to show our immediate concern toward our neighbors. Non-violence shows concern, not so much for your friend as for your enemy. When we demonstrate, our non-violence shows that we can disobey and alter without harming the individual. At least I hope that's what we show.[90]

Challenging authorities by technically legal action can also have some of this significance:

When I go near a voting registrar in Mississippi I feel I'm dueling with the whole history of my race and the white race. It gets you just like that, in your bones. You're not just a person who is scared. You're doing something for the books; for history, too.[91]

The religious crusade often provides its test through a "formula for witnessing": the member proclaims his faith, tries to convert others, and endures derision and opposition. A college Christian crusader says:

The arguments the crusader has learned to give for defending his faith tend to crystallize that faith in his own mind. . . . I was hesitant about trying to convert someone on the spot. . . . After my first successful conversion, I remember feeling a sense of righteousness and joy, also a sense of oneness with the crusade movement. This feeling was greatly reenforced during a "sharing" meeting the same day.[92]

Such tests of rightness are especially important in an alienated society, because what an alienated person wants is to be home and, once again, like the Boy Scout, to tread the straight and true path of merit badges or, like Galahad, to successfully sit in the siege perilous.

3. Another contribution of the crusade to new identity is that it helps, indeed requires, a person to break with the routines and obligations of normal life and start a new life. With the crucial step he puts his old life behind him, perhaps renounces friends, job,

church—much as does many a sect convert. Family and friends often object to the crusader devoting so much time, effort, and money, which is at the same time inconvenient to them and a sacrifice for him. So, during the time of the famous Sacco-Vanzetti case, men quit jobs and mortgaged their homes to "save Sacco and Vanzetti." It is significant that an investigator of the John Birch Society reported:

> Among the Birch Society leaders and regular members I interviewed most had no active religious affiliation—and none had more than nominal affiliation. Their membership in the John Birch Society was by far their most time- and interest-consuming voluntary association. The John Birch Society has become their church, accepted as God's vessel of salvation, as God present with them for guidance, for comfort, and for strength. Welch has become the revealer of God's eternal truths. . . .[93]

The justification for such renunciation is the nobility of the role undertaken, compared with the relative worthlessness of the relationships neglected. The crusader does not feel any more at fault for leaving old friends than would a monk for devoting himself to begging. Crusades vary, of course, in the degree to which they demand a break with normal obligations. Some, such as Billy Graham's or Moral Rearmament, make less demands than movements like Jehovah's Witnesses or the Communist Party; perhaps this is a fault in the former, namely, that the more truly crusade-like a movement is, the more demands it makes. A member of the John Birch Society said:

> I was told that if I should join I would inevitably lose some of my friends. This was to be expected. But I would be more than compensated by the new friends and the new purpose I would acquire.[94]

A college Christian crusader said:

> After I had become involved with the crusade on a regular basis, I noticed the tension between my old friends and activities and my new friends and activities. I tried to compromise my new beliefs when with my old friends . . . to reduce conflicts. . . . Trouble arose when I began to define my position in my social fraternity. As my fraternity brothers and I became better acquainted and began to communicate on deeper levels, I was defined as a Christian and typed as a crusader.[95]

So the crusader, once he has joined, even if still accepted by his former friends, feels dislocated and set apart. Jail experience, or suffering the status of outcast, of course, greatly helps the break with normal life:

> I wrote my book *Revelle for Radicals* in . . . jail. Sometimes the jailers would tell me to get out when I was in the middle of a chapter. I'd tell them, "I don't want to go now; I've got a couple of hours more work to do." . . . No revolution ever got off the ground until the status quo performed the essential service of taking the leader or the organizer out of action. He'd never do it voluntarily. Think of what that first jail experience during the Montgomery bus strike did for Martin Luther King. That was when he decided to go all-out for total integration. And he was a very different man after the Birmingham experience, as he has written in his "Letter from a Birmingham Jail." . . . He came to understand that the well wishers who say, "I approve of your objectives but not your tactics" are an anchor around your neck. He saw that revolutionary changes never occur without conflict. . . . Concern for your reputation is one of the worst prisons you can have. I had a give-and-take with some of Joe McCarthy's henchmen. . . . I told them, "Go ahead, call me up, smear me. You think I give a good goddam about it?" And they knew I meant it. So they backed off.[96]

Though set apart, he does not feel outcast or to blame, but may rebuke those who do not join him—as Martin Luther King said of churches which "remain silent behind the safe security of stained glass windows." He feels that others belong on *his* side, not that he has stepped out of bounds. If he feels set apart, it is by dignity and dedication to higher calling, rather like Sir Galahad among the sinful knights. So the set-apartness is not a loss of status but a gain. Though judged heretic, apostate, oddball, troublemaker, traitor by some, he breaks with normal life to embark on a new life—rather like a cultic rebirth.

4. As compensation for dislocation from the social structure, the crusade offers a reorientation of life with a sense of courage and purpose. A Jehovah's Witness, who left his job as a telephone company technician to devote his life to preaching, said:

> Until then, we seemed to have no purpose. We made money and spent it and had fun, but there was an emptiness in our lives. Everything in Jehovah's Witnesses is teamwork. It is a vast family pulling together with the precision of a well trained army.

The crusade converts the "cat on the street" in Watts, Los Angeles, into the young lion (Simba) of Black Nationalism. Its action on the mass[97] is that of a magnet on iron particles: it draws rioting mobs into disciplined regiments, "lost souls" into corps with trumpets and tambourines. This orientation is like a cultic one, except that it is directed toward action upon society—whether by agitation, evangelism, nonviolent pressure, or outright war. When a movement is at the same time religion and crusade, it is hard to tell how much of the identity reclamation is due to the cultic and how much to the crusading aspect. A perfect crusade offers the paradoxical combination of the joy of righteous combat with the promise of perfect peace. Whatever may be its effect upon society, it offers a cure for the individual's anomie.

5. Like the cultic path, the way of a crusader is not ordinary, but heroic. The difference between ordinary life and a heroic role is the difference between climbing stairs and climbing Mt. Everest. It is achievement which sets a person above others—the straight-and-narrow path, the bridge of swords over which the quest hero must crawl with bleeding hands. Defeat allows a crusader to think of himself not as loser but as martyr. Hence, the power of uplift comes from the inherent exultation of the heroic role: the sense of having fought the "good fight," identification with leaders even more heroic, and cancellation of any guilt by merit and suffering.

Therefore, one of the prime duties of a crusade leader is to provide a firm, inspiring model for his followers. He should be the first to swing the axe, begin the march, apply the boycott, go on the hunger strike, and the last to recant or retreat. His personal style should be austere, expressing devotion to the cause. Aggressive, forthright, opinionated, morally courageous individuals who despise compromise make the best crusaders—such figures as Carry Nation, Billy Graham, Malcom X, Martin Luther King, Robert Welch, Barry Goldwater—to all of whom the remark of a Goldwater follower in 1964 would be equally applicable: "What I admire most about him is his absolute honesty and idealism."[98] By his assurance he helps all of those around him to feel like new men: he is clear and they find out where they stand; he is firm and they become resolute; he is opinionated and they become sure of themselves; he "knows" and they understand. Thus a crusade leader refreshes identity; through him a mass can experience an uplift without personal contact, as is true of most symbolic leaders.[99]

This does not imply that crusade followers—though they get psychological rewards—have the same personal characteristics as the leader, however much they may identify with him. It would be a mistake to put all "fanatics" in the same mold. He is strong, they are dependent; he has initiative, they imitate; he is authoritarian, they are suggestible. Their strength, is a facsimile of his, produced partly by imitation, supported by whatever inner strength they may have. Likewise, what a leader gets out of a crusade psychologically must be distinguished from what his followers get: a mix in which for the former there is a greater amount of realization of abilities, and for the latter more moral confirmation.[100]

6. The heroic role by which the crusade takes a person away from his old life pits him against evils which he now sees clearly, though he may have been complacent about them before. We must, therefore, consider the contribution of the image of evil to identity. A heightened melodramatic image of an enemy at whom to lance, or of apocalyptic evil looming, gives a person not only a sense of battle but an elevated image of himself; he may feel the stature of the heroic role and gird himself to meet the evil. Indeed, the image of the villain changes the aspect of the whole world for the crusader. Thus, as Malcolm X's sister explained, once the "demonology" of the Black Muslims is accepted by any black man, he will never again see the white man with the same eyes. Likewise, the Ku Klux Klan leader complains of the moral menace of "strangers" who have taken over the land, invaded the cities, broken down moral standards, desecrated the Sabbath, and threatened Nordic Americans.[101] If the villain has changed the world for the worse, then getting rid of him will change it for the better. From attack on him, the crusade gains a purgative function, providing a relief rather like that of lancing a boil, both for the individual and for society. So the idea of cleansing or sweeping away evil in order to restore goodness and save society is part of the mystique of the crusade and puts it in the category of the ritual of purity and danger.[102] This is the (I think mistakenly called) "paranoid" mentality of people like Birchers and fluoridation fighters, which may reflect no more than a need for the ritual of a fight for the right and a little romance brought into otherwise meaningless lives.

7. Likewise, the vision of the good that will be achieved after the fight is over needs to be sharpened for the crusader. It need not be a

Utopia, but it should be purged of villains and radically improved. So the rebellious university student described the world he wanted after reform:

> Most middle-class students see their role as going back to supplant daddy when he retires. . . .What I want is a world where people are free to make the decisions that affect their own lives, a world in which they are not trapped on a vast merry-go-round of concealed power, not forced into situations where the choice is already made for them. I want a "participatory democracy" . . . a nonexploited system in which no one is making money off another man's work. I want people to be happy, too. More than anything else, I want a world where we're free to be human to each other.[103]

Without some such image, however short of pie-in-the-sky, no crusade would have the power to stir people, for getting rid of the villain is not enough unless there is a better world ahead.

As a result of such features—emotional revivalism, the feeling of return home, a test by which to prove oneself, the break with normal life, reorientation, the heroic role, the purgative function of the image of evil, and the vision of the good—the crusade is able to offer a deeper change of self-conception and identity than would be possible in ordinary life. So people who have participated in crusades tell of the changes that have occurred in their outlook. A university student rebel says:

> We're a new generation of people. . . .We have been fairly well off. . . . So it's interesting that while many of us have not gone through a war or had to fight through a long depression, more and more of us are getting very upset about the world around us. Today most people look at students who are involved in protest as though they were still searching for an identity and not yet adjusting to our social situation. They see us as "not quite balanced." My parents, for example, still think I'm going through a phase. This common view . . . completely misses the point. Many of us *have* found an identity. What we are trying to do now is to make our identity realizable. We've found possibilities for a brotherhood—for understanding a lot of things that people kind of feel are corny. Brotherhood is something you talk about in rhetoric, but in everyday life brotherhood and love and understanding are things that people get squeamish if you talk about. . . .The thing for me right now is the movement. That's an interesting word, if you think about it— movement. Because it is people in motion. It's not an end; it's not static. That's a very apt word for what we are doing.[104]

306   *Crusades*

A white schoolteacher tells how he got rid of his mental baggage in the civil rights movement:

> After a few days you throw out a lot of baggage, your habits and expectations, from running water and inside plumbing to brushing your teeth regularly; and you become "men against the sea"—a small group rowing against odds that are sometimes heavy . . . . You think of yourself as removed from a lot you once took for granted; when I go past a bank or a restaurant now, it's like I'm looking into another world . . . . I guess, in a nutshell, you become an outsider.[105]

An educated Negro tells how the Watts riot, in which he did not actively take part, gave him a renewed pride in Negro identity:

> He found himself joyously speaking the nitty-gritty Negro argot he hadn't used since junior high, and despite the horrors of the night, this morning he felt a strange pride in Watts. "As a riot," he told me, "it was a masterful performance. I sense a change there now, a buzz, and it tickles. For the first time people in Watts feel a real pride in being black. I remember, when I first went to Whittier, I worried that if I didn't make it there, if I was rejected, I wouldn't have a place to go back to. Now I can say: 'I'm from Watts.' "[106]

So even vicarious experience of a riot interpreted as an expression of "Black Power" can make a person feel differently about himself. More is to be expected from actual participation, as with the college Christian crusader who tried the "formula for witnessing": "Inside of one month, I am a completely different person."

Colorful changes of name and costume—fezes, Moslem or Swahili robes, white vestments, grand titles, army uniforms, silver shirts, and so on—may make clear the purpose of the crusade to change identity and the effect it is having on identity. Malcolm X tells how change of style, accepting Black Muslim name and symbolism, helped him to feel a new person:

> My application (for membership) had . . . been made, and I received from Chicago my "X" during this time. The X for the Muslim was a symbol for the true African family name that he never could know; it would replace the white-slave-master name which had been imposed upon my paternal forebears by some blue-eyed devil. It meant, the re-

ceipt of my X, that in the Nation of Islam thereafter I would be known
as Malcolm X. . . . Reginald wrote, "Don't eat anymore pork." I tried
it and did it, and for the first time in a long while I began to get a little
feeling of self-respect, though I hardly knew even how to identify the
feeling.[107]

When a crusading spirit enters a movement, its natural tendency
is to change the life style, often in the direction of puritanism and
austerity. So one sees how the crusade of Mao Tse-tung has
changed the identity as well as the politics of China: people are
uniformly clad, both sexes wear mannish haircuts and overalls;
bosoms and women's legs are completely covered up; fancy hairdos,
drainpipe trousers, pointed shoes, love songs, painting on handker-
chiefs, and other "bourgeois" extravagances are condemned;
children march in orderly ranks in the street; physical culture is so
strong that people shadowbox on the street; night life is virtually
nonexistent, prostitutes are "re-educated"; Shanghai becomes
"almost pasteurized."[108]

Helping identity change in any crusade is something that any
military or athletic organization has too: a comradeship of the elect,
the *esprit de corps* of veterans who have proven themselves and feel
they are an elite corps. Drawn into and accepted by this elite corps,
the crusader begins to feel he has gained something precious,
however unsuccessful the fight or the game. He has "earned his
letter," and his self-conception rises.

Changes of identity are not peculiar to crusades, but may be
found in many kinds of group activities. Almost anywhere one may
meet people who introduce one to a new way of life. Hero worship
is a common experience, outside as well as within crusades. Conversion experiences, also, can happen in many sectors of life, without
intense interaction, cultic ritual, or ordeals. Still, cults and crusades
are likely to maximize the factors which favor identity change. And
the crusde has its own special elements which give it immense
power to change identity, center a person, and provide an emotional payoff, win or lose. For this reason, crusaders can always
say, "It is better to have loved (a good cause) and lost than never to
have loved at all."

External Dramatic Functions   So much for the internal payoff.
There is also the impact of the crusade as drama on society-at-
large—namely, what the audience sees in *causes célèbres*, epic

struggles, martyrdoms, and historical "morality plays." Here we return to the framework of Chapter 7 and consider the crusade as a kind of vicarious identity voyage available to the mass audience which watches but does not participate. Doubtless the crusade teaches many more than it involves. The public first becomes aware of many important problems through the dramatic acts of crusaders—like the muckrakers, the efforts to save Sacco and Vanzetti, or the bus boycott of Martin Luther King. They see the sides of the issue more clearly after a crusade has highlighted it.

But from the standpoint of what crusades offer as vicarious experiences, I think it is useful to divide them into two types, based on categories used in Chapter 7: reinforcing and transcending. A crusade is reinforcing when it affirms some well-established moral truth, gives people a feeling that right is being restored. Then it functions for the audience at large as a kind of morality play. A battle to pass a law against obscene literature or an effort to elect a reform mayor to clean up dirty city politics might be seen in this light. Probably the civil rights issue in the United States today has the character, for the public at large, of a morality play—with opposite heroes and villains north and south of the Mason-Dixon Line. Likewise, Eisenhower's "crusade in Europe" had, from an audience standpoint, the character of a morality play in which, as ancient stories tell, suffering peoples are delivered from an ogre.

On the other hand, some of today's crusades, especially those of the new left—including a bewildering spectrum of "filthy speech" demonstrations, teach-ins, sit-down demonstrations, obstruction of munitions movements, draft-card burning, civil disobedience, student takeovers of schools, happenings, LSD festivals, agitation for sex freedom and legal "pot," style rebellion of beatniks and hippies—are hard to fit into the framework of moral reinforcement. Such movements probably strike the public first as absurd or dangerous; but, ultimately, they have a chance of conveying the message that there is more to be experienced, something around the corner which we do not quite see, that is inspiring these "troublemakers" to engage in their demonstrations and pitched battles. This is like a movie or novel—capable of giving the public a transcending experience in which more and more members of the audience will become aware of new kinds of values, many not supported by traditional morality or in opposition to it. This important aspect needs appropriate research: What is the symbolic message of the crusade? What psychological changes does it produce in the audience at large which watches, first in curiosity, then in derision or disdain, finally, perhaps, in sympathy? At some point in the development of a successful crusade, there is probably a turning point, at which the public ceases seeing it as a threat to morality and comes to see it as a gateway to new values. This must have happened during women's struggles to vote, bob their hair, smoke cigarettes, and wear clothing like men. Is it possible that crusades for things like legalized abortion or euthanasia will, as new heroes appear for these causes, lead the public to transcend its present attitudes on these matters?

At least one may say that crusading makes news interesting, providing a sense that something is happening—whether it is or not. Where something *is* happening—real gains in civil rights—crusading adds an element of drama and significance which mere pressure group politics and legislation would not. And, in a society where, in fact, little is happening, crusading—however futile realistically—can prevent a sense of total alienation and helplessness, create a feeling that "somebody is doing something," "somebody is on our side." Thus the underground movements, guerilla fighters, little forlorn groups of protesters and nonviolent resistors, by their mere presence and occasional appearance, can add to the morale of a larger body of sympathizers who are able to do nothing.

CONCLUSION

The main purpose of this chapter was to describe crusading as one of the main routes of identity transformation by mass action. Crusading has many things in common with cults, in terms of mystique and centering, but adds the element of the "sword" (vigorous action upon the social order). I have tried to show that the crusade is superior to ordinary practical work and bureaucratic organization as an identity-finding opportunity. Whatever may be said against a crusade, one cannot take up the lance without thrill or change. On the practical side, too, crusading releases enormous amounts of energy.

A main criticism of crusading is that it arouses a moralism in politics which may lead to fanaticism, sectarianism, extremism, even totalitarianism. Who wants to use a weapon that can escalate to such results?

Would society, then, be better off without crusades, introducing changes gradually by piecemeal measures and compromises which do not require fights? The gain, certainly, would be less disturbance to the status quo and less threat to democratic process. But there would be losses: reform would be intolerably slow for many people; politics would be less interesting and exciting; and one of the psychological bonds giving a mass society a feeling of togetherness would be gone. It is hard to imagine how boring and hopeless a society would be where no one cared enough to crusade about anything.

One cannot dismiss the possibility that we might lose the crusade as a social instrument. There is in our modern society a struggle between two opposed sets of forces. On the one hand, increased identity problems, violations of law, and sense of moral crisis favor crusading. On the other hand, increasing sophistication and alienation, weariness of repeating the same historical patterns, and, above all, pragmatism—which is antirighteous and sees nothing as right or wrong except in results work against the crusading spirit, creating a less favorable climate of opinion for it. We must admit that there is an inherent naïveté in crusading, so that at a certain point in sophistication people might find it impossible to believe that they could restore their identities or their society by such means. However, so long as the moral base, especially on the right, remains strong, there is no immediate danger of the end of crusading. Perhaps it would continue, even if there were no faith in its practical efficiency, because it provides such a good way to define oneself dramatically. In a modern mass society, crusading is especially important for its dramatic—as distinguished from its practical—contributions, giving people a sense of being part of something and overcoming alienation. Even if practical problems were being solved by other methods, we would probably keep up the show for the sake of the drama. Lacking "causes," would-be crusaders would look for them—and, perhaps not finding them, would make them. In today's alienated society, crusading in its dramatic aspect probably acts as an escape valve for tensions. However, there are always other outlets—such as style rebellion and cultism—which can use up as much social energy as crusading.

Finally, one thought always lingers behind any discussion of crusading as a type of moralistic activism. The ancient wisdom of Taoism proclaims: If you want something, do not strive, contend, and stir up crises. The battle is rarely won by the "winner." Proceed quietly, seeking a natural and easier "way." Be like water which flows through nets. This is a nugget of wisdom, a basic proposition about life, which no crusader has ever really faced up to—nor, judging by his actions, even understood. The reformer who wants action now—or keener identity from struggle—may not be interested in this point. But for those who want permanent and larger results, and have no burning identity problems to solve, it may be a very important point indeed.

PART III CONCLUSION

9   Symbolic Poverty and Balance

SYMBOLIC POVERTY

Man has entered an era in which he is making his own
environment. He prefabricates entire dwelling units, together with
their contents, and stacks them where he pleases. He creates artificial climates under geodesic domes. He fills the world with
synthetic goods, including replicas of nature. More than politics,
technology, architecture, and city planning seem to hold the
promise of Utopia.

    But he has not been so successful with making symbols; he has
had less success in fabricating symbols than things. Functional
design fights continually against the tendency of technology and
mass production to sameness—that stainless-steel sameness which
one so often feels in modern design, however conscientious the ef-

forts to vary it and give it identity. The loss of individuality in mass production is only part of the problem, however. Another—and to my mind more important—part is the assumption either that the environment of man is made up merely of things rather than of symbols, or that needed symbols can be arbitrarily designed and created as the occasion calls for it.

The first of these assumptions which helps to make a meaningless society is illustrated by commercial land use. When one looks at an activity like real estate development, one sees a class of professionals just moving things around without concern for symbols other than those found on the face of the dollar in their own pockets. And so much activity in America (even in public communication!) has only this object so that it is no surprise to find a lack of meaning. Nor do suburban developments with names like Golden Oaks or Sun City solve the problem of creating an environment of places with meaning for people to live in. Indeed, such developments, if more than mere labels, are skillfully designed pseudoplaces, like Disneyland, except that you stay there longer.

The other assumption, that one can invent symbols, is shown by the design of sanctuaries. Sanctuaries highlight the problem, because here the requirement that a building be a symbol as well as a thing is most plain. Yet how grotesquely inappropriate are many designs for new church buildings—both inside and outside— ranging from bareboards dullness and plainness to startling buildings that look like automobile engines or launching pads for rockets. Occasionally a designer intervenes to create a stunningly appropriate and expressive contemporary symbol—as in Coventry Cathedral using charred beams to memorialize the German bombing and also Christian forgiveness. But, more often, the shock and bewilderment of the public-at-large is testimony enough that the problem of creating meaningful common symbols of man's highest hope has not been solved. To repeat, the fault, as in the case of church building, is not ignoring symbolism, but the architect's or artist's presumption, once he strays from tradition, that he knows what a significant design is—that meaning is produced by a designer's will rather than by a crescive growth in the interactions and responses of people, as when sanctuaries become hallowed by use.

The price of innovation, when ones does not know how to create symbols, is symbolic barrenness. In the midst of this barrenness, artists, architects, public relations experts, musicians, and ministers are often called upon to provide some kind of meaning for an occasion—to give a public building dignity, to affirm a sense of purpose, to give some individual a feeling of importance. But few know whether such efforts are successful. And artists often have not lived up to their responsibility—whether from their own choice and fault, or from conditions beyond, and possibly stifling to, their creative powers—of finding out the symbols the public needs. A great many artists disdain the effort to create symbols; they are the first to admit their work has no meaning, beating critics to the punch. And how many of those who produce the new things that make up our life—manufacturers, fashion designers, builders, architects, city planners, legislators—worry about symbols, either the ones they are displacing or those they ought to be creating? Aside from the special field of semantics dealing with the communication of precise information, the public meaning of symbols has been badly neglected.

Although we enjoy many new and beautiful things, our country suffers from symbolic poverty, resulting from the assumption that things are enough and the ignorance of how to make symbols—on some occasions, the sheer murder of symbols. People look around at their world—at things manufactured, at things produced by artists, at organizations and relationships with people, at things they themselves are doing—not knowing what they mean. Few recognize the obligation to make and preserve public symbols, and fewer still know how to do it.

What is symbolic poverty? Not lack of factual information, but of kinds of symbols which make a person's life meaningful and interesting. At the discursive level, this is not so much in term of factual information as such things as stories, legends, romances, gossip, and conversation which is engaging and expressive of vital concerns rather than banal. But at the nondiscursive level modern society suffers a more serious poverty of symbols, including a lack of: reassurance from the gestures of others (that one is loved, understood, needed, somebody special)—what Eric Berne calls "strokes"; ritual which gives a person a sense of himself and fills his life with valid sentiments; place symbols, the familiar world where one belongs, home; the voice of the past, a sense of contact with prior generations; psychological payoffs in recognition for work; and, above all, centering.

Such things result from, or themselves constitute, interactional deficiencies. In a society like ours, which stresses abundance, it is especially painful to suffer identity deprivations from interactional deficiencies. The keenness of identity deprivation is due to the fact that we expect so much and get so little: we live in a society which extols, proclaims, teases, and gratifies the ego—but fails to sustain it with adequate interaction. Not only does our modern society fail to provide adequate interaction for the sick and deviant, but even the "successful" feel a kind of hollowness. As I pointed out in Chapter 1, identity is a delicate psychosocial equilibrium requiring various kinds of support for its maintenance. But in the very society that proclaims abundance for everybody, we see interactional and symbolic deficiencies: the boredom of mechanized sameness, both in job and at home; the wiping away of traditions and places; shallow, inconsistent relationships which, though labeled "friendships," are really impersonally categorical and changeable; an inability of people to get through façades and roles to each other; a piling up of impersonal information which fails to identify because it is not "mine" or "ours"; a weakness of basic social sentiments, such as love, loyalty, and faith; and a lack of ritual by which to intensify either social sentiments or a sense of one's own importance; and, finally, the perishability of fads and styles as status symbols, which, because they do not last, cannot be reliable pegs for identity.

In such a milieu, a man has little with which to identify himself. His family is a small, unstable group which, as sociologists say, is more voluntary association than an institution. His family name means little in a society in which people coming and going makes it impossible to build family reputation, and the whole question of kinship and progenitors is unimportant. Possessions can do little to identify a man when major items—even one's home—are replaced every few years and turnover is increased by abundance and faddism. Anyway, how can one get a sense of ownership of technology, which is made by others, is just like the property of millions of others, and becomes obsolescent before one can be attached to it? Place cannot provide identity when it becomes merely space, as I have explained in Chapter 1. One's job or business is the main peg of identification in modern society; but even this offers little to identity because for the majority it is only a category—such as a civil service rating—in an impersonal bureaucracy. Few, even among leaders of business, have personal reputations that amount to much; and, for almost all, loss of job by retirement or unemployment turns a person easily into "nobody." Above it all is the lack of mystique, of faith in something "more," so characteristic of secular society.

Such features are symbolic deficiencies when considered in contrast with the meaning that a human needs in his life; they are interactional deficiencies when seen in terms of the support and psychological payoff that a person needs from others. Such deficiencies, though glaringly accentuated in the United States, are characteristic of mass societies and may reasonably be predicted of all modern and modernizing societies sooner or later.

From the standpoint of social policy, the nub of the matter is that we do not know how to design a context of human relations in the abundance of a mobile, modernistic, traditionless society which will provide the individual with nondiscursive symbols to give him an interesting life and a satisfying identity.

This is the problem of banality. A person whose interactions lack psychological payoffs will find life unutterably boring. The success symbols, though he has them, will seem empty. Practical measures, such as economic progress, political reform, even welfare legislation, will seem irrelevant to him, because they do not deal with the real problem—of banality. He will, therefore, have a tendency to become a dropout or a deviant, turning to escapes or kicks for compensation. Deviants come from those who, in increasing numbers, feel themselves cut loose from attachments to the social system and so are likely to take directions of identity search of which squares (satisfied with the identity they get from the status quo) disapprove. They do not mind becoming visible—as oddballs, rebels, ego-screamers, faddists, and poseurs, whose experiments in self-revision represent the new romanticism.

My basic theory, which I have tried to justify in this book, is that a deviant has a special motive, an identity deprivation from which the square does not suffer. An ego-deprived person turns to a kick outside the accepted order when he cannot find a *summum bonum* within. The kick is for the deviant what conversion is for the cultist—his centering and salvation. An identity-deprived person takes kicks much more seriously than does someone who is satisfied with identity—what to the latter is merely fun is to the former his big moment. Because of this identity need, the deviant feels he has a right to deviate. His argument might be as follows: If the social order denies me a feeling of integrity as a person, something is wrong with *it;* therefore, I have a right to go outside its codes to the extent necessary to find myself. Such a point of view divides people—not between haves and have-nots, or political parties—but between those who feel dissatisfied with their identity and cheated by the social order—therefore searching, escaping, unconventional, rebel, extremist—and those who are satisfied with their identities because the psychological payoffs are satisfactory to them.

The former will be likely to turn to the responses and movements dealt with in this book—major kinds of mass response to symbolic poverty and banality. They may turn to cults. They may try voyages of identity through the roles of celebrities and heroes. They may try ego-screaming—in various kinds of style experimentation, faddism, posing, and rebellion. They may try to define themselves by action and ordeal; to return home morally by commitment to crusades. From the standpoint of the individual seeking to gain himself a more meaningful life, these are all searches. But from the societal standpoint, they are efforts to restore symbolic balance. Let us consider this.

SYMBOLIC BALANCE

The groping responses of the mass are natural efforts of people to find renewed identity: by fads and ego-screaming, as the declaration of a new person and a search for feedback, at least in terms of being noticed; by pose, as trying on a new identity to see if it will pass; by ritual, as the revitalization of emotional life, both for the person and for the group; by intense interaction, as in crowds, cults, group therapy, or crusades, which allow a person to break out of the shell of his old life; by thrill seeking in "fun"; and by vicarious thrills from voyages of identity by means of heroes and dramas while part of audiences. Such searches are like arrows to a target—some hitting, many missing. Especially is the search for the *summum bonum* (the basic problem of philosophy) through kicks, cults, and fads likely to be unsuccessful. But when, on the other hand, one of these directions of search begins to provide "hits" for many people, then we may presume that society will move in that direction. Such identity experimentation, however wasteful it may be for individuals, is an important process of social change.

Now, taking the viewpoint of the social order, such groping responses are an effort to restore symbolic balance. Whatever inadequacies have developed in the symbolism of the society will produce efforts to remedy these inadequacies with new symbols; from the standpoint of maintaining the symbols necessary to a social order, this could be likened to recharging a battery.

What is the symbolic balance? I see the social order as maintaining a balance of discursive and nondiscursive symbols, as explained in Chapter 3 on ritual. There I stated the theory that societies need both rational and nonrational consensus, the former maintained largely by discursive, and the latter largely by nondiscursive, communication. According to this theory, every society needs discursive and nondiscursive communication in a certain ratio, or balance, in order to preserve its two levels of consensus. There are, in other words, two communication feedback cycles—not necessarily separate—necessary to maintain the balance of discursive to nondiscursive symbols and rational to nonrational consensus. A shortage of either kind of message will produce natural responses, individually and collectively, to restore the lack. Such a shortage, or symbolic imbalance, can easily be illustrated on the side of factual information. Suppose an army is in a battle, and contact with headquarters has been lost. There will naturally be groping—through questioning, through rumor, through scouting and reconnaissance—to find answers to the questions: Where are we going? What is the plan?

But this is not the kind of imbalance we are concerned with in this book. We have, indeed, in most areas, a pileup of factual information—more than an individual can use to order his own life—along with a relative lack of message by which a person can identify himself. These are the symbols that need to be recharged.

Now, if the recharging were to be done at the discursive level, we would be concerned with institutions such as science, education, and public communication, as the main purveyors of factual information. We would endeavor not only to improve the collection and distribution of information, but to improve the semantic clarity of language and the media of information. It is, I would say, a part of the rationalistic fallacy to stress this kind of information when the problems of society are actually at a nondiscursive level. This over-

stress on rationality usually leads to movements of anti-intellec-
tualism in the name of all the neglected emotions.

Our concern here is what nondiscursive symbols need for maintenance, and what can be done to support them. It seems plain that
nondiscursive symbols are recharged primarily, not by information,
but by various kinds of enactments and interactions, in which
people have emotional as well as intellectual experiences—helped
by body language, gestures, and intonation of speech, dance and
other expressive arts; physical participation in roles; ritual; storytelling; and dramatic reenactment. Take, for example, an institution like the seder, by which Jews celebrate the Passover, a complicated and deeply moving ritual in which scriptures are read,
stories are told, food and wine are shared in a communion, and
traditional acts are performed. A similar example is provided by the
activities celebrating Christmas for Christians. Now, it may be
asked, as we did in Chapter 3, what information could possibly
take the place of such activities? What factual description, or set of
statistical tables, however accurate, could provide the emotional
meaning of actually participating in such events even when participants are unable to tell what happened afterward? Yet, in a very
broad way, this seems to be what is happening in our society: while
information piles up, the nondiscursive language and the interaction through which it is communicated dry up. We are not
using such things enough; business-like transactions tend to replace
them. In this sense, symbolic poverty (of nondiscursive symbols) can
occur in the midst of informational plenty.

But if maintenance and revival of nondiscursive symbols is the
problem, then we see that this is much more delicate and demanding than maintenance of discursive symbols, for which about
all that is required is information and definition. Nondiscursive
symbols require a favorable context of numerous delicate conditions
for successful replication. Very often they need: artistic skill; an
authentic cultural or group situation; authority to use or perform;
respect or docility in the audience (versus argument and criticism);
spontaneity and sincerity in interpersonal relations; support by the
roles of others in a cooperative act; and complex feedback at several
levels (including such things as tone of voice in the reciting of a
ritual, and performer's response to audience's response to performers). But, outside of church and the theatrical arts, few pay

much attention to such niceties of nondiscursive symbolism—in daily life or even on important occasions.

A more difficult problem is presented when successful enactment of nondiscursive symbolism requires authentic souvenirs and connection with the past. Here the loss of tradition in American life makes itself painfully felt, and enactment of symbolism requiring authentic souvenirs might require creating an entire environment or culture. Returning to the example in Chapter 1 of the New England farmer who lamented the destruction of his home town—the familiar places, sights, smells, sounds, people, and customs he knew from boyhood. These were essential souvenirs to him. How would one go about replacing or recreating such symbols—except by reconstructing an entire community, a whole past? But even if one were to attempt a brick-by-brick restoration of a home town, as in the case of Williamsburg, it is plain that this would not create an authentic symbolic environment, but only a pseudoplace.

Again, how does one recreate the nondiscursive language and recharge sentiments, so many of which seem to be weakening or dying in modern society—romantic love, happy marriage, parental authority, chivalry of males, the patriotic fervor of World War I, the old-fashioned Fourth of July, the sentiment of Christmas caroling? I mention these to illustrate how much easier it is for nondiscursive symbols to die on the vine than it is to resurrect them. Surely one cannot resuscitate such symbols merely by shooting people full of information "about" such things. Factual, historical, technical, discursive information is next to irrelevant for the meaning of nondiscursive symbols.

This is perhaps the predicament of our society: trying to replace dying nondiscursive symbols (some of which we call tradition, some of which we call human relations) by material comforts, technological efficiency and design, and impersonal information. For example, a psychiatrist tries to give insight through diagnosis and interview that might replace a lack of mother love; a theologian philosophizes about matters of faith. I suspect that, on the contrary, the very mechanical efficiency, ingenuity of design, and piling up of new information and things help to smother the nondiscursive symbols remaining.

If this trend toward smothering nondiscursive communication is to be offset, much more attention must be given to the nondiscursive dimension of interaction (some of which Edward Hall calls the silent language): more stress on messages that can be sent through touch, song, dance, miming, dramatic reenactment, ritual, and allegory. To restore symbolic balance, we need not only exploration of nondiscursive dimensions of communication, but a shift to greater emphasis upon such symbolism throughout life, including education, which should strive for appreciation of those cultural and artistic messages which cannot be contained in a mathematical formula or a multiple choice examination question. If we are to restore balance to our symbolically poor society, we should shift deliberately to types of symbolism which are somewhat disreputable according to the prevailing standards of modern society which appear to stress the discursive dimension at the expense of the nondiscursive dimension wherever possible. The difference in value attached to these two dimensions can be appreciated by listing words which apply to one and then the other: denotation versus connotation, concept versus mystique, logical thought versus prelogical or unconscious thought, fact versus allegory or metaphor, history versus myth, story versus poem, function of status versus prestige of status, technique versus ritual, cash value versus sentimental value, contract versus communion, and secular versus sacred. At the present time institutions emphasizing discursive communication— such as science, technology, and the market—are functioning more energetically and effectively than those which emphasize such things as art, poetry, ritual, and human relations.

We may mention two forces of the present which seem, for different reasons, to be doing much to break down sentiments, interfere with nondiscursive communication in human realtions, and, therefore, to be contributing to the symbolic imbalance of our society. One may be called the pornography of violence, cruelty, and sex, which, supplied so liberally in public communication, makes assaults on the more delicate of social sentiments in the name of "entertainment," "news (sensationalism)," "art," or "sport." The extreme profitability of such material tramples roughshod on sentiments and gives it an advantage in the market of images over conscientious efforts to build up wholesome sentiments. The second force is the effort to clarify symbols by stripping them of nondiscursive reference in the interest of scientific objectivity. For example, an ideal from religion or poetry might be subjected to logical or scientific analysis. All aspects which could be clearly defined would be considered and the rest ignored. This illustrates what might be called the positivistic fallacy: that all symbols can be reduced to discursive reference, and that those incapable of scientific operations are "meaningless." As one heavy-handed devotee of this idea put it, "If you can't put it into a table, it's literature and to hell with it!" While there may be some service, occasionally, to science in ignoring such nondiscursive values, carrying such an idea into the discourse of everyday life and the transactions of people with one another can only contribute to the emotional emptiness which is already past the balance point. It is already apparent that our educational institutions suffer a multiplication of factual information at the expense of nondiscursive reference, that the universities are felt to be dehumanized, subject to a split between what C. P. Snow calls the two cultures, and the student feels swamped with information that he cannot read fast enough, which he doesn't care about, and which gives him less time for "art" and "life."

Another thing contributing to symbolic imbalance is the inadequacy of the square view that everything is all right with the society morally and sentimentally—all you need is enforcement of the existing code. This view quite ignores the sincerity of the ego-screaming, and the desire of the new cults to find nondiscursive meanings, not offered sufficiently by the present social order for all its technology and abundance. The square view sees cultism and style rebellion as forms of escapism and nihilism, and feels a sense of moral outrage that is close to persecution and punishment of "sinners." The cultists and style rebels, on the other hand, see the practical measures of modern society—whether political, economic, educational, or welfare—as meaningless efforts to feed the body not the soul, perpetuating a dead system. Their cultic and rebellious styles, as they see it, are precisely the search for what the world needs, new nondiscursive symbols to once again make life meaningful rather than boring.

Whatever the truth, I think that, as soon as the problem of symbolic imbalance is recognized, we need to explore more frankly and boldly the nondiscursive aspects of symbols and directions of experience which will bring new life into nonrational consensus. Just as economic policies depend upon what the economic system needs, and political policies on what the government and national defense need, so symbolic policies depend upon what the symbolic balance needs. In general terms, this is to supply compensating measures to offset the disintegrating effects of modern trends such as mobility, modernism, acculturation, urbanization, and increasing impersonality on nondiscursive symbols.

In the interest of symbolic balance, at the very least, three policies seem to be called for. The first is attention to the importance of souvenirs of the past and symbols of place: intelligent cultural preservation and revivalism, historical study, and fostering localism as sense of place. Just as souvenirs of the past and symbols of place are reemphasized, there should be an effort to play down modernism when it reaches dogmatic proportions of a doctrine of sameness everywhere, up-to-the-minuteism, and irresponsible trampling on symbols. A second obvious major need of society is to encourage and support research in adequate interaction: the depth, range of feeling, and quality of relationships that humans need to be complete as persons (including such things as exploration of sensitivity and awareness, group and individual psychotherapy, and introducing the "cluster" principle in mass institutions). A third obvious direction that policy should take to restore symbolic balance is exploration of nonrational symbolization in music, dance, art, mysticism, ritual, and cultic inquiry and experiment (including such things as the insights offered by mind-changing drugs).

And it may be, too, that another direction by which to restore symbolic balance would be to take the emphasis off the ego, personal fulfilment and happiness—even, perhaps, off the problem of identity itself—by finding some way to give a person more of a sense of unity with other men. The principal religions of the world explain, paradoxically, that man achieves true realization of himself, not by accentuating and concentrating on his ego but by losing, subduing, or denying it—Buddhism goes so far as to say destroying it. If these religions are correct, then efforts to advertise and claim more for oneself—as in ego-screaming, faddism, and style rebellion—are pointless. It may be, on the contrary, that the identities we today base on fame, success, and personal distinction are precisely the least stable and most unsatisfying and that the real solutions to identity problems are in directions that our society has taught us to look on as destructive of the ego, as in martyrdom and self-sacrifice. It may be, indeed, that the whole problem of identity as Westerners know it is a false one; and that the Buddhist monk may be right when he says, "The man who knows that both mind and body are made up of fleeting, inconstant processes and who therefore clings to neither, never hoping to find an 'I' or 'myself' within them, is not dismayed as death approaches. Neither does the wise man think that the mind in any of its aspects is his own or his own self, nor does he identify the body as belonging to himself. Without attachment to mind or body he views them serenely with mindfulness and in this way he is not afraid."[1]

I do not claim to know the answers to these questions. But, presumably, if the policy of preserving symbolic balance were built into the society of the future, and specific remedies such as those outlined were found, the search would stop. People would be content with the identities they had or were gaining in everyday life. The rate of faddism would probably slow down. Ego-screaming and style rebellion would cease. There would be less mass worship of heroes and less of the "Mitty syndrome" in mass audiences. Dramas would supplement—but not provide an escape from—life. Ritual and ceremony on suitable occasions would be appreciated, and people would not feel it was boring but, on the contrary, deeply meaningful. Most of the oddball cults would dry up because the existing ones would be functioning well enough to supply a meaning to life. And there would be less of the crusading element in efforts to reform society because people would not be solving identity problems by participating in crusades.

I do not believe that symbolic balance would mean a static society, though it would surely mean a slower changing one. To some people, a slowly changing society is almost equivalent to a bad society. But, of course, the idea of symbolic balance which I am urging does not require that a society stop changing, but only that it consciously run on two wheels of symbolism, more or less geared to each other, rather than try precariously to go on one.

10 Perspective for Research on Symbolic Balance

I hope that the arrangement of materials in this book has helped the reader to see a little more plainly the thread of identity search in various forms of contemporary mass behavior. The "new thing" in the latter twentieth century seems to be increasing search for meaning in countless novel ways—outside the conventional avenues of politics, economics, welfare, and education.

Behind such a search, I suggested, is a poverty—or malady—of symbols, concerning such things as nonverbal interactions, sentiments, and mystiques, here characterized as an imbalance between discursive and nondiscursive symbols. Such a malady is not just a failure of particular interactions and personal efforts but a blight on the forest of meanings which a child needs to grow up into a man, a grandparent, finally an ancestor. Many of its causes are difficulties in the way of a person in a mass society finding meaning to, for, and in himself: dehumanized work, extreme impersonality, destruction of places, social mobility, lack of identifying ceremonies, pile-up of objective (meaningless) information, mediocrity of bureaucratic and white-collar self images, explosion of expectations from impact of mass communication and increasing leisure, and fragmentation of identity from multiplicity of personality models. Presumably controlling such factors could minimize identity problems. I would not, however, wish my proposals for study of symbolism to be taken as a panacea; it was not my intention to jam all the feet of a centipede into one boot.

Rather, from this survey I hope will come a perspective and some suggestions for research, one of which is to look into the symbolic balance of social systems. Societies, communities, and institutions need to be compared as to the kinds of symbolic balance and identity which prevail. The feedback cycles need to be studied. Do urbanization, advanced technology, and bureaucratization correlate with loss of symbolic balance and increasing identity problems? What can be done by ritual, changed interaction patterns, and improved feedback cycles to restore symbolic balance?

Symbolic balance includes variables discussed in this book, such as rate of fashion and fad change, ratio of tradition to innovation (in curricula for example), rate of destruction of places, proportion of impersonal to primary relationships, ratio of identifying to factual information, amount of identifying ceremony, ratio of ceremonial to matter-of-fact procedure, intensity of cult, ratio of mysticism to rationalism and science, ratio of reinforcing to seductive and transcending vicarious voyages in mass communication, rate of emergence of new types of heroes versus traditional heroes, the proportion of meaning to "noise" in art. These are social psychological measures of whether a world can easily be meaningful to a person and whether nonrational consensus is being recharged sufficiently to offset the impact of acculturation, science, and other processes which challenge the world as one knows it.

It is my hypothesis that identity problems emerge as a common man's problem in advanced technological societies, which make it likely that large numbers of people—not just a few mental cases—will have disturbed identity. Identity problems creep up like air pollution in advanced technological societies, unnoticed in the transition, because optimism about progress, exploding expectations, and enthusiasm for nationalistic movements offset the pangs of disintegration of traditional identities. Thus we may conceive of three general stages: (1) *Traditional Society,* with closely knit village, tribal, and family life; high prestige of elders and the past; roles fixed by custom, little question about identity; low exposure to mass communication and acculturation, so little psychological mobility; high birth rate, high infant and maternal death rate, low standard of living, and stable population. This is a society which expects little; its values are centered around the home. (2) *Transitional Society,* with extensive introduction of technology into industry and agriculture; population movement from villages to cities, growing urban mass (urbanization over 50 percent; rising standard of living, declining death rate, high birth rate, so population explosion; optimism, accent on progress, tradition viewed as an enemy, decline in prestige of elders and priests; increasing impact of mass communication (especially transistor radios and cinema); explosion of expectations and psychological mobility—children wanting what their parents never dreamed of; weakening in-group security; struggle for status symbols and wealth with thousands of strangers in the anonymous milieu of the city and the big factory and school; little research in the social and behavioral sciences. (3) *Advanced Technological Stage,* with automated technology and high standard of living, and much leisure; urban style predominating (hotel, apartment, and suburban living with commuter problem); low birth rate, children are expensive, small planned families, high educational expectations; fragile conjugal relationship; the social molecule dissolves into atomic individualism and aloneness not offset by impersonal voluntary associations, little security in the in-group; high impact of mass communication (radio, television, cinema, news, advertising seven nights a week, even in one's car); multiplicity of models and expectations, increasing psychological mobility ("I could be this, I should be that"); impersonal mass living denying recognition, identity problems multiplying, Mitty syndrome frequent; loss of symbolic balance and outbreak of meaning-seeking movements; mounting concern with human problems and social-psychological research. As this schema indicates, I see identity problems as a price of modernization.

If identity problems for the common man are the fruit of an advanced stage of modernization, then, if progress is to mean betterment of man, it must be redefined to include better ways of identity realization and a solution to the problem of symbolic balance.

It may take a Plato to work out the style and harmony for a society which does not close the door, even a little, to disturbances of identity such as we have considered in this book; but marches on, as rapidly as possible, to what may be some day one open world. However, I think that right now is the time for statesmen, city planners, architects, or whoever concern themselves with the design for living, to try to construct not just roads and buildings but a *meaningful place* for people to live in. To do this, they will have to collaborate with artists and other exponents of the spiritual order, and with psychologists and sociologists discovering—or redis-covering—in village, tribe, kibbutz, cult, or wherever, patterns of interaction that enable people to become meaningful to each other and have a sense of belonging in a place so attractive that they want to stay in it, so attractive that their children will not be bored with it and want to move on. The fact must be faced that it is possible to have more identity in a tribal village or in a slum than in a modern apartment building; and that it is possible to lose identity in a modernization program. Until research and design are focused with this in mind, there is little hope that modernization will do much to solve identity problems or related ones. Their solution will depend on whether we can redefine modernization not as mere material acquisition and endless fads, but as the construction of a symbolic environment satisfactory to and worthy of man.

Likewise welfare in an abundant society needs to be redefined to include identity realization. Research and reform should be focused beyond material deprivation and social injustice so that measures will provide identity solutions for the maximum number of people. We have, for instance, interpreted such things as slum riots, mod fashions, style rebellion, cults, and crusades, not as merely protests against material conditions or efforts to solve practical problems, but as searches for a fuller realization of oneself. Rock and roll, in this light, is not just an aberration in the history of music but a relatively successful realization of a new identity image for millions of teenagers: a new look, a new hedonistic-romantic style, a chal-lenge to adults, an aggressive release, a scene where one can gain the center of attention by making a loud noise and performing before others (an opportunity not for one but for quartets, for dozens). While it may not be an ideal solution to the identity problem of youth, it is at least a way of keeping them busy at something less destructive than gangfighting—a "moral equivalent of war." It needs to be studied sociologically to see what it has for identity that Beethoven, Strauss—even Gershwin, Mancini, and jazz—lack. Likewise, the presence of mystique in a sport, the devel-opment of cult around some drug, and a hysterical following of a popular idol show that identity solutions are being found. One should open one's eyes to what is sought here, and seek to incorporate equally successful realizations into reputable (square) institutions. As it is now, an expensive recreational, educational, or welfare program might lack the very features that make less reputable activities exciting. But what constructive program, lacking identity realization, can compete with a destructive or rebellious one that offers intense identity satisfactions to many people?

Conversely, reform should be careful in cutting out the irrational. As we have pointed out in the chapter on ritual, it is often the identity-realizing features of an institution, program, or curriculum that seem most senseless—a "cruel" fraternity initiation, a feud between cliques, a bit of mystical rigmarole, a sentimental custom, an over-long coffee break, frivolous social activity such as horseplay and joking. But the orderly, efficient mechanism may be precisely what denies identity satisfactions. Without research into identity-realizing values and processes (peak experiences) one does not know what to include and what to cut out.

Such considerations shift the focus of welfare in an abundant society. Are poverty measures called for? How do we know that urban renewal or a billion dollars for more students to attend mass universities will not make identity problems worse? If the salient point is that identity problems and movements are plentiful among the middle classes (perhaps as much so as among the lower), then the question one must ask is, What is the new kind of welfare that will aim not at jobs but at purposes, not at full dinner pails but full lives, at troubles affecting the middle as well as the lower class—not humiliating handouts to those painfully segregated as indigent?

Once the attack on social problems is focused on fuller identity for more people, many novel approaches and unexpected breakthroughs can be expected. What can one do in a slum that will also help identity in a suburb (not necessarily welfare checks or housing projects)? What can one do in an educational system (not necessarily improved textbooks, new dormitories, televised and computerized courses)? I am not in any sense deprecating practical measures but merely asking whether the problem is phrased in terms of what will give the most satisfactory identity to the most people? It is at least reasonable to expect better results when one zeroes in on the target.

If there is to be such a focus in human welfare, continual attention must be paid to two questions raised in this book: What measures are found scientifically to satisfy needs *faster* than they raise expectations and increase the frustration ratio? What measures will provide identity solutions to given categories of people when frustrations are mainly in this area? The latter will presumably aim at fulfilment in nondiscursive interaction, symbolism, and mystique.

Another suggestion for research is to detect and study emerging styles for hints of the future styles of modern man. We need to discover if there are *viable* identities for a rootless man who has abandoned commitment to local identities (family, tradition, community, ethnic group, class, work organization, church, nation)? Do jet set cosmopolitans, world tourists, vagrants, hippies, "rolling stones," playboys, faddists, poseurs, mass-communication addicts, cultists, humanists, existentialists indicate successful styles or merely the fumbling experiments of people with identity problems on a will-o-the-wisp search?

We may try to visualize some ascendant identity patterns of the world of tomorrow: perhaps a *cosmopolitan,* who identifies himself with all places and prides himself on sophisticated style rather than loyalty; a *rolling stone* who carries no identity but what is on his face and back, or in his suitcase; a *humanist,* who recognizes himself only as an individual with the burden of self-development within the ambiguous possibilities of "human," but who has enlarged his identity to the service of mankind rather than lapsing into irresponsibility. A broad possibility for many people is permanent *double identity:* having a secondary self at least as important as the one defined by work, education, and background. Leisure and psychological mobility may permit free development of a discontinuous secondary identity, so that it is not possible to tell who a man is from asking about his work and educational background, since it is equally important to ask about his secondary identity in sport, art, cult, and so on. Before, it was the privilege of a leisure class to cultivate interests which became more important than their formal statuses; but now the common man has an opportunity to have not only a hobby but a second life. Still other, rather less attractive, style possibilities, are: a *drug cultist,* who lives in self-induced trances, disengaged from obligations, on the minimum income provided by "scrounging" or the largesse of the welfare state; a *style poseur,* who lives only for the dramatic identities he can carry off in the night scene, by sartorial display, working just to make this possible; a *mass-communication addict,* who finds his primary identity in heroes and celebrities, in the vicarious voyages provided by television and cinema; a *mass nationalist,* who, having lost local roots and in-group security, finds his chief purpose in a national superself.

To conclude, I hope that these observations about identity problems of modern times will provide not reasons for melancholy but suggestions for a program of research into symbolic balance, new ways of identity realization, and emerging styles. If such values are missing from the equation of what we now call progress and welfare, let us find them and put them in.

NOTES

NOTES

PREFACE

1. Defined by Ralph Turner and Lewis Killian as relatively unorganized groups that, emerging from the mass, spontaneously develop norms and organization which contradict or reinterpret existing structure. *Collective Behavior* (Englewood Cliffs, N.J.: Prentice-Hall, 1957), pp. 3–4.
2. Herbert Blumer, "Collective Behavior," in R. E. Park (ed.), *Outline of Principles of Sociology* (New York: York: Barnes & Noble, 1939).
3. Collective behavior is defined by Neil Smelser as "an uninstitutionalized mobilization for action in order to modify one or more kinds of strain on the basis of a generalized reconstitution of a component of action." *Theory of Collective Behavior* (New York: Free Press, 1963), p. 71.

CHAPTER 1

1. Oscar Lewis, *The Children of Sanchez* (New York: Random House, 1961), p. 482.
2. Books such as Erving Goffman, *The Presentation of Self in Everyday Life* (New York: Doubleday, 1959), and Eric Berne, *Games People Play* (New York: Grove, 1965) reflect the sophisticated modern awareness of role-playing as distinct from what one is. Or take the treatment of conduct by a novelist like Marcel Proust.
3. Compare this with the following statement about the people who invented systematic philosophy: "A Greek takes no inventory of himself because from the time he was a baby his parents saw to it that he grew straight and hard, and because he knows himself to be a Greek." Margaret Mead (ed.), *Cultural Patterns and Technical Change* (New York: Mentor Books, 1955), p. 64. Of the many books commenting on the loss of assurance in modern societies, one might mention: Walter Lippmann, *A Preface to Morals* (New York: Beacon, 1960); Robert C. Angell, *Free Society and Moral Crisis* (Ann Arbor: University of Michigan Press, 1958); Pitirim Sorokin, *Crisis of Our Age* (Dutton, 1957); David Riesman et al., *The Lonely Crowd* (New Haven, Conn.: Yale University Press, 1950).
4. "An unhealthy self is at the heart of nearly all social discontent." Charles H. Cooley, *Human Nature and the Social Order* (New York: Scribner, 1922), p. 260.
5. "A person continually reappraises himself in the light of others' reactions." Anselm L. Strauss, *Mirrors and Masks, The Search for Identity* (New York: Free Press, 1959), pp. 44–131, 146–147.
6. "Almost all writers using the term imply that identity establishes WHAT and

WHERE the person is in social terms. It is not a substitute word for 'self.' Instead, when one has identity, he is SITUATED. . . . One's identity is established when others PLACE him as a social object by assigning him the same words of identity that he appropriates for himself or ANNOUNCES. It is in the coincidence of placements and announcements that identity becomes a meaning of the self." Gregory P. Stone, "Appearance and the Self," in Arnold M. Rose (ed.), *Human Behavior and Social Processes* (Boston: Houghton Mifflin, 1962), pp. 93–94.

7. "Past identities can be reconciled, made to appear uniform despite their apparent diversity. . . . A late convert to a sect may view most of his life as actually spent in the service of the Lord and regard the early wastrel years as a necessary preparation. . . . Biographers may give more unity to a career than was actually there." Strauss, pp. 146–147.

8. Strauss, pp. 42–43.

9. Charles Chaplin, *My Autobiography* (New York: Simon and Schuster, 1964; Pocket Books ed. 1966), pp. 94–95, 99–100, 138–140.

10. Chaplin, pp. 97–100.

11. Chaplin, pp. 138–140.

12. Francoise Gilot, "My life with Picasso," *Observer Magazine,* Nov. 29, 1964, p. 32.

13. S. A. Desick, "Jack Benny Plays a Labor of Love," San Diego *Union,* Jan. 2. 1966.

14. "Pablo had almost a reverence for Matisse. . . ." Gilot, *Observer Magazine,* Nov. 29, 1964, p. 32.

15. Carol Olten, "Satchmo," San Diego *Union,* July 25, 1965.

16. Donald Freeman, "A Certain Touch . . . That's Ahmed," Oct. 1, 1965.

17. So Saul Bellow's character Herzog "finds himself" after years of self-dissatisfaction: "Why must I be such a throb-hearted character. . . . But I am. I am, and you can't teach old dogs. Myself is thus and so, and will continue thus and so. And why fight it? My balance comes from instability. Not organization, or courage, as with other people. It's tough, but that's how it is. On these terms I, too—even I!—apprehend certain things. Perhaps the only way I'm able to do it. Must play the instrument I've got." Saul Bellow, *Herzog* (New York: Viking, 1961), p. 330. See also p. 340.

18. I am disregarding here the more severe mental disorders involving personal identity, such as depersonalization, amnesia, multiple personality, shellshock, and schizophrenia. See Tamotsu Shibutani, *Society and Personality, an Interactionist Approach to Social Psychology* (Englewood Cliffs, N.J.: Prentice-Hall, 1961), pp.453–465. Problems of identity are by no means congruent with mental disorder. As one psychologist, Robert E. Mogar, says: "It is now generally recognized that most recipients of psychotherapy are *not* suffering from traditional forms of neurosis and character disorder." Their problem, rather, is lack of meaning and self-fulfilment. Psychotherapists are "ill-equipped for such a *priestly* task." There "seems to be an incompatibility between psychotherapy, as traditionally conceived, and the nature of modern discontent." "Current Status and Future Trends in Psychedelic (LSD) Research," *J. Humanistic Psychology,* Fall 1965.

19. Erving Goffman, *Stigma: Notes on the Management of Spoiled Identity* (Englewood Cliffs, N.J. Prentice-Hall, 1963).

20. To be distinguished from sensitivity about honor or "face." Sensitivity about honor is due to responsibility for maintining a respected status. The aristocrat who defends his name by a duel may have a very firm identity—one established for centuries. Oversensitivity must be distinguished from normal "face work." See Erving Goffman, "On Face Work: an Analysis of Ritual Elements in Social Interaction," *Psychiatry*, Vol. 18, Aug. 1955, pp. 213–231.

21. Norman Mailer, "The White Negro," in *Voices of Dissent* (New York: Grove Press, 1954), pp. 197–214. In Jack Kerouac, *On the Road*, p. 148, the hero wishes he was a Negro, a Japanese, anything but a white man.

22. O. E. Klapp, *Symbolic Leaders* (Chicago: Aldine, 1965), pp. 18–101.

23. "It is primarily the inability to settle on an occupational identity which disturbs young people. To keep themselves together they temporarily over-identify, to the point of apparent complete loss of identity, with the heroes of cliques and crowds." Erik H. Erikson, *Childhood and Society* (London: Imago, 1953), p. 228.

24. George Eliot, *Middlemarch* (New York: Washington Square Press, 1963), pp. 760–761. Erikson says an identity crisis calls upon all the resources of an individual: he will defend his identity "with the astonishing strength encountered in animals who are suddenly forced to defend their lives." Erikson, p. 212.

25. Despair expresses the feeling that time is short, too short for the attempt to start another life, Erikson, p. 232.

26. Indeed, some of the identity problems have been attributed to the very rationality of bureaucracy and scientific techniques. See Eric Kahler, *The Tower and the Abyss* (New York: Braziller, 1957); Walter Lippmann, *A Preface to Morals* (Boston: Beacon, 1960); Herbert Marcuse, *One Dimensional Man* (Boston: Beacon, 1964); Floyd W. Matson, *The Broken Image; Man, Science and Society* (New York: Doubleday, 1964).

27. See Daniel Lerner, *The Passing of Traditional Society* (New York: Free Press, 1959).

28. James Baldwin and Richard Avedon, *Nothing Personal* (Baltimore: Penguin Books, 1964). No one has stated the Negro's dissatisfaction with his own identity better than James Baldwin: "Negroes want to be treated like men. People who have mastered Kant, Hegel, Shakespeare, Marx and Freud find this statement utterly impenetrable. A kind of panic paralyzes their features, as though they found themselves on the edge of a steep place. . . . Negroes want to be treated like men." James Baldwin, in Cleveland Amory (ed.), *Celebrity Register* (New York: Harper & Row, 1963).

29. E. U. Essien-Udom, *Black Nationalism* (Chicago: University of Chicago Press, 1962), p. 24.

30. Stuart E. Rosenberg surveys ambiguities and alternatives of Jewish identity, including: Jewishness, Judaism, political Zionism, Jewish anti-Semitism, the desire to assimilate as nationals; and, amidst all these perplexities, the remarkable fact that at least 2,500 Americans are converting to Judaism each year without proselytism—showing the "vitality of Judaism." (I would be inclined to add the seriousness of the identity problems of some non-Jews). *America is Dif-*

ferent, the Search for Jewish Identity (Camden, N.J.: Nelson, 1964), pp. 66, 74–75, 94–95, 126–128, 135, 144. Also see Allen Guttman, "The Conversions of the Jews," *Wisconsin Studies in Literature,* Vol. VI, 1965.

31. John W. Bennett et al., *In Search of Identity* (Minneapolis: University of Minnesota Press, 1958), pp. 110–199, 240–242.

32. See C. W. Mills, *White Collar* (New York: Oxford, 1951); and H. J. Friedsam, "Bureaucrats as Heroes," *Social Forces,* Vol. 32, 1954, pp. 269–274.

33. Russel Lynes, *The Taste-Makers* (New York: Harper & Row, 1954).

34. Cleveland Amory, *Who Killed Society?* (New York: Harper & Row, 1960), depicts the decline in authority of "old society" as social arbiter.

35. See David Riesman et al., *The Lonely Crowd;* Hendrik M. Ruitenbeek, *The Individual and the Crowd, a Study of Identity in America* (New York: New American Library, 1964); and many writings on alienation such as Maurice R. Stein et al. (ed.), *Identity and Anxiety; Survival of the Person in Mass Society* (New York: Free Press, 1960); Philip Olson (ed.), *Society, Changing Community and Identity* (New York: The Free Press, 1963). "We begin to conceptualize matters of identity at the very time in history when they become a problem. For we do so in a country which attempts to make a super-identity out of all the identities imported by its constituent immigrants; and we do so at a time when increasing mechanization threatens these essentially agrarian and patrician identities in their lands of origin as well." Erikson, p. 242. Melvin Seeman keenly explores the dimensions of inauthenticity and various responses of people to it in "Status and Identity: The Problem of Inauthenticity," *Pacific Sociological Review,* Vol. 9, Fall 1966, pp. 67–73.

36. Edward T. Hall, *The Silent Language* (New York: Doubleday, 1959).

37. Roger Eddy, "On Staying Put," *Mademoiselle,* May, 1966, pp. 108, 110. Another writer, Harvey Cox, comments on the destruction of "sacral space" (religiously significant place) by secularization, and recommends emphasis on "humanly significant space" to replace this loss. Harvey Cox, "The Restoration of a Sense of Place: a Theological Reflection on the Visual Environment," *Religious Education,* Jan. 11, 1966; reprinted in *Ekistics* (Athens, Greece), Vol. 25, no. 151, June 1968, pp. 422–424.

38. Shallowness of relationships ranks high among the images of Americans reported by foreign students at the University of California, Los Angeles. Richard T. Morris, *The Two-way Mirror, National Status in Foreign Students' Adjustment* (Minneapolis: University of Minnesota Press, 1960), pp. 120, 125.

39. "The Pleasures and Pains of the Single Life," *Time,* Sept. 15, 1967, p. 37.

40. Seeman discusses the problem of authenticity. I have referred to lack of authenticity in roles as pseudointegration in *Heroes, Villains, and Fools* (Englewood Cliffs, N.J.: Prentice-Hall, 1963) p. 110–116.

41. *Birth and Rebirth, the Religious Meanings of Initiation in Human Culture* (New York: Harper & Row, 1958), pp. xii, xiv, 3. Fred Davis and Virginia Oleson relate the identity stresses of student nurses to an absence of rites of initiation to minimize "the sense of discontinuity with a former identity, the mourning for a lost self." "Initiation in a Women's Profession: Identity Problems in the Status Transition of Coed to Student Nurse," *Sociometry,* Vol. 26, March 1963, pp. 98–99.

42. Alan W. Watts cites the mystical experiences of poets and religious sages to show that man's real identity is beyond ego, memory, consciousness, or any individual state; that it does not cease with death, and is reborn in new humans who do not remember the past. *The Supreme Identity* (London: Faber, 1950), pp. 76–298.

43. What Karl Popper refers to as the Platonic approach. *The Open Society and Its Enemies* (New York: Harcourt, 1952). Or fanaticism of the kind described by Eric Hoffer, *The True Believer* (New York: Harper & Row, 1951).

44. *Walden*, Ch. 2.

45. Erikson, p. 288; see also *Identity: Youth and Crisis* (New York: Norton, 1968).

46. Martin Buber postulates a human need for identity confirmation: "The wish of every man to be confirmed as what he is, even as what he can become, by men; and the innate capacity in man to confirm his fellow men in this way." "Distance and Religion," *Psychiatry*, Vol. 20, 1957, pp. 97–104.

47. A psychiatrist observes that patients borrow identity from their psychiatrist, and this is one reason why it is so easy to inflict a pseudoidentity on them. It is "inevitable that the patient will at some state begin to borrow his identity from the therapist. Indeed, the recovering patient will often appear to the outsider to be . . . a rag bag of oddly assorted scraps of theory, manner, and language filched from the therapist. . . . The therapist is . . . often forced, against his better judgment, to play the role of oracle or all-knowing authority." The thwarted identity need may become a "craving which, if unrecognized, will lead either to despair or illusion." Leslie H. Farber, "The Therapeutic Despair," *Psychiatry*, Vol. 21, Feb. 1958, pp. 7–20.

48. Everett C. Hughes, "What Other?" in Arnold Rose (ed.), *Human Behavior and Social Process* (Boston: Houghton Mifflin, 1962), p. 123. Albert K. Cohen describes the "gravitation" of those with status problems toward congenial groups. *Delinquent Boys* (New York: Free Press, 1955).

49. A public image or public self is shown as emerging in a dialectic of interaction between the public figure and his audience in O. E. Klapp, *Symbolic Leaders* (Chicago: Aldine, 1965), Ch. 2.

50. According to Charles H. Cooley, the lookingglass self is inseparable from the personal idea of the other. "Self and other do not exist as mutually exclusive facts." *Human Nature and the Social Order* (New York: Scribner's, 1922), pp. 118–134. G. H. Mead refers to the fed-back portion of the self as the "me." *Mind, Self and Society* (Chicago: University of Chicago Press, 1936).

51. See Pitirim Sorokin, *Altruistic Love* (Boston: Beacon Press, 1950), and *Reconstruction of Humanity* (Boston: Beacon, 1948). A study of popular culture in the nineteenth century suggests that there has been a decline of sentimentalism in America—especially in regard to religion, patriotism, reforming spirit, and the "softer emotions" such as romantic love and mother love. Carl Bode, *The Anatomy of American Popular Culture, 1840–1861* (Berkeley and Los Angeles: University of California Press, 1959), pp. xiii–xv. Many other writers have commented on the emotional shallowness, or affectlessness, of modern—perhaps especially American—life: for example, J. W. Krutch, *The Modern Temper* (New York: Harcourt, 1929); Aldous Huxley, *The Brave New World* (New York: Harper & Row, 1932; also Banton Books reprint.) Martha Wolfenstein

and Nathan Leites, *Movies, a Psychological Study* (New York: Free Press, 1950). Pamela Hansford Johnson argues that the pornography of cruelty so visible today is a symptom of creeping affectlessness—the "Affectless Society." *On Iniquity: Some Personal Reflections Arising Out of the Moors Murder Trial* (New York: Scribner, 1967). President Eisenhower deplores the decline of patriotic feeling: "Too many of us Americans have become so sophisticated that we are inclined to think of any honest emotion, including a public display of patriotism, as corny. It is hard for me to imagine anyone being ashamed of patriotism, yet there it is. And this attitude can scarcely fail to seep down to our children." Dwight D. Eisenhower, *Reader's Digest,* March 1963, p.78.

52. Karen Horney, *Neurosis and Human Growth* (New York: Norton, 1950).

53. Strauss, *Mirrors and Masks, The Search for Identity.*

54. For example, in Columbia University's "New Careers" program to educate successful people for diametrically different jobs. "The switchers mostly feel that their work has become a bore, a trap or a disillusionment." A 40 year-old company president said that he felt "wasted in working for material gain only." *Time,* Nov. 12, 1965, p. 89.

55. Arthur Koestler, *The Yogi and the Commissar* (New York: Macmillan, 1945).

56. Lawrence Lipton, *The Holy Barbarians* (New York: Messner, 1959; New English Library Edition, 1962), pp. 152–153.

57. Eve Curie, *Madame Curie* (New York: Doubleday, 1949), p. 158.

58. For example the legends of Perceval, Galahad, and Jason; the quest theme in literature is also exemplified by Don Quixote, Faust, and John Bunyan's Pilgrim. For treatment of this theme see David Malcolmson, *Ten Heroes* (New York: Duell, Sloan & Pearce-Meredith Press 1941), pp. 9–67; S. Swinscow, "The Holy Grail: Qui on en servait?" *Folk-Lore,* 1944, pp. 55:32.

59. Yvonne Lubbock, *Return to Belief* (London: Collins, 1961), pp. 9–10.

60. The Middle Way, *Journal of the Buddhist Society,* London, May 1966, p. 16.

61. Howard S. Becker distinguishes the moral crusader from a moral entrepreneur as an absolutist, fervent and self-righteous, who believes his mission is a holy one. *Outsiders* (New York: Free Press, 1963), pp. 147–148.

62. "Squares" or "straight," say beatniks and hippies.

63. Kornhauser's term for the unattached and uncommitted members of the population who are available for movements. See also K. Keniston, *The Uncommitted: Alienated Youth in American Society* (New York: Harcourt, 1965).

64. A. K. Cohen's term for the tendency of people with status problems to drift or congregate into congenial groups. Cohen, *Delinquent Boys.*

CHAPTER 2

1. We want to have "A Society from which no one is left out." F. D. Roosevelt.

2. *Time,* Aug. 4, 1967, p. 19.

3. Paul Jacobs and Saul Landau, *The New Radicals* (New York: Vintage Books, 1966; Pelican Books, 1967,), Ch. 2.

4. I do not imply that all members of the new left were well-to-do; SNCC, for example, a predominantly Negro organization, came from considerably poorer

strata than the predominantly white, middle-class SDS, as Jacobs and Landau point out, p. 26.

5. Jacobs and Landau, pp. 89–90.
6. Jacobs and Landau, pp. 105–106.
7. See Daniel Bell (ed.), *The Radical Right* (New York: Doubleday, 1964).
8. Seymour M. Lipset, "Radical Right Extremism," Lecture, San Diego State College, 1965; also Bell, pp. 332–335.
9. See K. Kenniston, *The Uncommitted: Alienated Youth in American Society* (New York: Harcourt, 1965).
10. *Time,* May 19, 1967, p. 138.
11. Herbert Gold, "Where the Action Is," *New York Times Book Review,* Feb. 19, 1967, p. 50. See also Fred W. Davis, "Focus on the Flower-Children, Why All of Us May Be Hippies Someday," *Trans-Action,* Dec. 1967, pp. 10–18.
12. *Understanding Media: The Extensions of Man* (New York: McGraw-Hill, 1964; Signet Books reprint), p. 36.
13. William Braden, *The Private Sea: LSD and the Search for God* (New York: Quadrangle, 1967); Alan Watts, *This Is IT!* (New York: Pantheon, 1960).
14. *International Herald-Tribune,* Aug. 1, 1967.
15. John Mackenzie, quoting Senator J. William Fulbright, *International Herald-Tribune,* Aug. 9, 1967.
16. Ben H. Bagdikian, *In the Midst of Plenty, The Poor in America* (Boston: Beacon Press, 1964).
17. Daniel Bell, *The End of Ideology* (New York: Collier, 1961). Chapter on decline of socialism in the United States.
18. So, for example, during the banking War of 1837, one might hear even banking interests using the Jeffersonian right to revolution in protest against the hard-money policy of President Van Buren: "It is our right and our duty to resist oppression. It is absolutely necessary that this right should be exercised at this moment. Revolution has no peculiar horror for those who feel that it now means the preservation of our Constitution and the protection of our lives and property. Our fathers exercised it and their descendants may and will resort to it when necessary." Arthur M. Schlesinger, Jr., *Age of Jackson* (New York: Mentor Books, abridged, 1949), p. 97.
19. M. D. Peterson, *The Jefferson Image in the American Mind* (New York: Oxford, 1962), pp. 201, 221, 308.
20. C. E. M. Joad, quoted by F. H. Taylor, "Modern Art and the Dignity of Man," *Atlantic,* Dec. 1948, p. 30.
21. Various aspects of the problem are discussed in: Daniel Bell, *The End of Ideology;* Pitirim Sorokin, *The Crisis of Our Age;* Walter Lippmann, *Preface to Morals,* and *The Public Philosophy* (Boston: Little, Brown, 1955); Arthur M. Schlesinger, Jr., "The One Against the Many," *Saturday Review,* July 14, 1962, pp. 9–11, 54–55; Joseph La Palombara, "Decline of Ideology: A Dissent and an Interpretation," *American Political Science Review,* Dec. 1966; Seymour M. Lipset, "Some Further Comments on the 'End of Ideology.' " *American Political Science Review,* Dec. 1966.
22. Richard Hofstadter, *The American Political Tradition* (New York: Knopf, 1948), p. vii.

23. Schlesinger, "The One Against the Many."
24. *Mirror For Man* (New York: Pocket Books, 1963), pp. 198–199.
24a The word "ekistics" is a term coined by the Greek architect and city-planner, Constantine Doxiades, for a program to redesign cities to the scale of man.
25. Says the travel folder: "Now, aren't you entitled to seven days of good food, festivities and fun to those pleasant places everyone is talking about? Of course, you are!"
26. For example, Ivo K. Fierabend and Rosalind L. Fierabend report a positive relationship between the political instability of various countries and a frustration ratio. "The notion of systemic frustration was defined as including those situations in which large strata of the population experience expectations, needs or aspirations which remain unmatched by equivalent levels of satisfaction. This type of gap between need or demand and achievement may most easily be identified among the ecological variables of political systems, especially in the socioeconomic sphere. . . . Identifying one form of systemic frustration as the ratio of social want formation to social want satisfaction, it was predicted that those countries in which this ratio was large would be more stable politically, whereas those in which the ratio was small, and hence the gap between wants and satisfactions was large, would exhibit a higher level of political instability. In order to test this prediction, a frustration index was calculated based on eight socioeconomic measures. . . . GNP and caloric intake per capita, physicians, telephones, newspapers and radios per unit of population, literacy level and level of urbanization. . . . The relationship yielded by correlating this frustration index, based on the years 1948–1955 to the political instability profile calculated for the time period 1955–1961, was Pearson $r = .499$, for the sample of sixty-one nations for which data were available on all indices . . . with a probability level of less than .001. . . . Specifically, the hypothesis was: the higher (lower) the social want formation in any given society and the lower (higher) the social want satisfaction, the greater (the less) the systemic frustration and the greater (the lesser) the impulse to political instability." "The Relationship of Systemic Frustration, Political Coercion, International Tension and and Political Instability: a Cross-National Study" (paper delivered to American Psychol. Assn., New York, Sept. 2–6, 1966). See also: Fierabend, "Aggressive Behaviors Within Polities, 1948–1962: a Cross-National Study," *Journal of Conflict Resolution,* Sept. 1966; and Betty A. Nesvold, *Modernity, Social Frustration, and the Stability of Political Systems: a Cross-National Study* (Master's Thesis, San Diego State College, 1964); James C. Davies presents a theory of revolution as resulting, not from absolute deprivation, but from an "intolerable gap between what people want and what they get." "Toward a Theory of Revolution," *American Sociological Review,* 27, 1962, pp. 5–19. " . . . The widespread unhappiness among transitionals in Egypt and Syria expresses the disjunction . . . between their empathy and their impotency." Daniel Lerner, *The Passing of Traditional Society* (New York: Free Press, 1958), p. 103. Hadley Cantril finds exploding expectations in societies like Brazil create a dangerous potential for the future. The danger is from optimism about the future combined with a sense of stagnation in the present and past. "Those who do rate themselves feel they have made little headway during the past five years and see Brazil as a nation

about at a standstill. . . . However people are optimistic about the future. . . . The picture is one of a people potentially ripe for political revolution if they should lose confidence that existing governments will find remedies. . . ." (p. 74) "In the study of the people of the Dominican Republic, we get an insight into the state of mind that breeds revolution and impels people to follow strong leaders unless the aspirations felt so intensely are rather immediately met. . . ." (p. 137) *The Pattern of Human Concerns* (New Brunswick, N.J.: Rutgers University Press, 1965).

27. S. M. Lipset and S. S. Wolin, *The Berkeley Student Rebellion* (Garden City, N.Y.: Doubleday, 1965), p. 219. Several popular songs expressing similar boredom with English middle class life can be found in a well known recording by The Beatles, *Sergeant Pepper's Lonely Hearts Club Album* (1967).

28. David A. Shannon, *The Decline of American Communism* (New York: Harcourt, 1959).

29. Viktor E. Frankl, *Man's Search for Meaning, an Introduction to Logotherapy* (New York: Washington Square Press, 1963), p. 169. Likewise, Rollo May says: "The chief problem of people in the middle decade of the twentieth century is emptiness." *Man's Search for Himself* (New York: Norton, 1953), p. 14.

CHAPTER 3

1. Lerner, *The Passing of Traditional Society* (New York: Free Press, 1958).

2. A survey of fashion consciousness among college students (San Diego State College, 1965, N=76 upper division sociology). Fifty-five percent said they tried to improve their status by fashion.

3. See John Fairchild, *The Fashionable World of Savages* (New York: Doubleday, 1965).

4. Advertisers recognize that people seek identities through purchase of commodities, fashions. Elbrun Rochford French (ed.), *The Copywriter's Guide.* (New York: Harper & Row, 1958), pp. 467–468.

5. Ernestine Carter, *The Times,* Sept. 13, 1964.

6. Drusilla Beyfus, "How to Tell a Boy from a Girl," *The Times Magazine,* (London) Sept. 20, 1964, pp. 46–47.

7. *Parade,* Feb. 7, 1965.

8. *Parade,* Feb. 7, 1965.

9. Murray Wax, "Themes in Cosmetics and Grooming," *American Journal of Sociology,* LXII, May 1957, pp. 558–593. An American woman views her body "as a craftsman views his raw material."

10. Advertisement for a hair tint, "Great Day."

11. "The Pretty Things," *The Times Magazine,* (London) July 12, 1964, p. 16.

12. See discussion of audience-directedness of modern society in O. E. Klapp, *Heroes, Villains and Fools* (Englewood Cliffs, N.J.: Prentice-Hall, 1963), Ch. 2.

13. Another way of saying this is that "Publi-ciety" is corrupting elite standards. Cleveland Amory, *Who Killed Society?* (New York: Harper & Row, 1960).

14. *Time,* Aug. 5, 1966, p. 32.

15. Lloyd Shearer, "Why They Dress This Way," *Parade*, Oct. 16, 1966, pp. 23–24.

16. Lawrence Lipton, *The Holy Barbarians* (New York: Messner, 1959; New English Library edition), pp. 17–18.

17. *The New York Times*, Aug. 6, 1966.

18. See my treatment of mockery of heroes in *Heroes, Villains and Fools*, Ch. 8

19. Enid Starkie, preface to Jules Amédée, *Barbey D'Aurevilly: the She-Devils* (London: translated by Jean Kimber).

20. Harold Finestone, "Cats, Kicks and Color." *Social Problems*. Hipster style was escapist in two ways: as a "cool" pose of "digging" the scene without engagement, and as a pseudo-Negroid identity for whites entering the world of the "cat." For the latter, see Norman Mailer, "The White Negro: Superficial Reflections on the Hipster," *Dissent*, Vol. 4, 1957, pp. 277–288.

21. Indeed, the zoot suit became a more and more explicitly rebellious and villainous symbol (a badge of delinquency and hoodlumism) as time went on. As its animosity to the square would become evident it subjected its wearers, whether or not Mexican-American or Negro, to attack and persecution. In riots the *zooter* symbol supplied "an objective tag with which to identify the object of attack." Ralph H. Turner and Samuel J. Surace, "Zoot-suiters and Mexicans: Symbols in Crowd Behavior," *American Journal of Sociology*, 62, 1956, pp. 14–20.

22. *The Times Magazine*, (London) Aug. 2, 1964.

23. "Mad New Scene on Sunset Strip," *Life*, Aug. 28, 1966, p. 80.

24. Beatnik poet Allen Ginsberg assumes role of guru, visits Tibet and Himalayas, bathes in holy water of Ganges, recites mantras, practices yoga and breathing exercises, has visions and illuminations, takes vow of poverty, plays the guru, holy man, to university students in lecture and poetry-reading tours. Barry Farrell, "The Guru Comes to Kansas," *Life*, May 27, 1966, pp. 79 ff.

25. "Hell's Angels," *Saturday Evening Post*, Nov. 20, 1965, pp. 32–39.

26. Kenneth Burke, *Permanence and Change* (New York: The New Republic, 1936). "Piety is a system-builder. . . . Piety is THE SENSE OF WHAT PROPERLY GOES WITH WHAT. And it leads to construction in this way: If there is an altar, it is pious of a man to perform some ritual act whereby he may approach this altar with clean hands. . . . Piety is a response which extends through all the texture of our lives . . . great areas of piety even at a ballgame. . . ." even in murder (pp. 100–102). "Refined critics, of the Matthew Arnold variety, assumed that exquisiteness of taste was restricted to the 'better' classes of people. . . . Yet if we can bring ourselves to imagine Matthew Arnold loafing on the corner with the gashouse gang, we promptly realize how undiscriminating he would prove himself. Everything about him would be inappropriate. . . . Consider the crudeness of his perception as regards the proper oaths, the correct way of commenting upon passing women, the etiquette of spitting. Does not his very crassness here reveal the presence of a morality, a deeply felt and piously obeyed sense of the appropriate, on the part of these men, whose linkages he would outrageously violate? Watch them—and observe with what earnestness, what *devotion*, these gashouse Matthew Arnolds act to prove themselves, every minute of the day, true members of their cult. Vulgarity is pious" (pp. 103–104).

27. See Howard S. Becker, *Outsiders* (New York: The Free Press, 1963). Seymour Rubenfeld, *Family of Outcasts* (New York: Free Press, 1965).

28. Even in prison uniforms, homosexuals make an effort to distinguish themselves: the "fag" or "queen" (effeminate male) by womanly walk, too-graceful gestures, coquettishness, dyeing his underclothing, curling his hair or coloring his lips with homemade lipstick; the "butch" by swaggering, sitting with knees apart, avoiding bras, and wearing belt low at the hips, and men's socks, underwear, and shorts. See David A. Ward and Gene G. Kassebaum, *Women's Prison* (Chicago: Aldine Publishing Co., 1965), pp. 103–107; and Gresham M. Sykes, *The Society of Captives* (Princeton, N.J.: Princeton University Press, 1958), p. 96. But, since such conspicuous mannerisms draw official attention, dramatizing oneself by "butch" or "fag" costume is dysfunctional in the prison setting. Ward and Kassebaum. pp. 103–107.

29. Call girls and party girls, of course, maintain a different professional image from whores. Harold Greenwald, *The Call Girl* (New York: Ballantine Books, 1958), pp. 23–27. It is in the latter category—among the true outcasts—that the flaunting use of style is most to be expected. It is one way of "finding oneself." Greenwald notes that prostitutes have vague self images and "seem to be in search of hints from the outside to tell them what role to play" (p. 119). The success of *Irma La Douce,* starring Shirley MacLaine, was due in part, I think, to its flaunting quality, the delight of seeing a person thoroughly herself, realize herself, by being explicit in a role which in America is usually hidden.

30. E. U. Essien-Udom, *Black Nationalism, A Search for an Identity in America* (Chicago: University of Chicago Press, 1962; Dell Books Edition), p. 97.

31. Georg Simmel, "Fashion," *American Journal of Sociology,* LXII, May 1957, p. 552.

32. *The Village Voice,* July 22, 1965.

33. See Alva Johnston, "The Downfall of Prince Mike," *Saturday Evening Post,* March 20, 1943, pp. 9 ff.; Robert Crichton, *The Great Impostor* (New York: Random House, 1959); Herbert Brean, "Marvin Hewitt, Ph(ony) D.," *Life,* April 12, 1954; Helene Deutsch, "The Impostor: Contribution to Ego Psychology of a Type of Psychopath," *Psychoanalytic Quarterly,* vol. 24, 1955, pp. 483–505.

34. *Time,* Aug. 27, 1965, pp. 65–67.

35. See the deviant subsocieties treated by A. R. Lindesmith and Anselm L. Strauss, *Social Psychology* (New York: Holt, Rinehart and Winston, Inc., 1968), Ch. 17; also Howard Becker, *Outsiders.*

36. See O. E. Klapp, *Symbolic Leaders* (Chicago: Aldine, 1965), p. 121; and Lillian Ross, *Portrait of Hemingway* (New York: Simon and Schuster, 1961).

37. Allen Geller, "An Interview with Allen Ginsberg," *Rogue,* June 1965, pp. 35 ff.

38. Klapp, *Heroes, Villains and Fools,* pp. 110–116.

39. Sumner noted frivolity and instability of fashions and fads but failed sufficiently to distinguish them from mores. He included them in the mores because of the similarity of their irrational authority ("there is no arguing with the fashion . . . the authority . . . is imperative . . . sanctions are ridicule and powerlessness . . . canons of criticism are set by fashion"); he noted, however, conflict of innovations with mores, and that fashions influence mores; but held that they could not

succeed if in conflict with mores. William G. Sumner, *Folkways* (New York: Ginn & Co., 1906), pp. 94, 168, 194–195. Herbert Blumer explicitly stated the function of fashion as a movement, "different from custom which . . . is static," because fashion "is based fundamentally on differentiation and emulation" in a class society. Fashion "contributes to the formation of a new social order" by expressing, shaping, and crystallizing new tastes. "Collective Behavior" in A. M. Lee, *New Outline of the Principles of Sociology* (New York: Barnes & Noble, 1946; originally published in 1939), pp. 217–218. The theory of secularization of society includes the idea of fashion replacing folkways.

40. Ailsa Garland, *Sun*, (London) Sept. 15, 1964.
41. Joyce Eggington, *Observer*, Sept. 27, 1964.
42. Brigid Keenan, *The Times Magazine* (London), July 19, 1964, p. 32.
43. *Observer*, July 12, 1964.
44. Brigid Keenan, *The Times Magazine* (London) Aug. 2, 1964.
45. Manchester *Guardian*, July 10, 1964.
46. Stanley Marcus, "Fashion Is My Business," *Atlantic Monthly*, Dec. 1948, pp. 43–44. Far from being a "dictatorship," fashion is a nerve-racking gamble involving guessing how people will make up their minds, according to Bernard Roshco, *The Rag Race* (New York: Funk & Wagnalls, 1963). The network of people interacting in the fashion system is seen as a "spirallike closed circuit" of producers, distributors, and consumers, by Rolf Meyersohn and Elihu Katz, "A Natural History of Fads," *Amerian Journal of Sociology*, LXII, (May 1957), p. 596. Elihu Katz and Paul F. Lazarsfeld point to the importance, not of high society, but of gregarious, young, upper-middle-class matrons in women's fashion leadership. *Personal Influence* (New York: Free Press, 1956).
47. I here follow Gregory Stone's distinction between uniform as a badge of social identity and status, and costume as assuming symbols of identity not one's own. "Appearance and the Self" in Arnold M. Rose (ed.), *Human Behavior and Social Processes* (New York: Houghton Mifflin, 1962), p. 113.
48. Amory, *Who Killed Society?*
49. *English Eccentrics*, pp. 20–21.
50. Lynes, Russell, *The Taste Makers* (New York: Harper & Row, 1954).
51. *Time*, Aug. 27, 1965, pp. 65–67.
52. Half a century ago Georg Simmel noted that fashion has "overstepped the bounds of its original domain . . . and has acquired an increasing influence over taste, over theoretical convictions, and even over the moral foundations of life." "Fashion," *American Journal of Sociology*, Vol. LXII, May 1957, p. 548.
53. Sir Herbert Read, "The Empty Landscape," *The Countryman*, Winter 1965, pp. 242–243.
54. Max Eastman analyzed a similar defeat of meaning in poetry in *The Literary Mind, Its Place in an Age of Science* (New York: Scribner 1935).

CHAPTER 4

1. I here follow Susanne K. Langer's distinction between discursive and nondiscursive symbols. Language conveys meaning (concepts) by denotation and con-

notation. But there is a "beyond" of semantics, which is meaningful, more than mere feeling, though we cannot talk about it by language. "Human thought is but a tiny, grammar-bound island, in the midst of a sea of feeling. . . . There are things which do not fit the grammatical scheme of expression . . . which require to be conceived through some symbolistic schema other than discursive language." *Philosophy in a New Key, A Study in the Symbolism of Reason, Rite and Art* (Baltimore: Penguin, Inc., 1948), pp. 70–71.

2. See O. E. Klapp, "The Fool as a Social Type, *American Journal of Sociology,* Vol. 55 (1949), pp. 157–162.

3. In classifying painting as nondiscursive language I do not imply that all art is, or must be, symbolic, merely that often it is. The question of significance in art is well treated by Charles W. Morris, *Signification and Significance* (Cambridge, Mass.: M.I.T. Press, 1964), pp. 65–80.

4. See, for example, David Efron and John P. Foley, Jr., "Gestural Behavior and Social Setting," in T. M. Newcomb and E. L. Hartley (eds.), *Readings in Social Psychology* (New York: Holt, Rinehart and Winston, Inc., 1947), pp. 33–40; Edward T. Hall, *The Silent Language* (New York: Fawcett World Library, Doubleday, 1959); Theodor Reik, *Listening With the Third Ear* (New York: Farrar, Straus, 1948).

5. "There is a symbolism and a definite meaning attached to every ceremony in the Mass. . . . Ceremonies assist in the evocation of appropriate attitudes . . . such as the attitude of reverence . . . adoration, thanksgiving, supplication, and propitiation. . . . There is a deepening of sense impressions, an enrichment and vivifying of mental imagery, and the establishment of sufficient apperceptive masses for the subsequent assimilation of abstract religious dogma, through the appeal made to the senses by . . . pictures, statues, frescoes, sculpturings . . . stained glass windows . . . music and song . . . gorgeous vestments, graceful and dramatic ceremonies . . . pageantry and pantomine. . . . They are the finished language through which the heart of the creature speaks to the heart of his God." Rev. John A. O'Brien, Ph.D., *Modern Psychology and the Mass* (New York: The Paulist Press, 1927), pp. 30–31.

6. Langer, pp. 70–71. Conventional terms of semantics and psychology for this realm include: connotation (versus denotation), intension (versus extension), apperceptive mass, emotive signification; in C. W. Morris' terminology, it would be the prescriptive and appraisive (versus designative) dimensions of signification, Morris, *Signification and Significance,* pp. 3–9; and *Signs, Language and Behavior* (New York: Braziller, 1955), pp. 60–91. Kenneth Burke calls it "Poetic Meaning." "The semantic ideal would attempt to *get a description* by the *elimination of attitude.* The poetic ideal would attempt to *attain a full moral act* by attaining a perspective *atop all the conflicts of attitude.* The first would try to *cut away,* to *abstract,* all emotional factors that complicate the objective clarity of meaning. The second would try to derive its vision from the maximum *heaping up* of all these emotional factors. . . ." Kenneth Burke, "Semantic and Poetic Meaning," in Donald E. Hayden and E. Paul Alworth (eds.), *Classics in Semantics* (New York: Philosophical Library, 1965), p. 305.

7. See Jane Belo, *Trance in Bali* (New York: Columbia University Press, 1960); Alfred Matraux, *Voodoo in Haiti* (New York: Oxford, 1959).

8. Exemplifying the difficulty of rationally explaining the meaning of unpleasant ceremonies: university students who were subjected to embarrassing initiations liked their groups better than students whose groups did not embarrass them. Elliott Aronson and Judson Mills, "The Effect of Severity of Initiation on Liking for a Group," *Journal of Abnormal and Social Psychology*, Vol. 59, 1959, pp. 177–181.

9. Charles Preston, *The Jokes Wagen Book* (New York: Geis Random House, 1966).

10. W. Lloyd Warner finds in Memorial Day a cult of the dead, whose culminating ritual is all elements of the community coming together for one symbolic act of solidarity: a procession of all as one group to the cemetery where "our dead" are honored. "An American Sacred Ceremony" in *American Life, Dream and Reality* (Chicago: University of Chicago Press, 1953) pp. 1–26.

11. Contrasting societal roles of white and black magic are shown in W. Lloyd Warner, *A Black Civilization* (New York: Harper & Row, 1937). Bronislaw Malinowski's theory of magic stresses its anxiety-relieving function. See Bronislaw Malinowski, *Coral Gardens and Their Magic* (London: G. Allen, 1935); Bronislaw Malinowski, *Magic, Science and Religion and Other Essays* (New York: Doubleday, 1954); and G. C. Homans, "Anxiety and Ritual," *American Anthropologist*, Vol. XLIII, 1941, pp. 164–172.

12. Arnold Van Gennep, *Rites of Passage* (Chicago: University of Chicago Press, 1960; original edition 1909); Frank W. Young, *Initiation Ceremonies, A Cross-Cultural Study of Status Dramatization* (Indianapolis: Bobbs-Merrill, 1965).

13. "The Coronation was the ceremonial occasion for the affirmation of the moral values by which the society lives. It was an act of national communion." Edward Shils and Michael Young, "The Meaning of the Coronation," *Sociological Review*, Vol. 1, 1953, pp. 63–81. See also Percy Black, *Mystique of Modern Monarchy* (London: C. A. Watts, 1953).

14. The criminal trial is like a morality play. It is not an efficient way of investigating what happened, but it satisfies a deep need for the appearance of justice and "presents the conflicting moral values of a community in a way that cannot be done by logical formalization." Thurman Arnold, *Fair Fights and Foul* (New York: Harcourt, 1965). In one aspect, the criminal court conviction is a status degradation ceremony, and may be analyzed dramatically along lines suggested by Harold Garfinkel, "Conditions of Successful Degradation Ceremonies," *American Journal of Sociology*, Vol. 61, 1956, pp. 420–424. See also O. E. Klapp, "Vilification as a Social Process," *Pacific Sociological Review*, Vol. 2, 1959, pp. 71–76. On law-enforcement functions of ritual of sorcery, see: E. E. Evans-Pritchard, *Witchcraft, Ordeals and Magic among the Azande* (Oxford: Clarendon Press, 1937); Reo Fortune, *Sorcerers of Dobu* (London: Routledge, 1932); Bronislaw Malinowski, *Crime and Custom in Savage Society* (New York: Harcourt, 1932); Ian Hogbin, *Law and Order in Polynesia* (London: Christophers, 1934); Warner, *Black Civilization*.

15. Klapp, "The Fool as a Social Type," also, "Heroes, Villains and Fools as Agents of Social Control," *American Sociological Review*, Vol. 19, 1954, pp. 56–62.

16. Marcel Mauss, *The Gift* (London: Cohen and West, 1954).

17. Monica Wilson, *Rituals of Kinship Among the Nyakyusa* (London: Oxford University Press for the International African Institute, 1957); Iwao Ishino, "The Oyabun-Kobun: A Japanese Ritual Kinship Institution," *American Anthropologist,* Vol. 55, Dec. 1953, pp. 695–707.

18. Ranging in significance from purification of a person or group from taboo violation to ritual rebirth. See Mary Douglas, *Purity and Danger, an Analysis of Concepts of Pollution and Taboo* (New York: Praeger, 1966); A. R. Radcliffe-Brown, *Taboo* (England: Cambridge, University Press, 1939); Mircea Eliade, *Birth and Rebirth.*

19. Aristotle, *Poetics.* For analysis of symbolic meanings of tragedy to Americans, see O. E. Klapp, "Tragedy and the American Climate of Opinion," *Centennial Review,* Vol. II, No. 4, Fall 1958, pp. 396–413; reprinted in John D. Hurrell, *Two Modern American Tragedies* (New York: Scribner, 1961).

20. Emile Durkheim, *Elementary Forms of the Religious Life* (New York: Free Press, 1947); A. Radcliffe-Brown, *Taboo,* and *Andaman Islanders* (New York: Free Press, 1948); Raymond Firth, *Elements of Social Organization* (Boston: Beacon, 1961), pp. 228–231; Max Gluckman (ed.), *Essays on the Ritual of Social Relations* (Manchester, England: Manchester University Press, 1962), and *Politics, Law and Ritual in Tribal Societies* (Chicago: Aldine, 1965); William A. Lessa and E. Z. Vogt (eds.), *Reader in Comparative Religion, an Anthropological Approach* (New York: Harper & Row, 1958); John J. Honigmann, *Theory of Ritual, a Book of Readings and Cases* (Chapel Hill, N.C.: University of North Carolina Bookstore, 1953).

21. Firth, *Elements of Social Organization,* pp. 63–65.

22. Following the theory of Robert E. Park. For a discussion of the scope of consensus as a social binder see O. E. Klapp, "The Concept of Consensus and Its Importance," *Sociology and Social Research,* Vol. 41, 1957, pp. 336–342. My earlier version of the function of ritual in maintaining nonrational consensus was *Ritual and Cult, a Sociological Interpretation* (Washington, D.C.: Public Affairs Press, 1956).

23. James S. Bossard and Eleanor S. Boll, "Ritual in Family Living," *American Sociological Review,* Vol. 14, 1949, pp. 463–469.

24. Ernest W. Burgess and Harvey J. Locke, *The Family* (New York: American Book, 1945), pp. 345–346.

25. There is a moderate (.4 Pearsonian) correlation between the amount of significant ritual and the solidarity of American families. O. E. Klapp, "Ritual and Family Solidarity," *Social Forces,* Vol. 37, No. 3, March 1959, pp. 212–214.

26. Newman quoted in O'Brien, p. 29.

27. And Sigmund Freud of the need to stop needing them, in *The Future of an Illusion.*

28. A. H. Whitehead, *Symbolism, Its Meaning and Effect* (New York: Putnam, 1959; originally published in 1927), pp. 60–81.

29. "Inefficiency of this sort occurs when the members of an organization become so preoccupied with meticulous application of detailed rules that they lose sight of the very purpose of their action." Peter M. Blau, *Bureaucracy in Modern Society* (New York: Random House, 1956), pp. 87–88. R. K. Merton refers to this as "displacement of goals whereby an instrumental value becomes a ter-

minal value." *Social Theory and Social Structure* (New York: Free Press, 1949), pp. 154–155.

30. As implied, for example, by Blau and by Merton; or Peter Berger's treatment of ritualism as part of the "okay world" of clichés which causes man to lead an "inauthentic life," *Invitation to Sociology* (New York: Doubleday, 1963), pp. 146–149. It is important to note that mystics have always believed that ritualism (say repetition of a mantra) leads to a higher authenticity than do logical clichés. Therefore, if we are to balance the claims of rationalism and mysticism, perhaps the best position is that both logic and ritual are subject to clichés but also are ways to authenticity.

31. Langer; Whitehead; Ernst Cassirer, *An Essay on Man* (New York: Doubleday, 1956), and *The Myth of the State* (New York: Doubleday, 1955); T. W. Arnold, *The Symbols of Government* (New York: Harcourt, 1962; 1935).

32. Marcuse; Matson; Karl Mannheim considers the possibility that mankind might lose the capacity for "reality-transcending" consciousness. *Ideology and Utopia* (New York: Harcourt, 1936), p. 236.

33. Kenneth Burke, *Permanence and Change* (Indianapolis: Bobbs-Merrill, 1954), pp. 286–287.

34. *The American Way of Death* (New York: Simon and Schuster, 1963); also Geoffrey Gorer, *Death, Grief and Mourning* (London: Cresset Press, 1965).

35. James H. Barnett, "The Easter Festival . . . a Study in Cultural Change," *American Sociological Review*, Vol. 14, 1949, pp. 463–469; and *The American Christmas: A Study in National Culture* (New York: Macmillan, 1954). See also Mark Benny, R. S. Weiss, Rolf Meyersohn, and David Riesman, "Christmas in an Apartment Hotel," *American Journal of Sociology*, Vol. LXV, 1959, pp. 233–240.

36. A survey of attitudes toward Christmas of 104 (41 male, 63 female) upper division sociology students and their friends, San Diego State College, 1966. The ten features of Christmas felt to be most important among 31 alternatives were (in rank order): (1) Christmas dinner together as family, (2) Christmas Eve together as family, (3) Christmas tree in home, (4) exchange of gifts among family members, (5) attending church on Christmas Eve, (6) decorating the tree by family members, (7) visiting and receiving visits of relatives and friends, (8) attending church on Christmas Day, (9) the Crèche (Biblical scene showing Christ child), and (10) special foods such as plumpudding, fruitcake, cranberries. The sentiments which subjects felt were most emphasized by Christmas were (in rank order) toward: (1) family, (2) friends, (3) Christ, (4) fellow man, (5) fun and merriment, (6) church—among 12 alternatives. Negative feelings toward Christmas were most frequently mentioned toward: (1) commercialization, (2) innovations, (3) loss of traditional features, (4) lack of real Christmas spirit, (5) economic strain, (6) rush and crowds of Christmas shopping.

37. Frank H. Ferris, in Judson T. Landis and Mary G. Landis (eds.), *Readings in Marriage and the Family* (Englewood Cliffs, N.J.: Prentice-Hall, 1952), pp. 133–138.

38. Sociologists have long noted the increasing secularization of marriage and declining familism. See Burgess and Locke, pp. 525–538.

39. Without attempting complete bibliography, we may mention a few examples of

literature which touch on the weakening of sentiments in modern life: home town nostalgia, Thornton Wilder, *Our Town;* effect of mobility on community sentiment, George Homans, *The Human Group* (New York: Harcourt, 1950), pp. 349–368; declining ability to work together, F. J. Roethlisberger, *Management and Morale* (Cambridge, Mass.: Harvard University Press, 1941); loss of fellow feeling, Pitirim Sorokin, *Reconstruction of Humanity* (Boston: Beacon) and *Altruistic Love* (Boston: Beacon, 1950); shallowness of emotion in movies, Martha Wolfenstein and Nathan Leites, *Movies, a Psychological Study* (New York: Free Press, 1950); decline of romantic love, Burgess and Locke, p. 368; comparative sentimentality of the pre-Civil War period, Bode; weakening of tragic feeling, J. W. Krutch, *The Modern Temper* (New York: Harcourt, 1929); loss of sentiment in modern scientific and technological society, Aldous Huxley, *Brave New World;* and the entire literature of alienation.

40. For example: "Foreigners . . . have been drawn by a feeling that in Greece life is lived more fully than elsewhere." Alexander Eliot, *Greece* (New York: Time, Inc., 1963), p. 118. "For the first time in my life . . . I . . . met men who were like men ought to be—that is to say, open, frank, natural, spontaneous, warm-hearted." Henry Miller, *The Colossus of Maroussi* (Baltimore: Penguin Books, Inc., 1950; 1941), p. 212.

41. Ritual symbolism of mass communication is explored in studies such as Peter Homans, "Puritanism Revisited: An Analysis of the Contemporary Screen-Image Western," *Studies in Public Communication* (University of Chicago), No. 3, Summer 1961; W. Lloyd Warner and W. E. Henry, "The Radio Day-Time Serial: a Symbolic Analysis," *Genetic Psychology Monographs,* Vol. 37, 1948, pp. 7–13, 55–64; W. L. Warner, *The Living and the Dead: A Study of the Symbolic Life of Americans* (New Haven, Conn.: Yale University Press, 1959); Helen M. Hughes, *News and the Human Interest Story* (Chicago: University of Chicago Press, 1940); Wolfenstein and Leites; Hugh D. Duncan, *Communication and Social Order* (New York: Bedminster, 1962).

42. O. E. Klapp, "The Folk Hero," *Journal of American Folklore,* Jan.–March 1949, pp. 17–25; "The Clever Hero," *Journal of American Folklore,* Vol. 67, 1954, pp. 21–34.

43. Lloyd Shearer, "The Biggest Box Office Draw of All Time," *Parade,* Dec. 18, 1966, p. 4.

44. Cooley's observations on formalism are worth repeating: "Much of what is unfree and unhuman in our modern life comes from mere inadequacy of mental and moral energy to meet the accumulating demands upon it. In many quarters attention and effort must be lacking, and where this is the case social relations fall to a low plane—just as a teacher who has too much to do necessarily adopts a mechanical style of instruction. So what we call 'red tape' prevails in great clerical offices. . . . (p. 56) A merely formal politeness goes with a crystallized society, indicating a certain distrust of human nature and desire to cloak or supplant it by propriety. (p. 198) . . . Too much mechanism in society gives us something for which there are many names . . . institutionalism, formalism, traditionalism, conventionalism, ritualism, bureaucracy, and the like. It is by no means easy, however, to determine whether mechanism is in excess or not. It becomes an evil . . . when it interferes with growth and adaptation . . . sup-

presses individuality and stupefies or misdirects the energies of human nature. (p. 342 . . . So long as spirit and symbol are vitally united and the idea is really conveyed, all is well, but so fast as they are separated the symbol becomes an empty shell, to which, however, custom, pride or interest may still cling. It then supplants rather than conveys the reality. Underlying all formalism, indeed, is the fact that it is psychically cheap; it substitutes the outer for the inner as more tangible, more capable of being held before the mind without fresh expense of thought and feeling, more easily extended, therefore, and impressed upon the multitude. Thus in out . . . architecture or literature we have innumerable cheap, unfelt repetitions of forms that were significant and beautiful in their time and place. The effect of formalism upon personality is to starve its higher life and leave it the prey of apathy, self-complacency, sensuality. (p. 343) . . . The apparent opposite of formalism, but in reality closely akin to it, is disorganization or disintegration, often, though inaccurately, called 'individualism.' One is mechanism supreme, the other mechanism going to pieces. . . ." (p. 347) Charles H. Cooley, *Social Organization* (New York: Charles Scribner's Sons, 1927).

45. Perspective by incongruity but pietistic outrage, in Kenneth Burke's terminology. *Performance and Change* (Indianapolis: Bobbs-Merrill, 1965; 1954).

46. Emile Durkheim, noting anomie and breakdown of the "collective conscience" associated with loss of tradition and rise of the new order of life (the division of labor), rejected the revivalist solution: "the remedy is not to seek to resuscitate traditions and practices which, no longer responding to present conditions of society, can only live an artificial, false existence," but to devise new institutions and codes. *The Division of Labor in Society* (New York: Free Press, 1947), p. 409.

47. Ralph Linton, "Nativistic Movements," *American Anthropologist,* Vol. 45, 1943, pp. 230–240. Revitalization: "a deliberate, organized, conscious effort by members of a society to construct a more satisfying culture." Anthony C. Wallace, "Revitalization Movements," *American Anthropologist,* Vol. 58, 1956, pp. 264–281.

48. According to Max Weber's well-known theory. Also Wallace.

49. As suggested in notes 10, 13, 19, 36, and 41 above. Also see Warren O. Hagstrom, "What is the Meaning of Santa Claus?" *The American Sociologist,* Vol. 1, Nov. 1966, pp. 248–252.

CHAPTER 5

1. Advertisement in London "tube," November 1964.

2. William James, *The Varieties of Religious Experience* (New York: Collins, Fontana Library Edition), p. 172.

3. Quoted by Richard Hofstadter, *The American Political Tradition* (New York: Knopf, 1948), p. 186.

4. Henry Anatole Grunwald, *Life,* May 31, 1954, p. 99.

5. Louis Schneider and Sanford Dornbusch, *Popular Religion, Inspirational Books in America* (Chicago: University of Chicago Press, 1958).

6. Paul Hutchinson, "Have We a New Religion?" *Life,* April 11, 1955, pp. 138.

7. Ray Bone, "We Witches Are Simple People," *Life*, Nov. 13, 1964, p. 62.

8. So a retired businessman speaks of the significance of symbolic nudity for him: "I was doing very well, but one day I had a vision of driving myself in top gear for a few more years and then dropping down dead. . . . I thought, 'to hell with all this.' I gave my business to my partner and . . . put my earnings into shares and a hotel that would produce enough income to meet my responsibilities, but would leave me free to see what life is all about. It sounds easy, but it was agonizing. I had to strip myself naked. It was like being reborn. I had to come to terms with myself all over again and I said, 'You're naked. Who are you? Put your clothes back on!'—so I did, but they were new clothes. Now I've written the best part of a book. When you're in business your outlook is narrow. All you're thinking is 'what's in it for me, Joe?' Before Joe didn't really exist, but you get out and suddenly everything and everybody has a new significance. You become alive. You start experiencing, and that's what I believe life is all about, experiencing." "Time For a Change," *Sunday Times Magazine*, Nov. 19, 1967, p. 71.

9. Norman Cohn, *The Pursuit of the Millennium* (London: Secker and Warburg, 1957); E. U. Essien-Udom, *Black Materialism* (Chicago: University of Chicago Press, 1962), p. 72; Vittorio Lanternari, *Religions of the Oppressed, a Study of Modern Messianic Cults* (New York: Knopf, 1963).

10. "The Devil . . . was God . . . incarnate; they adored him on their knees, they addressed their prayers to him." (28) In becoming witches, they renounced previous errors of faith and took vows (77). "The cult was organized in as careful a manner as any other religious community." (186) Accused witches "endured agonies of torture . . . like many a Christian martyr" rather than betray their leaders or give up their faith (59). Margaret A. Murray, *The Witch-Cult in Western Europe* (London: Oxford, 1921).

11. *Time,* April 30, 1965, p. 88.

12. Muggeridge, *Observer,* June 26, 1966.

13. The well-known tendency of sects to lose their "spirit" within a generation or so. See Ernst Troeltsch, *The Social Teaching of the Christian Churches* (New York: Macmillan, 1931), pp. 331–341; Bryan R. Wilson, "An Analysis of Sect Development," *American Sociological Review*, Vol. 24, Feb. 1959, pp. 3–15.

14. Gordon Allport, *The Individual and His Religion (1950).*

15. The Krishna Venta cult drew seekers from Baptist, Catholic, Congregational, Episcopal, Lutheran, Greek Orthodox, Christian Scientist, Latter Day Saints, Presbyterian, Quaker, Seventh Day Adventist, Pentecostal, and other established churches, as well as from sects like Jehovah's Witnesses. William R. Catton, Jr., "What Kind of People Does a Religious Cult Attract?"*American Sociological Review*, Vol. 22, 1957, pp. 561–566.

16. *Time,* July 25, 1949, p. 14. E. J. Hobsbawm describes the ritual of such brotherhoods. *Primitive Rebels* (Manchester, England: Manchester University Press, 1959), pp. 150–174.

17. J. Milton Yinger, *Religion, Society and the Individual* (New York: Macmillan, 1957), pp. 148–155; Howard Becker, *Systematic Sociology* (New York: Wiley, 1932), pp. 624–628; or C. S. Braden, who defines a cult as a "minority religious group . . . any religious group which differs significantly in some one or

more respects as to belief or practice from those religious groups which are regarded as the normative expressions of our total culture." *These Also Believe* (New York: Macmillan, 1949, 1960), p.xii. Ernst Troeltsch's distinction between "church" and "sect" is a partial source of this difficulty since, however valuable the distinction is, "cult" got drawn into the "sect" orbit in sociological usage and lost its right to refer to the established church of the majority. See Troeltsch, *The Social Teaching of the Christian Churches* (New York: Macmillan, 1931), pp. 331–341.

18. V. Ogden Vogt, *Cult and Culture* (New York: Macmillan, 1951).

19. This is implicit in Georg Simmel's view that religious attitudes are not unique to religious organization but find expression in many activities of life. Yinger, pp. 334–336.

20. "Their membership in the John Birch Society was by far their most time-and-interest-consuming voluntary association. The John Birch Society has become their church, accepted as God's vessel of salvation, as God present with them for guidance, for comfort, and for strength. Welch has become the revealer of God's eternal truths. . . ." J. Allen Broyles, *The John Birch Society* (Boston: Beacon, 1964), p. 122.

21. Rudolph Otto, *The Idea of the Holy* (London: Oxford, 1923; Roger Caillois, *Man and the Sacred* (New York: Free Press, 1959).

22. See Charles Nordhoff, *The Communistic Societies of the United States* (New York: Schocken, 1965; originally published in 1875); Mark Holloway, *Heavens On Earth: Utopian Communities in America 1680–1880* (London: Turnstile Press, 1951); Everett Webber, *Escape to Utopia: The Communal Movement in America* (New York: Hastings, 1959); Edward Deming Andrews, *The People Called Shakers* (New York: Dover, 1963); Robert V. Hine, *California's Utopian Colonies* (San Marino, Calif.: The Huntington Library, 1953); Elmer T. Clark, *Small Sects in America* (New York: Abingdon, 1949); Charles S. Braden, *These Also Believe* (New York: Macmillan, 1949); Brian Wilson, *Sects and Society* (Berkeley: University of California Press, 1961); Richard R. Mathison, *Faiths, Cults and Sects of America: From Atheism to Zen* (Indianapolis: Bobbs-Merrill, 1960); Marcus Bach, *Strange Sects and Curious Cults* (New York: Dodd, Mead, 1961).

23. Andrews, p. 133.

24. A hymn composed by Hannah Brownson, a Shakeress, in answer to stories that Shakers put some kind of seed into their cake that made members want to stay.

25. *The New Day,* Sept. 1, 1956, A.D.F.D.

26. William James, *The Varieties of Religious Experience* (New York: Modern Library, 1936; originally published in 1902), p. 193.

27. Kenneth Burke, *Permanence and Change* (New York: New Republic, 1936), pp. 100, 104–105.

28. Karlfried Graf von Durckheim, *The Japanese Cult of Tranquillity* (London: Rider & Co., 1960), pp. 38–39.

29. As a Japanese wise man said: "If something is to require religious significance, it need only be simple and capable of repetition." Durckheim, p. 27.

30. J. S. Slotkin, "The Peyote Way," in William A. Lessa and Evon Z. Vogt, *Reader in Comparative Religion* (New York: Harper & Row, 1958), pp.

482–485. See also David Aberle, *The Peyote Religion Among the Navaho* (Chicago: Aldine Co., 1965); William Braden, *The Private Sea, LSD and The Search for God* (New York: Doubleday, 1967); Timothy Leary, Ralph Metzner, and Richard Alpert, *The Psychedelic Experience, A Manual Based on the Tibetan Book of the Dead* (New York: University Books, 1964). Alcohol also has its cultic role as shown by the Dionysian and Bacchanalian ceremonies; or see Seth Leacock, "Ceremonial Drinking in an Afro-Brazilian Cult," *American Anthropologist,* 66, April 1964, 344–354.

31. Slotkin, pp. 484–485.

32. Mircea Eliade, *Shamanism, Archaic Techniques of Ecstasy* (London: Routledge, 1964).

33. Winthrop Sargeant, "Holy Man," *Life,* May 30, 1949.

34. Robert H. Lowie, "The Vision Quest Among North American Indians," Lessa and Vogt (eds.), pp. 181–190.

35. René Fulop-Miller, *Rasputin:The Holy Devil* (New York: Garden City Books, 1928), pp. 29–32.

36. Raymond Firth, *Elements of Social Organization* (Boston: Beacon, 1961, 3d ed.) pp. 228–231.

37. A. D. Nock, *Conversion* (London: Oxford, 1933), p. 7. Tamatsu Shibutani analyzes conversion as a transformation of identity in *Society and Personality* (Englewood Cliffs, N.J.: Prentice-Hall, 1961), pp. 523–532. Mass observation (43 observers) of Billy Graham "Crusade" in Madison Square Garden, N.Y., failed to find real conversions. "Decisions"—to come forward and fill out cards—were not life changes, but merely a gesture winning approval of audience and indicating participation in a larger cause. "The person so won is hardly the True Believer. . . . (Hoffer) The inquirers do not restructure themselves; they are not born again. The conventionality, the demand for a limited commitment, and the air of organization only strengthen their identifications with an accepted way of life already familiar to them." Appeal is not to down-and-outers but to members of established churches. The modern revival dramatizes religion and offers a "ritual confession and a ritual atonement" lacking in official Protestantism and Judaism. (Catholics were unimpressed.) Kurt and Gladys Lang, "Decisions for Christ; Billy Graham in New York," in Maurice R. Stein, and others. *Identity and Anxiety* (New York: Free Press, 1960), pp. 416, 425–426.

38. So Tamatsu Shibutani treats the conversion process as a change in significant others in *Society and Personality,* pp. 523–532. John Lofland and Rodney Stark have analyzed the social process in conversion of 15 cult members, holding that after the "turning point" (which I have called the centering experience), the new convert must get intensive interaction and support from the cult if he is to become a "deployable agent" (active convert). They distinguish stages in a sequence; for conversion a person must: (1) experience enduring, acutely felt tensions; (2) within a religious problem-solving perspective; (3) which leads him to define himself as a religious seeker; (4) encountering the D.P. (Divine Precepts) at a turning point in his life; (5) wherein an affective bond is formed (or pre-exists) with one or more converts; (6) where extra-cult attachments are absent or neutralized; (7) and, where, if he is to become a deployable agent (full

convert who helps cause, he is exposed to intensive interaction (close association with reciprocal support). "Conversion to a Deviant Perspective," *American Sociological Review*, Vol. 30, Dec. 1965, pp. 862–875. See also John Lofland, *Doomsday Cult, a Study of Conversion, Proselytization and Maintenance of Faith* (Englewood Cliffs, N.J.: Prentice-Hall, 1966).

39. W. Seward Salisbury, *Religion in American Culture* (Homewood, Ill.: Dorsey Press, 1964), pp. 57–58.

40. "Billy Graham, The Personal Story of the Man," *Reader's Digest*, 1956.

41. Roland Stevenson, quoted by Edmund Brucker, San Diego *Union*, July 10, 1949.

42. Interview with Mrs. K., White American, age 63, married 30 years, no children, before marriage a registered nurse.

43. Interview with mother of three children, age 40, former Baptist, converted to the Church of God.

44. Alan Watts, *This is IT* (New York: Pantheon, 1958).

45. H. G. Barnett, *Indian Shakers, A Messianic Cult of the Pacific Northwest* (Carbondale, Ill.: Southern Illinois University Press, 1957).

46. Hannah Whitall Smith, in Ray Strachey, *Religious Fanaticism* (London: Faber & Gwyer, Ltd., 1928), pp. 208–212.

47. Jack Kerouac, *On the Road* (New York: Signet Books, 1958), p. 11.

48. "Beyond Utopia: The Beat Generation," in Arnold M. Rose (ed.), *Human Behavior and Social Processes* (Boston: Houghton Mifflin, 1962), pp. 360–377. This is a good survey of beatnikism, with bibliography.

49. Max Weber, *The Sociology of Religion* (Boston: Beacon, 1963, 4th ed.), pp. 155–158.

50. *You May Survive Armageddon into God's New World* (Brooklyn, N.Y.: Watchtower Bible and Tract Society, Inc., 1955), pp. 364–366. (Italics mine.)

51. J. E. Esselmont, *Baha'u'llah and The New Era* (Wilmette, Ill.: Baha'i Publ. Committee, 1950), pp. 97–108.

52. *The Middle Way, Journal of the Buddhist Society*, August 1965, p. 86.

53. Essien-Udom, p. 211.

54. Marcus Bach, *Strange Sects and Curious Cults* (New York: Dodd, Mead, 1961), pp. 125, 136, 144–145.

55. Esselmont, pp. 320–321.

56. Essien-Udom, pp. 224–225.

57. Deindividualization, leveling of individuality; the opposite of adornment. Georg Simmel, *The Sociology of Georg Simmel*, (Kurt H. Wolff, ed.) (New York: Free Press, 1950), pp. 338–344, 372–73.

58. "A Girl Sets Out to be a Nun," *Life,* March 15, 1963, pp. 68 ff.

59. Bryan Wilson, *Sects and Society* (Berkeley: University of California Press, 1961), pp. 115, 149, 211.
For example: Richard Blum and Associates, *The Use and Users of LSD-25* (New York: Atherton Press, 1964); Timothy Leary, Ralph Metzner, and Richard Alpert, *The Psychedelic Experience, a Manual Based on the Tibetan*

60. *Book of the Dead* (New York: University Books, 1964); *ETCETERA, A Review of General Semantics; Special Issue on the Psychedelic Experience*, ed. by Robert E. Mogar, Vol. 22, No. 4; John Cashman, *The LSD Story* (Green-

wich, Conn.: Fawcett Publications, 1966); William H. McGlothlin, *Halluci-nogenic Drugs* (The Rand Corporation, P-2937, July 1964).

61. Quoted by S. I. Hayakawa, "The Quest for Instant Satori," *ETCETERA*, p. 390.

62. Foreword to Blum and associates.

63. Leary's own statement (rather more matter-of-fact and less inspired than those of most prophets) was: "I think that anyone who wants to have a psychedelic experience and is willing to prepare for it and to examine his own hang-ups and neurotic tendencies should be allowed to have a crack at it." "Interview with Timothy Leary," *Playboy*, Sept. 1966, p. 93.

64. Cashman, p. 60.

65. Joseph J. Downing, in Blum, pp. 164–165.

66. *Playboy*, Sept. 1966, p. 104.

67. *Playboy*, Sept. 1966, p. 106.

68. *Playboy*, Sept. 1966, p. 255.

69. Among LSD users there were no cases of addiction, but habitual users develop "a severe state of overenthusiasm" in which tendency to "make the drug ex-perience the center of all their activities." William H. McGlothlin, *Hallucino-genic Drugs* (Rand Corporation, P-2937, July 1964), p. 65 (quoting F. Barron, M. E. Jarvik and S. Bunnell).

70. Quoted in Cashman, p. 68. See also Watts, *This is IT* (New York: Pantheon, 1958), pp. 132–144.

71. Cashman, pp. 72–73.

72. Study of 71 acceptors and 47 controls (rejectors) showed: "Persons accepting the drug are more often dissatisfied with themselves and their lives than those re-jecting it. . . . Rejectors who had an equal number of sources of unhappiness perceived these to be outside themselves. . . . Acceptors . . . sought an uncertain adventure in self-change." Acceptors report beneficial results, emphasizing "self-change or goal-reduction." Richard Blum and Associates, pp. 115–116.

73. Willis W. Harman, "The Issue of the Consciousness-Expanding Drugs," *Main Currents in Modern Thought*, Vol. 20, No. 1, Sept.–Oct. 1963, p. 10.

74. The Tibetan Buddhist *Book of the Dead* is preferred. Leary, Metzner and Alpert.

75. Blum, pp. 72, 160.

76. *Time*, Sept. 23, 1966, p. 62.

77. Neil Smelser, *Theory of Collective Behavior* (New York: Free Press, 1963).

78. Cohen; Kornhauser; Liston Pope, *Millhands and Preachers* (New Haven, Conn.: Yale University Press, 1942).

79. J. H. Fichter, *Social Relations in the Urban Parish* (Chicago: University of Chicago Press, 1954), p. 188. Sociologists observe a general tendency of sect to routinize, formalize, and lose fervor as it becomes a church. Ernst Troeltsch made the classic distinction. Liston Pope describes the development from sect to church as a change, among other things, "from fervor in worship to restraint, from positive action to passive listening." *Millhands and Preachers* (New Haven, Conn.: Yale University Press, 1942), pp. 122–123. "The Sect maintains a moral community, excluding unworthy members . . . while the Church em-braces all who are socially compatible. . . . The Sect values fervor . . . while the

Church values passivity. . . ." Russell R. Dynes, "Church-Sect Typology and Socio-Economic Status," *American Sociological Review*, Vol. 20, October 1955, p. 556.

80. Of 259 girls polled at an upper class private English high school for girls, 143 said they would be "quite indifferent" to someone near them in an audience remaining seated during the playing of *God Save the Queen,* 1964.

81. *Tao Te Ching,* Ch. 38.

82. Audiences of Krishna Venta, a cult leader, contained people from many churches who "had strong religious interests that were not being satisfied through normal institutional channels." Catton theorizes that there is a "cult-prone" individual who is institutionally alienated but religiously intense. William R. Catton, Jr., "What Kind of People Does a Religious Cult Attract?" *American Sociological Review*, Vol. 22, 1957, pp. 561–566.

83. Bach, pp. 74–75.

84. Louis Schneider and Sanford M. Dornbusch, *Popular Religion, Inspirational Books in America* (Chicago: University of Chicago Press, 1958) pp. 23–24.

85. Eric Hoffer, *The True Believer* (New York: Harper & Row, 1951); Robert A. Nisbet, *The Quest for Community* (New York: Oxford, 1953).

CHAPTER 6

1. Some scholars assert that there is no sharp line between cult and play and that they have essential elements in common. Johan Huizinga holds that there is a continuity, indeed, an identity between play and cult, in such features as makebelieve, mystical "actualization," by re-enactment, even in seriousness and sacredness. *Homo Ludens, a Study of the Play Element in Culture* (Boston: Beacon, 1955), pp. 18–26. Adolph E. Jensen agrees with Huizinga, but distinguishes cult (the sacred feast) from other play by two things: "a deeper and more fundamental relationship to reality," and "a special psychological state . . . a spirit of celebration and solemnity" which "links all men to their gods according to their respective beliefs . . . thus cult is not just any order re-enacted but the true order, the order under which man lives and which shapes his image of reality" (p. 53). Cults or ceremonies are different from other parts of the social order in being "a *demonstration* of this order" through which "the community gains a heightened awareness of it. . . . Everyone knows the order and his role in it, but it is . . . necessary to raise it to a level of heightened awareness" (pp. 41–42). *Myth and Cult Among Primitive Peoples* (Chicago: University of Chicago Press, 1963; originally published 1951). One can make rather a similar argument to that of Huizinga concerning the continuity between cult and mass entertainment, namely that identity search can give the latter a more serious aim than is implied by the word "fun." Indeed, as we argue in Chapter 7 on celebrities, such a search can approach cult. On the other hand, Roger Caillois criticizes Huizinga's thesis of a continuity between play and sacred cult. "I do not believe that the various forms of play and religion, because they are separated with equal care in daily life, occupy equivalent situa-

tions with respect to each other, nor that for this reason they are identical in content. . . . The Sacred . . . is pure content—an indivisible, equivocal, fugitive, and efficacious force. Rites serve to capture, demonstrate, and guide it, for better or worse." pp. 157–158.

2. *Bulletin of the Society for Comparative Philosophy* (Sausalito, Calif., Winter–Spring 1967).

3. See George Lundberg, Mirra Komarovsky, and Mary McInerny, *Leisure, a Suburban Study* (New York: Columbia University Press, 1934), pp. 17–18; C. W. Mills, *Whitecollar* (1951), p. 238; Werner Sombart, *Vom Menschen* (Berlin: 1938), pp. 56–57; Eric Larrabee and Rolf Meyersohn (eds.) survey problems of leisure in *Mass Leisure* (New York: Free Press, 1958).

4. See Martha Wolfenstein, "The Emergence of Fun Morality," *Journal of Social Issues*, Vol. 7, 1951, pp. 3–16; Nelson N. Foote, "Sex as Play," in Larrabee and Meyersohn, pp. 335–340.

5. Abraham Maslow, *Toward a Psychology of Being* (New York: Van Nostrand, 1962), pp. 97–108.

6. Irving Babbitt, *Rousseau and Romanticism* (Boston: Houghton Mifflin, 1919), pp. 31–34, 52–55, 63–64, 182–183, 216; Jacques Barzun, *Romanticism and the Modern Ego* (Boston: Little, Brown, 1943), pp. 111–113. The new right to be fulfilled seems to have bloomed in the feminist movement, Christopher Lasch notes the "cult of self-fulfillment" in the feminism of the early twentieth century. *The New Radicalism in America* (New York: Knopf, 1965), pp. 46–47. A recent version is found in promotional copy of *Cosmopolitan Magazine:* "A girl can do almost anything she really wants to, don't you agree? . . . There's one magazine that seems to understand me–the girl who wants everything. I guess you could say I'm That Cosmopolitan Girl." *Time*, Feb. 9, 1968, p. 44.

7. The nature camps of the Club Méditerranée, Kathleen Halton, "Primitives of Cefalu," *The Times Magazine* (London), July 26, 1964, pp. 22 ff. William R. Burch explores "rituals of reindentification" in the American camping experience. "The Play World of Camping," *American Journal of Sociology*, Vol. LXX, March 1965, pp. 604–612.

8. Students of religion are beginning to explore the cultic aspects of sports—for example, Samuel Z. Klausner, "Religion and Emotional Valence: a Report on Sport Parachuting," delivered at meeting of Society for the Scientific Study of Religion, Berkeley, Calif., Dec. 27, 1965.

9. Sir John Hunt, interviewed by Kenneth Harris, *The Observer*, June 27, 1965.

10. Rod Pack interviewed by Donald Freeman, San Diego *Union*, March 5, 1965.

11. John Severson, Editor of *Surfer Magazine*, quoted in *Life*, Sept. 9, 1966, p. 37.

12. Interview with a San Diego, Calif., surfer, 1966. Other quotations from surfers illustrate the mystique: "I felt locked in life's bag."—"Just being out there with the waves is enough. Your parents, your school and your girl could all be bugging you, but when you're surfing, the waves demand all your attention. After three or four hours out there you're so excited you can't talk. Your mind is blown out."—"You become part of the ocean. . . . I would lose track of time, find an inner space, and find myself in myself."—"It offers complete dissassociation from society." *Newsweek*, Aug. 28, 1967, p. 41.

13. *Henderson the Rain King* (New York: Popular Library, 1963), p. 230.
14. *Observer Magazine,* Aug. 29, 1965, pp. 27–28.
15. Neil Feather, *Jazz and the White Americans* (Chicago: University of Chicago Press, 1962), pp. 60, 66–67. Cult-like features of jazz have also been pointed out by William B. Cameron, "Sociological Notes on the Jam Session," *Social Forces,* Vol. 33 Dec. 1954; reprinted in *Informal Sociology* (New York: Random House, 1963), pp. 118–130.
16. Jack Kerouac, *On the Road* (New York: Signet Books, 1958), pp. 106–107, 162, 170.
17. Lipton, p. 19.
18. Eliade, *Shamanism, Archaic Techinques of Ecstasy* (New York: Bollingen Foundation, Pantheon, 1964), pp. 168, 174–175.
19. *Chitty Chitty Bang Bang, The Magical Car* (New York: Random House, 1964), pp. 19–23.
20. F. W. Cozens and F. S. Stumpf, *Sports in America* (Chicago: University of Chicago Press, 1953), pp. 294–296.
21. *Life,* Feb. 12, 1965, p. 37.
22. Norman Poirier, "Discotheque, GoGo Madness Strikes and the Nation Gyres in a Frenzy," *Saturday Evening Post,* March 27, 1965, pp. 21–27.
23. Thomas Meehan, "A Night on the Wiggy Scene," *Saturday Evening Post,* Oct. 26, 1966, pp. 35–39.
24. Maslow; Marghanita Laski, *Ecstasy, A Study of Some Secular and Religious Experiences* (London: Cresset Press, 1961); Leary, Metzner and Alpert.
25. *Saturday Review,* Oct. 9, 1965, p. 41.
26. Kerouac, p. 148.
27. Lipton, p. 19.
28. *Time,* Dec. 11. 1964, p. 36. For the beatnik view of square, see Lipton, pp. 122–126.
29. Various dimensions of pain for identity realization are seen in the flagellant movements of the thirteenth and fourteenth centuries. Norman Cohn, *Pursuit of the Millennium,* Ch. VI; the Penitentes of New Mexico described in Bach; Lewis Yablonsky, *The Violent Gang;* and the literature on puberty initiations.
30. Howard S. Becker analyzes how the societal response *makes* a person deviant. *Outsiders* (New York: Free Press, 1963); see also Edwin Lemert, *Social Pathology* (New York: McGraw-Hill, 1951) for an account of secondary deviation.
31. William Raymond Smith, "Hepcats to Hipsters," *The New Republic,* April 21, 1958, pp. 18–20.
32. Harold Finestone, "Cats, Kicks and Color," in Howard S. Becker (ed.), *The Other Side* (New York: Free Press, 1964), pp. 285–294.
33. Charles Winick, "Physician Narcotic Addicts," in Becker, p. 271.
34. James Miller, "The World of Needle Park," *Life,* Feb. 26, 1965, p. 82.
35. "The four of us have had the most hectic lives. We have got almost anything money can buy. But when you can do that, the things you buy mean nothing after a time. You look for something else, for a new experience. It's like your Dad going to the boozer and you want to find out what the taste of drink is like. We have found something now which fills the gap. Since meeting His Holiness

(a Hindu seer, Maharishi Mahesh Yogi), I feel great." Ringo Starr of The Beatles, quoted in *Time,* Sept. 22, 1967, p. 58.

36. Barbara La Fontaine, "Fitness for Sale: The Girl Behind the Golden Door," *Life Special Report, The Healthy Life* (New York: Time, Inc., 1966), pp. 93–96.

37. J. E. Hulett, Jr., "The Kenny Healing Cult: Preliminary Analysis of Leadership and Patterns of Interaction," *American Sociological Review,* Vol. 10, 1945, pp. 364–372.

38. Wheelis.

39. "The Mystic More Freudian than Freud," *The New Republic,* May 1, 1965, p. 22.

40. See Carl M. Grossman and Sylvia Grossman, *The Wild Analyst: The Life and Work of Georg Groddeck* (New York: Braziller, 1965).

41. See Erving Goffman, "The Moral Career of the Mental Patient," *Psychiatry,* Vol. 22, No. 2, May 1959, pp. 123–142; Max Siporin, "Deviant Behavior Therapy in Social Work," *Social Work,* Vol. 10, July 1965, pp. 59–67.

42. For example, Daniel I. Malamud and Solomon Machover, *Toward Self-Understanding, Group Techniques in Self-Confrontation* (Springfield, Ill.: Charles C Thomas, 1965).

43. W. W. Meissner, *Group Dynamics in the Religious Life* (South Bend, Ind.: University of Notre Dame Press, 1965).

44. See Maslow; and, for general description of Synanon, Lewis Yablonsky, *The Tunnel Back: Synanon* (New York: Macmillan, 1965); and "The Anticriminal Society," in Donald M. Valdes and Dwight G. Dean, *Sociology in Use* (New York: Macmillan, 1965), pp. 160–173.

45. Edgar H. Schein, "Brainwashing," in Warren G. Bennis, et al., *Interpersonal Dynamics* (Homewood, Ill.: Dorsey Press, 1964), pp. 454–464; James Clark Moley, "Psychic Self-Abandon and Extortion of Confessions, *Interpersonal Dynamics,* pp. 439–453; and Robert J. Lifton, "Methods of Forceful Indoctrination," in Maurice R. Stein et al., *Identity and Anxiety* (New York: Free Press, 1960), pp. 480–492.

46. See: Hereward Carrington, *The Physical Phenomena of Spiritualism* (Boston: Turner & Co., 1907); F. S. Edsall, *The World of Psychic Phenomena* (New York: McKay, 1958); Eileen J. Garrett, *Beyond the Five Senses* (Philadelphia: Lippincott, 1957); and *Adventures in the Supernatural* (New York: Garrett Publications, 1949); Rosalind Heywood, *The Sixth Sense* (London: Chatto & Windus, Ltd., 1959); Peter Hurkos, *Psychic* (Indianapolis: Bobbs-Merrill, 1961); R. C. Johnson, *Psychical Research* (New York: Philosophical Library, 1956); G. Murphy and R. Ballou, *William James on Psychical Research* (New York: Viking, 1960); J. B. Rhine, *New World of the Mind* (New York: Sloane, 1953); R. Sudre, *Parapsychology* (New York: Citadel, 1960); and Gertrude Schmeidler and R. A. McConnell, *E.S.P. and Personality Patterns* (New Haven, Conn.: Yale University Press, 1958).

CHAPTER 7

1. Quoted BBC 1 television, Sept. 22, 1964.

2. *Time,* Feb. 1, 1960, p. 38.
3. Of a sample of San Diego school children asked to name heroes, only four of 37 seventh graders and none of the 22 eleventh graders mentioned parents.
4. For many of the statements from teenagers used in this chapter I am indebted to Marilyn Arfman and to students of San Diego State College.
5. See my *Heroes, Villains and Fools* (Englewood Cliffs, N.J.: Prentice-Hall, 1963) and *Symbolic Leaders* (Chicago: Aldine, 1965).
6. Warren J. Clear, "Glory Through Hara-Kiri," *Reader's Digest,* Aug. 1943, pp. 103–104.
7. Sigmund Freud, *The Future of an Illusion* (New York: Liveright, 1949), p. 22.
8. Lycurgus M. Starkey, Jr., *James Bond's World of Values* (Nashville, Tenn.: Abingdon Press, 1966).
9. *Life,* Nov. 11, 1966, p. 115.
10. Thomas Wolfe, *You Can't Go Home Again,* develops the same theme.
11. Marshall McLuhan's definition, *Understanding Media* (New York: McGraw-Hill, 1964; Signet Books, 1966), pp. 36–45.
12. The term used by Arthur Kornhauser to refer to readiness of people without fixed relationships to participate in social movements.
13. E. J. Kahn, Jr., *The Voice* (New York: Harper & Row, 1947), pp. 45–54, 68, 83–84.
14. *Time,* April 23, 1965, p. 60.
15. See the literature on hero and saint cults, particularly: L. R. Farnell, *Greek Hero Cults* (Oxford: Clarendon Press, 1921); S. Czarnowski, *Le Cult des Heros et les Conditions Sociales* (Paris: F. Alcan, 1919); H. Delehaye, *Sanctus* (Bruxelles: Societé des Bollandistes, 1927); and C. Gower, "The Supernatural Patron in Sicilian Life" (Chicago: unpublished Ph.D. Dissertation, University of Chicago, 1928); D. W. Riddle, *The Martyrs, a Study in Social Control* (Chicago: University of Chicago Press, 1931); and Dixon Wecter, *The Hero in America* (New York: Houghton Mifflin, 1941).
16. *Muhammed Speaks,* April 23, 1965, p. 6.
17. "The Idol Remembered," *Esquire,* July 1965, p. 84.
18. Alexander King, *Mine Enemy Grows Older* (New York: Signet Books, 1958), pp. 234–239.
19. See Malcolm Boyd, *Christ and the Celebrity Gods* (Greenwich, Conn: Seabury, 1958).
20. I have tried to analyze the nature of this "luck" in *Symbolic Leaders, Public Dramas and Public Men* (Chicago: Aldine, 1965), Ch. 2.
21. San Diego *Union,* June 16, 1965.
22. Walter Winchell, San Diego *Union,* July 11, 1965. Paul McCartney of The Beatles says: "The fan at my gate knows really that she's equal to me, and I take care to tell her that." Quoted in *Time,* Sept. 22, 1967, p. 57B.
23. Peter Bart, "The Image Polished," *Esquire,* July 1965, p. 80.
24. *Look,* June 29, 1965, p. 33.

CHAPTER 8

1. Volkmar of Gretz, an original crusader, quoted in James A. Michener, *The Source* (New York: Random House, 1965), p. 554.

2. He refers to a study by Leo Lowenthal and Norbert Guterman, *Prophets of Deceit* (New York: Harper & Row, 1949). As examples of persistent themes transcending particular historical eras (common to Populism and fascism) Hofstadter mentions: the conception of history as a conspiracy; the notion that the world is moving toward apocalypse; the attention to "greed and other personal vices" of wicked people rather than to structural analysis of the social system; and the concept of the "native simplicity and virtue of the folk." *The Age of Reform* (New York: Random House, 1955), pp. 72, 73.

3. Richard Hofstadter, *The Age of Reform* (New York: Random House, 1955), pp. 16–17.

4. Most often mentioned in 365 nominations of crusaders by 74 junior and senior students (36 males, 36 females), San Diego State College, 1966. See also crusaders mentioned in Klapp, *Heroes, Villains and Fools,* p. 46.

5. Klapp, *Heroes, Villains and Fools,* pp. 9–16.

6. Wendell Phillips Garrison and Francis Jackson Garrison, *William Lloyd Garrison, 1805–1879: The Story of His Life Told by His Children,* Vol. I (New York: Century Company, 1885), pp. 224–225.

7. Louis Rochames, *The Abolitionists* (New York: Capricorn Books, 1964), pp. 15–16.

8. Theodore Roosevelt, "The Man With The Muck-Rake," in John Eric Nordskog (ed.), *Contemporary Social Reform Movements* (New York: Scribner, 1954), pp. 386–387.

9. John A. Stormer, *None Dare Call It Treason* (Florissant, Mo.: Liberty Bell Press, 1964), pp. 228–237.

10. "The Migratory I.W.W." by J.H.B. The Rambler, a song, in Joyce Kornbluh (ed.), *Rebel Voices: an I.W.W. Anthology* (Ann Arbor, Mich.: University of Michigan Press, 1965).

11. Carleton Beals, *Cyclone Carry* (Philadelphia: Chilton, 1962); Heywood Broun, *Anthony Comstock* (New York: Albert & Charles Boni, 1927), pp. 15, 24–25, 36; Stewart H. Halbrook, "Bonnet, Book, and Hatchet," *American Heritage Magazine,* Vol. IX, No. 1, Dec. 1957, pp. 53–55, 120–121; Gustavus Myers, *History of Bigotry in the United States* (New York: Random House, 1943), p. 104.

12. Louis Filler, *Crusaders for American Liberalism* (Yellow Springs, Ohio: Antioch Press, 1939); Eric F. Goldman, *The Crucial Decade* (New York: Knopf, 1956); Peter Lyon, "The Herald Angels of Women's Rights," *American Heritage Magazine,* Vol. X, No. 6, Oct. 1959, pp. 18–21, 107–111; Peter Lyon, "The Honest Man, Peter Cooper," *American Heritage Magazine,* Vol. X., No. 2, Feb. 1959, pp. 5–11, 104–106; Louis Rochames, *The Abolitionists;* Anne Scott, "Saint Jane and the Ward Boss," *American Heritage Magazine,* Vol. XII, No. 1, Dec. 1960, pp. 12–17, 94–99; Alfred Steinberg, "Fire Eating Farmer of the Confederacy," *American Heritage Magazine,* Vol. IX, No. 1 Dec. 1959, pp. 22–25, 114–117; Forrest Wilson, *Crusader in Crinoline, the Life of Harriet Beecher Stowe* (Philadelphia: Lippincott, 1941); Elvi Whittaker and Virginia Olesen, "The Faces of Florence Nightingale: Functions of the Heroine Legend in an Occupational Subculture," *Human Organization,* Vol. 23, Summer 1964, pp. 123–130.

13. Margaret Sanger, *An Autobiography* (New York: Norton, 1938), pp. 104–105.

14. Heywood Broun, *Anthony Comstock* (New York: Boni, 1927), p. 15.

15. Peter Lyon, "The Herald Angels of Women's Rights," *American Heritage Magazine,* Oct. 1959, p. 111.

16. Erving Goffman's term.

17. Quoted by Richard Hofstadter, *The American Political Tradition* (New York: Random House, 1948), p. 271.

18. Herbert Hoover, "The Ordeal of Woodrow Wilson," *American Heritage Magazine,* Vol. IX, No. 4, June 1958, pp. 65–85.

19. Hofstadter, *The American Political Tradition,* p. 282.

20. William A. White, *Woodrow Wilson: The Man, His Times and His Task* (Boston: Houghton Mifflin, 1924), p. 377.

21. Hofstadter, *The American Political Tradition;* William Hanchett, "Abraham Lincoln and Father Abraham," *North American Review,* Vol. 251–252, March 1966, pp. 10–13.

22. Christopher Lasch, *The New Radicalism in America* (New York: Knopf, 1965), pp. 270–274.

23. R. G. Tugwell, in Abraham S. Eisenstadt (ed.), *American History* (New York: Crowell, 1962), Vol. II, pp. 366–386.

24. Hofstadter, *The American Political Tradition,* pp. 315–352.

25. Dwight D. Eisenhower, *Crusade in Europe* (New York: Doubleday, 1948), p. 473.

26. Along with the gang, sect, and militant labor union, political party and nation. A conflict group is defined as "an organization and orientation with reference to conflict with other groups of the same kind or with a more or less hostile social environment, as in the case of religious sects." Robert E. Park and Ernest W. Burgess, *Introduction to the Science of Sociology* (Chicago: University of Chicago Press, 1921), p. 646.

27. Bob Darke, *The Communist Technique* (London: Penguin, 1952), p. 12.

28. One of the main roots of the Peace Corps was William James's idea of a "moral equivalent of war," a "new outlet for heroic energy." He proposed a "peace army" to fight against poverty, disease, and ignorance. Roy Hoopes, "An Idea Whose Time Had Come," *1967 Peace Corps Reader* (Office of Public Information, Washington, D.C.), pp. 7–8.

29. Richard Collier, *The General Next to God* (New York: Dutton 1965), pp. 107, 109.

30. *Decision,* Sept. 1966, p. 8.

31. Howard S. Becker, *Outsiders* (New York: Free Press, 1963), pp. 147–163.

32. Indeed, in my opinion, a perfect crusade is a type of vilifying movement. See O. E. Klapp, "Vilification as a Social Process," *Pacific Sociology Review,* Vol. 2, No. 2, Fall 1959, pp. 71–76. This is the reason, in my opinion, why Eric Hoffer focuses on hate as a unifying force in fanatical movements. *The True Believer* (New York: Harper & Row, 1951), p. 89.

33. *The Menace of Darwinism* (Westwood, N.J.: Fleming H. Revell Company, 1922), pp. 15–17, 22–23, 49–51.

34. In Seymour M. Lipset and Sheldon S. Wolin (eds.), *The Berkeley Student Revolt* (New York: Doubleday, 1965), p. 216.

35. Peter H. Odegard, *Pressure Politics: The Story of the Anti-Saloon League* (New York: Columbia University Press, 1928); abridged and adapted in Leonard Broom and Philip Selznick, *Sociology* (New York: Harper & Row, 1955), pp. 291–296 (quote is from 294).

36. Whereas Kenneth Burke notes that the naturalistic or positivistic temper tends to "fragment" social evils in analysis and search for solutions; but "fragmentation makes for triviality . . . a kind of organized inanity that is socially morbid" and "the whole aggregate of petty fragmentary victimage may . . . require a 'total' victim, if it in turn is to be cured." *Permanence and Change* (Indianapolis: Bobbs-Merrill, 1954), pp. 286–287.

37. Richard Collier, *The General Next to God* (New York: Dutton, 1965), p. 160.

38. Including the sense of Georges Sorel, *Reflections on Violence* (New York: Free Press, 1950).

39. For example, the "traditionals" studied by Daniel Lerner, pp. 147–152, had too little empathy to imagine, let alone engage, in reforms and crusades . . . unless, perhaps, a holy war against infidels.

40. See the discussion of strains and "structural conduciveness" for collective behavior by Neil Smelser, *Theory of Collective Behavior* (New York: Free Press, 1963).

41. See Klapp, *Symbolic Leaders*.

42. Lerner, pp. 47–52.

43. Carl Bode, *The Anatomy of American Popular Culture, 1840–1861* (Berkeley and Los Angeles: University of California Press, 1959), p. xiv.

44. Richard Hofstadter, *The Age of Reform*, p. 3.

45. Hofstadter, p. 175.

46. Louis Filler, *Crusaders for American Liberalism* (Yellow Springs, Ohio: The Antioch Press, 1961, 2nd ed.), pp. 3–9, 17–18, 44–45, 153, 372–381.

47. Filler, pp. 372–376; also Hofstadter, p. 275.

48. Hofstadter, pp. 275, 279.

49. Hofstadter, pp. 205–207.

50. Arthur M. Schlesinger, Jr., "The New Deal in Historical Perspective," in Abraham S. Eisenstadt (ed.), *American History* (New York: Crowell, 1962), Book II, p. 349; Arthur S. Link, "Normalcy and the New Deal," explains the decline of progressivism in the twenties, *American History*, pp. 304–311; Hofstadter points out the decline of the crusading spirit, the discontinuity of the New Deal from progressivism, and the indignation of critics at its opportunism, *The Age of Reform*, pp. 310, 314–320.

51. Daniel Bell, *The End of Ideology* (New York: Collier, 1961), pp. 111–120, 275–298, 308–314. See also Edward Shils, "The End of Ideology?", *Encounter*, Nov. 1955, pp. 52–58; S. M. Lipset, "The End of Ideology?", in *Political Man* (New York: Doubleday, 1960); Robert Lane, "The Decline of Politics and Ideology in a Knowledgeable Society," *American Sociological Review*, Vol. 31, Oct. 1966, pp. 649–662.

52. *Time*, Feb. 25, 1966, p. 108. Bell analyzes the failure of American socialism, *The End of Ideology*, Ch. 12.

53. In Roy Newquist, *Counterpoint* (Skokie, Ill.: Rand McNally, 1964), p. 348.

54. Hofstadter, *Age of Reform,* p. 15.

55. See Seymour M. Lipset and Sheldon S. Wolin (eds.), *The Berkeley Student Revolt* (New York: Doubleday, 1965); Albert T. Anderson and Bernice P. Biggs (eds.), *A Focus on Rebellion* (San Francisco: Chandler Publishing Company, 1962). The actual extent of the student revolution was estimated by Joseph Katz and Nevitt Sanford to be not more than 15 percent of American college students socially involved. "Causes of the Student Revolution," *Saturday Review,* Dec. 18, 1965, p. 79.

56. A notable participant photographic study of "Vietnik" protest movement was done by Sam Angeloff, "How the Antiwar Marches Happen," *Life,* Dec. 10, 1965, pp. 108 ff.

57. Volunteers in Service to America, an organization to fight domestic poverty, parallel to the Peace Corps, headed by Glenn Ferguson, which during the first 11 months showed faster rate of recruitment than the Peace Corps.

58. See Louis E. Lomax, *The Negro Revolt* (New York: Harper & Row, 1962); Louis Ruchames, "Segregation and Discrimination in the Twentieth Century," in H. H. Quint et al. (eds.), *Main Problems in American History* (Homewood, Ill.: Dorsey Press, 1964), pp. 338–341; and William B. Cameron, *Social Movements* (New York: Random House, 1966), pp. 113 ff.

59. Richard Schmuck and Mark Chestler, "On Super-Patriotism: a Definition and Analysis," *Journal of Social Issues,* Vol. 19, April 1963, 31–50; Daniel Bell (ed.) *The Radical Right* (New York: Doubleday, 1963); Lawrence F. Schiff, "Dynamic Young Fogies—Rebels on the Right," *Trans-Action,* Nov. 1966, pp. 31–36; R. E. Wolfinger et al. in D. E. Apter (ed.) *Ideology and Discontent* (New York: Free Press, 1964); *Christian Anti-Communism Crusade News-Letter,* April 1962; Dr. Fred Schwartz, *You Can Trust the Communists* (Englewood Cliffs, N.J.: Prentice-Hall, 1960).

60. Trevor Armbruster, "Portrait of an Extremist," *Saturday Evening Post,* Vol. 237, Aug. 3, 1964, p. 80. Also see Margaret Long, "Imperial Wizard Explains," *New York Times Magazine,* July 5, 1964, p. 8. W. J. Cash analyzes the crusading spirit of the KKK as an "authentic folk movement" which gave a "coveted, splendid sense of being a heroic blade, a crusader" for White Supremacy, and asserted the "South's continuing identity." *The Mind of the South* (New York: Knopf, 1941), pp. 345–346.

61. Howard Zinn, *The New Abolitionists* (Boston: Beacon, 1966).

62. *Muhammed Speaks,* Aug. 2, 1963, pp. 1, 9.

63. A 23-year-old University of California English major, quoted by Jessica Mitford Truehaft, "The Indignant Generation," in Anderson and Biggs, pp. 159–160.

64. The speaker was a girl 16 years old, beginning her senior year in an American high school. She was good spirited, well adjusted, college bound, not in any sense a beatnik, nor did she have a radical ideology beyond the humanism referred to.

65. Edward M. Keating, "The New Left: What Does It Mean?" *Saturday Review,* Sept. 24, 1966, pp. 25–27, 64. See also Mitchell Cohen and Dennis Hale, *The New Student Left* (Boston: Beacon, 1966).

66. A trend actually beginning at the turn of the century, running from Jane Addams and Mabel Luhan to Norman Mailer and Reinhold Niebuhr, repre-

senting a fundamental shift in social criticism from politics to culture, morality, and alienation from politics. Christopher Lasch, *The New Radicalism in America (1889–1963): the Intellectual as a Social Type* (New York: Knopf, 1965).

67. *Newsweek,* June 27, 1966, p. 60. VISTA and Peace Corps recruitment, however, remained higher than ever.

68. *Time,* Nov. 18, 1966, pp. 95–96.

69. But even the John Birch Society was felt to be losing some of its zip and fervor by reproachful anticommunists. Two resigning members of the national council of the John Birch Society accused the leader, Robert Welch, of leading the Society away from militance into a purely educational role. One said, "The fight has gone out of Mr. Welch and the John Birch Society. The Society is becoming increasingly frustrating to its members and decreasingly disturbing to the enemy." *Time,* Sept. 9, 1966, p. 25.

70. Gerald N. Grob, "The Knights of Labor and the Trade Unions, 1878–1886," Abraham S. Eisenstadt (ed.), *American History: Recent Interpretations* (New York: Crowell, 1962), Book II, p. 110.

71. Peter H. Odegard, *Pressure Politics: The Story of the Anti-Saloon League* (New York: Columbia University Press, 1928).

72. See Crane Brinton, *Anatomy of Revolution* (Englewood Cliffs, N.J.: Prentice-Hall, 1952), pp. 118–131; and Eric Hoffer, *The True Believer* (New York: Harper & Row, 1951).

73. Hoffer, *The True Believer,* pp. 142–143.

74. *Society* (New York: Free Press, 1955), p. 26.

75. Annie Wittenmyer, *History of the Woman's Temperance Crusade* (1878); extract from R. E. Park and E. W. Burgess, *Introduction to Science of Sociology* (Chicago: University of Chicago Press, 1924, 2d ed.), pp. 898–905.

76. Joseph R. Gusfield, *Symbolic Crusade, Status Politics and the American Temperance Movement* (Urbana, Ill.: University of Illinois Press, 1963), pp. 110, 176.

77. E. J. Hobsbawm, *Primitive Rebels, Studies in Archaic Forms of Social Movements in the 19th and 20th Centuries* (Manchester, England: University of Manchester Press, 1959), p. 150.

78. Marxist antiritualism tries for "extreme matter-of-factness and colorlessness even in cloak-and-dagger activities," but "a certain amount of romanticism" compensates for tension. Hobsbawm, p. 173.

79. However the Black Muslims avoid the physical emotionalism of Negro revivalism. There is no singing. E. U. Essien-Udom, *Black Nationalism* (Chicago: University of Chicago Press, 1962), pp. 240–243.

80. Interview with Jehovah's Witness, housewife 26 years old, lower-middle class, four children, 1966.

81. Saul Alinsky, "The Professional Radical, Conversations with Saul Alinsky," *Harper's,* June 1965, p. 43.

82. Interview with College freshman, male, 18 years old, middle class, white, crusader for civil rights and voter registration, member of Students for Democratic Society, 1966.

83. Interview with housewife, 40 years old, lower-middle class, three children, crusader for Parents for Prayer, 1966.

84. Interview with College junior, female, 23 years old, middle class, crusader for civil rights, voter registration with SNCC, 1966.

85. *Autobiography of Malcolm X* (New York: Grove, 1964), pp. 1–11.

86. John R. Adams, *Harriet Beecher Stowe* (New York: Twayne Publishers, Inc., 1963), pp. 19, 25, 75.

87. Howard Romaine, student, University of Virginia, *Life,* April 30, 1965, p. 30.

88. William B. Cameron, *Social Movements* (New York: Random House, 1966), pp. 116–117.

89. Interview with SNCC crusader, white, female, age 23, middle class, college junior, 1966.

90. Garrett Lambrev, student, Stanford University, *Life,* April 30, 1965, p. 30.

91. A Negro student civil rights worker, quoted by Robert Coles, "A Psychiatrist Joins 'The Movement,' " *Trans-Action,* Jan.–Feb. 1966, p. 21.

92. Interview with male college Christian crusader, 1966.

93. J. Allen Broyles, *The John Birch Society* (Boston: Beacon , 1964), p. 122.

94. Interview with college senior, female, 1965.

95. Male, college junior.

96. Saul Alinsky, *Harper's* June, 1965, p. 47. "The Professional Radical, Conversations with Saul Alinsky."

97. For theory of the mass and availability of people for social movement, see Arthur Kornhauser, *The Politics of Mass Society* (New York: Free Press, 1959), which distinguishes between communal, pluralistic, and mass societies in terms of availability of people for movements. For basic theory of the mass and its "convergence" of interests, see Herbert Blumer, "Collective Behavior," in A. M. Lee (ed.) *Outline of Principles of Sociology* (New York: Barnes & Noble, 1946), pp. 185–189.

98. BBC 1 television, London, July 31, 1964.

99. See Klapp, *Symbolic Leaders.*

100. Eric Hoffer, *The True Believer* (Harper & Row, 1961), analyzes the reward of the "fanatic" as the assurance of sheep-like belief for which he surrenders his old spoiled identity. This, I think, is a little too strong to apply to all—perhaps even most—crusaders, many of whom, leaders especially, are markedly inner-directed.

101. Hiram Wesley Adams, Klan Imperial Wizard, quoted in Hofstadter *The Age of Reform,* pp. 295–296.

102. Mary Douglas, *Purity and Danger, an Analysis of Concepts of Pollution and Taboo* (New York: Praeger, 1966). In more mythic terms, the crusade is a repetition of the hero-monster-deliverance theme (St. George, Beowulf, Perseus, Sigird, Rama). See O. E. Klapp, "The Folk Hero," *Journal of American Folklore,* Jan.–March 1949, pp. 17–25.

103. David Smith, student, Tufts University, *Life,* April 30, 1965, p. 30.

104. Stephen Block, student, Williams College, *Life,* April 30, 1965, p. 30. A Columbia University student rebel, David Shapiro, remarked after the massive student takeover in April, 1968: "Since the demonstrations I have a new kind of faith in myself. It's like going from death to life. I'm becoming more alive. I'm able to be more tender toward people I love." *Time,* June 7, 1968, p. 44.

105. Quoted in Robert Coles, "A Psychiatrist Joins 'The Movement.' " *Trans-Action,* Jan.–Feb. 1966, pp. 24–25.

106. Quoted by Shana Alexander, *Life,* Aug. 27, 1965, p. 18.

107. *Autobiography of Malcolm X* (New York: Grove Press, 1964); see also C. E. Lincoln, *The Black Muslims in America* (Boston: Beacon, 1963); and E. U. Essien-Udom, *Black Nationalism.*

108. *Time,* July 31, 1964. p. 34; *Observer,* Dec. 13, 1964.

CHAPTER 9

1. Venerable Khantipalo Bhikku, "Instruction in the Dhamma," *The Middle Way,* (London), May 1966, pp. 3–4.

INDEX